Corporate Social Responsibility in the Global Business World

Asli Yüksel Mermod · Samuel O. Idowu
Editors

Corporate Social Responsibility in the Global Business World

 Springer

Editors

Asli Yüksel Mermod
Faculty of Economics and Administrative
  Sciences
Marmara University
Istanbul
Turkey

Samuel O. Idowu
London Metropolitan Business School
London Metropolitan University
London
UK

ISBN 978-3-642-37619-1   ISBN 978-3-642-37620-7 (eBook)
DOI 10.1007/978-3-642-37620-7
Springer Heidelberg New York Dordrecht London

Library of Congress Control Number: 2013945145

Printed on acid-free paper

Springer is part of Springer Science+Business Media (www.springer.com)

In memory of Professor (Dr.) Ali Sait Yüksel

Foreword

It was a great honor for me to be asked to write the foreword to a book which is dedicated to my late senior professor who taught me the basics of Financial Management almost 40 years ago.

When my colleague Dr. Asli Yüksel, one of Professor (Dr.) Ali Sait Yüksel's daughters asked me to write this foreword, I made a short research on the CSR literature in the context of global financial crisis under which we all have had to live since 2008, some nearly five challenging years. I saw that academics are asking questions like, "Did CSR play a significant role in the financial crisis?", "Why CSR failed to prevent global financial crisis?", "How corporate social irresponsibility contributed to the financial crisis?", "How we may reframe CSR or improve CSR frameworks to help prevent or mitigate any future financial and economic crisis?"[1] Dr. Kim Møller, CEO Oxford Group says that "in the past, in times of crisis, such as the one we are living through, companies would have reduced their commitments to CSR, or even abandoned it altogether. In reality, the evidence of the past six months suggests that the commitment to CSR is neither being reduced nor abandoned during this crisis—except in those cases of total bankruptcy".

According to KPMG[2] the proportion of the world's 250 largest companies issuing annual reports on corporate social responsibility has increased from 50 % in 2005 to 80 % in 2008. The main drivers for implementing CSR strategies have been from the perspective of risk management on the one hand and ethical considerations on the other. Investors, especially institutional investors, are also pushing for corporate social responsibility. According to the latest European study on sustainable and responsible investment (SRI) the average annual growth of SRI[3] investments is close to 50 %. Almost 20 % of all capital in Europe is now invested explicitly in the areas of environmental sustainability and social responsibility. Increasingly, investors are deciding to engage in a joint dialogue

---

[1] William Sun, Jim Steward, David Pollard; Reframing Corporate Social Responsibility: Lessons from the Global Financial Crisis.

[2] KMPG International "KPMG International Survey of Corporate Responsibility Reporting 2008", Geneva.

[3] Eurosif "European SRI Study 2008" Paris.

with the company in question, demanding that CSR policies and procedures be implemented and monitored by corporations.

The World Bank Institute offers the "Competitiveness and Corporate Social Responsibilities" course to explore both conventional and innovative policies, strategies, and actions associated with CSR. This is a response to the recent global financial crisis, recession, and shifts in political and economic power across countries, governments, and the private sector are rethinking the strategy behind their development and growth policies. Improved competitiveness at the national, sub-national, and corporate levels is seen as a key priority. At the same time, a growing number of countries and companies recognize the development and business benefits of socially and environmentally responsible policies and practices. Emerging evidence supports the idea that developing a long-term corporate strategy based on integrity and social values offers both business benefits to corporations and positive contributions to society.

In conclusion CSR is a hot topic of these crisis days. Therefore, a book such as this covering various aspects of CSR in the world of business will be a useful resource for practitioners, students, and business executives.

I congratulate the participating authors and the two editors for their valuable effort and recommend this book to all scholars, students, and practitioners in the field of CSR.

Prof. Dr. Necdet Şensoy
Board Member
Central Bank of the Republic of Turkey
Ankara, Turkey

Preface

Modern businesses are expected to be socially responsible regardless of their industry of operation or country of abode. The age of economic globalization, efficiency in information transfer, and the desire to make our world a more sustainable place of abode for everyone have all combined together to make it even more so.

The principles advocated by international organizations, global investors, governments, capital markets, etc., for corporations to ensure that they have in place a good system of governance have compellingly meant that global businesses can no longer continue to dream that irresponsible and reckless actions would help them to survive and prosper.

Interestingly, it has now become apparent that corporate entities in both developed and developing economies of the world are conscious of their social responsibilities to all their stakeholders. This is certainly a step in the right direction; our world can only be a better place for this generation and future generations of all living objects to exist in, if we all as individuals and corporate entities were to take issues relating to social responsibility very seriously.

Global businesses whether small, medium, or large have several parts to play in the debate on social responsibility. Effective individual and corporate actions on social responsibility are required by all, which perhaps explains why these two editors have taken the step to call for a book on *Corporate Social Responsibility in the Business World*. The book has been particularly fortunate in attracting interest from nine countries in five of the six continents that make up our world. The views expressed in each of the 19 chapters could therefore be said to be truly global. The main objective of the book was to gather together in a book the progress which corporations have made in the drive for sustainability and social responsibility over the last few decades.

It is hoped that our readers, regardless of their perspectives on CSR, would find the issues explored and discussed by contributors to each of the 19 chapters useful and of interest. We hope that the book provides useful information on corporate activities in the quest for a better understanding of how CSR has evolved in business and not for profit entities across the world since its relatively recent general global acceptance.

February 2013   Samuel O. Idowu
                                                              Asli Yüksel Mermod

Acknowledgments

We are extremely grateful to all our contributors who have made the publication of this book a reality. There are also others who have not featured directly in the book as contributors but have played some equally active parts in ensuring the publication of the book. We would also like to show our gratitude to them.

We are grateful to the following friends and colleagues, Kiymet Caliyurt—the President of the two Network Groups under the auspices of which the book was published. Our colleagues at Springer have been equally great in dealing with the technical aspects of publishing the book, we are deeply grateful to them.

The two editors would like to thank their respective families for their support and they would also like to thank their colleagues and friends who have supported them in seeing through the publication.

The next book in the Networks' series of books on CSR is on *Corporate Governance: An International Perspective* which will be edited by Caliyurt and Idowu.

Contents

Part V   CSR in Education and Socially Responsible Investment

About the Editors

Asli Yüksel Mermod is a Professor of Finance in the Faculty of Economics and Administrative Sciences at Marmara University, Business Administration Department Istanbul, Turkey. She started her academic career in 1996 after moving from a professional business career where she worked as a public relations manager in Istanbul Convention and Exhibition Center and as editor, copy writer, and accounts director in Mediart and Sanatevi Advertising Agencies. Besides Marmara University, Mrs. Yüksel Mermod also taught at Webster University in Geneva, Switzerland from 2004–2006, and still teaches as visiting professor at different universities such as Bahcesehir University—International Finance Department and Okan University—Social Sciences Institute as adjunct faculty. Mrs. Yüksel Mermod studied Economics (Volkswirtschaftslehre) at Konstanz University in Germany and graduated from Marmara University Economics Department. She completed her M.Sc. and Ph.D. in Finance from Marmara University Banking and Insurance Institute and is fluent in Turkish, English, and German. She is currently at an intermediate level in French.

Dr. Asli Yüksel Mermod's research areas cover Bank Management, CSR, Socially Responsible Investing, Brand Equity, Electronic Finance, and Financial Services Marketing. She teaches International Banking, International Finance, Project Finance, Bank Management, Principles of Finance and Financial Markets, and Institutions on undergraduate courses and Bank Funds Management, Project Finance and Management, Risk management in Banking on MBA, Ph.D., and Executive MBA classes. She has supervised four Ph.D. theses and 14 master's theses to date. She has published books on Bank Management, Service Marketing, Brands and Measuring Brands' Equity, Electronic Banking and Risks, Banking Law and Management in Turkey and also in Germany. She published in different national and international journals such as Internationale Wirtschafts-Briefe, Journal of Business Economics and Management, Journal of Internet Banking and Commerce, International Journal of Energy Sector Management, and Journal of Business and Economics Research. Dr. Yüksel Mermod also wrote chapters in many international published books. Besides her research and teaching responsibilities, Dr. Yüksel Mermod has been actively involved in administration at Marmara University. She was the Vice Director of Marmara University Institute of Social Sciences and was Erasmus-Socrates Program Coordinator for postgraduate students. She has key positions in some international scientific conference organizations in terms of organization and scientific committee membership, board of referees, and she has taken part in a number of book projects on CSR with internationally esteemed scholars.

Samuel O. Idowu is a senior lecturer in Accounting at the city campus of London Metropolitan Business School, London Metropolitan University, where he was course organizer for Accounting Joint degrees, Course Leader/Personal Academic Adviser (PAA) for students taking Accounting Major/Minor and Accounting Joint degrees, and currently Course Leader for Accounting and Banking degree. He is a fellow member of the Institute of Chartered Secretaries and Administrators, a fellow of the Royal Society of Arts, a Liveryman of the Worshipful Company of Chartered Secretaries and Administrators, and a named freeman of the City of London. Samuel has published about 40 articles in both professional and academic journals and contributed chapters in edited books and the Editor in Chief of two major global reference books by Springer—*Encyclopaedia of Corporate Social Responsibility* (ECSR) and *Dictionary of Corporate Social Responsibility* (DCSR). Samuel has been in academia for 25 years winning one of the Highly Commended Awards of Emerald Literati Network Awards for Excellence in 2008. In 2010, one of his edited books was placed in the 18th position out of 40 top Sustainability books by Cambridge University Programme for Sustainability Leadership. He has examined for the following professional bodies: the Chartered Institute of Bankers (CIB) and the Chartered Institute of Marketing (CIM) and has marked examination papers for the Association of Chartered Certified Accountants (ACCA). His teaching career started in November 1987 at Merton College, Morden Surrey; he was a Lecturer/Senior Lecturer at North East Surrey College of Technology (Nescot) for 13 years where he was the Course Leader for B.A. (Hons) Business Studies, ACCA, and CIMA courses. He has also held visiting lectureship posts at Croydon College and Kingston University. He was a Senior Lecturer at London Guildhall University prior to its merger with the University of North London, when London Metropolitan University was created in August 2002. He has served as an external examiner to a number of UK Universities including the University of Sunderland, the University of Ulster, Belfast, and Coleraine in Northern Ireland, and Anglia Ruskin University, Chelmsford. He is currently an External Examiner at the University of Plymouth and Robert Gordon University, Aberdeen, Scotland. He was also the Treasurer and a Trustee of Age *Concern*, Hackney, East London from January 2008 to September 2011. Samuel is on the Editorial Advisory Board of the Management of Environmental Quality Journal and International Journal of Business Management. He has been researching in the field of CSR since 1983 and has attended and presented papers at several national and international conferences and workshops on CSR.

Contributors

Dr. Maria Aluchna is an Associate Professor at the Department of Management Theory, Warsaw School of Economics, Poland. She specializes in corporate governance (ownership structure, board, executive compensation, transition economies) as well as in strategic management. Additionally, she researches in the field corporate social responsibility. She was awarded the Deutscher Akademischer Austauschdienst (DAAD) a study visit research scholarship by the Universität Passau and Polish-American Fulbright Commission scholarship to Columbia University, in the United States of America. She was also awarded the Polish Science Foundation young researchers for two consecutive years (2004 and 2005). Recently, within a grant financed by the EU she completed a visiting scholar's stay at London Metropolitan Business School in the UK and at University of Sydney Business School in Australia. Maria Aluchna teaches "Corporate Governance" (both in Polish and English), "Strategic Management" (in English) and "Transition in Central and Eastern Europe" (in English). She is the author of a number of articles in both national and international journals as well as conference papers. She was serving on two editorial boards in 2008 and was the Editor in Chief of the Warsaw Stock Exchange portal on corporate governance best practice. Currently, she is a consultant to a law firm Głuchowski, Siemiątkowski i Zwara and conducts research projects for the Capital City of Warsaw in Poland.

Asli Aybars is a Research Assistant at Marmara University; Turkey, in the Faculty of Business Administration. She worked as a Research Assistant in Bahcesehir University between 2007 and 2009. She is a Ph.D. Candidate of Accounting and Finance program at Marmara University and she is pursuing her studies in the area of Corporate Finance for her thesis. Some of her main areas of research are Financial Economy and Financial Markets with particular emphasis on the relationship between Corporate Social Responsibility, Sustainability and firms' financial performance.

Dr. Özlem Arzu Azer's research interests encompass political economy, strategy and finance. She earned her B.S. degree in Economics from Marmara University, Istanbul, Turkey her Master of International Banking also from Marmara University and her doctorate of Economics from Istanbul University. Her doctorate thesis was on the subject of globalisation, titled as "*The Transformation of Capital* *from Multinational to Supra-national between 1994—2005.*" She began her career as banker at Garanti Bank, Head Quarters and her banking career continued as the Divisional Manager of the department of Commercial Credit Quality Control, she continued her Banking career as a Vice President at Koçbank; in the Credit Assignment Department at the Demir-Halk Bank/Rotterdam, Netherlands, Vice President at the Commercial Credit Risk Management at the Denizbank and finally ended her banking career as Marketing Manager at the Arap Turkish Bank. After her 13 years career in banking, she worked as an Educational Consultant at the Boğaziçi Eğitim ve İletişim and gave some lessons on Analysis of the World Economy, The Credit Risk Management to private and public companies. She began her academic career as an Assistant Professor at Istanbul Arel University in 2009 and worked there for two years. She is still an Assistant Professor at Kadir Has University, a post she took up in May 2012.

Mara Del Baldo is an Assistant Professor of Small Business Management at the University of Urbino, Italy. Moreover she teaches Financial Accounting at the Department of Economics, Society and Business, at the same Univeristy. Her main research interests are in small business economics and management with particular focus on Corporate Social Responsibility and small entrepreneurs/SMEs' business ethics; entrepreneurial values and attitudes as drivers for the diffusion and implementing of CSR and sustainability in SMEs; SMEs strategies of qualitative development; networking processes and networking strategies for the development of SMEs and on Social and Environamental Accounting (SEAR). She is currently involved in diverse researches and projects on those topics. She is member of European Council for Small Business (ECSB); Centre for Social and Environmental Accounting Research (CSEAR), University of St Andrews, Scotland; EBEN Italia (European Business Ethics Network) and Editorial Board Member of several journals including the following (International Journal Piccola Impresa/Small Business; International Journal of Society Systems Science; Journal of Business Administration Research (JBAR); International Journal of Business and Management) as well as reviewer for different international journals. She has published in Italian and foreign journals as well as in national and international conferences proceedings.

Burcu Öğüt Çayözü She was born in 1981 in Istanbul, and completed her bachelor degree on Tourism Management Department at Dokuz Eylül University Faculty of Business in 2004. She worked in the hospitality sector for two years and then changed her target into the cosmetics market. She has obtained license in trichology after completing her theoretical and practical trainings in Turkey and in the Far East for five years. Meanwhile, she started pursuing her graduate level studies in MA in Production Management and Marketing at the Marmara University. Currently, she is working on her master's thesis on "Corporate Social Responsibility".

Emine Çobanoğlu Ph.D. She was born in 1965 in Istanbul, and completed her bachelor degree on Business Administration at Boğaziçi University, Faculty of

Economics and Administrative Sciences in 1987. She started her academic career as a Research Assistant at Marmara University, Department of Business Administration in 1994. She completed her Ph.D. in Marketing at Marmara University, Social Sciences Institute in 1998. Currently, she teaches at Marmara University, Department of Business Administration as an Associate Professor. Her research and teaching areas include sales management, organizational marketing, and social media marketing. She has book chapters in national and international books, and published articles in national and international journals.

Ioana Dragu is a Ph.D. Candidate at Babes-Bolyai University, Faculty of Economics and Business Administration, Accounting and Audit Department, Romania. She graduated with a degree in Finance and Banking English Line of Study within Faculty of Economics and Business Administration and then followed an M.B.A. of two years in Managerial Accounting, Audit and Control. She started her research in corporate reporting and disclosure when she was still a student. Currently she is writing her thesis on Integrated Reporting as the mixture between financial and non-financial information brought together, including in her topic sustainability and corporate social responsibility disclosure practices. She has published a series of papers on reporting practices and disclosure regarding financial and non-financial information. Her research interests incorporate CSR insights and their integration into standard reporting practices and information disclosure.

Aslı Küçükaslan Ekmekçi is a Professor of Management and Organization at Marmara University, Istanbul, Turkey. She has a doctorate degree in Business Administration. Her research interests are in management and organization, business administration, multinational management, international management and marketing. She has authored over 50 research papers in multiple editions and journals and books on these subjects.

İrem Eren Erdoğmuş Ph.D. She was born in 1976 in Istanbul, and completed her bachelor degree on Political Science and International Relations at Boğaziçi University, Faculty of Economics and Administrative Sciences in 1998. She started her academic career as a Research Assistant at Marmara University, Department of Business Administration in 1999. She completed her Ph.D. in Marketing at Boğaziçi University, Social Sciences Institute in 2005. Currently, she teaches at Marmara University, Department of Business Administration as an Associate Professor. Her research and teaching areas include brand management, services marketing, international marketing, emerging markets, and social media marketing. She has book chapters in national and international books, and articles in national and international journals, some of which include European Journal of Marketing, International Marketing Review, and Journal of Fashion Marketing Management.

Vanina Andrea Farber is the Professor and Chair of Sustainable Entrepreneurship and Social Inclusion at Universidad del Pacifico, Business Graduate

School, Peru. She is also a Lecturer at IE Business School, Spain. She holds a Ph.D. in Business Administration and M.A. in Economics from the University of Memphis, USA and a "Licenciatura" in Political Science from the University of Buenos Aires. She has worked as a consultant for different international organizations (ILO, UNDP, UNOPS, European Commission) and in Spain (IUDC UCM, Observatorio de Responsabilidad Social Corporativa de Madrid, Centro de Estudios Económicos Tomillo), applying quantitative methods to economic development and corporate social responsibility issues.

Mehpare Karahan Gökmen is a Research Assistant at Ondokuz Mayıs University, Turkey at the Economics and Administrative Sciences Faculty, Business Administration Department. She served as Research Assistant in Business Administration (English) department for four years between 2008 and 2012. Mrs. Karahan Gökmen received her B.A. in Business Administration (English) Department, Marmara University and her Master and Ph.D. degrees in Accounting and Finance (English), Marmara University. She graduated from Samsun Anatolian High School in Turkey. Her main areas of research are in Financial Accounting and Corporate Social Responsibility.

Phillip Gordon currently retired, has almost three decades of business and academic experience in the Bay Area. His business experience, in corporate information technology, was in regulated industries with major social responsibilities: financial services (Charles Schwab, Franklin Resources, and Wells Fargo) and health care (Kaiser). He consulted with a number of startups on business and technology strategy, including nonprofits. He founded and managed the Center For Socially Responsible Business at the Lokey Graduate School of Business, Mills College, including a continuing conference and speaker series. He taught at the Haas School of Business, University of California, USA, the Norwegian School of Management, UC-Berkeley, and the Lokey Graduate School of Business. His courses included Management Information Systems, Innovation and Entrepreneurship, Technology and Society, Social Networks, and Corporate Social Responsibility/Green Business. He holds a Ph.D. degree in Genetics from UC-Berkeley.

Carmela Gulluscio Assistant Professor at the Faculty of Economics, University Unitelma Sapienza of Rome, Italy. She holds a Degree in Business Studies magna cum laude, Università degli Studi Roma Tre, Italy and a Ph.D. in Business Studies, Università degli Studi Roma Tre. She specialized in Accounting (General Accounting Theory, Accounting for Public Administration, German Accounting, Social Accounting, Accounting History). Moreover, she conducts research on corporate social responsibility themes. She was visiting scholar at Ludwigs Maximilian University, Munich. She teaches "Economia aziendale", "Accounting" and "Audit". She is author of a number of national and international conference papers, and she has contributed to several academic books.

Ali Osman Gurbuz is presently working as Professor of Banking and Finance at Istanbul Commerce University, Turkey. He received his Ph.D. in Finance from Marmara University, Istanbul and worked as a Professor of Accounting and Finance at Marmara University. He worked as a Visiting Scholar at Purdue University (USA) and International American University in Cyprus. He specializes in firm valuation, corporate governance and investment analysis. He has published several books and articles in finance.

Hosei Hemat is a Ph.D. Candidate in the Discipline of Marketing at the Business School of the University of Sydney, Australia. She has completed a Master of Commerce degree with Honours and a Bachelor of Commerce degree at the Univeristy of Sydney Business School. Hosei has worked in Finance and Marketing at IBM Australia and is applying her experience to her research. Her research areas include international business and marketing. While her postgraduate honours degree focused on cross-cultural managerial risk-taking, her research for her Ph.D. revolves around cross-cultural consumer behaviour with great attention to industry relevance. She has also taken interest in CSR from a marketing perspective.

Abubakar Sadiq Kasum obtained his B.Sc. Accounting in 1999, M.Sc. Accounting in 2005 and Ph.D. Accounting and Finance in 2010. He became an Associate of the Institute of Chartered Accountant of Nigeria (ACA) in 2005. Between 1992 and 1994 he worked in Lagos Nigeria and observed the National service between 1999 and 2000. He is currently based in a faculty at the University of Ilorin, Nigeria, a job he took up in 2001. He has attended and presented papers at several international conferences and has published several articles in refereed academic journals. He is currently serving on the editorial boards of the International Journal of Critical Accounting and Contemporary Management Research. He served on the conference organizing committee for the 3rd Northern Regional District Accountants Conference and Member's Education and Training Committee of the national council, of the Institute of Chartered Accountant of Nigeria. He is one of the Editors of a forthcoming edited book on *Socio-Economic Dimensions of CSR, Gower, UK.*

Zuhal Yonca Odabaş is an Assistant Professor at the Department of Sociology, Atatürk University, Turkey. She specializes in sociology of disaster, sociology of health and illness, gender studies, and social problems. She stayed in Indonesia (2005−2006) with the Darmasiswa Program of Indonesian Government for ten months and conducted two researches about the social effects of Tsunami and Bird flu. She is the author of a number of articles for national and international journals as well as conference papers. She is one of the editors of Global Dialogue's Turkish version (an online bulletin of International Sociological Association). She is the member of European Sociological Association (ESA), International Sociological Association (ISA), and Sociological Association in Turkey. Currently, she teaches at Atatürk University, Department of Sociology, Turkey and conducts research projects.

Juliette Overland is a Senior Lecturer in corporate law at the University of Sydney Business School, Australia where she is also the undergraduate co-ordinator for business law. She has also lectured in corporate and commercial law at Macquarie University. Juliette's research and teaching expertise is in insider trading, securities regulation, corporate governance and corporate social responsibility, and she has published widely in these areas. Juliette also has extensive practical legal experience, having worked as a Senior Corporate Lawyer in top tier Australian law firms for more than 10 years before commencing her academic career. Juliette regularly consults to industry on legal issues within her areas of research expertise.

Dr. Mia Mahmudur Rahim is a Lecturer in law at Queensland University of Technology, Australia. He did his LLB with Honours and LLM from Dhaka University; LLM in International Economic Law from Warwick University, UK as a Chevening Scholar; MPA from LKY School of Public Policy with NUS Graduate Scholarship and Ph.D. from Macquarie University, Australia with the Research Excellence Scholarship. Before he joined the university, he was a Lawyer and Deputy District and Sessions Judge in Bangladesh. He also worked for the Law Commission and the High Court of Bangladesh. He is a member of the Center for Legal Governance of Macquarie University, Australia and Technical Committee for Asian Consumer Protection Research Network.

Adriana Tiron- Tudor Ph.D. is a Professor, at Babes-Bolyai University, Faculty of Economics and Business Administration, Accounting and Audit Department Romania, where she coordinates doctoral students in accounting, and is actively involved in the development of the Romanian accounting profession. A graduate of Babes Bolyai University with a Ph.D. in Accounting, Mrs. Tiron-Tudor received her expert accountant designation from the CECCAR in 1995. She has lectured extensively at national level on financial management, internal audit and control topics for public entities, and on public sector accounting standards. In 2006, she contributed to the implementation of the accrual accounting system in Romania by being involved in the training of practitioners, especially for local governmental administrations. Since 2008, she has also been a member of the Fédération des Experts Comptables Européens (Federation of European Accountants, or FEE) Public Sector Committee. She became a member of the International Public Sector Accounting Standards Board (IPSASB) in January 2012. She was nominated by the Body of Expert and Licensed Accountants of Romania (CECCAR). She has also made several publications relating to government accounting and standard setting in the public sector.

Patrizia Torrecchia Temporary Research Associate at *Dipartimento di Scienze Economiche, Aziendali e Finanziarie*, Università degli studi di Palermo, Italy. She holds a Degree in Business Studies*magna cum laude*, Università degli studi di Palermo and a Ph.D. in Business Studies, Università degli studi di Messina. She specialized in Accounting (General Accounting Theory, Accounting for Public Administration, Social Accounting, International Accounting) as well as in

Accounting History. Additionally, she conducts research on corporate social responsibility themes. She was awarded from Università degli studi di Palermo scholarship for research stay at Saïd Business School, Oxford, and also from Bonino-Pulejo Foundation (Messina) scholarship for research stay at Bocconi University, Milan. She received Società Italiana di Storia della Ragioneria (SISR) award for *Best doctoral thesis*. She is author of a number of international conference papers as well as national ones, and she has contributed to several academic books.

Prof. G. José Vargas-Hernández is a member of the National System of Researchers of Mexico and a zresearch Professor at University Center for Economic and Managerial Sciences, University of Guadalajara. Professor Vargas-Hernández has been a Visiting Scholar at IURD-UCBerkeley and has a Ph.D. in Public Administration and a Ph.D. in Economics. He has undertaken studies in Organizational Behavior and has a Master of Business Administration and a Bachelor in Commercial Relations. Professor Vargas-Hernández has received awards from AGBA Distinguished Scholar. 2011, 2010–2011 Emerald/EMRBI Business Research Award, Global Strategic Management, Inc., Washington, D.C. (2009), Academia de Ciencias Administrativas, México (2007), Global Business and Economic Development (2004), Allies Academies, International Business Academy (2002), among others.

Dr. Ülkü Yüksel is a Senior Lecturer (Associate Professor) at the University of Sydney Business School, Marketing Discipline, Sydney, Australia since 2004. She made the move from industry to academia after a 13-year-long professional business career in the international services sector. Her research revolves around the application of consumer marketing concepts in various contexts; including services marketing, international business and cross-cultural consumer behaviour.

Introduction

Issues involving corporate social responsibility and good corporate governance have shaken our world to its very roots for a number of years. We now know the serious damage that bad corporate governance on the part of corporations could cause everyone living in our world, even those who live in the remotest parts of the world who have little or nothing to do with economic globalization. The effects of the financial crisis which commenced in 2008 still linger on despite all global efforts to put things right.

The crisis has made it more apparent to us all that global businesses have the power to make things very pleasant or most unpleasant for all either by their responsible or irresponsible actions. What was probably not apparent to us all until now was the length of time it could take for the unpleasantness to remain with us. Governments of countries have been forced to make many unpleasant economic decisions which have made them unpopular amongst their citizens. Countries which had competently managed their economic affairs for centuries with little or no problems have been made to appear as mediocre in managing the business of government. Social unrests as a result of economic woes and hardships have pervaded many countries and their cities in Europe and other parts of the world. Several countries have seen their creditworthiness downgraded by credit raters as if countries were individuals unable to manage their financial affairs. The leading nation of the world, the United States of America, has not been immune from it all. It has also been badly bruised because of the global financial downturn. Some country leaders who had ruled their countries with an iron hand and no questions were asked by citizens for decades were toppled, killed, or are presently paying the price of irresponsibility in solitary confinement in prisons or awaiting trials. Many developing nations continue to suffer in silence with no one noticing them as a result of these problems, all because of what?—The failure on the part of businesses to behave in a socially responsible manner.

To argue that social irresponsibility on the part of businesses was a general problem prior to the emergence of the crisis would be totally incorrect. This was because many businesses in different parts of the world were and still are doing their utmost in respect of corporate social responsibility, but it must be remembered that a basket of eggs only needs to have a couple of bad eggs in it for it to be described as a basket of bad eggs. It is therefore clearer to us now that it would certainly be inadequate for 99 % of global businesses to be socially responsible and the remaining 1 % to be socially irresponsible; our world would still remain a socially irresponsible world and the threat of financial crisis and all its peculiar economic woes would never go away. We need all businesses—100 % of them to be socially responsible, that is our contention and we strongly believe in that argument.

Idowu (2010) notes that those at the helm of managing the affairs of corporate entities need to behave responsibly and ethically at all times, behaving responsibly can only create sustainable value for companies which take this suggestion on board. The collapse of several of the so-called "good, successful and profitable" businesses in both the advanced and less advanced countries of the world a few years back has confirmed that cutting corners and behaving unethically is a more expensive way of running the business and would inevitably lead to disasters, damage reputations, unsettle stakeholders' lives, and result in loss of confidence. See the issues and consequences of high profile corporate collapses in different parts of the globe such as Polly Peck (UK), Enron (USA), Royal Ahold (The Netherlands), Parmalat (Italy), China Aviation Oil (China/Singapore), HIH Insurance (Australia), and Satyam (India) just to mention a few.

We have all got to behave responsibly in whatever spheres of life we find ourselves, regardless of whether we are businesses or individuals, that is what our world needs—another contention of these two editors and authors of this piece. Idowu (2010) argues that over the last few years, corporate entities around the world have identified the value creating ability of CSR and many corporate entities have consequently started to weave the so-called triple bottom line idea—economic, social, and environmental (ESE) considerations into their strategies. Of course, what constitutes CSR actions as noted in the *Global Practices of CSR*, Idowu and Leal Filho (2009), depends on a series of factors and circumstances that a country finds itself at any given point in time which requires CSR-related actions; that message has hopefully been understood by all. Interestingly, several scholars and authors have identified different issues that fall within the domain of CSR. These issues have no limit; see for example Kotler and Lee (2005). These CSR issues would change from time to time depending on the nation's social, economic, and environmental problems of the time which also suggests that corporate leaders need to be innovative in dealing with finding solutions to these issues; after all the intention should be to create sustainable values which all stakeholders can easily identify with and could help these stakeholders to meet their respective needs.

This book, *Corporate Social Responsibility in the Global Business World*, provides an insight into how issues relating to CSR have been inculcated into business strategies around the world. The book has been fortunate in the sense that its contributors, who are scholars and professionals in their different fields around the world, have each provided an account of how CSR has either changed or redirected thoughts in different corporate entities. They have expressed from their own viewpoint how corporate entities, both profit seeking and not-for-profit, are demonstrating the positivity they are giving back to society in return for the privileges noted by Lantos (2001).

The book has been divided into five parts, each part focusing on issues that have been grouped together for convenience. Part I—Professionals' CSR—which comprises three chapters; Part II—Corporate Governance and Financial Crisis—looks at these issues in four chapters; Part III—Not-for-Profit Sector and SMEs—considers CSR from these perspectives in three chapters; Part IV—Ethics, Morality and CSR—explores these issues in six chapters; Part V—CSR in Education and Socially Responsible Investment explores these issue in three chapters.

The very first chapter, *Cause Related Marketing and CSR* by Hosei Hemat and Ulku Yuksel provides a holistic view of cause-related marketing (CRM) which has been used as a business strategy by companies for more than three decades to encourage customers to make donations toward good causes by helping not-for-profit organizations. This is one of the philanthropic dimensions of CSR, these two authors note.

In Chap. 2 on *Integrating Best Reporting Practices for Enhancing CSR*, Ioana-Maria Dragu and Adriana Tiron-Tudor look at the contribution of CSR to International Accounting Standards in corporate reporting from the perspective of Integrated Reporting, a growing area in CSR reporting. The chapter seeks to present co-ordinates of CSR practices and ultimately performs an analysis of the insights into corporation practices by determining the level of their CSR disclosures of these corporations.

Chapter 3 by Asli Ekmekci entitled *An Examination of the Relationship Between Companies' CSR Activities and Consumers Purchase Behavior*, explores the role of companies' CSR activities in the purchase orientation of consumers. The chapter, which stems from a study of Turkish companies listed on the Istanbul Stock Exchange, notes that companies' CSR activities influence consumers' purchase pattern of these companies' products and services.

Giallonardo and Mulino in Chap. 4 *CSR in a Model of Heterogeneous Firms' Financial Constraints and Economic Crisis*, develop a model on strategic CSR and vertical product differentiation in a context of heterogeneous firms and monopolistic competition based on Mélitz (2003) model. The chapter argues that in times of crisis under certain conditions the attention devoted by firms to CSR has the capability of being strengthened.

In Chap. 5 by Mia Rahim entitled *The Impact of CSR on Corporate Governance*: *The Rise of Standardization of CSR Principles*, argues that the synergy between CSR and Corporate Governance (CG) has changed the commercial environment since it has brought about a complex and dimensional focus of modern businesses. This has encouraged corporations of today to concentrate on meeting their triple bottom line's key performance indicators. The chapter investigates how CSR has impacted on CG in its quest to contribute to the rise of standardization of CSR practices.

Maria Aluchna in Chap. 6 entitled *The Corporate Declaration Versus Corporate Practices*: *The Financial Crisis Perspective*, explores the reasons and causes of the current financial global financial meltdown on the economies of the developed nations of the world. The chapter casts some doubt on the effectiveness of the regulatory and governance standards on global financial markets. Aluchna also notes some structural and governance failures which occurred as a result of unethical and irresponsible behaviors on the part of some corporate executives in addition to poor systems of corporate governance in both listed companies and financial institutions. Aluchna identifies that there are lessons which could be learnt from corporate governance issues in each of the following companies: Bears Stearns, Lehman Brothers, Goldman Sachs, AIG, and General Motors.

In Chap. 7 entitled *CSR Reporting and Directors' Duties: The Australian Experience*, Juliette Overland argues that CSR has the potential to impact significantly on the conduct of global business. She notes that the growth in international trade has enabled all and sundry to be aware of the impact of corporate behavior on all aspects of society. Overland notes that many businesses, regardless of where they are based or their industry of operation are keen to act responsibly. Two CSR issues of great importance to business, Overland notes, are the public disclosure and reporting of issues that impact on CSR (CSR Reporting) and the relationship between CSR and Directors' duties and the impact it could have on the corporate decision-making process.

Patrizia Torrecchia and Carmela Gulluscio in Chap. 8 *Social Responsibility: The Italian Case Within Public Administration*, examine the Italian perspective of CSR and CSR Reporting in the Public Sector in Italy. The chapter describes the concept of CSR in terms of how it is perceived in the Italian Public Administration; it analyzes the characteristics of social reporting in two public sector organizations which operate in Italy and underlines stakeholders' role in the Italian CSR reporting framework.

In Chap. 9 of the book, entitled *To the Root of Entrepreneurial Values—The Relationship with the Territory as a Driver for the Development of CSR: An Analysis of the Experiences of Italian SMEs*, Mara Del Baldo reflects on the contributions of SMEs in spreading the philosophy and practices of governance directed toward CSR and Sustainability. The chapter provides the findings of a study of a sample of SMEs in the Marche region of Italy. The chapter is a recommended read for anyone interested in how SMEs are faring in the CSR debate in Italy.

In Chap. 10; a second chapter by Patrizia Torrecchia and Carmela Gulluscio on *CSR and Healthcare Public Sector: Some notes on the Concept of 'Value,'* the chapter outlines the concept of 'value' from the standpoint of the public sector. The chapter suggests a shift from the established doctrine for making the expectations of multiple stakeholders to converge.

In Chap. 11 by Phillip Gordon entitled *The Two Walmarts*, Gordon notes that Wal-Mart has gained a significant reputation as both a sustainable business and a proponent of, and leader in, sustainability. But in reality there appears to be some good actions in its drive for sustainability toward a group of its stakeholders but with some actions which could be perceived as its inability to demonstrate sustainability toward other groups of its stakeholders. There appears to be a policy of two-in-one when it comes to CSR by the company, argues Gordon.

Chapter 12 by Kaplan and Odabas entitled *Cultural Heritage and Women*: *The Case of Beypazari*, provides the authors' findings of a study in Ankara's Beypazari County, Turkey, on the role of women who produce and sell traditional labor products for commercial purposes. The authors present *Women's* perspective of goods and services which fall under the area of cultural heritage.

Vanina A. Farber in Chap. 13 entitled *The Challenges of a Peruvian Inclusive State*, explores the challenges that Peru faces in its attempt to become an inclusive state. The chapter analyzes various dimensions of social inclusion in terms of the economic, social, political, and cultural rights of Peruvian citizens. Farber argues that for the State of Peru to realize its ambition of an Inclusive State, it must move from the rhetoric of social inclusion to a functional design and practice of collaborative government and social responsibility.

In Chap. 14 entitled *The Dynamics Behind the 'Moral Corruption' of the Financial System*, Özlem Arzu Azer argues that the current global financial crisis has its roots in the corrupt practices during the transformation of the world economic system of the 1980s.

In Chap. 15 on *The Responsibilities of Corporations*: *An Analytical Approach*, Abubakar Kasum appraises the responsibilities of businesses using a just and fair approach with regard to the relationship they have with all stakeholders. Kasum argues that there are three responsibilities of business enterprises namely; primary, secondary, and tertiary. The chapter notes that if businesses do the right things at all times, there will be no need for anyone to compel anybody to be responsible as these responsibilities would be met naturally with no coercion.

Eren-Erdoğmuş et al. in Chap. 16 on *Success in Philanthropic CSR*: *The case of* Turkey, consider the practice of CSR from its philanthropic dimension in Turkey—an emerging economy and shed some light on some philanthropic activities which have become prominent and sometimes criticized in debate on CSR in Turkey. The chapter looks at two large Turkish companies which have been known to have good reputations in philanthropic CSR.

In Chap. 17 entitled *Fostering Management Education for Professional* Integrity: *The Case of the Centre for Economic and Managerial Sciences, University of Guadalaraja, Mexico*, José G. Vargas-Hernández analyzes the case of management education for professional integrity from a Mexican University perspective. The chapter uses the ethnographic research method to document its findings from a study.

In the penultimate chapter on *Do Institutional Investors Prefer to Invest in Socially Responsible Companies ?* An empirical analysis, Gurbuz et al. note that CSR has become an indispensable item on corporate agendas even though the discipline has been on the corporate scene for well over three decades. They argue that socially responsible investors are now very keen to ensure that those companies they invest in take their triple bottom line issue very seriously. The chapter provides findings from an empirical study carried out on shares listed on the Istanbul Stock Exchange by Institutional Investors.

In the final chapter, Yuksel-Mermod and Idowu look at socially responsible investing from the global perspective with special reference to Turkey. These two authors argue that SRI is now one of the trendiest investment approaches of our time simply because it has the capability of improving corporate reputation and credibility.

A careful read through of the issues noted in this introductory chapter to each of the 19 chapters featured in this book should hopefully reveal that these chapters have one common theme and message; that CSR is an important discipline in modern business. Modern corporate entities are all aware of the value creating capability of CSR even in times of financial downturn. Elkington's Triple bottom principle has gone a long way to reorient modern businesses that success is no longer measured only in terms of the Income Statements or what is happening to the share price on the stock market; in any event a company that is perceived to be socially irresponsible would have an unsatisfactory P and L Account result and lower share price at the stock exchange. It is now no longer a case (as was previously believed) that it is only society which benefits from corporate entity's CSR actions but the entity actually helps itself to operate sustainably and consequently do well because of its triple bottom line actions (Elkington 1997). Malloch (2013) argues that the concept of CSR and its various theories and practices are part and parcel of corporate behavior, governance, and wider understandings of society and business. This goes a long way to confirm that large corporations and SMEs of our era must be socially responsible, since it is good for business.

A series of corporate governance failings by those at the helm of control and directing the affairs of some large companies in different countries around the world have led to corporate scandals and collapses in recent times. These have led to governments, stock exchanges, and other interested parties to embark on issuing Corporate Governance Codes and Guidelines for listed companies to follow, see for example Cardbury Report 1992, or more recently, the Combined Code 2009 in the UK, the OECD Seven Corporate Governance Principles 1999 and 2004, and several others in countries around the world. Issues relating to corporate governance failings affect all economies of the world regardless of whether these are developed, developing, or emerging—it is a global issue. This is therefore one of the reasons why the next book in the series will be on *Corporate Governance*. The book will explore how some countries of the world are dealing with the issue of best practice in their corporate governance.

Samuel O. Idowu
Asli Yüksel Mermod

References

Elkington, J. (1997). *Cannibals with forks: The triple bottom line of 21st century business*. Oxford: Capstone.

Idowu, S. O., (2010). Professionals' perspectives of CSR: An introduction. In S. O. Idowu & W. Leal Filho (Eds.), *Professionals' perspectives of corporate social responsibility*. Heidelberg: Springer.

Idowu, S. O. & Leal Filho, W. (2009). Global practices of CSR in context. In S. O. Idowu & W. Leal Filho (Eds.), *Global practices of CSR*. Heidelberg: Springer.

Kotler, P. & Lee, N. (2005). *Corporate social responsibility*. Hoboken: John Wiley.

Lantos, G. P. (2001). The Boundaries of strategic corporate social responsibility. *Journal of Consumer Marketing, 18*(7), 595–612.

Malloch, T. R. (2013). 'Foreword—corporate social responsibility: Key issues and debate'. In S. O. Idowu, N. Capaldi, L. Zu & A. Das Gupta (Eds.), *Encyclopedia of corporate social responsibility*. New York: Springer.

Part I
Professionals' CSR

Chapter 1
A Critical Review of Corporate Social Responsibility Practices from a Marketing Perspective: Is Cause-Related Marketing Really a 'Win–Win–Win' Situation?

Hosei Hemat and Dr. Ulku Yuksel

Abstract This chapter provides a holistic overview of cause-related marketing (CRM) as a corporate social responsibility strategy. CRM is a partnership entailing a company making donations to a non-profit organisation (NPO) depending on a consumer purchase of a CRM-labelled product or service (Varadarajan and Menon 1988). The chapter provides a detailed definition of CRM and distinguishes it from other popular strategic forms of giving such as philanthropy and sponsorship. Further, the chapter offers a consolidated overview of consumer expectations and behaviours in regard to CRM based on academic literature and commercial survey results. In addition, real-world examples of CRM campaigns are provided and critically analysed. The chapter critically reviews the positivist claim that CRM is a 'win–win–win' strategy, where all parties (i.e., firms, NPOs and customers) involved in CRM campaigns experience a variety of benefits. While the chapter acknowledges that potential benefits may be derived by all parties involved in CRM campaigns, it also provides an overview variety of potential risks and costs associated with CRM campaigns, which illustrates that not every party involved may 'win'. The chapter's objective is not to conclude that potential risks or costs outweigh the benefits of CRM, but instead to suggest that potential negative factors should be considered when developing CRM campaigns.

1.1 Introduction

According to global Corporate Social Responsibility (CSR) consultancy Cone Inc., 93 % of consumers globally expect firms to display CSR by going beyond the minimum standards required by law to operate responsibly by changing their

H. Hemat (✉) · Dr. U. Yuksel
The Discipline of Marketing, The University of Sydney Business School, Sydney, Australia
e-mail: hhem3223@uni.sydney.edu.au

A. Yüksel Mermod and S. O. Idowu (eds.), *Corporate Social Responsibility in the Global Business World*, DOI: 10.1007/978-3-642-37620-7_1,
© Springer-Verlag Berlin Heidelberg 2014

business practices and lending support to address social and environmental issues (Cone Inc. 2011). Only 6 % of consumers agreed with economist Milton Freedman (Cone Inc. 2011) that a company's only responsibility is to its shareholders by purely focussing on profit maximisation (Carroll and Shabana 2010). Similarly, there is increasing literature that argues for the business case of CSR and that CSR is a key factor for building long-term competitiveness (Porter and Kramer 2006). In fact, 68 % of companies are utilizing CSR as an opportunity for corporate growth (Pohle and Hittner 2008).

As a response, many companies incorporate such consumer expectations not only through corporate philanthropy/donations, but also increasingly through marketing communications and promotions with social dimensions by applying so-called cause-related marketing (CRM) strategies (Drumwright 1996). CRM is a partnership entailing a company donation to a not-for-profit organisation (NPO) dependent on a consumer purchase of a CRM-labelled product or service (Varadarajan and Menon 1988). CRM is a widely-used marketing tool, which acknowledges "not only that business success is compatible with the public good, but that both can be achieved in unison" (Varadarajan and Menon 1988, p. 72) achieving social and economic goals. In fact, CRM is the fastest growing marketing strategy, which demonstrates its relevance and potential that managers attribute to it (Chang 2008).

An example of some well-known health-related CRM campaigns would be in partnership with cancer research foundations, where companies around the world such as Avon, Mount Franklin, Estee Lauder and Revlon make donations toward cancer research foundations based on sales of their CRM labelled products (Polonsky and Wood 2001). This usually involves incorporating some pastel pink colouring or a pink ribbon in their product/service characteristics, which has become synonymous with the "fight for breast cancer" globally (Lubitow and Davis 2011). An example of a popular Australian CRM campaign is the Mount Franklin Spring Water (owned by Coca-Cola Amatil) partnership with the National Breast Cancer Foundation (NBCF) during 2006–2011. As part of this partnership Mount Franklin water has transformed their water bottle lids (see Fig. 1.1) from blue to pastel pink during the breast cancer awareness month of October, which led to a AUD $ 1.35 million donation by Mount Franklin to the foundation (Mount Franklin 2012).

The increased use of CRM has been triggered by factors relating to business, NPOs and government, which include shifts in the macro-environment, competitive challenges, increased demands of consumers and decreased government support for non-profit organisations. Firms tend to increasingly face saturated markets and a difficult task of differentiating their offerings, which is intensified by strong local and international competition (Westberg 2004). Accordingly, firms use new strategies to develop a sustainable competitive advantage, while being more accountable for expenses (Polonsky and MacDonald 2000). Similarly, NPOs also face pressures to find alternative ways of funding as government support generally declines (Andreason 1996).

Fig. 1.1 Mount Franklin water bottles in partnership with the National Breast Cancer Foundation. *Source* Mount Franklin Website (2008). Available from: http://mountfranklin. mccann.com.au/2008-the-power-of-positivity/

Further, consumers are more demanding not only in terms of price and quality but also of a firm's CSR efforts (Ptacek and Salazar 1997). Accordingly, today's marketplace is characterised by steady increases in competition, product parity and consumer expectations (Westberg 2004), where CRM is often applied and referred to as a unique win–win or win–win–win strategy (e.g., Westberg 2004; Ptacek and Salazak 1997) for the company, the NPO and the customer. Accordingly, companies would enjoy the benefits of building/differentiating their brands, improving their corporate image and publicity, improving employee morale, and increasing sales revenue, while the NPOs would receive increased funding and public receptivity to their causes and customers would feel better about themselves through their CRM labelled product purchase (e.g., Berglind and Nakata 2005; Varadarajan and Menon 1988).

Essentially, CRM involves companies communicating through their advertising, packaging, and promotions their CSR, which is their affiliation with their NPOs or support for causes. Key is to attract customers who are seeking to make a difference in society or the environment through their purchasing (Bronn and Vrioni 2001). However, consumers are critical of companies who make claims relating to their contribution to social causes (Bronn and Vrioni 2001). Accordingly, there are risks and costs associated with CRM strategies, which may prohibit a win–win–win situation for parties involved. It is important to note that the win–win–win approach to CRM follows a very optimistic/positivist view disregarding the potential risks and costs involved. For example, NPOs may pursue CRM partnerships with businesses at the expense of pursuing individual donors, which has been questioned as a sustainable approach (Andreason 1996). Similarly, a poor fit between the two partners may damage the business' or the NPO's reputation and integrity. There is also the potential risk that consumers perceive businesses as exploiting a not-for profit cause (Webb and Mohr 1998). Accordingly, it is important to view any CRM campaign critically to understand whether a win–win–win situation is in fact evident.

Therefore, this chapter provides an overview of CRM as a popular marketing strategy used by businesses as part of their overall CSR efforts. It provides a consolidated overview of consumer expectations and behaviours in' regards to CRM based on academic literature and commercial survey results. In addition, real-world examples of CRM campaigns are provided and critically analysed. Further, the positivist claims relating to CRM strategies are reviewed, while acknowledging the potential risks, costs and issues associated with such strategies. The objective is not to conclude that potential risks or costs outweigh the benefits of CRM, but instead that potential negative factors should be considered when developing CRM campaigns.

1.2 CRM as a Unique Marketing Strategy

Firms have a variety of different options to choose from when they decide to donate or lend support to social or environmental causes. Drumwright and Murphy (2001) suggest that there are 10 socially oriented marketing activities, which include: philanthropy, strategic philanthropy, sponsorships, company advertising with social dimensions, cause-related marketing, licensing agreements, social alliances, corporate volunteerism, strategic corporate volunteerism and enterprises. The three most popular are arguably philanthropy, sponsorships and CRM. While CRM is the focus of this chapter, it is important to note the features that differentiate CRM from other popular CSR strategies. Accordingly, the following section provides a brief overview of key features of CRM, philanthropy and sponsorship.

1.2.1 CRM

The concept of *CRM* was first introduced by American Express as part of a marketing campaign in 1983. The campaign's objective was to increase the number of new customers and increase credit card usage (Westberg 2004). American Express developed a campaign connecting these financial objectives with a commitment to donate funds toward the restoration of the Statue of Liberty: US $0.01 for each use of a card and US $1 for each new customer during the last quarter of 1983. The campaign was attributed with a 28 % increase in card usage when compared to the same period of the preceding year along with a significant increase in new customers. Accordingly, American Express donated US $1.7 million to the Statue of Liberty—Ellis Island Foundation. The campaign was considered a win–win situation for both, the company and the NPO—Ellis Island Foundation.

The concept of CRM is a relatively new concept in the academic literature. The first scholars to focus on CRM were Varadarajan and Menon (1988), who acknowledged the emergence of this marketing communications tool with the following definition:

> Cause-related marketing is the process of formulating and implementing marketing activities that are characterised by an offer from the firm to contribute a specified amount to a designated cause when customers engage in revenue-providing exchanges that satisfy organizational and individual objectives (p. 60).

CRM is based on the notion of "doing well by doing good", where CRM strategies are developed to primarily achieve company objections through a partnership or support of a cause or NPO. CRM is an attractive alternative for companies that are under pressure to generate a return for every investment (Cunningham 1997), which supports the business case for CSR in general. "The business case for CSR refers to the 'business' justification and rationale; that is, the specific benefits to businesses in an economic and financial ('bottom-line') sense that would flow from CSR activities and initiatives. In some cases, the effect of CSR activities on firm financial performance may be seen clearly and directly" (Carroll and Shabana 2010, p. 95).

1.2.2 Philanthropy

Philanthropy is the oldest form of corporate giving and is based on altruism, where a company gives "…cash or kind- without an expectation tied benefit" (Collins 1994, p. 226). It involves "returning or investing a share of the company's profits into the community" (Mescon and Tilson 1987, p. 49). Such donations to an NPO or cause are based purely of a firm's wish to be a good corporate citizen without seeking any association with the NPO (Shaw and Post 1993). However, many firms do seek to benefit from, for example, an improved image/reputation from their philanthropic giving by publicising their association with the NPO/cause. This is then referred to "pseudo-altruism" (Collins 1994, p. 227), where the philanthropic donations are in fact financially driven, which is also referred to as strategic philanthropy.

1.2.3 Sponsorship

Sponsorship has been acknowledged as being a commercial activity primarily that moved away from doing good for society to doing financially well for companies (Polonsky and Wood 2001). It involves either providing "financial or in kind to an activity by a commercial organisation for the purposes of achieving commercial objectives" (Meenaghan 1983, p. 9). The type of events/organisations that are sponsored can range from sports, entertainment, causes, arts, festivals, fairs and membership organisations (IEG 2012). The firm uses the sponsored event and association to support specific company, marketing or media/PR efforts. An example of a 35 year long-standing global partnership is McDonald's sponsoring the International Olympic Committee until 2020, the former reportedly pays "US $100 m for each two-game deal of one winter and summer" (BBC 2012). As a top partner, McDonald's has exclusive branding rights and was one of the few branded food suppliers during the London Olympics.

Similarly, IBM has been the Official Technology Partner of the Australian Open for the 18th year in 2011 by providing technical services such as IBM solutions that capture, analyse and distribute data on almost every aspect of the Australian Open (IBM 2011). In return, the IBM sponsorship is publicised in the media and IBM logos are displayed throughout tennis courts to encourage the association of the partners in spectators' minds.

It is important to note that sponsorship would not be considered pseudo-altruism as companies explicitly sponsor to benefit from these events. According to global sponsorship consultancy IEG, despite economic uncertainty global sponsorship spending is forecasted to grow by 4.9 % to $51 billion in 2012 (IEG 2012).

In summary, while CRM, philanthropy and sponsorship are all valid CSR activities, the latter two differ in their objectives and execution from CRM and thus, are not to be confused with CRM.

1.3 Major Types of CRM Strategies

There are several major types of CRM strategies according to Polonsky and Speed (2001). They derived the following four aspects to categorise each strategy:

- Type of target consumer (existing or new).
- Type of required customer action (purchase or purchase with secondary action).
- Nature of firm's financial commitment (unlimited or capped).
- Required leveraging activities.

1.3.1 Broad-Based CRM

These campaigns are considered the simplest form of CRM. Companies make an unlimited donation for CRM products and services purchased, which allows targeting new and existing customers (Polonsky and Speed 2001). Advertising would be required as a leveraging activity. However, other promotional activities, such as including packaging information and/or point of sale information about the campaign, can be added to strengthen the firm-cause association (Polonsky and Speed 2001). An example could be a car firm donating $100 per car sold for a given time period to a cause.

1.3.2 Limited CRM

These campaigns are very similar to broad-based programs; however, they differ in the company's financial commitment. With limited CRM, the company donation is capped, which increases the return on investment for the firm given no donations will be made when sales exceed the predetermined capped level. Companies sometimes provide a minimum donation amount, which would increase the perceived sincerity of the campaign (Polonsky and Speed 2001). This would be captured in the "fine-print", but if the cap is set too low it may seem that the company is exploiting the association between the firm and the cause purely for its own gains (Speed and Thompson 2000). An example could be that a fast moving consumer goods company donates 7 % of their sales of its products of up to $30,000 to a cause/NPO.

1.3.3 Market-Focused CRM

These campaigns involve tailored leveraging activities that target new customers, which can be either capped or uncapped in terms of financial commitment. Secondary consumer behaviour (action) may be required when targeting new customers (Polonsky and Speed 2001). For example, a company aiming to target male customers may choose to work with a male associated cause or include vouchers in advertising in male oriented magazines, which once redeemed will affect the company's donation. This allows companies only to donate, when the targeted customers purchase a product as well as redeem their vouchers. Thus, market-focused programs require more tailored promotions than the other CRM programs, which may also involve sales promotions. Accordingly, such programs can be used to achieve firm objectives, while limiting donations and increasing returns on donations for firms (Polonsky and Speed 2001). An example of a market focused campaign could be American Express' campaign, which involved donating US $1 toward the restoration of the Statue of liberty for each new customer (Westberg 2004).

1.4 CRM and Consumer Behaviour

1.4.1 Public Opinion Studies on CSR/CRM Consumer Attitudes and Behaviour

This section draws on empirical academic research and on commercial public opinion studies to provide an overview of consumer trends, expectations and behaviour that generally encourage companies and NPOs to engage in CRM.

Table 1.1 2011 Cone Inc. consumer insights

	Develop partnerships (%)	Raise Awareness and educate (%)	Make donations (%)
Be more likely to trust a company	56	51	47
Want to purchase the company's products/ services	52	48	43
Be more loyal to the company (i.e., Continue buying the company's products/services)	49	48	43
Want to engage with the company beyond their purchases (e.g., Donate their own money or volunteer for the company)	37	33	33
Recommend the company and its products/ services	54	49	46
Want to work for the company	41	41	34
Feel good about the company operating in their communities	56	55	50

Percentage who strongly agree
Source Cone Inc (2011), p. 19

Cone Inc. and Echo research conducted an extensive study involving 10,000 consumers in the world's ten largest countries by GDP (e.g., USA, UK, Germany, China, India, Brazil and China) to reveal consumer attitudes toward socially responsible firms and their CSR expectations (Cone Inc. 2011). According to their findings, if a company addresses issues that consumers find most important, it may be rewarded with their trust, loyalty, advocacy, engagement and increased sales as illustrated by the findings in Table 1.1 (Cone Inc. 2011).

Specifically, they found that "when price and quality are equal, 94 % of consumers are likely to switch brands to one associated with a good cause" (Cone Inc. 2011, p. 21). In fact, 76 % of these consumers noted that they have actually switched brands in the past 12 months (Cone Inc. 2011). Similarly in 2011, 93 % of consumers indicated that they would buy a product/service associated with a cause compared to 56 % of consumers in 2008, which signals a major rise in this consumer attitude. The finding that 81 % of consumers would actually donate to a charity supported by a company they trust (Cone Inc. 2011) may be of particular interest for NPOs. But maybe most importantly, the study also found that 93 % of consumers are prepared to boycott a company for irresponsibility or deceptive business practices, of which 56 % already boycotted companies in the past (Cone Inc. 2011).

1.4.2 Empirical Research on Effect of CRM on Consumer Attitudes and Behaviour

This section reviews academic research on the effect of CRM on consumer attitudes and their intention to purchase, which are both important indicators of consumer purchase behaviour (Westberg 2004). As mentioned, CRM is a marketing communications tool, which focuses on changing and/or enhancing brand attitude and/or motivate purchase.

Similar to public opinion polls, academic literature generally supports the impact of CRM on consumer attitudes and/or behaviour (e.g., Drumwright 1996) as well as consumer support for CRM and companies employing CRM (e.g., Ross et al. 1992). Fundamentally, successful CRM strategies rely on socially conscious consumers, who are defined as follows by Webster (1975):

> The socially conscious consumer can be defined as a consumer who takes into account the public consequences of his or her private consumption or who attempts to use his or her purchasing power to bring about social change (p. 188).

1.4.2.1 Brand Image and Brand Attitude

Brand image and attitude are two of the key objectives of firms in using CRM strategies. A brand image is defined as a sign, symbol, name, design or a combination of these, which identifies products/services of a company and thus, differentiates the company from other competitors (Armstrong et al. 2011). Brand image consists of "…perceptions about a brand as reflected by the brand associations held in consumer memory" (Keller 1993, p. 3). A high brand awareness and positive brand image ideally increase the likelihood of brand selection as well as consumer loyalty, while decreasing exposure to marketing strategies of competitors (Keller 1993).

Fombrun and Shanley (1990) found that a company's commitment to a social cause affected how customers viewed the company. In addition, several studies confirmed that consumers will use their purchasing power to reward or punish companies based on their CSR efforts (e.g., Sen and Bhattacharya 2001). In fact, Ross et al. (1992) reported that half of respondents previously bought a product or service mainly due to their wish to support a NPO/cause.

Berger et al. (1999) investigated the effect of the persuasiveness of print advertising with CRM claims on brand attitude and purchase intention compared to print advertising without CRM claims. They found that information related to the CRM strategy enhanced consumer involvement with the advert. In cases, where the advert was viewed positively, there was higher involvement with the advert and thus, more positive brand attitudes and buying intentions.

Furthermore, Bloom et al. (2006) compared CRM to sponsorship and found that CRM was more effective at product choice. In fact, Pracejus and Olsen (2004) found that respondents made trade-offs for CRM donations regarding other service or product characteristics. Further, Arora and Henderson (2007) found that CRM strategies enhance consumer product quality perceptions and reduce price sensitivity. More recently, Henderson and Arora (2010) found that presence of CRM improved brand choice probabilities within a product/service category. They also confirmed that this leads to spill-over effects to other product/service categories.

Krishna and Rajan (2009) also confirm this and reported that 67 % of participants were willing to pay a higher price for products/services with CRM elements.

1.4.2.2 CRM: Strategic Fit

Academics and practitioners both identified the strategic fit between the firm/brand and the NPO/cause as a critical success factor for a CRM campaign (e.g., Adkins 1999). Consumers should perceive an affinity between the selected cause and the product or service (Westberg 2004). Accordingly, when selecting CRM partnerships both parties are advised to find an NPO/firm where some synergy is evident with the company's products. Consumers view CRM campaigns more positively if an obvious connection between the two parties exists (Andreason 1996).

1.4.2.3 Consumer Scepticism

In addition, the level of consumer scepticism toward CRM has been investigated by several academics (e.g., Webb and Mohr 1998; Ross et al. 1992; Andreason 1996). Consumer scepticism is often reflected in consumers voicing their scepticism about a firm's motivation to use CRM campaigns, especially when the company promotes their partnership with the NPO (Webb and Mohr 1998). Consumer scepticism is evaluated on the basis of whether consumers view the CRM campaign to benefit the cause or to exploit the cause (e.g., Ross et al. 1992; Andreason 1996; Webb and Mohr 1998). In fact, Webb and Mohr (1998) found that 50 % of their respondents held negative attitudes toward CRM campaigns mostly due to scepticism regarding the implementation and/or cynicism toward the company's motivation. Similarly, 50 % of the respondents also perceived that the company's motivation is self-serving (Bronn and Vrioni 2001). Thus, consumers with high levels of scepticism are less likely to react positively to CRM programs than consumers with low levels of scepticism. Accordingly, consumer scepticism can influence consumer purchase decisions, which requires practitioners to have a comprehensive understanding of the level of consumer scepticism in their target audiences (Bronn and Vrioni 2001).

1.5 Benefits and Objectives for Firms, NPOs and Consumers

As mentioned earlier, CRM campaigns are referred to as win–win–win strategies for all parties (i.e., firms, NPOs and consumers) involved (e.g., Ptacek and Salazak 1997). The following section builds on this notion and provides a detailed overview of benefits that fims, NPOs and consumers may derive from participation in CRM campaigns. The section concludes with some CRM examples where win–win–win situations were in fact achieved.

Table 1.2 Business CRM objectives

Revenue generation	Corporate image	Brand equity
Generate incremental revenue	Enhance corporate image	Increase brand awareness
Attract new customers	Improve social responsibility	Increase brand recognition
Retain existing customers	Counter negative publicity	Enhance brand attitude
Increase market share	Pacify customer groups	Differentiate brand
Competitive edge	Attract and retain employees	Attract media attention
Improve customer loyalty	Favourably influence external stakeholders (i.e., Government)	

Source Westberg (Westberg 2004)

1.5.1 Firms: Objectives and Benefits

1.5.1.1 Firm CRM Objectives

As previously noted the business case for CSR is usually 'bottom-line' based for firms. CRM as a subset of CSR is not immune to stand the business case and must meet objectives relating to corporate, marketing and/or individual product strategies. While the strategies are different in nature, they tend to share three main aspects: revenue generation, corporate image and brand equity (Westberg 2004). Table 1.2 summarises specific company CRM objectives for each of these aspects:

To realise such objectives, US companies spent US $1.68 billion in 2011, which is predicted to grow to US $1.73 billion in 2012 and was the fastest growing category in the IEG sponsorship tracking report (IEG 2012). As noted previously, the primary motivation for CRM strategies is usually to create a positive response from consumers or potential new customers, which will eventually result in an increase of sales revenue. But despite such advantages of CRM, it carries risks, which will be discussed in a later section of this chapter.

1.5.2 Firm Benefits from CRM Campaigns

Benefits can be of financial and non-financial nature for companies using CRM strategies. CRM campaigns may stimulate an increase in sales revenue (Ptacek and Salazar 1997) as consumers perceive that in buying a CRM associated product, they contribute to society. Further, the CRM partnership between the firm and the NPO may lead to product differentiation allowing customers to distinguish between two relatively identical products (Webb and Mohr 1998).

Further, CRM campaigns assist firms in changing their corporate image (Strahlevitz and Myers 1998), which will indirectly lead to further sales to consumers wishing to buy from more socially responsible firms, who perceive a value that is added to the product due to the CRM campaign.

They may also be increased publicity for firms, where some CRM campaigns may enable companies to directly communicate to an NPO's supporters, which may not have been possible with traditional advertising (Polonsky and Wood 2001), which in turn enables direct access to potential new customers.

In addition, CRM may have benefits for the company internally as it allows employees and staff to see that their employer cares (Mullen 1997). In fact, companies engaging CRM strategies have experienced increased employee morale and motivation, particularly when senior management is seen to be actively engaging in CRM/CSR activities. As a result, employee loyalty and/or pride may increase if the company is involved in CSR programs generally (Mullen 1997). For example, Avon employees have experienced increased pride in representing their company to women as it donates to breast cancer research through their CRM campaign (Davidson 1997). This may also lead to increased employee performance (Polonsky and Wood 2001).

1.5.3 NPO Benefits from CRM Campaigns

There are a number of benefits that arise for NPOs out of a CRM partnership with companies. CRM may lend some causes/NPOs legitimacy in marketplaces which previously may not have been the case; NPOs may now be viewed as feasible partners for companies and no longer as "beggars" asking for corporate donations (Weeden 1998).

Financially, CRM campaigns lead to monetary payments for causes directly obtained from donor companies (Drumwright 1996). Accordingly, the financial benefits received from CRM partnerships allow NPOs to support their causes, groups, individuals and the environment that rely on them.

Other benefits may be of non-financial nature, where the donor company provides volunteers to the NPOs and senior executive staff may provide managerial assistance within the program, which may enhance the managerial skills for the NPO internally (Polonsky and Wood 2001). CRM partnerships may also enhance the NPOs image and provide publicity in cases, where the NPO's aim is to communicate a message to change consumer behaviour such as getting consumers to exercise more (Polonsky and MacDonald 2000). This way the message is being communicated, which would be a key NPO objective in such instances.

1.5.4 Consumer Benefits from CRM Campaigns

Some of the benefits CRM campaigns give consumers are in form of additional details and sometimes additional perceived value depending on the consumer (Webb and Mohr 1998). If consumers want to buy from socially responsible companies, then CRM may facilitate to differentiate between similar companies/

brands. Consumers may also think that they are contributing to society by buying a CRM associated product/service.

Further, consumers are consistently pursued for donations directly by different NPOs, which may lead to "donor-fatigue" (Murphy 1997). This may lead to consumers reducing or stopping their donations as they think they have donated enough or may get tired of the constant requests for support by different NPOs (Polonsky and Wood 2001). However, through CRM associated product purchases customers may not experience "donor-fatigue" as they are not pursued to buy such products but do so at their own discretion.

Consumers buy products/services that are most likely part of their regular shopping items. The only decision to be made relates to switching the brand for a product similarly priced, which may encourage consumers to buy the CRM product. Therefore, consumers may prefer CRM labelled/associated products as they do not necessarily have to change behaviours and, while contributing to a cause/NPO (Ptacek and Salazar 1997). Further, while consumers usually make small donations, through continued purchase of a CRM associated product/purchase they will have the feeling of doing good continuously and donated more overall (Polonsky and Wood 2001).

Overall based on the above, CRM can be worthwhile for NPOs, firms and consumers involved, which is why it is often referred to as a win–win–win strategy. However, it is paramount to consider where CRM may have negative results for the parties involved, which is discussed in a later section.

1.5.5 'Win–Win–Win' CRM Campaign Example: Subaru's "Share the Love" Campaign

To conclude this section, a successful CRM campaign by Subaru in partnership with five charities is reviewed as an example of a 'win–win–win' CRM campaign. It illustrates the 'win' for the NPOs, Subaru and its customers.

1.5.5.1 Campaign Details

In 2008 in the USA, Subaru launched its "Share the love" campaign in partnership with five NPOs: ASPCA Big Brothers and Big Sisters of America, Habitat for Humanity, Meals on Wheels, and National Wildlife Foundation (Jones 2012). As part of this campaign, Subaru would donate US $250 in total for each car sold or leased. The campaign ran for about 2 months (Jones 2010), which is an example of a broad-based CRM campaign. The customer would choose which charity/NPO gets the US $250 with the option of splitting the money between the charities. If no preference is indicated, Subaru will split the US $250 equally and donate it to each NPO on behalf of the customer.

1.5.5.2 'Win' for Subaru (Firm)

In the wake of the financial crisis, the year 2008 was characterised by decreased consumer spending in all industries including the car industry, which saw an industry decline of about 18 % in car sales according to Subaru's CEO Mahoney (Jones 2010). However, despite the industry decline Subaru was the only car company to grow in this climate; its market share grew to 2 %, which led to its highest market share at the time. Mahoney attributed the growth and performance partly to its "Share the Love" CRM campaign (Jones 2012). He also noted that they decreased their incentive costs, which may be an indication of their CRM campaign working successfully as a differentiating factor in the consumer purchase decision. Further, Subaru's association with these five NPOs would have resulted in an improved brand image as a socially responsible company. The variety of charities would have also allowed Subaru to reach different target audiences with its CRM campaign as well as help deter sceptics of thinking that Subaru only partners with marketable causes.

1.5.5.3 'Win' for NPOs:

Subaru's "Share the Love" campaign resulted in US $4.6 million in donations to the 5 NPOs: ASPCA, Big Brothers and Big Sisters of America, Habitat for Humanity, Meals on Wheels, and National Wildlife Foundation (Jones 2012). Each NPO would also have benefited from an improved brand image and publicity due to the success of the campaign. Further, Subaru has allowed for donations to a variety of different NPOs that support different causes. Accordingly, this would have led to a greater balance in their giving rather than choosing the most marketable NPO as a partner based on firm profit-maximisation objectives, which is a common practice with CRM campaigns (see section on issues, costs and risks of CRM).

1.5.5.4 'Win' for Customers

Similar to Subaru and their NPO partners, Subaru's customers also benefited from the campaign in a number of ways. Firstly, the amount of the donation of US $250 per sold/leased car is a significant amount when compared to other CRMs where transaction based donations are usually relatively low and in the category of fast moving consumer goods. Thus, consumers may feel more charitable and "better" about themselves with such a comparatively large amount. Secondly, consumers have the choice to donate to one of five different charities or split the amount as preferred, which is rare when it comes to CRM. CRM campaigns usually do not offer customers such flexibility. Another benefit to this feature is that customers are being actively engaged in the donation process, which will not only enhance their experience but also increase their feeling of having contributed to the cause

Fig. 1.2 "Share the Love" CRM Campaign. *Source* Cima Systems (2012)

directly as part of the execution/implementation. Overall, customers benefit from the campaign as the various NPOs support causes that contribute to society, of which customers are a part of.

1.5.5.5 Continuous 'Win–Win–Win': "Share the Love" CRM Replicated 2008–2013

The success of Subaru's "Share the Love" campaign that has resulted in 'win–win–win' outcomes for all parties involved has been replicated for every year since 2008. Subaru has run its campaign for at least four years now, generating US $20 million in donations to various NPOs (Cima Systems 2012). Figure 1.2 is a picture of their 2011–2012 campaign which replaces three of the original five 2008 NPOs. For the 2012–2013 campaign, consumers were asked to help Subaru choose two out of six pre-selected NPO options by voting on Facebook for the preferred charities until 26th August 2012 before the campaign starts running in November 2012 (Subaru Subaru's Share the Love Event 2012). Involving consumers in the choice of charities and in the implementation by allowing them to choose what charity to donate to increases consumer engagement and attachment to the CRM campaign.

1.6 Criticisms, Risks and Costs Related to CRM

As noted, while there are significant benefits for the different parties (i.e., NPOs, firms and customers) involved from CRM strategies, there are also some criticisms, costs and risks that may prohibit the so-called win–win–win situation for all parties involved. Hence, the following section discusses such criticisms, costs and risks associated with CRM.

Polonsky and Wood (2001) have referred to situations where firms employ tactics such as CRM to increase corporate returns "without a corresponding benefit to consumers or society" (p. 8). They coined such situations as an "overcommercialisation of corporate giving activity" (p. 8), where the social element of giving is exploited. Accordingly, they identified such situations that require practitioner attention.

1.6.1 Overstated Perception of Corporate Generosity

Consumers are misled in cases when companies participate in activities where their generosity/giving is overstated, which may be due to companies trying to maximise their returns on their giving, resulting in an unfair benefit to the firm (O'Sullivan and Murphy 1998). This may lead to consumers shifting their buying of CRM products/services in favour of such firms, which leads to fewer donations to other causes that do not engage in overstating their generosity (Polonsky and Wood 2001).

Similarly, some consumers may perceive certain causes as receiving enough support due to the overstated corporate support, which may lead to consumers directing their donations to other causes (Andreason 1996). This may not harm consumers or other causes, but it may have a negative effect for causes associated in CRM campaigns where firms overstate their support. They may be perceived as needing no further assistance, which ultimately may lead to less funding leaving the NPO unable to support their cause/constituencies.

According to Polonsky and Wood (2001) anecdotal evidence that two-stage CRM campaigns which require secondary consumer behaviour/action may be explicitly designed to exaggerate firm generosity or at least limit firm donations. In such campaigns, firms only donate when consumers buy a product/service and undertake a secondary consumer action such as submitting voucher codes online. However, this requirement may not always be very clear to consumers at the time of purchase and thus, such secondary behaviour may not take place. Accordingly, firm donations to the NPO are reduced, while firm generosity is overstated (Polonsky and Wood 2001).

1.6.2 Shifting in Donations

From a firm's perspective a shift in donations may occur, where firms now engage in more and more strategic giving such as CRM as it will provide firms with a return on their investment (e.g., Ptacek and Salazar 1997), which may result in a reduction of a firm's philanthropic donations, which are based on altruistic reasons

(Collins 1994). This would result in a shift in the type of donations. However, a shift in the type of causes/NPOs that companies support may also occur. Companies may choose an NPO not based on the social good that can be achieved but rather because of its marketability as more publicity and sales can be generated (Davidson 1997). Thus, other deserving NPOs may not be considered as partners for CRMs but instead more marketable causes/NPOs will be chosen as CRM partners as their better public profile allows them to be a better marketing vehicle for companies (Polonsky and Wood 2001). For example, breast cancer as a cause may receive more donations than prostate or ovarian cancer as it is more marketable.

1.6.3 Strategic Mis-Fit Between NPO and Firm

As noted earlier, the strategic fit between the NPO and firm is a key success factor for a CRM campaign. Affinity and synergy should exist between the NPO and the firm as consumers view campaigns more positively, if there is an obvious connection between the two parties (Westberg 2004). Accordingly, a strategic mis-fit would imply that consumers cannot perceive an affinity between the cause and the product/service/brand/firm, which would consequently result in consumers viewing such CRM campaigns more negatively.

CRM campaigns are a type of brand alliance, where both firms and NPOs need to protect their brand equity (Andreason 1996). Thus, a mis-fit may come at a cost for both the NPO's and firm's brand equity, if popular media publicises a mis-fit or if consumers' perception of the individual parties is affected due to a strategic mis-fit. A loss in credibility is particularly damaging for an NPO and will affect its long-term ability to fund their cause as their firm and individual donations will decrease (Abrahams 1996). For example, an environmental NPO that forms a partnership with a company that is actually polluting the environment may suffer significantly as it may also lose its core supporters (Coddingtion 1993). While the loss for NPOs may be significant, it is important to note that the firm itself will also suffer because in this case, it would be accused of hypocrisy since the fit between the two parties would not be perceived as an obvious connection. This practice, where firms use green and eco-friendly marketing to attract customers although their products, services and firm business practices are actually harming the environment, is referred to as 'green-washing' (Lubitow and Davis 2011).

1.6.4 "Pink-Washing" with Breast Cancer Research

A similar concept to green-washing, is called 'pink-washing' which describes "activities of companies and groups that position themselves as leaders in the struggle to eradicate breast cancer while engaging in practise that may be contributing to rising rates of the disease" (Malkan 2007, p. 75). Companies will incorporate the colour pastel pink or a pink ribbon into their products or services because they are synonymous with the "fight against breast cancer" (Lubitow and Davis 2011). As mentioned in the introduction, many firms choose NPOs associated with breast cancer research, which may be partly due to the fact that for example, "one in nine women will develop breast cancer in their lifetime" (NBCF 2012). Such statistics make it a marketable cause for companies who seek to work with causes that will have a large target audience. Furthermore, women generally do the grocery shopping for households and many firms of fast moving consumer goods choose to team up with breast cancer related causes as they may appeal to women's emotions and fears (Lubitow and Davis 2011).

One CRM campaign that has been accused of pink-washing was a result of KFC's and the NPO Komen's partnership in the USA. Komen is an NPO that funds research and community-based grants in the fight against breast cancer (Komen 2012). In 2010, KFC and Komen launched a CRM campaign in a bid to raise a record-breaking US $8.5 million in donations by donating US $0.50 to Komen for every pink bucket of chicken purchased as depicted in Fig. 1.3 (Hutchison 2010). "KFC has over 5,000 restaurants nationwide, 900 of which are in communities that Komen currently has no presence or outreach in, so when the fast food chain expressed interest in a partnership, Komen took it as an opportunity to connect and educate" (Rader cited in Hutchison 2010). However, this CRM campaign has been widely criticised as hypocritical as KFC and Komen are raising money for women's health (i.e., breast cancer) by selling products that are harmful to women's health (Hutchison 2010). In fact, "according to medical experts, there is an established connection between eating fatty, high caloric food and the risk for breast cancer" (Hutchison 2010), which is in line with the number one advice by cancer researchers to keep a healthy body weight to prevent cancer (Rock cited in Hutchison 2010). Due to this fact this particular CRM campaign seems to undercut the actual cause. Further, according to Hutchison (2010) the campaign has also caused a public outcry on social media, where people are "furious" about the campaign. In addition, Hutchison (2010) notes that some people expressed having lost their faith in Komen, who used to be a respectable advocacy group, which is now however, being questioned due to this campaign.

This example shows that both Komen's and KFC's brand image and credibility have been negatively affected by their CRM partnership, which arguably did not lead to win–win–win situation. While there was a large donation by KFC of US $4.2 million as a result of the campaign (Komen 2010), it falls short of their target of US $8.5 million, which is arguably due to the negative publicity the CRM campaign received. Further, the long-term damage to the brand image and credibility may exceed such short-term financial gains as it may make raising funds in the future difficult for Komen. Consumers may also feel that the firm and the cause/NPO have misled them, leading to an increase in consumer scepticism (Polinksy and Wood 2001). Accordingly, it is crucial that potential CRM partners understand and evaluate the fit between the cause and the firm.

Fig. 1.3 KFC and Komen CRM Campaign. *Source* Examiner (2010)

1.6.5 Variable Duration of CRM Partnerships

Another issue that may arise from CRM campaigns is the long-term feasibility of an NPO, if it relies too heavily on firm donations (Andreason 1996). In an environment where firms are increasingly pressured for returns on investments, partnerships may be stopped by firms, if their targets are not met (Polonsky and Wood 2001). Alternatively, firms may switch NPOs to one that promises higher returns on investments and is generally a more marketable cause.

If firms terminate their CRMs without switching, then the effect is a loss to the cause and society. However, if the firm switches NPO partners then the overall benefit to society remains unchanged (Polonsky and Wood 2001). However, in the latter case, this may have significant long-run effects for the NPO and its existence potentially, if it mostly relies on CRM donations. Thus, NPOs should never solely focus and rely on funding generated through CRM campaigns. They should not neglect their individual donor base, which usually attributes to most of their funding (Polonsky and Wood 2001).

1.6.6 Reductions in Corporate Donations

Another potential risk for NPOs related to CRM campaigns is that companies' return on donations may increase, while companies decrease their actual donations (Gray 1997). Employing CRM programs where secondary consumer action is required, may allow firms to increase their sales and/or improve their image while minimising their donations through such strategies (Polonsky and Wood 2001). This may be intentionally or unintentionally but may lead to consumers being exploited or misled (e.g., Andreason 1996). Overall this will have a direct effect on the NPO's funding, although in some cases increased publicity may lead to increased individual donations (Polonsky and Wood 2001).

1.6.7 Restrictions Imposed on NPOs by Firms

Given that for firms and for NPOs, CRM partnerships are brand alliances, firms may restrict activities of NPOs as firms may exploit their power as donors in the partnership (Andreason and Dumwright 2000). For example, a firm may stipulate that they have an exclusive partnership with the NPO. This prohibits the NPO to work with other firms in CRM campaigns, which restricts the NPO's options to work with any other potential donor firms leading to an increased dependence on one CRM partner firm (Polonsky and Wood 2001).

1.6.8 CRM Paradox

Competition for charitable organisations is generally very high. Generally, governments, individuals and firms support NPOs. Governments fund NPOs the most, followed by individuals and then firms (Polonsky and Speed 2001). Flaherty and Diamond (1999) found that consumers feel that they "have fulfilled their philanthropic obligations" when purchasing through CRM campaigns, which means no (or less) individual separate donations will be made. CRM makes philanthropic giving easy for individuals; it becomes a 2-in-1 activity, with the primary activity usually being grocery shopping. For example, consumers may choose some products such as German firm DANONE's Volvic Mineral Water, who teamed up with UNICEF in a CRM campaign to help provide clean water to rural areas in Africa (Just Drinks 2008). Consumers who would choose to buy Volvic water will "Drink 1 and give 10", which will lead to donations to UNICEF who build clean water wells in Africa. This purchase may come at a slight premium compared to other water brands and consumers may feel satisfied with their donations.

Further, Krishna (2011) found that CRM campaigns reduce individual giving overall, even if the Volvic water for example came at no premium price. It can decrease total contribution to the cause instead of increasing it, which is referred to as the CRM paradox (Krishna 2011). Consumers feel satisfied with their giving through CRM campaigns and will not give to charities directly. Usually individual direct giving to NPOs would exceed amounts that firms would donate to on behalf of consumers through their purchases as these are usually amounts such as for example, US \$0.50 cents per KFC pink chicken bucket (Hutchison 2010). This would have a direct impact on charities' funding because traditionally individual donations are higher than corporate donations (Polonsky and Wood 2001). NPOs should consider this fact and ensure that their efforts are not solely focussed on CRM partnerships. They should still pursue individual donors given it is their second largest donor base.

1.7 Conclusion

In conclusion, this chapter has provided a critical review of cause-related marketing as one of many corporate social responsibility strategies. CRM was distinguished from sponsorship and philanthropy as a distinct form of giving. The chapter then presented both public opinion and empirical research supporting the use of CRM. Further, the motivations and objectives of NPOs, firms and customers to participate in CRM campaigns were discussed. Examples from around the world of successful and questionable CRM campaigns were reviewed.

While there can be significant benefits that may lead academics and practitioners alike to assume a win–win–win outcome for all parties involved, the chapter focuses on potential issues, risks and costs that need to be taken into consideration when developing and implementing CRM campaigns. The potential issues and risks indicate that there may not always be a win–win–win situation as indicated throughout the chapter. In fact, it seems that more often the NPO and the customer are at risk due to the overcommercialisation of CRM campaigns by firms. However, this chapter is not to deter NPOs from the use of CRM campaigns but instead provides a holistic view of CRM and its benefits and risks. Taking both risks and benefits into considerations, may ensure that NPOs and firms form partnerships with the best possible returns on investments for all partners involved. Accordingly, a critical approach towards any CRM campaign claiming win–win–win outcomes is encouraged.

References

Abrahams, B. (1996). Profit from principles. *Marketing*, 22–23.

Adkins, S. (1999). The wider benefits of backing a good cause. *Marketing*, 20–21.

Andreason, A. R. (1996). Profits for nonprofits find a corporate partner. *Harvard Business Review*, 47–49.

Andreason, A. R., & Drumwright, M. E. (2000). Alliances and ethics in social marketing. In A. K. Andreason (Ed.), *Ethical issues in social marketing* (pp. 95–124). Washington, DC: Georgetown University Press.

Armstrong, G., Adam, S., Denize, S., & Kotler, P. (2011). Principles of marketing (5th ed.) Pearsons Australia, Frenchs Forest.

Arora, N., & Henderson, T. (2007). Embedded premium promotion: Why it works and how to make it more effective. *Marketing Science, 26*(4), 514–531.

BBC. (2012, Jan 13). London 2012 McDonald's extends Olympic sponsorship. *BBC*. Retrieved May 23, 2012, from http://www.bbc.co.uk/news/business 16547045.

Berger, I. E., Cunningham, P. H., & Kozinets, R. V. (1999). Consumer persuasion through cause-related marketing. *Advances in Consumer Research, 26*, 491–497.

Berglind, M., & Nakata, C. (2005). Cause-related marketing: more buck than bang? *Business Horizons, 48*, 443–453.

Bloom, P. N., Hoeffler, S., Keller, K. L., & Meza, C. E. B. (2006). How social-caused marketing affects consumer perceptions. *MIT Sloan Management Review, 47*(2), 49–55.

Bronn, P. S., & Vrioni, A. B. (2001). Corporate social responsibility and cause-related marketing: an overview. *International Journal of Advertising, 20*, 207–222.

Carroll, A. B., & Shabana, K. M. (2010). The business case for corporate social responsibility: A review of concepts, research and practice. International Journal of Management Reviews (Blackwell Publishing Ltd, Oxford).

Chang, C. T. (2008). To donate or not to donate? Product characteristics and framing effects of cause-related marketing on consumer behaviour. *Psychology and Marketing, 25*(12), 1089–10110.

Cima Sysems (2012). Share the love event. Blog posted January 9, 2012. Retrieved April 22, 2012 from http://blog.cimasystems.net/2012/01/09/subaru-share-thelove-event/.

Coddington, W. (1993). Environmental marketing: Positive strategies for reaching green consumers. New York.

Collins, M. (1994). Global corporate philanthropy and relationship marketing. *European Management Journal, 12*(2), 226–233.

Cone Inc. (2011). Cone/Echo global CR opportunity study. Retrieved April 21, 13, 2012 from http://www.coneinc.com/globalCRstudy.

Cunningham, P. (1997). Sleeping with the devil? Exploring ethical concerns associated with cause-related marketing. *New Directions for Philanthropic Fundraising, 18*, 55–76.

Davidson, J. (1997). Cancer sells. *Working Woman, 22*(5), 36–39.

Drumwright, M. E. (1996). Company advertising with a social dimension: The role of noneconomic criteria. *Journal of Marketing, 60*(October), 71–87.

Drumwright, M. E. & Murphy, P. (2001). Corporate societal marketing. In P. N. Bloom & G. T. Gundlach (Eds.), *the* H*andbook of marketing and society* (pp. 168–83). Thousand Oaks, CA: Sage.

Flaherty, K., & Diamond, W. (1999). The impact of consumers' mental budgeting on effectiveness of cause-related marketing. *American Marketing Association Conference Proceedings, 10*, 151–152.

Fombrun, C., & Shanley, M. (1990). What's in a name? Reputation building and corporate strategy. *Academy of Management Journal, 33*(2), 233–258.

Examiner. (2010). KFC buckets for a cure help fight breast cancer: KFC promotes pink buckets on Facebook 16th April 2010. Retrieved May 15, 2012 from http://www.examiner.com/article/kfc-buckets-for-a-cure-help-fight-breastcancer-kfc-promotes-pink-buckets-on-facebook.

Gray, S. (1997). Tracking big business donations. The Chronicle of Philanthropy. November 27.

Henderson, T., & Arora, N. (2010). Promoting brands across categories with a social cause: Implementing effective embedded premium programs. *Journal of Marketing, 74*(6), 41–60.

Hutchison, C. (2010). Fried chicken for the cure. April 24, 2010. *ABC News.* Retrieved May 15, 2012 from http://abcnews.go.com/Health/Wellness/kfcfights-breast-cancer-fried-chicken/story?id = 10458830#.UGZB8a5tmSp.

IBM. (2011). IBM and Australian open 2011. Retrieved May 24, 2012 from http://www.australianopen.com/en_AU/event_guide/ibm.html.

IEG. (2012). Economic uncertainty to slow sponsorship growth in 2012. Retrived May 15, 2012 from http://www.sponsorship.com/About-IEG/PressRoom/Economic-Uncertainty-To-Slow-Sponsorship-Growth-In.aspx.

Jones, P. (2010). Cause marketing saves subaru money and generates $5 million for 5 charities. *Cause-related marketing BlogSpot.* Retrieved April 18, 2012 from http://causerelatedmarketing.blogspot.com.au/2010/12/cause-marketing-saves-suburu-money-and.html.

Jones, P. (2012). Has Subaru's 'Share the Love' Cause Marketing Promotion Boosted its Net Promoter Score? *Cause-related marketing BlogSpot.* Retrieved April 18, 2012 from http://causerelatedmarketing.blogspot.com/2012/02/has-subarus-share-love-cause-marketing.html#ixzz2XtFn8IED.

Just Drinks. (2008). US: Volvic, UNICEF launch initiative for clean water for Africa. Retrieved April 17, 2012 from http://www.google.com.au/url?sa=t&rct=j&q=&esrc=s&source=web&cd=1&v d = 0CB0QFjAA&url = http%3A%2F%2F www.justdrinks.com %2Fnews%2 Fvolvic-unicef-launch-initiative-for-clean-water-for africa_id92700.aspx&ei = Y2hmUMK8 HMySiQei9oHgDw&usg = AFQjCNFW wA_uwdk6ub0b_4fNi5fEzuA.

Keller, K. L. (1993). Conceptualizing, measuring, and managing customer-based brand equity. *The Journal of Marketing, 57*(1), 1–22.

Komen. (2010). KFC presents to Susan G. Komen for the Cure® a check for more than $4.2 Million: single largest donation in organization's history. Retrieved April 28, 2012 from http://ww5.komen.org/KomenNewsArticle.aspx?id=6442452377&terms=kfc.

Komen. (2012). About Us. Retrieved May 14, 2012 from http://ww5.komen.org/AboutUs/AboutUs.html.

Krishna, A. (2011). Can supporting a cause decrease donations and happiness? The cause marketing paradox. Retrieved May 18, 2012 from http://philanthropy.com/blogs/prospecting/files/2011/03/cause_marketing_JP_2011.pdf.

Krishna, A., & Rajan, U. (2009). Cause marketing: Spillover effects of cause-related products in a product portfolio. *Management Science, 55*(9), 1469–1485.

Lubitow, A., & Davis, M. (2011). Pastel injustice: the corporate use of pink washing for profit. *Environmental Justice, 4*(2), 139–144.

Meenaghan, T. (1983). Commercial sponsorship. *European Journal of Marketing, 17*, 5–43.

Malkan, S. (2007). *Not just a pretty face: The ugly side of the beauty industry* (p. 75). Vancouver: New Society Publishers.

Mescon, T. S., & Tilson, D. J. (1987). Corporate philanthropy a strategic approach to the bottom-line. *California Management Review, 29*(3), 49–61.

Mount Franklin Website (2008). *The Power of Positivity.* Retrieved 10 may 2012, from http://mountfranklin.mccann.com.au/2008-the-power-of-positivity/.

Mount Franklin (2012). *Our partnerships.* Retrieved May 10, 2012, from http://mountfranklinwater.com.au/our-wellbeing/our-partnerships/.

Mullen, J. (1997). Performance-based corporate philanthropy: how 'giving smart' can further corporate goals. *Public Relations Quarterly, 42*(2), 42–48.

Murphy, D. (1997). Mutual attractions. *Marketing*, October 2, pp. 30–33.

NBCF. (2012). About breast cancer. Retrieved May 15, 2012 from http://www.nbcf.org.au/Research/About-Breast-Cancer.aspx.

O'Sullivan, P., & Murphy, P. (1998). Ambush marketing: The ethical issues. *Psychology and Marketing, 15*(4), 46–57.

Pohle, G. & Hittner, J. (2008). *Attaining sustainable growth through corporate social responsibility.* IBM Institute for Business Value. Retrieved April 15, 2012, from http://www-935.ibm.com/services/us/gbs/bus/pdf/gbe03019-usen-02.pdf.

Polosky, M. J., & Macdonald, E. K. (2000). Exploring the link between cause-related marketing and brand building. *International Journal of Nonprofit and Voluntary Sector Marketing, 5*(1), 46–57.

Polonsky, M. J., & Wood, G. (2001). Can the overcommercialisation of cause-related marketing harm society? *Journal of Macro Marketing, 21*(1), 8–22.

Polonsky, M. J., & Speed, R. (2001). Linking sponsorship and cause-related marketing: Complementarities and conflicts. *European Journal of Marketing, 35*(11/12), 1361–1385.

Porter, M. E., & Kramer, M. R. (2006). Strategy and society: The link between competitive advantage and corporate social responsibility. *Harvard Business Review, 84*(12), 78–92.

Pracejus, J. W., & Olsen, G. D. (2004). The role of brand/cause fit in the effectiveness of cause-related marketing campaigns. *Journal of Business Research, 57*(6), 635–640.

Ptacek, J. J., & Salazar, G. (1997). Enlightened self-interest: Selling business on the benefits of cause-related marketing. *Nonprofit World, 15*(4), 9–13.

Ross, J. K., Pattersn, L. T., & Stutts, M. A. (1992). Consumer perceptions of organizations that use cause-related marketing. *Journal of the Academy of Marketing Science, 20*(Winter), 93–97.

Sen, S., & Bhattacharya, C. B. (2001). Does doing good always lead to doing better? Consumer reactions to corporate social responsibility. *Journal of Marketing Research, 38*(2), 225–243.

Shaw, B., & Post, F. R. (1993). A moral basis for corporate philanthropy. *Journal of Business Ethics, 12,* 741–751.

Speed, R., & Thompson, P. (2000). Determinants of sports sponsorship response. *Journal of the Academy of Marketing Science, 5*(1), 59–70.

Subaru Subaru's Share the Love Event. (2012). Retrieved April 29, 2012 from http://minnesotachevycadillacsubaru.clementsauto.com/159/subarus-sharethe-love-event/.

Strahilewitz, M., & Myers, J. G. (1998). Donations to charity as purchase inceptives: How well they work may depend on what you are trying to sell. *Journal of Consumer Research, 24,* 434–446.

Varadarajan, P. R., & Menon, A. (1988). Cause-related marketing: A co-alignment of marketing strategy and corporate philanthropy. *Journal of Marketing, 52,* 58–74.

Webb, D. J., & Mohr, L. A. (1998). A typology of consumer responses to cause-related marketing: From skeptics to socially concerned. *Journal of Public Policy and Marketing, 17*(2), 226–238.

Webster, F. (1975). Determining the characteristics of the socially conscious consumer. *Journal of Consumer Research, 2,* 188–196.

Weeden, C. (1998). *Corporate Social Investing.* Berrett-Koehler Publishers, San Francisco, CA.

Westberg, K. J. (2004). *The impact of cause-related marketing on consumer attitude to the brand and purchase intention: a comparison with sponsorship and sales promotion.* PhD Thesis.

Chapter 2
Integrating Best Reporting Practices for Enhancing Corporate Social Responsibility

Ioana-Maria Dragu and Adriana Tiron-Tudor

Abstract The importance of the current research lies in its contribution to international accounting literature in the field of accounting and corporate reporting. The study should hopefully become a starting point for future research debate on integrating reporting practices to enhance corporate social responsibility. By amplfying the advantages of developing CSR practices, we similarly seek to increase awareness about *integrated reporting* in order to hopefully increase the number of companies that would voluntarily adopt corporate social responsibility accounting. Which we believe this action would create value and benefit stakeholders and companies which choose to adopt this type of reporting. The main objective of this chapter is to present the coordinates of corporate social responsibility practices and ultimately to perform an analysis of the insights of corporations' practices, by determining the level of their CSR disclosures.

2.1 Introduction

CSR concept is generally defined as actions taken by an organization that aim to achieve sustainable results by employing best practice and standards in its dealings with isuues relating to Social, Economic and Environmental (SEE) impacts of its activities. Although the notion of corporate responsibility is relatively new, the affiliated practices and policies have been around for over 200 years Idowu (2011). The main roles and responsibilities are always discussed within the context of the corporation, society and environment.

While companies measure their performance based on criteria such as the price of goods and servuces, quality of service, and how competitive they are in terms of

I.-M. Dragu · A. Tiron-Tudor (✉)
Faculty of Economics and Business Administration, Babes-Bolyai University,
Cluj-Napoca, Romania
e-mail: adriana.tiron.tudor@gmail.com

A. Yüksel Mermod and S. O. Idowu (eds.), *Corporate Social Responsibility in the Global Business World*, DOI: 10.1007/978-3-642-37620-7_2,
© Springer-Verlag Berlin Heidelberg 2014

their rivals, the not for profit organizations often use the three Es. (efficiency, effectiveness and economy) or simply the 'value for money' (VFM). How can the corporation perceive the supplemental advantages, of economic, environmental, and social nature, that would make the company better off in the eyes of its stakeholders? Such elements would comprise community support, better trade-mark identity, reduced costs by eliminating wastes or improved working conditions. Nowadays, customers, investors, governments and employees understand the need for a corporate social responsible behavior. Within the business environment, reputation has become a primary quality, and CSR practice represents its prerequisite.

The positive CSR experiences build trust and understanding from stakeholders' side. Corporate social responsibility is perceived as an important and integral part of the day to day activities of a company. Therefore, a responsible business leads to an enlargement of its activities ending with a sustainable result.

This chapter presents the context within which corporate social responsibility practices operate in the global business environment. We start from the various definitions of the concept of CSR, and then describe its main elements, as well as the international guidelines regulating the field. Further on, we highlight the reasons behind the practice corporate responsibility and the benefits that derivable from it. On the background of CSR overview, we perform a literature review on the most relevant studies on CSR disclosure and then we introduce the notion of integrated report as the link between financial and non-financial information.

2.2 Corporate Social Responsibility: Definition, Core Elements and International Guidelines

International literature discusses three visions on CSR, namely (Benabou and Tirole 2010): (1) increasing profit as a result of incorporating a socially responsible behavior; (2) sacrificing profit in favor of sustainability as a result of stakeholders' pressure, and (3) engaging in socially and environmentally beneficial activities in priority to profit targets as a company initiative. *Corporate social responsibility* represents the responsible behavior of corporations that generate welfare and profit for stakeholders. Hopkins (2003) defines CSR from the perspective of both social and economic dimensions, focusing on stakeholder equality. Through CSR, organizations have become aware of the impact of their operations on society and environment. Dahlsrud (2008) and Marsden (2001) argues that corporate social responsibility means achieving profit by employing a socially responsible behavior that demands accountability and transparency towards stakeholders and future generations (Andersen 2003). Therefore, corporate social responsibility should be undertaken on a voluntary basis (Dahlsrud 2008; Piacentini et al. 2000). CSR contributes to sustainable development by enhancing economic, social and environmental benefits for stakeholders. In addition, by reducing the negative effects and increasing positive contributions on society (Pinney 2001) and environment, corporations actually engage in a socially responsible behavior. Dahlsrud (2008); Lea (2002) and Van Marrewijk (2003) define CSR as the process of integrating both social and environmental elements into business operations and stakeholders needs.

CSR implementation varies by company and country. Incorporating many additional subjects- *organizational governance, human rights, labor practices, environment, fair operating practices, consumer issues, community involvement and development*—corporate social responsibility has the main purpose of maintaining the path to sustainability (Financial Times Lexicon, Corporate Social Responsibility CSR—Global Executive MBA). Please see a pictorial form of CSR and its core elements in Fig. 2.1.

The field of social responsibility has a generally recognised and used set of guidelines *ISO 26000* issued in 2010. According to the standards, CSR is derived from the notion to re-affirm that our future as a sustainable society can be only be achieved through a general respect for human rights, sustainable environmental operating practices, consumer issues, community involvement and development, organizational governance.

2.3 The Key Drivers for CSR Reporting

The practice of CSR is determined by certain factors that inspire corporate entities to exibit socially responsible behaviors: stakeholder value creation, increase in profit, reputation, efficiency, investments, human and intellectual capital, low risk level and high ethical standards. Investors have become more aware of good practices in terms of social responsibility. They came to the understanding that

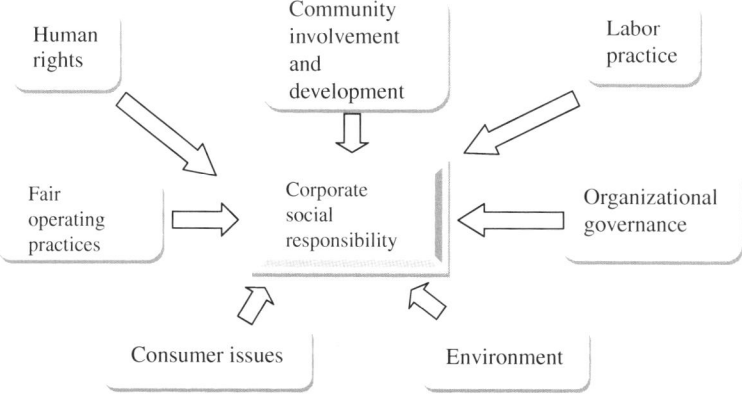

Fig. 2.1 CSR core elements (*Source* Designed by the authors)

good financial performance is driven by effective corporate social responsibility actions. An organization's CSR practice can determine its positive reputational effects in terms of its relationships with suppliers and clients. In addition, employees feel motivated and proud to be involved with socially responsible corporate entities. From a client perspective, reputation is, indeed, an essential aspect that companies should be aware of. Therefore, corporations need to understand the importance of building a socially responsible image for its selective, sophisticated and sensible clients. Further more, corporate social responsibility contributes to improvements in the efficient use of resources by conserving the environment and recycling, thus adopting an eco-efficient strategy. Cooperation between management and employees is also necessary for enhancing efficient productivity. Along with cooperation, working conditions, training and development, employee engagement in community related issues contribute to employee retention, as motivating factors. Organizations that fail to implement CSR policies are placing themselves in a position of losing their reputation, as the are likely to find it difficult to enage in dialogues with their stakeholders. Effective communication with stakeholders is needed in order to provide indormation about an organization's commitment to corporate social responsibility practices.

Yongqiang (2011) outlines the main reasons that drive CSR reporting, in the form of stakeholder pressure (Crowther 2003; Idowu and Towler 2004), regulations enforcement (Holcomb et al. 2007), and not at least, reputation (Brammer and Pavelin 2005). Eventually stakeholder pressure resulting from governments and banks that demand corporate disclosure, society that needs to be informed about corporate responsibility practice, and customers that are interested in both social and environmental issues (O'Rourke 2004). Arjaliès and Péan (2009) argue that CSR reporting is determined by both external and internal motivations. In an attempt to study corporate social responsibility integration within organizations' strategy, they found that those internal factors that contribute to the adoption of CSR involve innovation, increase in efficiency, value adding, while the external factors represent customers' needs, environmental organizations, and reputation.

2.4 Background on CSR: Prior Studies

Academics and scholars have developed various research directions in the field of corporate social responsibility. Two empirical studies on UK companies show that some organizations tend to report separately on their CSR practices, while others choose to disclose this type of information within their annual report and accounts (Idowu and Towler 2004), and that small and medium sized enterprises are in line with multinationals in regard to social reporting habits (Parsa and Kouhy 2008).

Employing the methodology of content analysis, Mirfazli (2008) notes that 43 corporations from Indonesia; register significant disclosures about the environment

(14.3 %), society (14.7 %), customer (19.4 %) and labor (51.6 %). A similar study (Thompson and Zakaria 2004) demonstrates that in Malaysia companies maintain a certain interest for disclosing information related to the environment, community involvement, products, customers, and employees. Out of 250 companies, 16 % disclosed environmental information, 22 % presented their initiatives for community development, 24 % provided details about products and consumers, and while a higher percentage (40 %) disclosed human resource aspects. Investigating reports on human resource, Vuontisjarvi (2006) performed an analysis on 205 organizations in Finland. The findings demonstrate relevant disclosures on training, employee involvement and participation, working environment, intrinsic motivation, and other elements related to employees. However, the majority of companies from the sample failed to include quantitative indicators that would have added consistency to their reports. Perrini (2006) studied 90 European companies affiliated to the Ethical Index Euro, aiming to identify the denominations of the reports that presented the corporate social responsibility practices implemented by the organization. The observations generated six different report names: social report, social and environmental report, environmental report, sustainability report, HSE report. In addition, the research highlights the position of various stakeholders.

Engaging in a critical disclosure analysis, Nielsen and Thomsen (2007) referred to 6 Danish companies whose reports diverge from the perspectives of topic and length, while maintaining the particular elements of stakeholder primacy, plans for the future, the information being presented in the right context. Paul et al. (2006) develops a comparative case study on 10 corporations from Mexico, showing that although the percentage of CSR adopters is still very small, information related to stakeholders is disclosed within all the sample reports, and the majority of companies hold ISO 9000 and ISO 14000 certifications, as well as many awards for acting socially responsibly. In addition, organizations mention their concern for the environment, and their initiatives for community involvement, donations and volunteer acts.

2.5 Non-Financial Reporting Initiatives

The most prominent non-financial reporting initiatives emanate from some international organizations located in different parts of the world, for eample the Global Reporting Initiative, AccountAbility or Climate Disclosure Standards Board and several others.

Eccles and Saltzman (2011) provide an analysis of non-financial reporting tendencies within the business world. These scholars highlighted large discrepancies between Europe and other continents, as the European Commission highly promotes non-financial information disclosure. Contrary to European countries, Japan, China and the US maintain low disclosure levels of non-financial reporting. In 2009, an estimated number of 1,400 organizations were disclosing non-financial reports, while in 2010 this number has has increased by 29 %. Therefore, we can expect that reporting would eventually shift to a mixture of financial and non-financial elements, being presented in an integrated form (Eccles and Saltzman 2011).

The notion of *integrated reporting* has evolved from the triple bottom line (Elkington 1997, being inoculated by scholars and academics in their studies on corporate reporting (White 2005; Eccles et al. 2010). The IIRC- International Integrated Reporting Committee was set up with the purpose of establishing a common framework for integrated reports: "The goal of the IIRC is not to increase the reporting burden on companies and other entities. Rather, it is to … help us all make better decisions about the resources we consume and the lives we lead" (Ian Ball, CEO of the International Federation of Accountants and Co-Chair of the IIRC Working Group).

The main benefits derived from publishing integrated reports involve good reputation, engaging with stakeholders, better allocation of resources, meeting investors' needs of ESG—environmental, social and governance- disclosure, compliance with regulation issued by stock exchanges, standards, guidelines, frameworks (Eccles and Saltzman 2011). However, limitations still exist in the form of low adoption level for integrated reporting, lack of assurance for non-financial information, missing more specific standards, frameworks, guidelines.

2.6 Methodology

The research methodology involves both qualitative and quantitative methods. Our primary purpose was to obtain an image on how corporations report on their CSR practices, and, most importantly, how they integrate non-financial information—mainly CSR—with financial matters. Therefore, we performed a two year analysis of those organizations that publish integrated reports and disseminate the information disclosed in them, in order to obtain an understanding of what corporate responsibility expects from those corporations that choose to report on this aspect of their activities. Issues concerning the length and complexity of the CSR information, peculiarities of the information presented in reports and finally the degree of CSR disclosure were analysed. The qualitative research of CSR information analysis assumes an evaluation of the most relevant CSR coordinates noted by the UN Global Compact as Universal Principles (Selvi et al. 2010): *human rights, labour standards, environment and anti-corruption.*

In order to estimate the level of corporate social responsibility actions taken by a corporation, we performed a quantitative analysis of the information disclosed and therefore determined a disclosure index for the main categories of the Universal Principles. According to the UN Global Compact (Selvi et al. 2010), namely: *human rights, labour standards, environment and anti-corruption.* The formula for the Disclosure Index can be described as follows:

$$DI_{csr} = \Sigma(d_i \text{ effectively disclosed})/\Sigma (d_i \text{ all possible cases of disclosure}) \quad (2.1)$$

In the function above, we denote with 1 the case when a certain category of each of the issues involved (human rights, labour standards, environment or anti-corruption) is disclosed and with 0 when they are not mentioned. Thus, the minimum amount for DI will be 0 and the maximum 1.

2.6.1 Sample Selection

Our sample was made up of integrated reports and our choice was based on the fact that companies which publish integrated reports have also adopted CSR reporting. We selected 24 corporations that produce integrated annual reports. Data gathering was been performed for the period 2009–2010. At the stage of collecting the information and implementing our analysis, the reports for 2011 were not available. We obtained the annual reports for years 2009 and 2010 directly from the companies' websites, and actually downloaded our primary data from the section on investor relations. We also considered the report denomination that could explain a tendency for the volume of corporate social responsibility information. Each report was been double checked by the authors for the afore-mentioned CSR elements, namely: human rights, labour standards, environment and anti-corruption. Besides the information quantity, was also analysed for its consistency and complexity. The relevance of our research derives from conveying an image with regard to CSR disclosure that should illustrate how companies understand the benefits of corporate responsibility acts in terms of its conse-quential effects on reputation and corporate performance. The companies cover 10 activity sectors, namely: banking and insurance, chemicals, telecommunications, cosmetics, energy, electricity and electronics, medicine, mining, entertainment, metals and platinum, retail, information technology. When studying the perspec-tive of international organizations upon integrated reports, we discovered that this reporting trend has emerged from corporate reporting practices. The document presented by PwC "11 Reporting Tips", provides examples of companies that successfully implements integrated reporting elements. The South African Institute of Chartered Accountants (SAICA) presents a list of companies that publish integrated annual reports , South Africa itself being a state in which integrated reporting is already mandatory, while Sweden, Spain, US, Brazil, Australia, UK, and even China, are intending to regulate this field (Eccles et al. 2010). The chosen sample provides the opportunity to observe the evolution of CSR practices, as well as new emerging trends in reporting, as there are more and more corporations which are embedding the use of integrated annual reports into their reporting practices.

2.6.2 Results

Our study in this area has revealed a series of interesting results that are summarized below, in a number of tables. There are a few *caveats* to note. First, it must be mentioned that some reports were not available in a pdf format, and so were excluded from the analysis (RB Platinum annual report 2009 and UTC 2009 and 2010 annual reports). Secondly, for the other remaining companies, we performed the disclosure analysis by searching for each of the CSR elements and extracting the corresponding information from the report and the page source. This detailed overview conveyed the opportunity to prepare a qualitative study that focuses on the complexity and relevance of the information as well as disclosure extension.

Further on, our examination starts with report denomination. This perspective of the methodology has also been used by Perrini (2006) in his study. Unlike Perrini (2006) whose observations revealed six different report names: social report, social and environmental report, environmental report, sustainability report, HSE report, we found that corporations following integrated reporting trends choose various titles for their integrated reports, from the simple *annual report*, to *report, annual report and accounts, sustainability report, corporate accountability report, integrated annual report,* or *sustainable development report.*

Previous research studies in the field of corporate social responsibility have involved CSR disclosure (Mirfazli 2008; Thompson and Zakaria 2004; Vuontisjarvi 2006). Considering the background literature in the field of CSR and accountability, we were intending to add to knowledge in the field of CSR and integrated reporting, a pioneer segment that has not been debated yet by academicians and scholars in their research. Therefore, we analyzed corporate disclosure of corporate responsibility elements- *human rights, labour standards, environment and anti-corruption,* in order to establish whether or not non-financial information was able to integrate well with the financial information in a single, integrated report.

Moving further, we were also intending to discuss our results. It appears that the shift to integrated reporting has generated a great amount of environmental related information, as corporations have chosen to reserve reasonabl number of pages in their annual reports to issues concerning the environment. Therefore, environmental and accountability issues are put in priority to others. The elements of anti-corruption and human rights are put next to environmental data and information. We noticed that when these elements are disclosed, organizations provide detailed explanations for their policies and practices. Issues relating to labour standards are disclosed last and therefore are not given extended coverage as the previous elements in the reports. We can add that organizations can still improve their CSR reporting, as we detected variations in the disclosure levels from one year to another. If the first two parameters- human rights and labour standards, have shifted backwards, for environmental and anti-corruption related information we found this action to say that some sound progress appears to have been made in this regard.

However, the results show that corporate social responsibility information is generally presented in high proportion. In addition, the figures demonstrate medium and high levels of disclosure for CSR related issues. We believe that by disclosing corporate social responsibility related information, corporations are better placed to respond and address to a more than obvious stakeholder pressure for CSR practices.

Tables 2.1 and 2.2 present the information we have extracted from the annual integrated reports and show how corporations have chosen to present their CSR views. Being knowledgeable of what a good reputation means, organizations are able to respond to the needs and expectations of their stakeholders.

The next section of our study covers the analysis on CSR disclosure levels. Further more, we present our findings for the main CSR coordinates: human rights, labor standards, environment, and anti-corruption. In 2009, most of the integrated reports of the sample companies (95.45 %) disclosed environmental information, 68.18 % was attributed to human rights disclosure, anti-corruption was presented in 50 % of the cases, while for labor standards we noted that, that was only 45.45 % disclosure level. The disclosure index proves that corporate social responsibility information is represented by at least one of the four items, as the index receives the values of 0.25; 0.5; 0.75; or 1. Six out of our sample firms have presented all the required elements and obtained a disclosure index of 1, while five disclosed just one element. The others are medium-level or above medium form the perspective of CSR disclosure (0.5 or 0.75) (Table 2.3).

In 2010, we noted full disclosure for environmental elements, while labor rights and anti-corruption incorporate similar levels (65–70 %) and labor standards present only 40 % disclosure. Seven companies out of the total sample have complete disclosure on the four elements of CSR. Four corporations imply a value of only 0.25 for the disclosure index meaning that they mention just one item out of four. Five organizations maintain a medium disclosure of 0.5 and the remaining six sample companies register a disclosure index of 0.75 being situated above medium (Table 2.4).

2.7 Conclusions

This chapter focuses on corporate social responsibility disclosure practices. The study incorporates best practice examples from corporations that produce integrated annual reports. In essence, we try to estimate how companies have managed to integrate CSR information with their traditional main report. We analyzed four main dimensions of the corporate social responsibility behavior, namely human rights, labor standards, environment and anti-corruption. These items have been used in previous research to test the level of CSR disclosure (Selvi et al. 2010). After evaluating a sample of 24 annual integrated reports, we note evidence of

Table 2.1 CSR disclosure within 2009 annual reports

Company	Report denomination	Human rights	Labor standards	Environment	Anti-corruption
AEP	Annual report	–		Pages 6–134	–
Altron	Annual report	Human rights in operations outside of South Africa, page 68	Relevant employment legislation, the basic conditions of Employment Act, The Labour Relations Act, The Employment Equity Act and the Skills Development Act, AR, page 64	Managing the environmental impact of its businesses, page 77	–
Amlin plc	Annual report	South African Human Rights Commission, page 18	–	Page 52	–
Anglo Platinum	Annual report	Page 6	–	Page 33	–
BASF	Report	Pages 15–98	Labor standards and laws, page 16	Page 91	Pages 15, 16, 120, 121
Capita Group	Annual report and accounts	Diversity, inclusion and human rights, page 37	UK, European and Indian employment law as well as international human rights legislation, International Labour Organisation standards, page 37	Controlling our environmental impacts, page 38	–
Eskom	Annual report	Pages 22–26	The United Nations Global Compact—we will continue to demonstrate leadership in the 10 principles relating to labour standards, the environment and anti-corruption, page 17	The United Nations Global Compact—we will continue to demonstrate leadership in the 10 principles relating to labour standards, the environment and anti-corruption, page 17	The United Nations Global Compact—we will continue to demonstrate leadership in the 10 principles relating to labour standards, the environment and anti-corruption, page 17

(continued)

Table 2.1 (continued)

Company	Report denomination	Human rights	Labor standards	Environment	Anti-corruption
Gold Fields	Annual report	Page 59	–	Page 71, 75–82	Page 64
Great Portland Estate	Annual report	–	–	Pages 35–36	–
Implats	Annual report	Pages 76–79			
Logica plc	Annual report and accounts	–	–	Page 73—improving environmental sustainability	–
Massmart	Annual report	–	–	Page 7	–
Metso Corporation	Sustainability report	Page 11, the foundation of our code of conduct is the UN's Universal Declaration of Human Rights, the UN's Global Compact initiative, and the International Labor Organization's (ILO) declara-tion on Fundamental Principles and Rights at Work.	International Labor Organization's (ILO)	Pages 6–27	SO3 Employees trained in organization's anti-corruption policies SO4 actions taken in response to incidents of corruption GC 10 work against corruption in all its forms, including extortion and bribery, pages 8–9, 147, 148
National grid	Annual report and accounts	The Human Rights Campaign's Equality Index in the US, page 35; human rights issues- page 90;	–	The environment and climate change—page 90; safety, health and environmen; Changing our energy landscape- pages 8-10	–

(continued)

Table 2.1 (continued)

Company	Report denomination	Human rights	Labor standards	Environment	Anti-corruption
Natura	Annual report	*Our essence integration program, Page 43—the new employees are taught Natura's relationship principles, which are inspired by the Declaration of Human Rights… programs on human rights for the security personnel; raise awareness on human rights, violence, peace culture and of responsibility; pages 41, 45, 50, 55, 59, 61, 62, 139*	–	*pages 19-92*	*Although there are no specific training courses on issues related to corruption and human rights, in the Integração Nossa Essência program, page 43; pages 17, 41*
Novo nordisk	Annual report	*Pages 28–31*	*Page 90*	*Pages 8, 9*	*Pages 28, 90*
Philips	Annual report	*Maplecroft Human Rights Risk Indexes; human rights, labor, the environment and anti-corruption, page 215, 232*	*International Labor and Civil Society Organizations, page 215*	*Human rights, labor, the environment and anti-corruption., page 215*	*Human rights, labor, the environment and anti-corruption. Page 215*

(continued)

Table 2.1 (continued)

Company	Report denomination	Human rights	Labor standards	Environment	Anti-corruption
Potash group	Sustainability report	*Human rights issues and policies, page 24, 67, 84, policies and practices of HR (page 94) compliance with human rights policies (page 95) human rights performance (page 182)*	*Provincial labor legislation, page 92*	*Environmental overview (pages 100–104), environmental performance (pages 105–123)*	*Risks related to corruption, page 183; anti-corruption policies and procedures and actions taken in response to instances of corruption (page 184)*
RB platinum	Not available in pdf format				
Standard bank	Annual report	–	–	*Our environmental impacts, page 65*	*Has a "zero tolerance" approach to fraud and corruption, Page 154*
UTC	not available in pdf format				
Vodacom	Annual report	–	*Industry standards; the relevant labour legislation, page 87*	*Containing our impact on the environment, page 91*	*Corruption, money laundering and terrorism, page 239*
Wolesely	Annual report and accounts	–	*Relation to labour standards, Page 48*	*The group's approach to environmental measures is set out in the corporate responsibility report on pages 39–49.*	*Prevention of fraud and corruption, page 41*
Xstrata plc	Annual report	*Page 39*	–	*Enviromental incidents, greenhouse gas emissions, page 33*	–

Source Designed by the authors, based on the information extracted from the annual integrated reports

Table 2.2 CSR disclosure within 2010 annual reports

Company	Report denomination	Human rights	Labor standards	Environment	Anti-corruption
AEP	Corporate accountability report	*Page 42*	–	*Pages 22–27, 30*	*Pages 42–44*
Altron	Integrated annual report	*Human rights and fair labour practices, page 74*	*Basic Conditions of Employment Act, The Labour Relations Act, The Employment Equity Act and The Skills Development Act, page 60*	*Pages 68-74*	*The company's policies on bribery, fraud, corruption and ethics, page 75*
Amlin plc	Annual report	–	–	*Pages 49, 81*	–
Anglo Platinum	Sustainable development report	*Page 102*	–	*Environmental footprint page 108*	–
BASF	Annual report	*Human rights: Universal Declaration of Human Rights, page 19; security: observance of human rights, page 92*	*Aadherence to internationally recognized labor standards, page 204*	*Pages 91–101: Environment and safety*	*Pages 19, 120: corruption*
Capita group	Annual reports and accounts	–	–	*Controlling our environmental impacts Continue to measure and assess our carbon footprint (tonnes CO_2 eq. page 42*	–
Eskom	Integrated report	*Social performance indicators: human rights (HR), page 82*	*Abour laws, page 87*	*Environmental compliance— Minister of Water and Environmental Affairs, page 88*	*Anti-corruption clause, page 293*
Gold fields	Integrated annual report	*Pages 146, 147, 175*	*Pages 142–154*	*Pages 67–90*	*Page 172*
Great Portland Estate	Annual report	–	–	*148 h of environmental and sustainability training, Page 40: environment and the Portfolio, page 41*	–
Implats	Integrated annual report	*Page 112*	–	*Environmental review—entire section, page 118*	*Corruption and fraud -entire section, page 140*
Logica plc	Annual report and accounts	–	–	*Pages 9, 14, 25*	–

(continued)

Table 2.2 (continued)

Company	Report denomination	Human rights	Labor standards	Environment	Anti-corruption
Massmart	Annual report	–	Page 27	Page 27	–
Metso corporation	Annual report	The foundation of our code of conduct are the UN's Universal Declaration of Human Rights, The UN's Global Compact Initiative, which we have endorsed, and The International Labour Organization's (ILO) declaration on fundamental principles and rights at work, page 15	We comply with the ten principles of the UN's Global Compact initiative in the areas of human rights, labor standards, the environment and anti-corruption, Page 15	Ppage 18; 26–29—environmental solutions; page 22—environmental technology	We comply with the ten principles of the UN's Global Compact Initiative in the areas of human rights, labor standards, the environment and anti-corruption, Page 15
National grid	Annual report and accounts	In the US, we scored 100 % in the US Human Rights Campaign's 2008 Corporate Equality Index—page 36; security and human rights issues—page 95	–	Significant environmental incidents—page 38; protecting the enviroment; pages 38–47	–
Natura	Report	Employees—topics related to human rights, page 46; all our new employees learn our relationship principles, which are inspired by the declaration of human rights; page 62, suppliers- aspects related to human rights, pages 63, 97, 139	–	Constantly deliver superior results and relevant value in the economic, social, and environmental dimensions. pages 4;Actions and greater awareness concerning the socio-environmental cause are revealing examples of the emergence of a change in the direction of civilization. We must therefore mobilize society to build an agenda of transformation.- page 6; biodiversity and reduced the environmental impact of our products, pages 7, 10	We have no specifi training on issues related to corruption and human rights, page 46; the integrity policy against corruption and bribery—page 74; combating corruption—page 139

(continued)

Table 2.2 (continued)

Company	Report denomination	Human rights	Labor standards	Environment	Anti-corruption
Novo nordisk	Annual report	Universal Declaration of Human Rights, page 31, reporting on business strategies and activities on human rights, labour standards, environment and anti-corruption. Danish Financial Statements Act (FSA), section 99a, page 94	Reporting on business strategies and activities on human rights, labour Danish Financial Statements Act (FSA), section 99a, page 94	Reporting on business strategies and activities on human rights, labour Danish Financial Statements Act (FSA), section 99a, page 94	Reporting on business strategies and activities on human rights, labour Danish Financial Statements Act (FSA), section 99a, page 94
Philips	Annual report	Page 48- human right abuses; page 207—sustainability statement	Standards, environment and anti-corruption. Companies that subscribe	Standards, environment and anti-corruption. Companies that subscribe	Page 207—sustainability statement
Potash group	Sustainability report	Pages 67, 84 training in human rights; human rights policies and practices, page 94-181, human rights performance, page 182	–	Page 16, environmental performance—pages 188-194	Risks related to corruption, anti-corruption policies and procedures pages, actions taken in response to instances of corruption, page 184
RB platinum	Integrated annual report	Protecting community human rights (see page 35), protecting employee human rights (see pages 30–34 Ethics and human rights, page 90	–	Environmental performance, page 11	Managing and providing advice on the company's finances, putting in place policies, procedures and systems to protect the company from fraud and corruption. ensuring economic sustainability and managing relations with investors (See pages 52–61)
Standard bank	Annual integrated report	–	National economic development and labour council, Page 112	Environmental report, page 118	Has a zero tolerance approach to fraud and corruption. Page 196

(continued)

Table 2.2 (continued)

Company	Report denomination	Human rights	Labor standards	Environment	Anti-corruption
UTC	Not available in pdf format				
Vodacom	Annual report	*Privacy is a fundamental human right, page 54; complying with all applicable human rights, page 57*	–	*Impact on environment, page 48*	*Vodacom has established the anti-CMT compliance programme as an explicit process to manage risk associated with corruption, money laundering and terrorism ('CMT'), page 54*
Wolesely	Annual report and accounts	–	–	*The Group's approach to environmental management is set out in the Corporate responsibility report on pages 37 and 38*	*corruption and fraud, page 33*
Xstrata plc	Annual report	–	–	*Pages 25, 39–40, 44–46*	*A global bribery, fraud and corruption policy that updates our existing Fraud Policy and procedures has been developed, page 8*

Source Designed by the authors, based on the information extracted from the annual integrated reports

Table 2.3 Disclosure index 2009 annual reports

Company	Report denomination	Human rights	Labor standards	Environment	Anti-corruption	DI
AEP	Annual report	0	0	1	0	0.25
Altron	Annual report	1	1	1	0	0.75
Amlin plc	Annual report	1	0	1	0	0.5
Anglo platinum	Annual report	1	0	1	0	0.5
BASF	Report	1	1	1	1	1
Capita group	Annual report and accounts	1	1	1	0	0.75
Eskom	Annual report	1	1	1	1	1
Gold fields	Annual report	1	0	1	1	0.75
Great Portland Estate	Annual report	0	0	1	0	0.25
Implats	Annual report	1	0	0	0	0.25
Logica plc	Annual report and accounts	0	0	1	0	0.25
Massmart	Annual report	0	0	1	0	0.25
Metso corporation	Sustainability report	1	1	1	1	1
National grid	Annual report and accounts	1	0	1	0	0.5
Natura	Annual report	1	0	1	1	0.75
Novo nordisk	Annual report	1	1	1	1	1
Philips	Annual report	1	1	1	1	1
Potash group	Sustainability report	1	1	1	1	1
RB platinum	Not available in pdf format					
Standard bank	Annual report	0	0	1	1	0.5
UTC	Not available in pdf format					
Vodacom	Annual report	0	1	1	1	0.75
Wolesely	Annual report and accounts	0	1	1	1	0.75
Xstrata plc	Annual report	1	0	1	0	0.5
		68.18 %	**45.45 %**	**95.45 %**	**50.00 %**	

Source Authors' compilation

integration of CSR information within the annual report. Our arguments are covered by the large quantity of non-financial information allocated for the disclosure of human rights, labor standards, environment and anti-corruption. We have also computed a disclosure index for each of the sample companies in order to estimate the CSR disclosure level. The results show relevant disclosure with boundaries of between 0.25 and 1, meaning that at least one of the four elements is well represented in every corporation from our database.

Table 2.4 Disclosure index 2010 annual reports

	Report denomination	Human rights	Labor standards	Environment	Anti-corruption	DI
AEP	Annual report	1	0	1	1	0.75
Altron	Annual report	1	1	1	1	1
Amlin plc	Annual report	0	0	1	0	0.25
Anglo platinum	Annual report	1	0	1	0	0.5
BASF	Report	1	1	1	1	1
Capita group	Annual report and accounts	0	0	1	0	0.25
Eskom	Annual report	1	1	1	1	1
Gold fields	Annual report	1	1	1	1	1
Great Portland Estate	Annual report	0	0	1	0	0.25
Implats	Annual report	1	0	1	1	0.75
Logica plc	Annual report and accounts	0	0	1	0	0.25
Massmart	Annual report	0	1	1	0	0.5
Metso corporation	Sustainability report	1	1	1	1	1
National grid	Annual report and accounts	1	0	1	0	0.5
Natura	Annual report	1	0	1	1	0.75
Novo nordisk	Annual report	1	1	1	1	1
Philips	Annual report	1	1	1	1	1
Potash group	Sustainability report	1	0	1	1	0.75
RB platinum	Integrated annual report	1	0	1	1	
Standard bank	Annual report	0	1	1	1	0.75
UTC	Not available in pdf format					
Vodacom	Annual report	1	0	1	1	0.75
Wolesely	Annual report and accounts	0	0	1	1	0.5
Xstrata plc	Annual report	0	0	1	1	0.5
		65.22 %	**39.13 %**	**100.00 %**	**69.57 %**	

Source Authors' compilation

Therefore, we predict that integrated reporting trends will lead to the concise and clear presentation of the most relevant CSR information. In addition, more corporations will become aware of their accountability and eventually enhance corporate social responsibility behavior and best practice. By disclosing non-financial information related to CSR organizations provide a clear view of their practice demonstrating stakeholder engagement and aiming to meet stakeholders' needs and expectations.

References

Andersen K.I. (2003).The Project. http://www.aiesec.dk/projects/rexpect/Theproject.htm# Definition [23 May 2003]

Arjaliès, D.L. & Péan, J.M. (2009).*CSR: A new business model for multinational companies? A study of the management systems used by the French CAC 40 companies to integrate CSR into their strategy: Working Paper, CSR&Management Systems.*

Benabou, R., & Tirole, J. (2010). Individual and corporate social responsibility. *Economica, 77,* 1–19.

Brammer, S., & Pavelin, S. (2005). Corporate reputation and an insurance motivation for corporate social investment. *Journal of Corporate Citizenship, 20,* 39–51.

Crowther, D. (2003). Corporate social reporting: Genuine action or window dressing? In D. Crowther & L. J. Rayman-Bacchus (Eds.), *Perspectives on corporate social responsibility* (pp. 140–161). Aldershot: Ashget Publishing Limited.

Dahlsrud, A. (2008). How corporate social responsibility is defined: an analysis of 37 definitions. *Corporate Social Responsibility and Environmental Management, 15,* 1–13.

Eccles, R., & Saltzman, D. (2011). Achieving sustainability through integrated reporting. *Stanford Social Innovation Review, 2011,* 56–61.

Eccles, R. G., Krzus, M. P., & Tapscott, D. (2010). *One report: Integrated reporting for a sustainable strategy.* NJ: Wiley.

Elkington, J. (1997). *Cannibals with forks: The triple bottom line of 21st century business.* Oxford: Capstone.

Financial times Lexicon, Corporate Social Responsibility CSR—Global Executive MBA.

Holcomb, J. L., Upchurch, R. S., & Okumus, F. (2007). Corporate social responsibility: What are top hotel companies reporting? *International Journal of Contemporary Hospitality Management, 19*(6), 461–475.

Idowu, S. O. (2011). An exploratory study of the historical landscape of corporate social responsibility in the UK. *Corporate Governance, 11*(2), 149–160.

Idowu, S. O., & Towler, B. A. (2004). A comparative study of the contents of corporate social responsibility reports of UK companies. *Management of Environmental Quality: An International Journal, 15*(4), 420–437.

Lea R. (2002).Corporate Social Responsibility, Institute of Directors (IoD) member opinion survey. IoD: London. http://www.epolitix.com/data/companies/images/Companies/Institute-of-Directors/CSR_Report.pdf [23 June 2003].

Marsden C. (2001).The Role of Public Authorities in Corporate Social Responsibility. http://www.alter.be/socialresponsibility/people/marchri/en/displayPerson [23 June 2003]

Mirfazli, E. (2008). Corporate social responsibility (CSR) information disclosure by annual reports of public companies listed at Indonesia Stock Exchange (IDX). *International Journal of Islamic and Middle Eastern Finance and Management, 1*(4), 275–284.

Nielsen, A. E., & Thomsen, C. (2007). Reporting CSR—What and how to say it? *Corporate Communications: An International Journal, 12*(1), 25–40.

O'Rourke, D. (2004). Opportunities and obstacles for corporate social responsibility reporting in developing countries, University of California, Berkeley for the Corporate Social Responsibility Practice of the World Bank Group.

Parsa, S., & Kouhy, R. (2008). Social reporting by companies listed on the alternative investment market. *Journal of Business Ethics, 79,* 345–360.

Paul, K., Cobas, E., Ceron, R., Frithiof, M., Maass, A., Navarro, I., et al. (2006). Corporate social reporting in Mexico. *The Journal of Corporate Citizenship, 22,* 67–80.

Perrini, F. (2006). The practitioner's perspective on non-financial reporting. *California Management Review, 48*(2), 73–103.

Piacentini, M. G., MacFadyen, L., & Eadie, D. R. (2000). Corporate social responsibility in food retailing. *International Journal of Retail and Distribution Management, 28*(10), 459–469.

Pinney, C. (2001). Imagine Speaks Out. How to Manage corporate social responsibility and reputation in a global marketplace: The challenge for Canadian business. http://www.imagine.ca/content/media/team_canada_china_paper.asp?section=media[23 June 2003].

Selvi, Y., Wagner, E., & Türel, A. (2010). Corporate social responsibility in the time of financial crisis: Evidence from Turkey. *Annales Universitatis Apulensis Series Oeconomica, 12*(1), 281–290.

Thompson, P., & Zakaria, Z. (2004). Corporate social responsibility reporting in Malaysia: Progress and prospects. *Journal of Corporate Citizenship, 13*, 125–136.

Van Marrewijk, M. (2003). Concepts and definitions of CSR and corporate sustainability: Between agency and communion. *Journal of Business Ethics, 44*, 95–105.

Vuontisjarvi, T. (2006). Corporate social reporting in the European context and human resource disclosures: An analysis of Finnish companies. *Journal of Business Ethics, 69*, 331–354.

White, A. L. (2005). Fade, Integrate or Transform? The Future of CSR. *Business for Social Responsibility*. http://www.bsr.org.

Yongqiang, G. (2011). CSR in an emerging country: A content analysis of CSR reports of listed companies. *Baltic Journal of Management, 6*(2), 263–291.

Chapter 3
An Examination of the Relationship Between Companies' Corporate Social Responsibility (CSR) Activities and Consumers' Purchase Behavior

Aslı Küçükaslan Ekmekçi

Abstract This research study investigates the relationship between companies' corporate social responsibility (CSR) activities as a marketing strategy and consumers' purchase behavior orientation towards companies' products and services. The main aim of the study is to explore the role of companies' CSR activities in the purchase orientation of the consumers for the products of companies. Based on the previous literature sources and empirical research findings about the relevant subject, it is assumed that the consumers' purchase behavior orientation would be one of the consequences of companies' CSR activities that are undertaken as a marketing strategy. In order to get meaningful data about the subject, a study in Turkish context was conducted on one main holding group that has well-known CSR projects in Turkey. After a review of previous empirical and theoretical studies, general explanations about the subject were made which obtained data for understanding the main proposition of the current study.

3.1 Introduction

The rationale of this study is to investigate the relationship between companies' corporate social responsibility (CSR) activities as a marketing strategy and consumers' purchase behavior orientation towards these companies' products and services. The main aim of the study is to explore the role of companies' CSR activities in the purchase orientation of the consumers for the products of these companies. Based on the previous literature sources and empirical research findings about the relevant subject, it is assumed that the consumers' purchase behavior orientation would be one of the consequences of the companies' CSR

A. K. Ekmekçi (✉)
Department of Business Administration, Faculty of Economics and Business
Administration, Marmara University, Istanbul, Turkey
e-mail: aslikucukaslan@yahoo.com

A. Yüksel Mermod and S. O. Idowu (eds.), *Corporate Social Responsibility in the Global Business World*, DOI: 10.1007/978-3-642-37620-7_3, © Springer-Verlag Berlin Heidelberg 2014

activities that are done as a marketing strategy. Therefore it is found meaningful to investigate how companies' CSR activities relate with the consumers' purchase orientation towards the companies' products.

In this study we handle the issue of corporate social responsibility first of all, being the independent variable, which has become one of the recently outstanding concepts in corporate management with the change of public priorities. It is obvious that public opinion makes a shift and goes away from thinking that a company's financial and legal responsibilities are the prevailing and most important responsibilities towards a concern for ethical responsibilities with a strong impact.

In this respect, the main purpose of this study is to develop a customer response framework to social responsibility activities of the corporations in the context of customer purchase behavior and orientation taking into consideration a range of moderating factors. It is expected that this study will provide marketing managers as well as company managers a coherent understanding of customer perceptions, motives, attitudes and behavior regarding social responsibility.

3.2 Literature Review

It is recognized that while corporate social responsibility (CSR) is an important issue for the organizations, most of the research studies about CSR were done in different types of business and industries. The role of the holding groups' businesses in an increasingly dynamic context in Turkey is now being questioned, including how companies' socially responsible approaches that operate under these holding groups might affect the perception and orientation of the consumers.

In Turkey, the leaders of the social responsibility concept has been holdings such as Koç, Sabancı, Eczacıbası, Yasar, Dogan Holding with their charities and projects and then other companies have followed the trend (Büyük 2006, p. 2). These companies have realized the short term and long term benefits associated with being socially responsible, therefore they invest large amounts of their budget for such projects and campaigns.

According to a research conducted in 2004 among 1665 Turkish consumers by GFK a marketing research company, consumers think that priority for social responsibility projects must be given to mainly education and health, followed by environmental issues (Artiegitim 2005, p. 2). Sabancı Holding, Koç Holding, Arçelik, Ülker, Turkcell, Eczacıbası, Bosch, and Dogan Holding were placed at the top of the list of the most admired companies that have social responsibility projects.

Furthermore, another research study conducted in 2005 by Capital magazine with the contribution of Metro Group The aim was to understand how consumers perceive the social responsibility efforts of companies and to help companies to develop their strategies and establish an effective communication with their consumers. 1,320 Turkish consumers were interviewed. According to the results of the research, Sabancı Holding was placed at the top of the list of most successful companies in almost all areas of social responsibility followed by Koc Holding. Eczacıbaşı was also found to be successful in the education, arts and health areas.

In this context, in the light of the preliminary literature survey, it is proposed that the concept of corporate social responsibility should be described in order to understand the socially responsible attitudes of the three main holding groups of companies in Turkey. Respectively, we believe that it is necessary to examine the literature on Corporate Social Responsibility and the consumer purchase behavior orientation. Therefore, in this section of the study, the corporate social responsibility as a marketing strategy and the consumer purchase behavior will be described conceptually with the previous literature implications.

3.3 The Concept of Corporate Social Responsibility and its Importance

Corporate social responsibility (CSR) has been defined differently in the literature. One of the definitions says, CSR is the duty of the organization to respect individuals' rights and promote human welfare in its operations (Manakkalathil and Rudolf 1995). As cited in the Article of Sen and Bhattacharya, CSR has also been decsribed as prosocial corporate endeavors (as cited in Murray and Vogel 1997) or corporate social performance (Turban and Greening 1997), it has traditionally been conceptualized broadly as "both managerial obligation to take action to protect and improve both the welfare of society as a whole and the interest of organizations" (Davis and Bolmstrom 1975, p. 6). Although there are many conceptualized views of Corporate Social Responsibility in the literature, but the definition adopted by Brown and Dacin as the company's "status and activities with respect to its perceived societal obligations"(Dacin and Brown 1997) interests this author.

Today, it is generally accepted that organizations have many responsibilities. In addition to legal and financial responsibilities, they also have social, environmental and ethical responsibilities towards their stakeholders. For instance, retailers use many social responsibility activities to attract customers and to fulfil their ethical duties. Social responsibility activities may come in many guises e.g. making donations to charities, managing sports activities or financial sponsorhip of sporting events, healthcare and educational institutions. The forms of business activities in this area can be divided into business sectors for example retail, chemicals (including pharmaceuticals), construction, high technology, banking, utilities, business services, etc. Similarly, we can view social performance according to its effectiveness on communities, the environment or employees' welbeing (Brammer and Pavelin 2004).

After 2000s, it was realized that global corporations should have formulated strategies which would have reduced the adverse impacts of corporate activities on the environment (Valentine and Fleischman 2007; Quaak et al. 2007; Maignan and

Ferrell 2004). Such strategies would have alleviated the resulting social, ecological and economic problems currently affecting our world. Besides, it was also also indicated that companies had responsibilities for taking corrective actions about these problems and CSR should have contributed to reducing community problems, create value for society, and improve social concerns of the individuals within a community, Quaak et al. 2007, p. 293.

While there is no generally accepted definition of corporate social responsibility, the World Business Council for Sustainable Development (WBCSD) has defined CSR as "the commitment of business to contribute economic development, working with employees, their families, the local community and society at large to improve quality of life" (WBCSD 2000). Another definition of corporate social responsibility says that it is "the degree of moral obligation that may be ascribed to corporations beyond simple obedience to the laws of the state" (Kilcullen and Kooistra, 1999, p. 158). This definition suggests, corporations have a duty not to cause damage or harm to others. Furthermore, according to Carroll's "pyramid of corporate social responsibility", a hierarchy of responsibilities involving economic, legal, and more socially oriented ones of ethical and philanthropic responsibilities were implied (Carroll 1991, p. 40).

Carroll (1991) mentioned that CSR involves "economic, legal, ethical, and discretionary expectations that society has of organizations at a given point in time". Therefore, several programs and projects that which companies put in place in response to these basic expectations were developed in order to meet their economic and social obligations stakeholders and the general society. This action of course gives the organization the opportunity to be more value oriented or gives it a morally-based foundation within its community (Valentine and Fleischman 2007, p. 159; Swanson 1995, p. 43; Wood 1991, p. 692).

On the other hand, CSR activities may be motivated by self-interest, societal pressures based on institutional economics, or by a desire to assist stakeholders when such help is not required and lies outside of traditional profit-making motives (Valentine and Fleischman 2007, p. 159; Swanson 1995). Besides, CSR efforts "focus on establishing legitimacy" (Wood, 1991, p. 692) and "fit between society's expectations of the business community and the ethics of business" (Zenisek 1979, p. 362 as cited in Valentine and Fleischman 2007, p. 159) to enhance the organization. This is especially so in situations where social responsibility creates a crucial relationship "based on give and take between stakeholders and companies" (Tuzzolino and Armandi, 1981, p. 22). Therefore, in this study, relevant assumptions were based on the stakeholder theory that is considered for integrating the relationship between the social responsibility of companies and individuals' purchase behavior orientation.

Besides, Maignan and Ferrell (2004) have taken an overview of the evolving perspectives about CSR. In its earliest views, CSR was characterized by a sense of social obligations, "to follow those lines of action which are desirable in terms of the objectives and values of the society" (Bowen 1953, p. 6 as cited in Balmer et al. 2007, p. 9). Later, Carroll (1977) provided contributions to this idea and proposed a model involving four different categories of CSR that are described as economic, ethical, legal, and philanthropic responsibility.

According to these theorists' implications, corporations' social responsibility expects them to create economic value for the stakeholders (Balmer et al. 2007, p. 10). In addition, corporations are legally required to comply with existing laws. The ethical responsibilities of a corporation mean that, that corporation should engage in what is right, just, and fair, despite the fact that it is not necessarily bound with any of its existing legal framework. Besides they are the responsibilities, which come from specific cultural contexts (Balmer et al. 2007, p. 10). Philanthropic or discretionary responsibilities, arise out of the philosophical, ethical tradition of being concerned with what is good for society as a whole, and provide a justification for companies to improve the quality of life for different stakeholders, society, and the environment (Balmer et al. 2007, p. 10; Swanson 1995, p. 50)

Additionally, Buchholz (2004, p. 131) has argued for another category and within the framework of this contemporary CSR view, that companies' stakeholder obligations require them to focus on various societal concerns (Buchholz 2004). Buchholz and Rosenthal (2005, p. 144) explained the relational understanding of managing for stakeholders as follows:

"While a company must be able to compete to survive, survival requires growth, growth requires enhancement of a relational web, and the direction growth takes evolves through the self direction of the company's community dynamics. Moreover, community growth cannot be measured in economic terms alone, because it involves the enrichment of human life in its entirety. The moral meaning of the company is rooted in the community dynamics by which life thrives and in which the experience of value and its sustainability emerges" (Buchholz and Rosenthal 2005, pp. 144–145).

In this context, it can be mentioned that today, organizations have many responsibilities apart from their legal and financial responsibilities; social and ethical responsibilities are also very important in corporate and marketing management, especially multinational companies which use many socially responsible activities to attract customers and to fulfil their ethical duties. Socially responsible activities include philanthropic activities and may be in the form of donations to charities, managing sports activities or financial aids to sporting events, health or education institutions. (Brammer and Pavelin 2004)

Actually, it was stated that "compamies in retail industry displayed higher rates of social responsibility when compared to those in other industries" (Lerner and Fryxell 1988). Therefore, we can assume that corporate characteristics like the type of business activity play a very important role in the corporate social responsibility and consumers' perceptions and purchase orientation relationships. In addition, a company's industry, its size may also have a role in impacting on the nature of the relationship between social performance and corporate reputation (Brammer and Pavelin 2004). Large companies are first of all more commercially vulnerable to adverse reactions, larger companies are more diversified across the geographical areas, so they are subject to demands for social responsiveness and lastly large organizations are more accountable to individuals and local communities (Lerner and Fryxell 1988). Thus we will take the size of organization and the characteristics of the organizations into account while evaluating the corporate social responsibility activities in this study.

3.4 The Concept of Consumer Purchase Behavior

According to statements made by Rodríguez-Pinto et al. (2008, p. 154), companies do business in a dynamic and changing environment full of competition, uncertainities, and rapid technological change. At this point, the effective positioning of products, the effective determination of the factors influencing consumer behaviors, and the effective understanding of consumers' perception of CSR dimensions in the market can be considered as the critical factors for the achievement of the success of these companies.

Investigating the factors influencing consumer behavior is based on the principle of dealing with necessities. Briefly, identifying the factors influencing consumer behaviors is the process of demonstrating the different dimensions that impact the buying behaviors of the consumers. Moreover, identifying the factors influencing consumer behaviors is the process of identifying the potential customers and their specific characteristics and determining the likely factors that influence their purchase behavior. The key to a successful identification is the ability to capitalize on similarities within a consumer category that are important from a marketing point of view (Piercy and Morgan 1993, p. 123). The aim of this process or period is to build up a marketing mix and brand management program that will adjust better to individuals' needs ad perceptions in choosing a market section.

In marketing and management literature it is often mentioned that giving importance to understanding corporate social responsibility perceptions throughout the customer relationships and building the social marketing and customer relations processes on the basis of these considerations are essential for the companies to identify the customers' perceptions, expectations, and various consumer behavior patterns (Kotler and Zaltman 1971, p. 5; Drumwright and Murphy 2000, p. 164).

There are a number of studies about the influence of CSR perceptions on consumer behavior which show that different people react differently to products and services and the social responsibility activities of companies (Drumwright and Murphy 2000, p. 164), further, Eves and Cheng (2007) have implied the influence of values and perceptions of individuals on the purchase decisions of the consumers.

It is indicated that; it is certainly reasonable to inquire about the consumers' shopping behaviors, such as the motivations underlying where they shop and why they shop and what they buy (Sidin et al. 2008, p. 7). Many factors interplay to affect consumers' decision making process that can directly influence their purchase behavior (Sidin et al. 2008, p. 7)

Therefore, according to previous studies of the literature, it is recognized that research studies have linked several individual perceptions in the studies related to consumer behavior such as purchasing, societal influence, changes in attitude, company preferences, concerns about a company's identity and/or corporate activities, etc. (Mowen and Speers 1999; Keaveney and Parthasarathy 2001; Keh and Xie 2008). At this point, it is assumed that in order to understand why consumers behave the way they do, it is important to look at what factors influence individuals in their subsequent behaviors. As the researchers have addressed, it can be claimed that there is the relevance of companies' perceived corporate social responsibility activities as part of their marketing strategy in determining the consumer behavior patterns. Therefore, it can be proposed that there is an association between consumers' perceptions of corporate social responsibility activities and consumer purchase behavior orientations.

3.5 The Conceptual Framework of the Study

Depending on the preliminary literature survey and based on the literature implications about the subject the proposed conceptual framework of this study was given in order to understand the proposed relationships between the concepts. According to our proposed framework the CSR activities of the company as a marketing strategy can be assumed to be a determinant of consumers' purchase behavior orientation which is relevant for the specific unit of context and unit of analysis. Therefore, a survey will be conducted in order to understand how the consumers perceive and respond to the communicated CSR activities of the case company.

It should be implied that corporate social responsibility is one of those corporate initiatives practiced by marketers throughout the marketing management process. It was once noted that, societal marketing calls upon marketers to build social and ethical considerations into their marketing practices (Kotler and Zaltman 1971, p. 5). Therefore, in the next section, corporate social responsibility will be taken as a dimension of societal marketing in this study and corporate social responsibility will be reflected in marketing practices by companies adopting a societal marketing focus.

Since profit seeking organizations aim of profit works in collaboration with the desire to contribute towards social welfare is taken into consideration which is rather different when it comes to not-for-profit organizations, societal marketing fits the corporate social responsibility activities context emphasized in this study.

In the literature, there is evidence which suggests that the collaboration of the role of other moderating and mediating variables within the conceptual framework of CSR and consumer purchase behavior. For instance, some studies have found corporate reputation as a mediating factor that affects the relationship between

CSR activities of the companies and the individuals' purchase orientation (Zeithaml, Parasuraman and Berry 1996; Morgan and Hunt 1994; Capozzi 2005). Additionally, it was noted that the individual perceives companies' CSR projects with the mediating role of some factors like customer loyalty, commitment etc. Thus, if customers think that a company is reputable, they then feel committed to it and they show they demonstrate this through purchase behavior. (Zeithaml et al. 1996; Morgan and Hunt 1994; Capozzi 2005)

To further support this argument, Bartikowski and Walsh suggest in that, depending on the contingency theory (e.g., Heider 1946; Osgood and Tannenbaum 1955), that people prefer the presence of harmony between their beliefs, attitudes and behaviors in order to avoid any discomfort in their feelings. Thus, if customers have a good perception about a company, they have commitment to that company and they continue their purchase (Bartikowski and Walsh 2009). Moreover, Morgan and Hunt (1994) claimed that customer commitment as a mediating factor increases efficiency, productivity and effectiveness. Furthermore, Raj (1982) notes that customer loyalty is a sign for the future purchase behavior of the customers (Bartikowski and Walsh 2009). Thus, it can be suggested that all these clues and factors mean that if customers have a positive perception about a company and about its products, services and social responsibility activities, they are likely to be loyal and committed to that company and would be more willing to purchase these companies' products and services.

After an analysis of the literature we diverted our attention to the role of different factors, how the CSR activities of companies have contributed to customers behavioral patterns.

In this context, based on the literature examination, it can be suggested that corporate social responsibility activities have been an important factor to be analyzed by researchers. Especially, the effects of CSR on consumer behavioral patterns are worthy research in order to illuminate the path of the managers of companies and to motivate them to organize and put in place CSR activities to improve the reputation of the company and to make financial gains through increased consumer purchasing habit or behavior towards their products or services.

Becker-Olsen et al. (2005) state that consumer expectations would most likely be related to companies CSR profile. These scholars have noted an increase in this over the past 5–10 years. First, the number of companies with social responsibility programs grew, second, more companies continue to communicate their efforts with the public and thirdly, consumer groups continue to promote companies' wrongdoings and have called for large-scale boycotts (Becker-Olsen et al. 2005). İt is also stated that there is managerial and empirical evidence that companies with insufficient CSR records experience negative results (Becker-Olsen et al. 2005).

Interestingly, there is another study result in the literature, that shows that more than 80 % of respondents believe that companies should engage in social initiatives and 76 % felt those initiatives would be beneficial to these companies, later it was also found that 52 % of respondents would boycott irresponsible acts by companies in terms of their CSR activities, if they would find any alternative companies (Becker-Olsen et al. 2005).

By looking at the literature it can be found that, according to the social identity theory, buyers are willing to identify or build connection with highly-reputable sellers, which can facilitate their self-definition process (Pratt 1998; Bhattacharya and Sen 2003 as cited in Keh and Xie 2008

In this respect, it can be mentioned that in the literature, there is a body of research findings that constitute a basis for the relationship between the companies' social responsibility and the community's perceptions, intentions, preferences and purchase orientation towards these companies' products and services as there are evidences that indicate the analysis of corporate social responsibility projects and consumer behaviour (Tench et al. 2007; Li 2007; Chung and Poon 1996). Therefore, it was mentioned by studies that corporations perceive social responsibility as a marketing strategy and perceive how their socially responsible manners and attitudes towards the social and environmental issues will influence the individuals' preferences and purchase orientation.

Therefore, depending on the literature it can be said that, according to the social identity theory, the consumers have orientation and preferences towards highly reputable companies' products and services (Pratt 1998 and Bhattacharya and Sen 2003 as cited in Keh and Xie 2008).

At this point, in this study a conceptual model was developed after reviewing the literature on corporate social responsibility, marketing strategy and consumer purchase behavior. The model was developed in order to examine the hypothesized relationship between the independent and dependent variables of concern. This hypothesized relationship will be tested on data collected from the participants of the survey.

Accordingly, the proposed conceptual framework of this study can be presented as a model in Fig. 3.1.

Figure 3.1 gives the proposed conceptual framework of the study noted in this chapter. In this context, the study's intentions and previous research studies help to indicate the hypotheses of this study. Thus, the following hypotheses (H) which have been constructed in order to measure the relationship between the variables

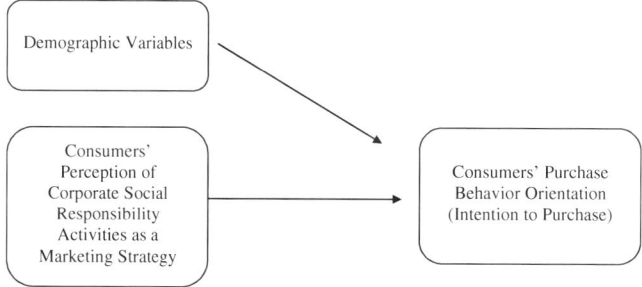

Fig. 3.1 The proposed conceptual framework of the study

can be proposed. Upon the proposition of "the overall perception related to the CSR activities of the relevant company involving the factors namely philanthropy, community, youth education, youth health and environment is related with the consumers' purchasing preferences", Hypothesis 1 was generated.

Hypothesis 1 At least one of the CSR perception factors has a relationship with the consumers' purchase behavior of the products and services of the company.

In order to test whether the CSR factors have a relationship with the purchase behavior orientation, the following hypothesis was generated.

Hypothesis 2 A company's CSR activities as a marketing strategy has a positive relationship with the consumers' purchase behavior orientation.

3.6 The Research Methodology

3.6.1 The Aim of the Research

This study aims to investigate the relationship between the corporate social responsibility activities of chosen company's and customers' purchase behavior. In this study, we have used two main variables to conduct our research. Thus, the focus of the study was on a special holding group famous with its endless reputable corporate social responsibility activities in Turkey, namely Sabancı Holding Group was taken as our subject, in our attempt to measure these variables and their relationships with each other, if any.

Within the framework, the research was seeking to examine the importance of corporate social responsibility activities as a par marketing strategy in the context of Turkey. Further, it sought to identify the consumer perceptions and expectations as well as the main CSR projects of Turkish companies. Therefore, the main purpose of the survey was to measure consumers' perceptions of the relevant company's CSR activities and customers' purchase behavior orientation towards the company's, brands, and products and services of the Holding group. Thus, measurement was based on the dimensions of perceived corporate social responsibility activities and consumers' purchase behavior orientation.

3.6.2 The Sample

In this study, convenience sampling was used. The study was conducted in Turkish Context. The data about the consumer purchase behavior orientation were gathered from individuals working in the academic sector (universities) in Istanbul.

Holding companies which have CSR projects in Turkey were investigated through secondary sources such as company records, industrial publications, annual marketing research reports, etc.

3.6.3 The Procedure

The primary data was collected through questionnaire (Bryman and Bell 2007). Questionnaires were distributed to participants working in two public universities of Istanbul who were believed to be potential customers of the selected holding groups of companies. Thus the survey was cross-sectional. Later, these questionnaires were returned by hand to the researcher by these individuals—the subject. The study was applied to individuals working in two big government universities in Istanbul. The preconditions for the study were that those individuals filling in the questionnaires must be customers of the selected holding group of companies.

3.6.4 The Measures and Data Analysis Methods

The data were obtained through the official web pages of the Holding company, other official web pages that contain news and information about the relevant company's socially responsible behaviors and facilities relevant to the issues. Besides, the data were obtained by searching the news and facilities archives of the company.

Moreover, a structured questionnaire was used in the survey. The survey instrument was in three different parts, measuring different variables of the research model. The objective was to examine individuals' perception of the holding groups' corporate social responsiveness; in order to allow the relationship between these variables to be seen after the survey.

Individuals' perception of the relevant company's social responsiveness and CSR projects will be measured by the corporate social responsibility items developed by Mohr and Webb (2001) which were also used by Walker (2009) in a dissertation. The items were modified in order to turn them into a perceived social responsibility scale and an additional subscale was added concerning the holding groups' corporate social responsibility campaigns. The subscales were identified as philanthropy, community, youth education, youth health and environment.

The second part of the questionnaire aims to measure the purchase behavior orientation of the individuals towards the products and services of these holding companies. Thus, the last variable of the model, purchase behavior orientation is considered to be the dependent variable. The items are used in a dissertation written by Xu (2009). The purchase behavior orientation was measured to test the hypotheses claiming that the corporate social responsibility perceptions influence the purchase orientation of the customers positively.

The third part of the research study aims to measure the demographical data of the participants.

Within the data analysis method, firstly, frequency analysis and descriptive evaluations were used to describe the participants according to demographic characteristics. After that, various statistical methods such as factor analysis and reliability analysis, Regression Analysis were used through computer statistical package for social sciences (SPSS).

3.7 Research Findings and Results

3.7.1 Frequency Distributions of the Participants

Descriptive information about the sample is displayed in the following tables. Table 3.1 provides information about gender characteristics; Table 3.2 provides age characteristics; Table 3.3 gives the educational level; Table 3.4 presents the/ occupation status; and Table 3.5 provides the marital status of the respondents.

As noted in table above, 50 % of the respondents consisted of females and 50 % consisted of males. The results show that majority of the respondents (76 %) fall into the 22–35 age group, thus it can be said that a younger demographic profile participated in the survey.

As depicted in Table 3.3, all of the respondents (100 %) are university graduates. Doctorate graduates consist of 25 %. It's seen that in general terms that education demography of the participant was high. The reason was because the survey was conducted among the university lecturers, research assistants, associate

Table 3.1 Gender of the respondents

Gender	Frequency	Percentage
Male	100	50
Female	100	50

Table 3.2 Age of the respondents

Age	Frequency	Percentage
22–25	55	33.3
26–35	75	42.3
36–45	33	12
46–55	27	8
56–70	10	4.5

Table 3.3 Education level of the respondents

Education	Frequency	Percentage
University	200	100
Post graduate	125	75
Doctorate	75	25

Table 3.4 Position/
occupation levels of the
respondents

Position	Frequency	Percentage
Research assistant & lecturer	122	52.3
Associate professor	57	11.3
Professor	21	5.3

Table 3.5 Marital status of
the respondents

Marital status	Frequency	Percentage
Married	100	50
Single	100	50

professors and professors. As further noted in Table 3.4, 52.3 % of the respondents work as research assistants and lecturers in the relevant university whereas 11.3 % are associate professors and 5.3 are professors.

In Table 3.5 it is seen that married and single participants are equal within the research context as half of the sample are married (50 %) and half are single.

3.8 Descriptive Analyses of the Participants

Descriptive analyses were conducted on the research dependent and independent variables in order to explain the mean and standard deviation of the variables.

Respondents were asked the importance of each variable mentioned in the Table 3.6 while they made a purchase. The responses were measured by a 5-point Likert scale ranging from very important to not important at all. Table 3.6 shows the means and standard deviation values of the importance of purchase criteria of the respondents while buying a product. As it is seen in Table 3.6, among all items, quality came out to be the most important criteria while making a purchase with

Table 3.6 Considering your purchase criteria while buying a product, how important or unimportant are the following criteria for you?

Importance of purchase criteria	Mean	Standard deviation
Price	4.39	0.830
Quality	4.72	0.571
Brand	3.35	1.121
Promotions	4.00	0.999
Discounts, sales promotions	2.71	1.154
Product previous experiences	4.59	0.771
Company image	3.93	0.936
Social responsibility concerns of the company	3.94	1.042
Salesman	3.84	1.036
Personal recommendations	3.49	1.033

the highest mean score o 4.72 followed by previous experience and price. In terms of importance, the social responsibility activities of the company was ranked 5th.

Respondents were asked their level of agreement or disagreement with social responsibility efforts of companies and their own attitude towards social responsibility on a 5-point Likert scale. The negative statements' answers were recoded to obtain positive statements. The range of the responses' mean values has changed between 2.50 and 4.72. The statements "A company which acts with the aim of contributing to society has a positive image for me" and "Social responsibility projects are among the principal duties of companies" got the highest mean scores (4.72 and 4.59 respectively). This statement also obtained the low standard deviation values (0.571 and 0.771) which imply that respondents agreed upon these statements.

3.9 Analysis of Data

3.9.1 Reliability Analysis

Cronbach alpha method was used for the reliability analyses for the "Perceptions of Company's Corporate Social Responsibility profile" and consumer purchase behavior scale and scientifically high internal consistency was found for the present study. The Cronbach alpha is 0, 859 for the perception of CSR scale and 0, 866 for the consumer purchase behavior scale. Thus, the scales are found reliable.

3.9.2 Factor Analysis

Factor analysis was performed for both of the perception of CSR and the purchase behavior questionnaires.

3.9.2.1 Factor Analysis of the Perception of Corporate Social Responsibility Responsiveness Questionnaire

As was mentioned in the previous section, individual's perception of the company's social responsiveness and CSR projects were measured by the corporate social responsibility items (Interval—Q26–Q33). The items were been modified by the researcher in order to turn it into a perceived social responsibility scale and an additional subscale was added concerning the relevant holding group's (Sabancı Holding) corporate social responsibility activities/projects/campaigns. The subscales used were philanthropy, community activities, youth education, youth health and environmental issues.

Table 3.7 Perception of CSR Activities Factor Analysis Report

Factor Name	Factor Loadings	Cronbach α
Factor 1		
Community	0.742	0.859
Factor 2		
Youth education and health	0.678	
Factor 3		
Environment	0.650	
Mean = 3.114		
Kaiser–Meyer–Olkin measure of 0.806		
Sampling adequacy		
Bartlett's test of sphericity approx. Chi Square 6614.016		
df 351		
sig. 0.000		

In order to understand how variance can be partitioned, component analysis was performed on data set. This statistical method was chosen in order to explain as much of the variance as possible using the fewest number of components. The total variance explained in the study can be seen in the Table 3.9. In the study, Kaiser R rule, which is the most widely used rule and basically proposed to drop all components with eigenvalues under 1.0, was used to decide how many factors to retain.

At this point, in our analysis, Kaiser–Meyer–Olkin Measure of Sampling Adequacy of the Perception of CSR questionnaire was found as 0.806 which is over the acceptable level (>0.50). This indicates that the sample was adequate in order to apply factor analysis. The Bartlett Test of Sphericity was found to be 0.000 which represents a meaningful factor analysis.

After the factor analysis of 8 items which was used in order to assess the CSR perceptions of the individuals, it has been found that the 3 factors explained 76.442 % of the total variance. In this study, after the factor analysis it has been found that the 3 factors explained the total variance as presented in Table 3.9.

The items which have loadings of less than 0.50 and which have low reabilities have been extracted from factor analysis.

These 3 factors are named as Community (Q26, Q27, Q28), Youth education and health (Q29, Q30, Q31), and Environment (Q32, Q33). The CSR perceptions Factor Analysis Report can be seen in Table 3.7.

3.9.2.2 Factor Analysis of the Consumer Purchase Behavior Questionnaire

Kaiser–Meyer–Olkin Measure of Sampling Adequacy of the consumer purchase behavior questionnaire was found as 0.833 which is over the acceptable level (>0.50). So the sample was adequate to apply factor analysis. The Bartlett Test of Sphericity was found to be 0,000 which represents a meaningful factor analysis.

Table 3.8 Consumer Purchase Behavior Factor Analysis Report

Factor Name	Items	% of the variance explained	Cronbach α
Purchase behavior orientation	Q34 While I am at a shopping to buy a product, probably I will have tendency to prefer the products of one of the companies of Sabancı Holding Group	64.330	0.866
	Q35 It is a big probability that I will prefer to buy any product which was produced or sold by Sabancı Holding Group's companies		
	Q36 It is a big probability that I will directly buy any product which is produced by Sabancı Holding Group's companies		

Mean = 2.979

Kaiser–Meyer–Olkin measure of 0.833

Sampling adequacy

Bartlett's test of sphericity approx. Chi Square 6925.022

df 366

sig. 0.000

After the factor analysis of 3 items (Q34–Q35–Q36) which were used in order to assess the intention to purchase of the respondents, it has been found that one factor explained 64.330 % of the total variance. As a result of factor analysis, none of the items which are related with consumer behavior have been excluded, so 3 items were used for assessing that variable. The consumer purchase behavior Factor Analysis Report can be seen in Table 3.8.

At this point, according to the results of the factor analysis, while testing the hypothesis, all factors have been put into analysis on their own. As the factors "Community", "Youth education and health", and "Environment" exactly fit the scale used for CSR concern in the design of the questionnaire, two factors –philanthropy and community- have been merged to measure "CSR activities concerning community" as we have named; and two other factors -youth education, youth health- have been merged to measure "CSR activities concerning youth education and health" as they were named. Consequently Fig. 3.2 shows the modified research model of perceived CSR activities and intention to purchase after the factor analysis.

3.9.2.3 Regression Analysis

Table 3.9 shows the model summary of regression analysis and Table 3.10 presents the regression analysis outcomes of CSR perception and consumer purchase behavior. In Tables 3.9 and 3.10, it can be seen that, R Square is 0.627, F is 33.771

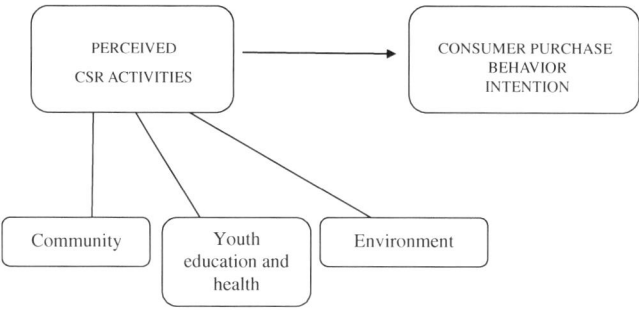

Fig. 3.2 Modified research model of perceived CSR activities and intention to purchase after the factor analysis

Table 3.9 Model summary of regression analysis

Model	R	R square	Adjusted R square	Std. error of the estimate
1	0.792[a]	0.627	0.608	0.48173

[a] Predictors: (Constant), community, youth education & health, environment

Table 3.10 Regression analysis of CSR perception and consumer purchase behavior

Model		Sum of squares	df	Mean square	F	Sig.
1	Regression	70.735	9	7.837	33.771	0.000[a]
	Residual	42.004	181	0.232		
	Total	112.540	190			

[a] Predictors: (Constant), community, youth education & health, environment
[b] Dependent Variable: consumer purchase behavior

and Significance level is 0,000. Table 3.11 presents the coefficients of regression analysis. According to the results of Table 3.11, it can be mentioned that the regression results show that the independent variables jointly explained 62,7 % of the variance in the dependent variable, consumer purchase behavior orientation. ($F = 33,771$, $p < 0, 05$).

Table 3.11 Coefficients of regression analysis

Dependent variable: consumer purchase behavior

Independent variables	Beta	t value	P value
Constant		−0.080	0.936
community	0.213	2.911	0.004
Youth education and health	0.116	2.217	0.028
Environment	0.232	3.808	0.000

$R = 0.792$; $R^2 = 0.627$; F Value $= 33.771$; P Value $= 0.000$

As a result, it can be implied that, the purchase behavior was significantly explained by all three independent variables—community, youth education and health, and environmental concern - as assumed in the generated hypothesis of this study.

3.9.2.4 Independent Samples T-Test

In order to see the effects of one's gender on his/her purchase behavior, Independent Samples T-Test is conducted to search the difference in the purchase behavior orientation of the participants belonging to their gender.

Independent Samples T-Test was conducted in order to test whether there is a difference between males and females in terms of purchase behavior orientation. Table 3.12 shows the purchase behavior summary results according to the gender factor. Table 3.13 provides the independent sample T-Test results of gender and purchase behavior.

According to the results of the above Tables 3.12 and 3.13, it can be suggested that the F value of 0,060 is not significant (p = 0,807 > 0, 05). Thus, results of the T-Test showed that there was no difference between the males and females in terms of purchase behavior orientation.

Table 3.14 shows the purchase behavior summary results according to the marital status factor. Table 3.15 presents the independent sample T-Test results of marital status and purchase behavior.

According to the results of above Tables 3.14 and 3.15, it could be seen that the F value of 0.089 is not significant (p = 0.766 > 0.05). Thus, the results of the T-Test showed that there was no difference between married consumers and single consumers in terms of purchase behavior orientation.

Table 3.12 Males and females purchase behavior summary

	Gender	N	Mean	Std. deviation	Std. error mean
Purchase behavior orientation	Female	100	3.0714	0.79060	0.10207
	Male	100	3.1341	0.76208	0.06658

Table 3.13 Independent sample T-Test of gender and purchase behavior

		Levene's test for equality of variances		T–Test for equality of means				
		F	Sig.	t	df	Sig. (2-tailed)	Mean difference	Std. error difference
Purchase Behavior	Equal variances assumed	0.060	0.807	−0.522	189	0.603	−0.06270	0.120120
	Equal variances not assumed			−0.515	110.796	0.608	−0.06270	0.12186

Table 3.14 Marital status and purchase behavior summary

	G	N	Mean	Std. deviation	Std. error mean
Purchase behavior	Married	100	3.1133	0.75488	0.07009
	Single	100	3.1032	0.81826	0.11135

Table 3.15 Independent sample T-Test of marital status and purchase behavior

		Levene's test for equality of variances		T-Test for equality of means				
		F	Sig.	t	df	Sig. (2-tailed)	Mean Difference	Std. Error Difference
Purchase behavior	Equal variances assumed	0.089	0.766	0.079	168	0.7	0.01013	0.12774
	Equal variances not assumed			0.077	64.431	96.345	0.01013	0.13157

Furthermore, in order to see the effects of occupation/position and educational level of the participants on purchase behavior, One-Way ANOVA was conducted. Table 3.16 shows the consumer purchase behavior results according to the current position factor. Table 3.17 provides the consumer purchase behavior results according to the educational level of the respondents.

As it is seen on Table 3.16, according to One-Way ANOVA test findings, the F values of 1.574 is not significant ($p = 0.197 > 0.05$). Thus, the purchase behavior of the participants doesn't vary according to the current occupation/position worked in the relevant sector.

As it is provided on Table 3.17, according to One-Way ANOVA test results, the F values of 1.566 is not significant ($p = 0.,201 > 0.05$). Hence, the consumer purchase behavior of the respondents doesn't vary according to their education level.

Table 3.16 One-way ANOVA between current position and consumer purchase behavior

	Sum of squares	df	Mean square	F	Sig.
Between groups	2,771	13	0.924	1.574	0.197
Within groups	109,768	187	0.587		
Total	112,540	200			

Table 3.17 One-way ANOVA between education level and consumer purchase behavior

	Sum of squares	df	Mean square	F	Sig.
Between groups	2,766	12	0.945	1.566	0.201
Within groups	119,661	188	0.681		
Total	121,533	200			

3.9.2.5 Results of Hypothesis Testing

In order to test Hypothesis 1 and its sub-hypothesis, Multiple Regression Analysis was conducted.

- H0: The three independent variables (Community concerns/Youth eductaion and health concers/Environmental concerns) will have no significant relationship with the consumer's purchase behavior of the products and services of the relevant company.
- Ha: At least one of the CSR perception factors has a relationship with the consumer's purchase behavior of the products and services of the relevant company.

According to the results of the Tables 3.11 and 3.12, it could be seen that significance level of the regression model was 0.000. Hence, at least one of the CSR activities perception factors has a relationship with the consumer's purchase behavior of the relevant company's products and services. Therefore, H0 is rejected and Ha is accepted.

Sig. $= 0.000 < 0.05$ **reject H0; Accept Ha**

As Hypothesis 1 has been supported and it has been found that at least one of the CSR activities perception factors has a relationship with the consumer's purchase behavior, the significance levels of the each independent variable in the regression model should be examined.

H0: The consumers' CSR activities perceptions do not have a positive relationship with the purchase behavior of wine brands.
Ha: The company's CSR activities as a marketing strategy has a positive relationship with the consumers' purchase behavior orientation.

Sig. $= 0,028 < 0.05$ **reject H0; Accept Ha**

In this context, according to the findings and the results, it can be suggested that Hypothesis 2 has been supported at the 0.05 significance level (Youth education and health concerns: Beta $= 0,116$, t: 2.217, p $= 0.028$; Community concerns: Beta $= 0.213$, t: 2.911, p $= 0.004$; Environmental concerns: Beta $= 0.232$, t: 3.808, p $= 0.,000$). Therefore, it can be indicated that there is a positive relationship between the consumers' CSR activities perceptions with the purchase behavior of the relevant company's products and services.

As it was indicated before, independent variables perceived community concerns, perceived youth education and health concerns, and perceived environmental concerns are found to explain the 62.7 % of the variance in the dependent variable consumer purchase behavior. (F $= 33.771$, p < 0.05).

3.10 Conclusion and Discussion

The findings in the present study demonstrate that perception of company's perceived CSR attributes is a contributing factor towards the purchase of identified company's products, services, and brands among the Turkish consumers. In other words, perceptions of the company's CSR attributes can impact on consumers' purchase behavior towards the products and services produced and sold by the relevant company in Turkish context. Perception of CSR activities concerning community, perception of CSR activities concerning environment, and perception of CSR activities concerning youth education and health are found to have positive significant relationships with consumer purchase behavior orientation of the company's products and services.

Among the factors of the perceived CSR activities, community concern is found to be one of the factors that support consumer purchase behavior orientation towards the company's products. A significant positive relationship was found between the perceived community concerns and consumer purchase behavior in the context of Turkey. Previous studies also suggest that consumers will be more oriented towards the purchase of certain brands and products if they perceive their associations and have awareness about that company's CSR efforts and activities related with community and society (Mowen and Speers 1999; Keaveney and Parthasarathy 2001; Keh and Xie 2008).

Therefore, it can be implied that consumers' positive perceptions of a company's CSR responsiveness related to community issues and problems can lead to their purchase behavior or intentions to purchase the relevant company's products. For that reason, it can be suggested that companies that want to have greater consumer preferences towards their products, services, and brands should engage in relationship-oriented behaviors like, creating social awareness, social responsiveness, and social responsibility projects (Drumwright and Murphy 2000; Eves and Cheng 2007; Valentine and Fleischman 2007).

Another CSR activities perception which was found to have an impact on consumer purchase behavior of in this study is the factor which is referred to as perceived CSR activities concerning youth education and health. It is generally known that there is high attention for the primary education of children and especially education of girls as well as the education and health improvement of youth among Turkish citizens (Demir and Paykoç 2006, p. 648). Therefore, it is thought that companies, especially the large companies in Turkey have a crucial role to play in creating social consciousness about children, youth education and health issues in terms of their social responsibility activities.

Consistent with this suggestion, as a result of our research, the multiple regression findings have indicated a significant positive relationship between perceived CSR activities concerning youth education, health and environmental issues and consumer purchase behavior. Thus, it can be said that perceived CSR activities concerning youth education and health of a company increases the purchase orientation level of the consumers towards the products of that company in Turkish context. This finding is consistent with previous findings. Balmer et al. (2007) and and Deresky (2000) have also indicated that the perceived CSR responsiveness and efforts concerning societal problems, health and education, and environment impacts the consumer purchase behavior in a positive way. Brammer and Pavelin (2004) have stated that perceived CSR activities of any company may lead to the preference and purchase of a certain product of a company. Therefore, it can be suggested that the consumers will be more oriented and prefer to buy the products which they perceive as having a positive image and CSR concerns about the relevant company.

In that respect, it can be implied that consumers' positive perceptions of a company's effective CSR activities can impact their purchase behavior towards the relevant company's products and services. For that reason, it can be suggested that the producers and companies in Turkey should try to find out the social, educational, and environmental issues which require CSR related actions, and then develop CSR activities around those issues. Itt is further suggested that companies should view CSR matters as a part of their overall corporate strategies both in the short term and long term.

Another important result was obtained when the dependent variable was taken as consumer purchase behavior and independent variables being community concerns, youth education and health concerns, and environmental concerns. The results of the regression analysis showed that predictors of consumer purchase behavior orientation are some of the factors regarding social responsibility, strongest predictor being the environmental concern. Although community concern was a strong predictor of consumer purchase behavior, it came out significantly to predict consumer purchase behavior with a less degree than the environmental concerns. Environmental concerns as a CSR responsiveness and as a marketing strategy being the strongest predictor is as expected since a close relationship exists between social responsibility marketing strategies involving environmental protection and environmental issues that should be applied by companies and consumer purchase behavior.

Although it is not the central concern of this research study (and thus not the subject of formal hypotheses), the current findings reveal that there is no significant difference found between males and females and married and single participants. Thus, it can be mentioned that our study shows that there is no difference between males and females and singles and married individuals in terms of purchase behavior in Turkish context. In contrast to several previous studies about the subject of CSR perception ad purchase behavior, gender, marital status, positional level, and educational level did not have a role in the purchase behavior of the relevant company's products in the present research undertaken in Turkey. One reason which be could responsible for relates to the samples used in other previous studies were in a common country, common city, region and culture, while the sample used in this present study was consumers in Istanbul and working as academicians in two selected government universities.

Consequently, it is suggested that the findings and the framework of this study is important in terms of explaining the sequence that must be followed while setting marketing strategies regarding corporate social responsibility. The study involves expectations from the company that it should invest in CSR activities and campaigns and it should inform the customers so that knowledgeable and conscious customers would participate be involved in more of purchasing activities. It is believed that in turn, the company will gain a positive image, a positive outlook and increase its purchased intention for its products, brands, and services.

References

American Marketing Association. (1985). The definition of marketing. Marketing News, March 2.
Balmer, J. M. T., Fukukawa, K., & Gray, E. R. (2007). The nature and management of ethical corporate identity: A commentary on corporate identity, corporate social responsibility and ethics. *Journal of Business Ethics, 76*, 7–15.
Bartels, R. (1974). The identity crisis in marketing. *Journal of Marketing, 38*(4), 73–76.
Bartikowski, B., & Walsh, G. (2009). Investigating mediators between corporate reputation and customer citizenship behaviors. *Journal of Buisness Research, 21*, 55–69.
Bayraktar, S. (2006). Social responsibility projects as a marketing strategy: a recycling approach from the customer's perspective. Unpublished Master Thesis, M.U. Social Sciencies Institute, Istanbul.
Becker-Olsen, K. L., Cudmore, A. B., & Hill, R. P. (2005). The impact of perceived corporate social responsibility on consumer behavior. *Journal of Buisness Research, 59*, 46–53.
Bryman, A., & Bell, E. (2007). *Business research methods.* New York: Oxford University Press.
Buchholz, R. A. (2004). The natural environment: Does it count? *Academy of Management Executive, 18*(2), 130–133.
Buchholz, R. A., & Rosenthal, S. B. (2005). Toward a contemporary conceptual framework for stakeholder theory. *Journal of Business Ethics, 58*, 130–148.
Capozzi, L. (2005). Corporate reputation: our role in sustaining and building a valuable asset. *Journal of Advertising Research, 45*(3), 290–293.
Carroll, A. B. (1977). *Managing corporate social responsibility.* Boston: Little, Brown and Company.
Carroll, A. B. (1991). The pyramid of corporate social responsibility: toward the moral management of organizational stakeholders. *Business Horizons, 34*, 39–48.
Cavana, R., Delahaye, B. L., & Sekeran, U. (2001). *Applied business research: Qualitative and quantitative methods.* Australia: Wiley.
Chung, S. S., & Poon, C. S. (1996). The attitudinal differences in source separation and waste reduction between the general public and housewives in Hong Kong. *Journal of Environmental Management, 48*, 215–227.
Collis, J., & Hussey, R. (2003). *Business research* (2nd ed.). New York: Palgrave Macmillan.
Davis, D. (2000). *Business research for decision making* (5th ed.). Duxbury: Thomson Learning.
Deresky, H. (2000). *International management: Managing across borders and cultures.* NJ: Prentice Hall.
Drumwright, M. E., & Murphy, P. (2000). Corporate societal marketing. In P. N. Bloom & G. T. Gundlach (Eds.), *The handbook of social marketing and society.* CA: Sage Publications.
Jayne, V. (2001). Positive partnering. *New Zealand Marketing Magazine, 19*(11), 24–27.
Kaplan, D. (2002). How to play the name game with women, men. *Adweek New England Edition, 36*, 3.
Keaveney, S. M., & Parthasarathy, M. (2001). Customer switching behavior in online services: An exploratory study of the role of selected attitudinal, behavioral, and demographic factors. *Journal of Academy of Marketing Services, 29*(4), 374–390.

Keh, H. T., & Xie, Y. (2008). Corporate reputation and customer behavioral intentions: The roles of trust, identification and commitment. *Industrial Marketing Management, 38*(7), 732–742.

Kilcullen, M., & Kooistra, J. O. (1999). At least do no harm: sources on the changing role of business ethics and corporate social responsibility. *Reference Services Review, 27*(2), 158–178.

Klein, J., & Dawar, N. (2003). Corporate social responsibility and consumers' attributions and brand evaluations in a product–harm crisis. *International Journal of Research in Marketing, 21*(3), 203.

Kotler, P., & Levy, S. J. (1969). Broadening the concept of marketing. *Journal of Marketing, 3*, 10–15.

Kotler, P., & Zaltman, G. (1971). Social marketing: An approach to planned social change. *Journal of Marketing, 35*, 3–12.

Lazer, W. (1969). Marketing's changing social relationship. *Journal of Marketing, 33*(January), 3–9.

Lerner, L. D., & Fryxell, G. E. (1988). An empirical study of the predictors of corporate social performance: a multi-dimensional analysis. *Journal of Buisness Ethics, 7*, 951–959.

Li, Z. (2007). Media performance and global policy making: A comparative study of press coverage on global warming. Unpressed Dissertation, University of Pennsylvania.

Luck, D. J. (1969). Broadening the concept of marketing too far. *Journal of Marketing, 33*(3), 53–55.

Luck, D. J. (1974). Social marketing: Confusion compounded. *Journal of Marketing, 38*(4), 70–72.

Maignan, I., & Ferrell, O. C. (2004). Corporate social responsibility and marketing: An integrative framework. *Journal of the Academy of Marketing Science, 32*(1), 3–19.

Manakkalathil, J., & Rudolf, E. (1995). Corporate social responsibility in a globalizing market. *SAM Advanced Management Journal, 47*, 29–32.

Mohr, L. A., & Webb, D. J. (2001). Do consumers expect companies to be socially responsible? The impact of corporate social responsibility on buying behavior. *Journal of Consumer Affairs, 35*, 45. (URL:http://www.allbusiness.com/periodicals/article/782502-2.html).

Morgan, R. M., & Hunt, S. D. (1994). The commitment–trust theory of relationship marketing. *J Mark, 58*(3), 20–38.

Mowen, J. C., & Speers, N. (1999). Understanding compulsive buying among college students: a hierarchical approach. *Journal of Consumer Psychology, 8*, 407–430.

Nowicka. P. (2002). Cause related marketing, reaping the benefits. *Ethical Corporation Magazine*, 30–32.

Artıeğitim D. (2005). Sirketler egitime destek için yarısıyor. URL:http://www.egitimedestek.meb.gov.tr/haber.php?id=96.

Büyük, S.S. (2006). Sosyal sorumlulukta Türkiye'nin liderleri. Capital. URL:http://www.capital.com.tr/haber.aspx?HBR_KOD=3362.

D'Silva, S. (2005). Use of societal concept of marketing in corporate image building URL: http://www.indiainfoline.com/bisc/sydfac06.html.

Piercy, N. F., & Morgan, N. A. (1993). Strategic and operational market segmentation: A managerial analysis. *Journal of Strategic Marketing, 1*, 123–140.

Quaak, L., Aalbers, T., & Goedee, J. (2007). Transparency of corporate social responsibility in Dutch breweries. *Journal of Business Ethics, 76*, 293–308.

Raj, S. R. (1982). The effects of advertising on high and low loyalty consumer segments. *Journal of Consumer Research, 1982*, 77–89.

Rodríguez-Pinto, J., Rodríguez-Escudero, A. I., & Gutiérrez-Cillán, J. (2008). Order, positioning, scope and outcomes of market entry. *Industrial Marketing Management, 37*, 154–166.

Saunders, M., Lewis, P., & Thornhill, A. (2009). *Research methods for business students* (5th ed.). England: Pearson Education.

Sidin, S. M., Rahman, M. A., Rashid, Z. A., Othman, N., & Bakar, A. Z. A. (2008). Effects of social variables on urban children's consumption attitude and behavior intentions. *Journal of Consumer Marketing, 25*(1), 7–15.

Steiner, G. A. (1971). *Business and society*. New York: Random House.

Swanson, D. L. (1995). Addressing a theoretical problem by reorienting the corporate social performance model. *Academy of Management Review, 20*(1), 43–64.

Takas, A. (1974). Societal Marketing: A businessman's perspective. *Journal of Marketing, 38*, 2–7.

Tench, R., Bowd, R., & Jones, B. (2007). Perceptions and perspectives: corporate social responsibility and the media. *Journal of Communication Management, 11*(4), 348–360.

Tuzzolino, F., & Armandi, B. R. (1981). A need-hierarchy framework for assessing corporate social responsibility. *Academy of Management Review, 6*(1), 21–28.

Valentine, S., & Fleischman, G. (2007). Ethics programs, perceived corporate social responsibility and job satisfaction. *Journal of Business Ethics, 77*, 159–172.

Walker, M.. (2009). Assessing the influence of corporate social responsibility on consumer attitudes in the sport industry. Ph.D. dissertation, The Florida State University, United States—Florida. Retrieved December 15, from Dissertations & Theses: Full Text.(Publication No. AAT 3282675).

Wood, D. J. (1991). Corporate social performance revisited. *Academy of Management Review, 16*(4), 691–718.

World Business Council for Sustainable Development (WBCSD). (2000).

Xu, B. (2009). New product creativity orientation: Consumers' view of new product creativity and consumer purchase intention. Ph.D. dissertation, New Mexico State University, United States—New Mexico. Retrieved December 30, from Dissertations & Theses: Full Text.(Publication No. AAT 3367536).

Zeithaml, V. A., Parasuraman, A., & Berry, L. L. (1996). The behavioral consequences of service quality. *Journal of Marketing, 60*, 31–46.

Media Cat. (2001). Sosyal Sorumluluk. URL:http://euspk.ege.edu.tr/makale/Sos_Sor.doc.

Sevier, R. (2005). A new definition of marketing: the AMA's update can mean enormous opportunities for higher education. University Business. URL: http://findarticles.com/p/articles/mi_m0LSH/is_3_8/ai_n13254488.

Part II
Corporate Governance and Financial Crisis

Chapter 4
CSR in a Model of Heterogeneous Firms, Financial Constraints and Economic Crisis

Luisa Giallonardo and Marcella Mulino

Abstract The paper develops a model considering strategic CSR and vertical product differentiation in the context of heterogeneous firms and monopolistic competition, based on the strand of literature on heterogeneous firms in international trade pioneered by Mélitz (2003). We seek to provide some understanding as to which of the features influence corporate CSR performance, factors which motivate firms to engage it and the strategies firms adopt in order to approach it. The results change if we introduce more realistic hypothesis, for example, the financial constraint firms face or the presence of economic cycles. We suggest that it is possible in times of crisis under certain conditions that firms attention for CSR can in fact be strengthened.

4.1 Introduction

The economic theory approached the phenomenon of Corporate Social Responsibility (CSR) only recently, through the analysis of wider and wider ethical behavior in society.

The discipline of CSR is often linked to the concept of "strategic CSR", which is crucial in the process of understanding most of the scientific articles in this field.

In 1970, Milton Friedman stated that "there is one and only one social responsibility of business—to use its resources and engage in activities designed to increase its profits so long as it stays within the rules of the game, which is to say, engages in open and free competition without deception or fraud" (Friedman 1970 and 1977), thus originating the idea of strategic CSR.

L. Giallonardo (✉) · M. Mulino
University of L'Aquila, Aquila, Italy
e-mail: luisa.giallonardo@univaq.it

A. Yüksel Mermod and S. O. Idowu (eds.), *Corporate Social Responsibility in the Global Business World*, DOI: 10.1007/978-3-642-37620-7_4,
© Springer-Verlag Berlin Heidelberg 2014

This last theory admits the existence of CSR only if its main objective is the firm's: profit maximization. So "responsibility as social purpose consists of the research of profit and CSR activities are a consequence of incentives coming from the markets (goods, work, capital), where the firm is located" (Sacco and Viviani 2005). Therefore Friedman's idea of strategic CSR is based on the conceit that firms are not altruistic at all; on the contrary they look only at the increasing of profits.

Shareholders elect managers who aspire to achieve the best results in terms of profits. According to Sacconi (2005), managers would not have the task to "pursue morally valuable social causes" and so they would not "tamper prices", without considering the effects on the market and consumers.

CSR products can be defined as the goods produced by undertaking CSR activities; *ceteris paribus*—all other things remaining equal—those products are more desirable than traditional goods. This means that CSR increases consumers' demand and firms strengthen their market shares if engaging in CSR activities.

This sequence is often called "bottom up pressure", underlining that CSR starts from consumers' initiative in appreciating it. In other words, consumers keep being sensitive to social responsibility before firms do. Firms incorporate this fact in their profit maximization calculation. The bottom up pressure principle can be formalized introducing CSR in the demand function, which obviously influences the process of profit maximization.

A simple way to formalize CSR and quantify its value is to consider it as a product differentiation criterion. The economic literature about product differentiation distinguishes between horizontal or vertical product differentiation. In the first case consumers don't necessarily prefer to have a higher share of CSR than a lower one, once they have defined their optimal quantity of CSR; while in the second case it is unanimously recognized that a higher quantity of CSR gives a higher value to the product.

Horizontal differentiation approach can be justified taking into account the possibility that a number of consumers are against CSR and consequently do not prefer it. An example of this case can be found in those who believe that CSR has to be a feature external to the firm, stating that only public institutions are supposed to protect the rights and duties stemming from CSR.

This idea is based on Friedman's conceit of CSR too. As described above, according to Friedman, a purpose of the firm other than profit maximization would be inconsistent with shareholders' aim. So managers, elected by these shareholders, are not usually delegated to undertake CSR projects and they are not expected to do that. For this reason some people could believe that firms do not have either the competence or the capability to engage in socially responsible initiatives and, above all, they would not have a relevant impact on sustainable development of society.

For those consumers demand for CSR products is very poor. They would pay a very high psychological cost when they buy from firms with more ethical than they like.

On the contrary a vertical differentiation approach is based on the awareness that, at given equal prices, a consumer is indifferent between the product with his preferred CSR contents and the more ethical one. In this case the consumer accepts to have more CSR than the preferred, if it is not costly.

Intermediate positions admit the existence of heterogeneous (admitting horizontal features too) consumers along an ethical segment of vertical differentiation (Becchetti et al. 2007).

Empirical literature shows a widespread preference among consumers for firms with ethical behaviour (Becchetti and Rosati 2005, Becchetti et al. 2006), thus contrasting the neoclassical theory. So it would seem unrealistic to believe that *ceteris paribus* consumers prefer renouncing to CSR.

For this reason, as most of the literature does, we will use a vertical differentiation approach to modelize CSR, considering this last as a product characteristic increasing the quality.[1]

Several authors have studied the phenomenon of CSR in an oligopoly market (Manasakis et al. 2007) or spatial models of differentiation in a duopoly market (Becchetti et al. 2005b; Becchetti et al. 2005a).

We believe it would be very interesting to find results in terms of CSR performance in a competition context.

For this reason, we consider the strand of literature concerning models of perfect and monopolistic competition incorporating vertical product differentiation applied to international trade, considering quality in the products as an important feature for intra-trade flows (Hummels and Klenow 2005; Hallak 2006; Cavallaro and Mulino 2009; Melitz 2003). CSR can be formalized as quality in those models.

Following that theoretical approach, product differentiation has a double dimension, given by variety and quality. Firms choose to increase the qualitative characteristics of the products in order to conquer market shares in the country and abroad. On the other side consumers evaluate positively the quality and choose their goods not only on the basis of relative prices, but of relative prices weighted for the quality too.

Most recent developments of this kind of models start from Mélitz (2003) and consider heterogeneous in productivity firms behaviour. Among other works following this approach we find Johnson (2008) and Kugler and Verhoogen (2008), who incorporate quality in the model under the hypothesis of heterogeneity and monopolistic competition. Also Baldwin and Harrigan (2007) obtain that the optimal level of quality varies positively with firm productivity, as a higher product quality causes higher marginal costs.

In the next section we discuss the idea of similarity between CSR and quality in terms of theoretical effects. CSR and quality can easily be considered at the same way both in consumers' preferences and in production side, even if they are different phenomena.

---

[1] The differences and similarities between CSR and quality are described in the next section of the paper.

In the context described, we will endeavour to understand which features influence CSR performances, why firms engage CSR and the strategies firms use in order to approach to it.

After that, we will change some of the hypothesis.

First, we will consider the presence of a financial constraint, influencing firms' credit access. We will show that it could decrease firms' willingness to engage in CSR projects in the whole market.

We will refer to literature about financial constraints (Grossman and Helpman 1991; Kaplan and Zingales 2000; Michie 1998). Moreover it is important to consider the work of Gorodnichenko and Schnitzer (2010), who study the effects of constraints on innovation of the firms in a context of open economies and development differences between the countries.

So we will introduce the scarcity of internal resources of firms. This could change the optimal CSR level.

Finally, the relationship between CSR and economic cycles is considered. In particular, the effects of a global crisis on CSR choices are explored. We identify a negative relation between the reduction of aggregate income in times of recession and the intensity of preference for CSR. This would create a positive effect on CSR optimal level in times of crisis contrasting the opposite effect due to the drop of the demand of goods. This last, on the contrary, influences the resources of firms which become less willing to pay for CSR costs.

We show that under certain conditions the first effect can prevail and so attention for CSR results strengthened in times of crisis.

This section helps us also to characterize better CSR and differentiate it from quality as explained in the next paragraph.

So the structure of the paper is the following: in the first section we make some points about the connection between CSR and quality in order to study the characteristics of the goods.

In the second section we present our model distinguishing the demand side, the production side and the optimal choice of firms in terms of CSR.

In the third section we analyze the effects of financial constraints on firms CSR performances and in the fourth one we raise the problem of CSR and the global crisis.

4.2 CSR and Product Quality

The first aim of the paper is to introduce ethical standards in production and understand how much SR content can be optimal for firms. As explained in the introduction the literature we will refer to is pionerized by Mélitz (2003), with the consideration of the stochastic evolution of firm productivity from Hopenhayn (1992).

Quality is often considered in the models of heterogeneous firms and, before introducing CSR, it is convenient to analyse its similarity with quality.

Of course CSR and product quality are two different features among consumers' preferences and in the production function of the firms, even if they are interrelated and correlated according to the prevalent definitions of CSR.

The definitions of CSR we find in the literature include several actions with social characteristics that a firm can undertake. McWilliams and Siegel (2005) define CSR as "situations where the firm goes beyond compliance and engages in actions that appear to further some social good, beyond the interests of the firm and that which is required by law" and they recognize that a socially responsible (SR) firm will produce "incorporating social characteristics or features into products". This means that the products of socially responsible firms have a higher qualitative level. In this sense CSR can be considered a component of the quality.

At the same time in Becchetti and Ciciretti (2010) the "product quality" is listed among the main "criteria of social responsibility". In this vision CSR includes product quality among the socially oriented actions of a SR firm.

CSR can also be considered a special kind of quality. The same authors (Becchetti and Ciciretti 2010) talk about "social quality" as the ethical value of a firm.

On the contrary Boehe and Cruz (2010) distinguished CSR by quality and innovation as differentiation criteria. Quality is related to "several product characteristics, such as product performance, durability, reliability, and consistency with specifications", for example. Innovation, or R&D intensity, "includes product and process engineering" and for this reason it can be considered a characteristic of the product as well.

Accepting the definition from McWilliams and Siegel 2005, quality, innovation or CSR are all differentiation criteria, but the three concepts are extremely different each other.

Moreover it is possible to show that there is a positive correlation between quality differentiation and CSR product differentiation and between innovation differentiation and CSR product differentiation.

So we can build our model using CSR as a differentiation criterion. And it is easy to show that the same setting can be applied considering quality or innovation as differentiation criteria instead of CSR.

Only at the end of the paper CSR plays a peculiar role in the model: when we analize the link between CSR and the crisis. In this case quality and innovation can not have the same role as CSR, so the model can not be applied to them. This compelled us to characterize the analysis for CSR only.

4.3 The Model

We work in a scenario of closed economy with heterogeneous firms which show firm level productivity differences. We hypothesize a monopolistic competition market with vertical differentiation in CSR. The heterogeneity in productivity concerns capability to realize different levels of utility at equal cost or the same utility at higher costs. The productivity differences are independent on product differentiation.

4.3.1 Demand

Households have a preference for diversity and therefore derive utility from the consumption of differentiated varieties of products, which substitute imperfectly for each other.

Preferences of the representative consumer among varieties are described by the following constant elasticity of substitution (CES) utility function:

$$U_i = \left[\sum_j \left(s_j^\lambda C_j \right)^{\frac{\theta-1}{\theta}} \right]^{\frac{\theta}{\theta-1}} \tag{4.1}$$

where s_j is the CSR content of variety j measured in utility per physical unit, assumed to be observable to all, with $s_j \geq 1$ and j indexes an individual variety among the set of available varieties, C_j is the quantity consumed measured in physical units, and $\theta > 1$ is the elasticity of substitution between varieties. The parameter $\lambda > 0$ captures the intensity of the consumers' desire for the CSR content of goods.[2] The CSR content of each product j is a demand shifter: higher CSR goods yield higher consumption utility per unit consumed.

The representative household earns profit flows π_i and labor income w_i by supplying her unit labour endowment L in a competitive labour market. We assume that consumers own an equal share of each firm, so that profits of firms will be equally distributed among the consumers.

Maximizing the representative consumer's utility we have the following demand function for a particular variety j:

$$C_h = \frac{p_h^{-\theta} s_h^{\lambda(\theta-1)}}{P} R \tag{4.2}$$

Where R is the aggregate income, p_j is the price of variety j, P is an aggregate quality-adjusted price index, defined as:

$$P = \sum_j \left(p_j / s_j^\lambda \right)^{(1-\theta)} \tag{4.3}$$

---

[2] Following Hallak (2006), λ may be assumed to be positively linked to the consumer's real income. This statement will be inverted in the last paragraph of the paper about the effects of crisis.

4.3.2 Production

The product is differentiated and each variety is produced by a single firm in monopolistic competition. Productivity is heterogeneous, so upon paying a fixed fee F_e required for entry, firms are endowed with a firm-specific productivity parameter (a_j) that is randomly drawn from a continuous probability distribution $G\,(a)$. Firms with low productivity exit the market and the remaining firms maximize their profits by taking the number of firms N as given. Each firm chooses its optimal price, decides whether to enhance its product with CSR and, if so, the level of the ethical standards.

The first case we analyze concerns an economy without CSR, that is, an economy where consumers are not sensitive to SR, so that $s_j = 1$ in (4.1).

Labour is homogeneous and it is the only factor of production; yet, productivity may raise physical output for a given level of labour input. Entry in the differentiated product sector is costly as each firm incurs a production start-up cost F_e of units of labour, equal for all firms. So firms with low productivity (high marginal cost) exit the market. Subsequent production exhibits constant returns to scale, so that, upon entry, the production of physical units is

$$Y_j = a_j l_j \tag{4.4}$$

The corresponding total cost is $TC_j = F_e + w l_j$ and the marginal cost (equal to unit labour requirement) is

$$c_j = \frac{w}{a_j} \tag{4.5}$$

where w is the common wage Profit maximization subject to technological and demand constraints yields the standard result that equilibrium prices are a constant mark-up over marginal cost, with the size of the mark-up depending on the elasticity of substitution between varieties:

$$p_j = \frac{\theta}{\theta - 1} \frac{w}{a_j} \tag{4.6}$$

Profits of the firm are given by the following expression:

$$\pi_0 = p_j Y_j - \frac{w}{a_j Y_j} \tag{4.7}$$

The second case we analyze concerns the possibility for the firm to pursue ethical standards in production. This happens when consumers are sensitive to SR, so $s_j > 1$ in Eq. (4.1). Firms face the new demand curve and base their calculations on it.

Besides the fixed cost F_e, in this case, we add a fixed cost F_s in units of labour of switching to ethical standards and a cost that varies only with respect to the level of SR the firm chooses to undertake. Upon deciding to pursue SR, the production function becomes:

$$Y_j = \frac{a_j l_j}{s_j^\eta} \tag{4.8}$$

and the corresponding marginal cost is

$$c_j = \frac{w}{a_j} s_j^\eta \tag{4.9}$$

with $0 < \eta < 1$ and $\eta < \lambda$. Such a parameter represents the elasticity of marginal cost with respect to the level of SR: we assume that when the firm increases the level of ethical content in the good it produces there is a less than proportional increase in the unitary cost.

The total cost $TC_j = wl_j + F_e + f\left(s_j\right)^\delta + F_s.$[3]

Moreover we impose $0 < (\theta - 1)(\lambda - \eta) < \delta$ (Johnson 2008). This means that fixed costs are always increasing in quality and the elasticity of substitution θ is not so high to create benefits of CSR "overwhelming" the cost of CSR. This condition will assure that the CSR optimal level is positive.

Combining the total cost with the production function we have

$$TC_j = \frac{w}{a_j} s^\eta Y_j + F_e + f\left(s_j\right)^\delta + F_s \tag{4.10}$$

the total costs the firm has to pay.

4.3.3 Optimal CSR Level Choice

Firms choose the level of CSR solving a profit maximization problem.

Through this procedure we are able to show the following proposition

Proposition 1 *If and $\eta < \lambda$ and $0 < (\theta - 1)(\lambda - \eta) < \delta$, heterogeneous firms facing a demand of consumers sensible to CSR and a cost structure given by Eq. (4.9) choose a level of CSR s_j^* given by the following*

$$s_j^* = \left\{ \left(\frac{w}{a_j}\right)^{1-\theta} \frac{(\theta - 1)^\theta (\lambda - \eta)}{\delta f \theta^\theta} \frac{R}{P} \right\}^{\frac{1}{\delta - (\theta - 1)(\lambda - \eta)}} \tag{4.11}$$

Proof The profits of firms are

---

[3] It can be useful alternatively to specify the variable cost for CSR as $f(s - 1)^\delta$. In that case we would be able to describe the model for $s \geq 1$, without distinguish the two cases, as the costs are null when $s = 1$.

$$\pi_j = p_j Y_j - \frac{w}{a_j} s^\eta Y_i - F_e - f s_j^\delta - F_s \tag{4.12}$$

Firms choose the amount of s_j maximizing the above profits.
That value is simply the solution of the following maximization problem

$$\begin{cases} \max \pi_j = p_j Y_j - \frac{w}{a_j} s^\eta Y_i - F_e - f s_j^\delta - F_s \\ \text{s.t. } Y_j = C_j \\ \quad C_j = \frac{p_j^{-\theta} s_j^{\lambda(\theta-1)}}{P} R \\ \quad p_j = \frac{\theta}{\theta-1} \frac{w}{a_j} s_j^\eta \end{cases} \tag{4.13}$$

That solution, given by Eq. (4.11), is positive for $\eta < \lambda$.   □

Proposition 1 *Tells us that CSR increases with productivity a_j, in fact a higher productivity causes a reduction of costs and prices so that firms can produce more and pay for more CSR. CSR increases also with λ, the intensity of ethical features in consumers' demand. As η and δ indicate the incidence of CSR respectively on total variable and sunk costs, it is easy to show how CSR decreases with them. Moreover the amount of CSR increases with the aggregate income. This means that CSR would be a luxury for consumers and it would be reserved to the richest.*

In the last section of the paper this feature will be better discussed, relating it to the debate on CSR performances during an economic crisis. Empirical studies show ambiguous results about the phenomenon of CSR during a recession. For this purpose it is relevant to evaluate consumers' sensitiveness for ethical issues in times of crisis.

4.4 CSR and Financial Constraints

In order to introduce a financial constraint in the model and analyze the effects on the solution, we suppose that firms don't necessarily have enough cash-flow to engage in CSR activities, so considering the possibility they ask for external finance.

Given the cost of external finance γ and the probability that the firm has to ask for it q, referring it to a share β of costs, we have the following total costs:

$$TC_{\gamma j} = \frac{w}{a_j} s^\eta Y_j + F_e + f(s_j)^\delta + F_s + \gamma \beta \left[f s_j^\delta + F_s \right] \tag{4.14}$$

Proposition 2 *Given Eq. (4.7), heterogeneous firms, facing a demand of consumers sensible to CSR, will find optimal to engage in CSR if and only if*

$$\pi_{0j} \geq \frac{s_j^* \phi + \Phi}{s_j^{*(1-\theta)(\eta-\lambda)} - 1}$$

with

$$\phi = (1 + (1 - q)\gamma\beta)f$$

$$\Phi = F_e + (1 + (1 - q)\gamma\beta)F_s$$

and being π_{0j} the amount of profits that the firm can obtain without CSR.

Proof If the firm decides to engage in CSR, it will derive two possible profits: the first one (π_0^s) would be achieved when the firm has not to recur to external finance and the second one ($\pi_{\cdot j}^s$), on the contrary, would be aggravated by the cost of external finance.

In particular we will have

$$\pi_{0j}^s = p_j Y_j - \frac{w}{a_j} s^\eta Y_j - F_e - fs_j^\delta - F_s \tag{4.15}$$

and

$$\pi_{\cdot j}^s = p_j Y_j - \frac{w}{a_j} s^\eta Y_j - F_e - fs_j^\delta - F_s - \gamma\beta\left[fs_j^\delta + F_s\right] \tag{4.16}$$

So total expected profits of the firm are

$$E\left(\pi_j^s \big| s_j\right) = q\pi_{0j}^s + (1-q)\pi_{\cdot j}^s =$$
$$= p_j Y_j - \frac{w}{a_j} s^\eta Y_j - F_e - fs_j^\delta - F_s - (1-q)\gamma\beta\left[fs_j^\delta + F_s\right] \tag{4.17}$$
$$= p_j Y_j - \frac{w}{a_j} s^\eta Y_j - \phi s_j^\delta - \Phi_s$$

Equation (4.17) represents the quantity to maximize in choosing the level of CSR s_j.

The new problem to solve is similar to problem (4.13), given consumers' demand and equilibrium prices:

$$\begin{cases} \max E\left[\pi_j^s \big| s_j\right] = p_j Y_j - \frac{w}{a_j} s^\eta Y_j - \phi s_j^\delta - \Phi_s \\ s.t. \quad Y_j = C_j \\ C_j = \frac{p_j^{\theta} s_j^{\lambda(\theta-1)}}{P} R \\ p_j = \frac{\theta}{\theta-1} \frac{w}{a_j} s_j^\eta \end{cases} \tag{4.18}$$

The solution of the problem is given by the following expression for s_j:

$$s_j^* = \left\{ \left(\frac{w}{a_j}\right)^{(1-\theta)} \frac{(\theta-1)^\theta(\lambda-\eta)}{\delta\theta^\theta(1+(1-q)\gamma\beta)f} \frac{R}{P} \right\}^{\frac{1}{\theta-(\theta-1)(\lambda-\eta)}} \tag{4.19}$$

Equation (4.19) can be substituted in the maximized function in order to compare the resulting profits with profits without CSR π_0.

We have

$$E\left[\pi_j^s \middle| s_j^*\right] = \pi_0 \left(s_j^{*(1-\theta)(\eta-\lambda)} - 1\right) - \phi s_j^{*\delta} - \Phi_s \tag{4.20}$$

From the comparison follows that $E\left[\pi_j^s \middle| s_j^*\right] \geq \pi_0$ if and only if the following inequality holds

$$\pi_0 \geq \frac{\phi s_j^{*\delta} + \Phi_s}{s_j^{*(1-\theta)(\eta-\lambda)} - 1} \tag{4.21}$$

That is the thesis of *Proposition 2*.

Proposition 2 shows that if profits without CSR π_0 are particularly high, then CSR costs are not very relevant for the firm. The firm will find convenient to undertake CSR projects, despite the financial constraint.

It is important to note that the optimal level of CSR with financial constraints (Eq. 4.19) is lower than the one of *Proposition 1*. The reason is that in the first case the firm pays the costs of financing, being forced to reduce the resources addressed to CSR.

So the conclusion is that when financial constraints hold, only high profit firms will be able to engage in CSR.

This result confirms the conclusion described in the previous paragraph for consumers that CSR is a luxury for firms too. In fact CSR increases with consumers' income and with firms' profits when there are financial constraints.

4.5   The Effects of the Crisis

In this section we aim to investigate what are the effects on the optimal level of CSR when the economy faces a global crisis.

In particular we wonder: in times of crisis do firms reduce their engagement in terms of CSR or do they increase it?

On a theoretical point of view two opposite behavior have well-founded justifications.

In the one side it is plausible that a firm facing frequent oversupply problems, liquidity deficiency, credit access difficulties and labor disputes do not have the necessary resources to undertake ethical projects. However it is also admissible that the market shows a higher sensitiveness toward more ethical than economic topics, being compelled to suffer demand decreasing of traditional products because of income reduction. For this reason consumers could consider more important the interest of firms to social problems and hope that institutions in the economy (not only public institutions but also firms and households) could ensure economic and environmental sustainability in the society.

The concourse of both effects should take to a positive or negative net result.

The recent empirical analysis is rather limited in this field and shows ambiguous results (Karaibrahimoglu 2010).

However empirical works about the stock market reaction to the financial crisis show that investors could consider more important CSR features in their evaluations after a failure of a company (the case of Lehman Brothers) with low CSR rating (Becchetti et al. 2010).

For this reason it would possible that a firm in times of crisis will face a drop of income decreasing the demand for its goods, but also a higher sensitiveness to CSR in the demand function.

This effect would be captured by a negative relation between the intensity of the consumers' desire for the CSR content of goods and the aggregate income, which will be negatively influenced in times of crisis:

$$\lambda = \lambda(R), \text{ with } \lambda'(R) < 0 \tag{4.22}$$

This relation is inverted with respect to the one of Hallak (2006) in which preference intensity for quality is positively related to income. Thus in this context we are able to characterize better CSR and differentiate it from quality.

If so, quality can be considered a luxury good, but CSR is not necessarily like that. The optimal level of this last depends positively on aggregate income as we showed at the end of Paragraph 2, but not only. There could be also a negative effect given by the above relation (Eq. 4.22). If it holds the final effect of a reduction of aggregate income on the optimal CSR level is not necessarily negative.

Let assume for example that the form of Eq. (4.22) is

$$\lambda(R) = \frac{\lambda_0}{R} \tag{4.23}$$

The following statement will hold.

Proposition 3 *If $\eta < \lambda(R)$ and $0 < (\theta - 1)(\lambda(R) - \eta) < \delta$, heterogeneous firms facing a cost structure given by Eq. (4.9) and a demand of consumers with sensitiveness to CSR depending on aggregate income according to Eq. (4.23), improve their optimal level of CSR when this last decreases.*

Proof Given the optimal CSR level of *Proposition 1* (Eq. 4.11) we can evaluate its derivative in aggregate income $\frac{\partial s_j^*}{\partial R}$ to find that it is negative[4]:

---

[4] The calculation of Eq. (4.24) is available in Appendix.

$$\frac{\partial s_j^*}{\partial R} < 0 \qquad (4.24)$$

□

This result can be interpreted as follows.

It is quite obvious that economic crisis could discourage firms' engagement in CSR because these last are compelled to cut costs in their budget. As CSR is costly it could be considered as a "luxury" that they can pay for in recession times. We will refer to this last as the first effect of crisis.

A second feature to consider is the decreasing demand during the crisis. That is consumers would not be willing to pay a higher price for CSR products if they have to face a reduction of income. This would bring CSR influence on the demand to drop and so the supply would answer with less CSR too, according to the principle of inverted "bottom up pressure". This effect is captured by the variable s in the demand function.

The attention for social themes and sustainability, on the contrary, could be increased in those recession periods. This is a third possible effect of the crisis. That is consumers would be more sensitive to social responsibility because of the reduction of income and so they would look for CSR projects more than in times of economic growth. This higher sensitiveness would feed the "bottom up pressure" principle and would intensify the producers' answer in terms of social responsibility. The third effect is captured by the function $\lambda(R)$ and its influence of the aggregate demand.

Proposition 3 shows that if $\lambda(R)$ has the structure of Eq. (4.23), then the third effect will prevail on the first and the second.

This means that CSR can help the economy to overcome the crisis.

Nevertheless it is more and more recognized among the scholars the fundamental role of CSR and in general of the civil economy in times of crisis (Becchetti 2009).

Before the more recent global financial crisis the world focused on values at the opposite of the ones supported by the civil economy and this could be the reason of the general lack of trust in the markets.

The result is that consumers could start trusting more social responsible firms than traditional ones and choose them after experiencing the issues of a severe financial crisis.

4.6 Conclusions and Future Developments

The paper develops a model of vertical product differentiation with CSR as a differentiation criterion. The scenario consists of heterogeneous firms under the hypothesis of monopolistic competition, differently from standard literature, in which prevail oligopoly settings. We show how CSR can be influenced in the market by several variables in demand or supply side. In particular we find a positive correlation between income and CSR and between profits and CSR, which take us to the conclusion that CSR can be considered a luxury for consumers and for firms.

The analysis is deepened wondering if it is convenient for firms to focus on CSR even if governments are facing a recession.

In the paper we include some important considerations into the model to analyze that statement, for example considering that in times of crisis consumers, but also institutions, are more sensitive toward SR than in periods of growth.

For this reason we suppose that, because of the reduction of income, the market shows a higher sensitiveness toward ethical topics than in growth periods. So consumers could appreciate the interest of the firms toward social problems and support institutions ensuring economic and environmental sustainability in the society.

The result is that CSR not necessarily decreases during recessions.

These aspects can be deepened considering what happens to CSR when firms face financial constraints in times of crisis. In that case firms will have less financial resources to spend for CSR but they will have to satisfy more SR consumers at the same time.

Moreover in the third section we show that high initial profits firms can more easily undertake CSR than low profits ones when financial constraints hold in the market. This happens because more ethical firms can have very easy access to financial markets if we admit the existence of ethical finance. This last is for definition directed to socially responsible firms and to ethical projects of firms.

So the concept of ethical finance would let us better specify CSR in our model, distinguishing it from quality and innovation.

References

Baldwin, R. & Harrigan, J. (2007). Zeros, quality and space: Trade theory and trade evidence. *NBER Working Papers* 13214.

Becchetti, L. (2009). Oltre la crisi nella società del rischio: il ruolo dell' economia civile. *AICCON—Università di Bologna, Working Paper no.* 62, Marzo.

Becchetti, L., Ceniccola, C., Ciciretti, R. (2010). Stock market reaction to the global financial crisis: the role of corporate governance and product quality ratings in the lehman brothers' event. *Sustainable Investment and Corporate Governance Working Papers 2010/14, Sustainable Investment Research Platform.*

Becchetti, L., Ciciretti, R. (2010). L'etica che ci salverà. *Dossier CSR,* no. 48, Maggio.

Becchetti, L., Federico, G., Solferino N. (2005a). The game of social responsibility: A product differentiation approach. *Working Paper no.* 15, *Cleonp, University of Forlì.*

Becchetti, L., Giallonardo, L., Tessitore, M.E. (2005b). Corporate social responsibility and profit maximizing behaviour. *AICCON—Università di Bologna, Working Paper no.* 21, *Ottobre.*

Becchetti, L., Giallonardo, L., Tessitore, M.E. (2007). On ethical product differentiation with asymmetric distance costs. *Rivista di Politica Economica.*

Becchetti L., Cremonese L., D'Achille E., Meo P., Venturini L. (2006). Le preferenze e la spesa dei consumatori equosolidali: un'analisi empirica sui consumatori italiani. In L. Becchetti, M. Costantini , (Eds.) *Il commercio equo e solidale alla prova dei fatti: dai consumatori del Nord ai produttori del Sud del mondo, Mondatori*.

Becchetti, L., & Rosati, F. (2005). Globalisation and the death of distance in social preferences and inequity aversion: empirical evidence from a pilot study on fair trade consumers. *The World Economy, 30*(5), 807–830.

Boehe, D.M., Cruz, L. B. (2010). Corporate Social Responsibility, Product Differentiation Strategy and Export Performance. *Journal of Business Ethics*.

Cavallaro E., Mulino M. (2009). Technological catching up, competitiveness and growth. *Journal of International trade & EconomicDevelopment*, 505–525.

Friedman, M. (1970). The social responsibility of business is to make profits. New York review, 13 Settembre, in Hoffman W. M., Frederick R. E. (a cura di) *Business Ethics*, Mc-Graw Hill, 1995.

Friedman M. (1970) The social responsibility of business is to make profits. In G.A. Steiner, J.F. Steiner (Eds.) *Issues in Business and society*, New York: Random House.

Gorodnichenko, Y., Schnitzer, M. (2010). Financial constraints and innovation: Why poor countries don't catch up. *NBER Working Papers* 15792.

Grossman, G., & Helpman, E. (1991). *Innovation and growth in the global economy*. Cambridge Massachusetts: MIT Press.

Hallak, J.-C. (2006). Product quality and the direction of trade. *Journal of International Economics, 68*(1), 238–265.

Hopenhayn, H. (1992). Entry, exit, and firm dynamics in long run equilibrium. *Econometrica, 60*, 1127–1150.

Hummels, D., Klenow, P. (2005). The variety and quality of a nation's exports. *American Economic Review,* 95(3): 704–723 (June).

Johnson, R. (2008), *Trade and prices with heterogeneous firms. Mimeo, University of California at Berkeley*.

Karaibrahimoglu, Y. Z. (2010). Corporate social responsibility in times of financial crisis. *African Journal of Business Management, 4*, 382–389.

Kaplan, S. N., & Zingales, L. (2000). Investment-cash flow sensitivities are not valid measures of financing constraints. *The Quarterly Journal of Economics, 115*(2), 707–712.

Kugler M, and Verhoogen E. (2008). The quality-complementarity hypothesis: Theory and evidence from colombia. *NBER Working Paper no.* 14418.

Manasakis, C., Mitrokostas, E., Petrakis, E. (2007) Corporate social responsibility in oligopoly. *Working Paper no.* 707, *University of Crete, Department of Economics*.

McWilliams, A., Siegel, D. S., Wright, P.M. (2005) Corporate social responsibility: strategic implications. *Rensselaer Working Papers in Economics, May* 2005.

Melitz, M. (2003). The impact of trade on intra-industry reallocations and aggregate industry productivity. *Econometrica, 71*(6), 1695–1725.

Michie, J. (1998). Introduction: The internationalisation of the innovation process. *International Journal of the Economics of Business, 5*(3), 261–277.

Sacco, P.L., Viviani, M. (2005). La Responsabilità Sociale d'Impresa. Un percorso a partire dal dibattito italiano", *AICCON—Università di Bologna, Working Paper no.* 11, *Aprile* 2005.

Sacconi, L.(2005). Etica degli Affari. In Sacconi, "*Guida critica alla Responsabilità Sociale e al governo d'impresa", cap.* 17, *Bancaria editrice, Roma,* 2005.

Chapter 5
The Impact of Corporate Social Responsibility on Corporate Governance: The Rise of Standardization of CSR Principles

Mia Mahmudur Rahim

Abstract The synergy between corporate social responsibility (CSR) and corporate governance (CG) has changed the commercial environment. It has developed a complex and multi dimensional organizational phenomenon that could be defined as the extent and the way in which a business corporation can pragmatically respond to its consumer and society. This synergy has joined the political endeavours to make corporations more attuned to public, environmental and social needs. It has standardized CSR principles and created the agencies specialized in broader ethical considerations of business corporations. This chapter deals with these issues. It assesses how the impact of CSR on CG has contributed to the standardization of CSR principles and the rise of agencies specialized in facilitating social responsibility performance of business corporations.

5.1 Introduction

The synergy between corporate social responsibility (CSR) and corporate governance (CG) has changed the global commercial environment. It has developed a complex and multi-dimensional phenomenon in organizations that could be defined as the extent and the way in which a global business enterprise can pragmatically respond to its consumer and society. It has joined the political endeavours to make enterprises more attuned to public, environmental and social needs by pursuing acceptable principles of corporate governance as a vehicle that encourage management to consider broader ethical considerations (McBarnet et al. 2007; Vogel 2006).

M. M. Rahim (✉)
Queensland University of Technology, Queensland, Australia
e-mail: mia.rahim@qut.edu.au

A. Yüksel Mermod and S. O. Idowu (eds.), *Corporate Social Responsibility in the Global Business World*, DOI: 10.1007/978-3-642-37620-7_5,
© Springer-Verlag Berlin Heidelberg 2014

With the development of this synergy, big enterprises, retailers and brands have created mechanisms of corporate governance that seek to engender investor accountability and stakeholder engagement. Such mechanisms include CSR board committees, company units dealing with business ethics, corporate codes of conduct, non-financial reporting practices and stakeholder complaint and dialogue channels, among others.

Business enterprises incorporate CSR practices into their self-regulation as these practices help them to secure their long-term profit, brand image and high-standard managerial efficiencies. Most of the large enterprises have developed their own code of conducts that deals with their and their suppliers strategies for social responsibility performance. The interest of global business enterprises, retailers and brands (as global buyers) to ensure CSR practices within their supply chains is increasing (Forstater et al. 2006). With the rise of sensitive consumerism and competition for getting market shares, their interests to ensure that CSR issues are dealt with by every supplier within their chains has increased too. In a survey of approximately 400 CEOs and top executives participating in the United Nations Global Compact 2, it was found that: "more than 9 out of 10 corporate leaders are doing more than they did five years ago to incorporate environmental, social, and political issues into their firms' core strategies" (Oppenheim et al. 2007).

Focusing on the demand of specialized services for CSR practices and third party accreditation of social responsibility performance, most of the business enterprises have started depending upon the organizations experts on CSR issues and have the credentials for certifying CSR performance of enterprises. Corporate self-regulation, nowadays, is less involved in the process for communicating the CSR performance to the business constituents. They depend upon the standardization organizations for this communication; by acquiring appropriate affiliations from the standardization organizations, business enterprises demonstrate that they are able to implement CSR related compliances. Thus the impact of CSR on CG and the strategic approach of business enterprises to response to this impact have contributed to the development of standardization of CSR practices. This has also contributed to the creation of many organizations whose role is to process and accredit CSR practices for the business enterprises. Business enterprises take assistance from these organizations; they depend on their accreditation system to ensure that their self-regulation and their supplying enterprises are able to implement standardized CSR practices.

Given this backdrop, the aim of this chapter is to provide an assessment of the development of standardization of CSR principles for corporate self regulation. It proceeds as follows. First, it highlights the percept of CSR and its core principles. Second, it describes corporate governance and its synergy with CSR. Third, it discusses the impact of this synergy on business strategies related with social responsibility performance. At this stage it highlights the engagement of corporate self-regulation with CSR practice in business operations. Fourth, it critically explicates the nexus of corporate self-regulation and the rise of standardization of CSR practices; this section also highlights the core function of some standardization organizations. Finally, it concludes that the impact of CSR on CG is a vital factor for the rise of standardization of CSR principles that links CSR values to economic incentives and disincentives and indirectly mandates and monitor self-regulated responsibility of business enterprises.

5.2 CSR and Its Core Principles

The main construction of this chapter does not intensively relate with the philosophies in CSR and CG. It mostly depends upon the effects of CSR demands on the corporate strategies. Hence, this section is not going to provide a thorough discussion on the definition of CSR and CG as this is believed to be a study in itself; and in this chapter distinction is made between different terms of CSR.

5.2.1 Corporate Social Responsibility

Corporate social responsibility (CSR)[2] is an increasingly essential issue for the business enterprises (Moon and Vogel 2008; Vogel 2006; Kakabadse et al. 2005). It is a fluid concept (Hopkins 2004; Van Marrewijk 2003). Its interchangeable and overlapping character is dominant in its definition. To some scholars, this concept resembles the source of competitive advantage; to others, it is "an important response to the increasing demands of key stakeholders such as employees, investors, consumers and environmentalists" (Bagi et al. 2004). Again, the precepts of CSR change with each generation, and its criteria may change according to the society in question (Kakabadse et al. 2005). Given this, this concept can be described using a number of terms: corporate citizenship, the ethical corporation, corporate governance, corporate sustainability, socially responsible investment, corporate accountability and so on, and there is no overall agreement on its definition (Blowfield and Frynas 2005; Services 2006; Matten and Moon 2007). The underlying notions of these terms are inwardly consistent and converge on some common qualities and similar elements. In a broader sense, CSR is about the impact of business on a society or, in other words, the role of business enterprises in the development of the society. In its narrower sense, it is a complex and multi-dimensional organizational phenomenon in which an organization is consciously responsible for its actions and non-actions and the impact of this on its stakeholders.

5.2.2 Core Principles of CSR

Though the definitional construct of CSR has not yet been settled (Bhattacharya and Sen 2004; Carroll 1999; Crowther and Capaldi 2008), it has been recognized as a long-term business strategy. Its different approaches balance business enterprises' economic rights with their social and environmental obligations. CSR relates these approaches with corporate strategies observing four core principles. These principles are vital to incorporating its ethos in any corporate strategy. The principle of the societal approach is that business enterprises should contribute to building better societies, and they should therefore integrate social concerns into their core strategies consider the full extent to their impact on communities (Cacioppe et al. 2008). More particularly, this principle requires business enterprises to uphold labour rights and human rights, and to engage with any other relevant ethical issues (Carroll 1999; Garriga and Melé 2004; Valor 2005; Van Marrewijk 2003). The economic principle emphasizes the efficiency of business enterprises in producing goods or providing services without violating social or environmental values (Elkington 1998; Rogers and Ryan 2001; Juholin 2004). Thirdly, the environmental principle holds that business enterprises should not harm the environment to maximize their profits, and they should play a strong role in repairing any environmental damage caused by their irresponsible use of natural resources (McAdam and Leonard 2003; Matten and Moon 2007). The fourth principle is the stakeholder approach, it holds business enterprises responsible for taking the legitimate interests of their stakeholders into account (Freeman and Velamuri 2008; Jamali 2008). These principles are the drivers of the sources of different CSR practices; they are important elements for initiating any strategies for developing CSR practices.

5.2.3 Business Case of CSR Principles

Business enterprises performance of social responsibilities could be viewed in three major ways. First, business enterprises face trade off between social responsibilities and financial performance. Second, cost for performing social responsibilities is minimal and business enterprises can strategically be benefited from these expenses. Third, cost for performing these responsibilities is significant but could be offset by a reduction in other managerial costs. These views hold that business societies have agreed that they have responsibilities to societies and these responsibilities could be turned as tools for their profit maximization. With this understanding, business societies and scholars considerably shifted their focus and devoted more into the creation of strategies to relate business case with these responsibilities.

Hence, the understanding of social responsibilities of business enterprises mentioned above is not beyond criticism. Friedman vividly differs with the above mentioned views and argues that business enterprises have only one social responsibility which is to maximise profits. In the societies, as he points out, every group has specific function and hence business enterprises' main function is to do business for generating returns for their investors. In other words, he is against the trend that accepts the business enterprises performing social responsibilities other than engaging themselves for generation of more profits for their stockholders.

This trend, according to him, thoroughly undermines the very foundation of the free society. At this point, it is interesting to note that he has not directly denied the positive relationship between the business case and corporate social responsibilities. He, in fact, heavily emphasises on the direct commercial activities of business enterprises (Friedman 2007, p. 133) and convicts that performing social responsibilities ends in decreased profit margin for business. Those arguing in this line, also argue that business enterprises that incur cost for performing social responsibilities put them in economic disadvantages compared to other less socially responsible enterprises, which in turn hampers the effectiveness of market (Henderson 2002; Bradgon and Marlin 1972; Vance 1975).

However, there are strong criticisms of these contentions. The advocates of CSR criticise the arguments of Freedman as they believe that performing social responsibilities has never been non-profit oriented activities for business enterprises. They argue that proper business strategies can keep the explicit cost of social responsibilities (Weiser and Zadek 2000) minimal and can create benefits out of these responsibilities. For example, socially responsible actions in terms of employee morale always raise employees' productivity and face relatively less labour problems. On the other hand, low performance of social responsibilities could raise doubt about the abilities of business enterprises to produce quality products and because of this doubts, customers may not favourable disposed of their products. Paul Samuelson supports the efforts of enterprises to engage in social performances, as he writes, 'a large corporation these days not only may engage in social responsibility, it had damn well better try to do so' (Samuelson 1971, p. 24).

Business enterprises engage in CSR because it leads them to profit (Porter and Linde 1995, p. 3). In other words, business enterprises need to avoid the risk of punishment from the consumers' side. They are always at the risk of getting punishment by the consumers and constituencies if they do unethical business operations. In 1990s, for instance, business enterprises like Nike and Walmart lost a considerable portion of their market share as the consumers of their products marked their labour management discriminatory and unfair (Stengel 2009, p. 28). This has passed a strong message to the business enterprises and pushed them to hold more socially responsible business strategies. Business enterprises, therefore, are more eager to have visible efforts to meet their social responsibilities. In 1992, for instance, Gap developed sourcing guidelines; in 1996 developed its code of conduct and since 2004 has been publishing the information about its suppliers. Timberland now discloses the material and energy usages for each pair of its shoes (Stengel 2009, p. 28). The underlying objectives of these types of corporate strategies is related with their need to relate more with the social activities, so that they could improve their standing with more important constituencies like bankers, investors, government officials, larger scale of customers etc. These constituencies are strong factors in investment decisions and could be the best source of capital. Therefore, performing social responsibilities could improve business enterprises' abilities to maximise their returns. This view has already been endorsed by the European Commission; one of its CSR related Green Paper stated:

[a]s companies themselves face the challenges of a changing environment in the context of globalisation and in particular the Internal Market, they are increasingly aware that corporate social responsibility can be of direct economic value. Although the prime responsibility of a company is generating profits, companies can at the same time contribute to social and environmental objectives, though integrating corporate social responsibility as a strategic investment into their core business strategy, their management instruments and their operations. (…) Where corporate social responsibility is a process by which companies manage their relationship with a variety of stakeholders who can have a real influence on their license to operate, the business case becomes apparent'(European Commission 2001b, p. 5–7).

Freeman contested the profit maximizing approach of business enterprises and argued that these enterprises are also responsible to consider the legitimate interests of their stakeholder who are affected or could be affected by their enterprenual achievement. While extending the stakeholder notion in CSR, he did not ignore companies' business profits and wealth creation initiatives. Rather, he noted that CSR makes a balance between business profit and stakeholder interests as the companies have immense influence on the lives of stakeholders (Post et al. 2002). After Freeman, the stakeholder notion in CSR has extended and got new dimension with the societal notion of CSR. Societal notion in CSR (as the broader view of stakeholder approach) suggests that business enterprises as an integral part of society should perform their responsibility to the society as a whole. The performances of these responsibilities are depended upon convincing financial pay off that these responsibilities can create. To add these two factors— performance of social responsibilities and financial pay off—business enterprises have to evaluate the effects of its decisions on the external social system in a manner that their decision accomplish social benefits along with the traditional economic gains (Davis 1973, p. 313). This is because, the denial of social responsibility may cause financial loss to a business enterprise. For instance, low levels of social responsibility performance may increase a business enterprise's financial risk as potential investors may relate their managerial inefficiencies with their less socially responsible performance. Again, along with the investors, other constituencies may be less interested in less socially responsible business enterprises since these important business stakeholders may anticipate an increase of management cost owing to lack of their (business enterprises) socially responsible performance as most of these types of enterprises are usually subject to fine, law suits, boycott etc.

The type of correlation between business case and social responsibilities of business enterprises in different real world situations is utmost important. To relate this type, over the past few decades several theoretical frameworks on the relationship between social or environmental and financial performance have emerged and approached in different ways to prove the sound economic rationale for corporate social responsibility. Particularly, from the beginning of 1990s, business case through CSR has got more attention from the corporate sector (Holliday 2002; Holliday et al. 2002; Schmidheiny 1992; World Business Council for Sustainable Development 1999), its stakeholders, the academic community (Bonifant et al. 1995; Dechant and Altman 1994; Hart 1995; Porter 1987; Porter and Van der Linde 1995; Shrivastava 1996; Zadek 1999) and consultancies (Elkington 1992).

Almost all of these factors and actors refer to the relationship between social and financial performance (Carroll 1999; Wood 1991). This has been reflected in many indexes of business competitiveness. These indexes frequently include the principles of CSR though not directly but as 'soft' issues. For example, IMD embodied 'value-in-society', attitudes towards gender and other aspects of discrimination as criterion for measuring competitiveness of business enterprises. Responsible behaviour is another major criterion as this criterion is an important source for creating positive impact on workforce motivation, innovation and brand recognition in business. The crux of including such CSR oriented criterions is that these criterions score positively towards economic competitiveness and do not constrain productivity.

Griffin and Mahon (1997) studied the correlation of business case and CSR practices. After an evaluation of 62 studies spaning 25 years of research, they found that 33 studies demonstrated a positive correlation between social and financial performances of business enterprises. This finding was re-evaluated and the number of researches that showed positive correlation has increased. These researches are from the real world and followed by established methodologies. For example, a meta-analysis conducted by Frooman concludes that good corporate social performance leads to good corporate financial performance (Frooman 1997). To establish this conclusion, six chemical industries were reviewed and concluded with 'hope for those of us who believe in some positive relationship between corporate financial and social performance' (Griffin and Mahon 1997, p. 27). *Fortune* reputation ratings over an 11 year period also find evidences of positive relationship between social and financial indicators (Preston and O'Bannons 1997, p. 428; Waddock and Graves 1997a; Pava and Krausz 1996; Preston and O'Bannon 1997, McGuire et al. 1988; Kraft and Hage 1990; Stanwick and Stanwick 1998). While designing a CSR framework in Europe, the European Commission identifies that the basis of this framework should be 'a structural and partnership based approach between business and their various stakeholders' (European Commission 2002, p. 22) and 'a concerted effort by all those concerned towards shared objectives' (European Commission 2002, p. 10). The objective for laying such basis is to foster the linkage amongst the CSR principles, economic progress through increased competitiveness of business enterprises, public policy and societal progress.

All sorts of economic competitiveness require dynamic and enterprising business community. This is nurtured and enabled in large part by markets that encourage and reward innovation, minimise costs and allow business to focus on the challenges of securing viability and success. Performing corporate responsibilities incur costs for the enterprises as well as ensures sustainable profit range and brand reputation. Therefore, CSR practices and business case management of business enterprises must progress hand in hand. A growing number of enterprises are following this perspective. They are more closely integrating CSR principles into key aspects of their governance and management strategies. Their abilities to handle the main intangibles are more important than before; their success also depends upon their clear understanding of societies changing demands. In the recent past, for example, British Petroleum commits to 'go beyond' petroleum and the Ford Motor Corporation set its vision to become a provider of mobility (Swift and Zadek 2002).

5.3 Synergies Between CSR and CG

With the increase of the business case of CSR practices, the evolving interplay between CG and CSR has also increased (Mitchell 2007). The synergies between CSR and CG could be traced back into their core features. Both these business regulation mechanisms hold economic and legal features. They could be altered through the socio-economic process within which the product market competition is the most powerful force (Shleifer and Vishny 1997a, b). They are complementary and are closely linked with this force. Their objectives are not concurrent; they could act as tools for reaching each other's goals, though their setups as corporate frameworks are different. CSR operates in a free-form, whereas CG issues operate within well-defined and accepted structures (Mitchell 2007).

CG is an umbrella term (Shleifer and Vishny 1997a, b; Turnbull 1997; Hart 1995a, b; Becht et al. 2003; Daily et al. 2003; Bebchuk et al. 2009). In its narrower sense, it describes the formal system of accountability of corporate directors to the owners of companies. In its broader sense, the concept includes the entire network of formal and informal relations involving the corporate sector and the consequences of this relation for the society in general. These two senses are not concurrent, but rather are complementary. CG has been described as the ways in which suppliers of finance to corporations assure themselves of getting a return on their investment (Shleifer and Vishny 1997a, b). However, it could also implicate "the whole set of legal, cultural, and institutional arrangements that determine what publicly traded corporations can do, who controls them, how that control is exercised, and how the risks and returns from the activities they undertake are allocated" (Blair 1995). Taking both the senses together, corporate governance is no longer merely about maximizing stock-value; rather, it concerns the relationships among the many players involved (the stakeholders) and the goals for which the corporation is governed.

CSR and CG are strongly related with the market competition, and hence, they act as strong drivers to develop the required framework by which a business enterprise can demonstrate its responsibility to society through its performance. In this framework, CG largely contributes by reconciling the tension between corporate governance's engagement with shareholder and stakeholder interest; it has become attuned to constituency concerns in corporate governance. CSR assist CG to direct corporate management to have suitable self-regulated 'strategy to make the ultimate goals of corporations more achievable as well as more transparent, demonstrate responsibility towards communities and the environment, and take the interests of groups such as employees and consumers into account when making long-term business decisions' (Gill 2008). Jamali (2008) has nicely summarised this relationship in a chart; below is the modified version of that chart.

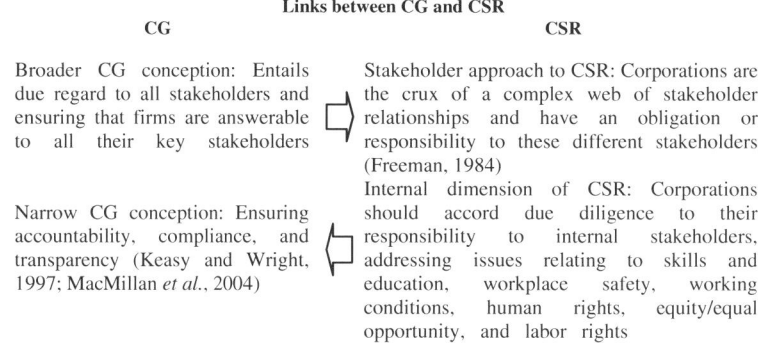

Links between CG and CSR

CG	CSR
Broader CG conception: Entails due regard to all stakeholders and ensuring that firms are answerable to all their key stakeholders	Stakeholder approach to CSR: Corporations are the crux of a complex web of stakeholder relationships and have an obligation or responsibility to these different stakeholders (Freeman, 1984)
Narrow CG conception: Ensuring accountability, compliance, and transparency (Keasy and Wright, 1997; MacMillan *et al.*, 2004)	Internal dimension of CSR: Corporations should accord due diligence to their responsibility to internal stakeholders, addressing issues relating to skills and education, workplace safety, working conditions, human rights, equity/equal opportunity, and labor rights

Source: Jamali *et al.*, (2008, p 446)

This synergy has gradually extended the narrower meaning of corporate governance. It adds the agency focus to corporate ethics and accountability (Mitchell and Diamond 2004), and it relies on the 'business judgment' of corporate governance to ensure this accountability (Rahim and Alam 2013). It finds 'corporate self-regulation' as its dominant expression in the field of corporate conduct. On the ground, by adding issues such as human rights, workers' rights and environmental protection with 'self-regulation', CG gained the opportunity to develop stakeholder engagement programs that could increase their competitiveness and to launch a marketing campaign that could emphasize their humanistic, democratic values as 'corporate citizens'. Business enterprises are coming out from the philanthropic approach to fulfill their social responsibilities and are taking such initiatives that could link their sustainable business case with the local social and economic development. Their initiatives seeking to develop mutually beneficial business with the poor, whether as consumer or producer, are progressing (Bendell et al. 2011). Unilever's Project Shakti, EDF's Access to Energy Programme and the Grameen Danone Limited Food Partnership are some prominent examples of such corporate initiatives (Prahalad 2004; Bendell et al. 2011).

Corporate self-regulation has gradually absorbed the ethos of this synergy. For instance, many business enterprises have appropriate measures to internalize the costs externalized to the environment due to their business operations (Vogel 2006). These initiatives are not driven mostly by laws; rather, they are driven by the corporate conscience to reduce costs as well as to contribute to environmental development. Wal-Mart has recently taken initiatives to 'green' its stores to reduce its energy and labour use. Between 2003 and 2008, Gap Inc. cut its greenhouse-gas emissions by 20 % and eliminated child labour from its suppliers (Sustainability Initiatives 2013). 3M's 3P program—'Pollution Prevention Pay'—helped the enterprise discover a huge savings that it had previously overlooked. John Deere's recent foray into renewable energy is another prime example. Other than selling tractors, it provides financial support and consultation to help farmers to harvest using wind energy. This may seem an odd fit, but the venture has become a source of value innovation as well as a way to meet social responsibilities: it is helping farmers to survive and is creating a new revenue stream for the company.

5.3.1 Impact of This Synergy on Business Strategies

Advocates of the synergies between CSR and CG believe that the corporate governance that holds the principles of CSR offer opportunities to business enterprises for greater market access, cost savings, productivity and innovation, as well as broader social benefits such as education and community development. The impact of this synergy has mostly been reflected through the development of 'self-regulation' regime in business environment as it has been an increasingly important part of business regulation (Rahim and Wisuttisak 2013). At the individual business enterprise level, the notion of corporate self-regulation usually enshrines either through its own code of conduct or through its incorporation of any multi-stake holder initiative and guideline prepared by any other social or commercial organization.

The codes are the main self-regulatory instruments for business enterprises; business enterprises address the social, environmental and human rights and economic externalities through their codes. Hence, these codes are largely focused on those sectors where brand reputation and export orientation are vital. Codes related with the labour issues usually incline with the footwear, garment, sporting goods, toy and retail sectors while those related to environmental aspects are likely to be noticed in oil, chemical, forestry and mining (Utting 2005). Sources suggest that the world's larger multinational business enterprises/buyers have taken the lead in adopting such codes which can hold the ethos of this synergy and can be an alternative means of regulation (Levis 2006; Hu Xiaoyong 2006).

Principles (as similar as code of conduct) of Fish4Ever may be a good mention at this point. Fish4Ever, a famous brand of sea food products with the target of fulfilling its 90 per cent turnover by the organic and/or sustainable products, has a clear policy that restricts it from selling any endangered fish declared by IUCN and other reputed NGOs (Fish4Ever 2013). According to these principles, it does not relate with any supplier that does not respect employee/workers rights or does not ensure fair pay and treatment to employees or workers (Fish4Ever 2013). For instance, to get Skipjack tuna, they consciously look for suppliers who have ability to relate sustainability and ethical practices with the product quality and process efficiency (Fish4Ever 2013).

Adidas Group, the owner of Adidas and Reebok brands, has more than 1,120 independent factories (on 31 December 2009) in 68 countries, has responded to this synergy through its standards, guidelines and principles to deal their social, ethical, and environmental issues (Adidas 2013). For instance, 'Workplace Standard' settled by Adidas, mainly set forth the Group's position on a number of challenging labour issues workers can face. These issues include the working hours, fair wages, freedom of association, child labour etc. (Adidas 2013). This Group prepares suitable guidelines and training programmes for its suppliers to minimize their business operations' impact on the environment. This guideline emphasizes its suppliers to get into its environmental management systems. This system is mandatory for its suppliers. By imposing this system in supplier's enterprises, Adidas is trying to tackle pollution and to ensure that its products are environmentally safe.

Gap Inc., one of the most popular brands as well as the biggest retailer of garments in the world, identified six factors in the garment suppliers that influence their supplier selection criterion, those factors are: (a) inefficient process and operation practices; (b) poor supervisory and management skills; (c) lack of full assessment of capacity and capability; (d) insufficient modern technology and equipment; (e) lack of regards for the right of workers; (f) insufficient under-standing of labour laws and standards. At this point it could assume that this buyer is less interested in those suppliers who are heavily related with these factors. This has been reflected when it clearly mentioned that 'poor factory working conditions are simply unacceptable' (Gap 2013).

The impact of the synergy of CSR and CG on the corporate self-regulation particularly of the big business enterprises helps the incorporation of CSR prin-ciples at the core of the business strategies. As mentioned above, business enterprises' response to this incorporation by developing their own codes. How-ever, such incorporation has not successfully met the CSR demands to them. The codes of conducts of different business enterprises are prepared to meet the very specific circumstances of individual enterprises and those are usually meant to serve the business interest of their respective business enterprises. Amongst the critiques with respect to codes of conduct, the following two sets are vital. The first set of critiques is concerned about legal pluralism and the free market ideology underlying self-regulation (Blackett 2000). Based on the percepts of legal plu-ralism and free market ideology, as it is argued, the economic players in the private sphere use this form of self-regulation to fulfill their own interests. This form creates the tendency that alleges private ordering systems pursue their own policies rather than public policy goals (Plzer and Scheuer 2003). The second critique contends that, the codes have practically failed to actually improve corporate behavior worldwide, thus are hypocritical in their purpose (Locke and Romis 2006). Indeed, many agree that the codes, even after being supported by a strong monitoring system, might not generate ground-level change, unless companioned by befitting changes in business culture and decision-making. In these circum-stances, business enterprises are depending on the third parties which have expertise and credentials in CSR strategies. Indeed, this move has contributed to the creation of many organizations engaged in checking the corporate self-regu-lation performance in CSR issues. Business enterprises relate with the activities of these organizations and especially the large business enterprises who are also the global buyer depend on them to ensure that their suppliers are fulfilling or are able to fulfill CSR practices following a set of international standards commonly known as multi-stake holder codes. These codes help the diverged CSR practices to be bundled into some 'generic management systems standards' (Gawel 2006). The impact of CSR on CG is an important issue as this impact drives business enterprises to create commercial value of the multi-stakeholder codes generated by the standardization organizations.

5.4 The Rise of the Standardization of CSR Principles

Standardization means the process to reach a standard. Standard could be termed as a limited set of solutions to actual and potential matching problems and balancing the need of the party or parties for whom they are meant. Standard could also be taken as solutions that intends and expects repeated or continuous use for a certain period. Standard Australia defines standard as a 'published document which set out specifications and procedures designed to ensure that a material, product, method or service is fit for its purpose and consistently performs the way it was intended to' (Standard Australia 2002). Therefore, in narrow sense, standard is a set of criteria that is meant to check the requirement and expectations of organizations. In broader sense, particularly while dealing with CSR issues, standard refers to CSR norms, rules, agreement, guidelines and codes directed for benefits for the party or parties involved. Vries termed standardization functions as a 'lubricant for modern industrial society' as these initiatives can facilitate contact, co-operation and trade throughout the world (Brunsson and Jacobsson 2000; Vries 1999).

Amongst the sources of CSR standardization, multi-stake holder initiative or codes are prominent. These codes are the product of concerted initiatives amongst the corporate stakeholders, such as, companies, trade unions and other worker's association, governmental agencies, NGOs and academics (Vries 1999). ISO Standard Series, SA 8000, AA1000, ETI Base Code are some prominent multi-stakeholder initiatives developed by the standardization organizations.

ISO Standard Series is considered to be the best product of International Organization for Standardization. Amongst this series of standards, the best known standards are the ISO9000 and ISO14000. These are practiced by more than a million organizations in 175 countries (ISO 2013). **ISO9000** family deals with **'quality management' to make enterprises capable of providing consistent and conforming products.** It provides guidelines to enterprises to (a) fulfill customers' quality requirements; (b) meet regulatory requirements; and to (c) attain long-lasting improvement of its performance to reach these objectives (ISO 2013). **ISO14000** family addresses **'environmental management' (ISO 2013).** This standardization initiative is basically related with environmental aspects of business enterprises. ISO14001 particularly deals with companies' environmental policies; helps to assess the legal and voluntary obligations of companies for the environmental aspects; and prescribes management to take appropriate internal audits to publish reports on companies' environmental performance.

SA8000 is initiated by the Council on Economic Priorities Accreditation Agency. It is based on the international agreement on human and labour rights. It is a universal standard aimed at safeguarding the fundamental rights of workers and employees in enterprises. According to this standardization initiative, business enterprises need to develop their management systems in such a way that they include policies on and procedures for ensuring human and labour rights. It prescribes a 'social management system' to facilitate continuous improvement in fulfilling labour rights related compliance of enterprises. Global buyers/retailers depend on this agency's accreditation to be sure that their supplier enterprises meet the basic standard for a safe and healthy working environment, including safe drinking water, clean rest room facilities, applicable safety equipment and necessary training. They require this accreditation also to be ensured that supplier enterprises address non discrimination, freedom of association and compensation provisions with at least some discretionary income.

AA1000 is developed by the Institute of Social and Ethical Accountability. It is a set of principles for processing social and ethical accountability of business enterprises. It is comprised of two main parts. The first part institutes the main principles for Social and Ethical Accounting, Auditing and Reporting and the second part mentions the principles for standardizing the process that addresses the core areas of planning, accounting, auditing, reporting and stakeholder engagement (Belal 2008). AA1000 provides guidelines to prepare process to ensure accountability in business plans and strategies to include stakeholders in the core of corporate governance. It's principles for process standards states that it engage stakeholders to determine 'the scope of the current process in terms of the stakeholders, geographical locations, operating units and issues to be included, and identifies how it plans to account for any excluded stakeholders, operations, locations or issues in future cycles' (AccountAbility 1999).

ETI Base Code is developed through a 'partnership between retail and consumer goods companies, NGOs, trade unions and the UK government' (Bagi et al. 2004). According to this Code, transnational corporations are liable to maintain 'ethics' in business and corporate responsibility, and for promotion of workers' rights and human rights in general. The companies that are certified by this initiative have to ensure that they have programs in their workplace to ensure that (a) workers choose their employment freely; (b) workers enjoy freedom of association and can bargain collectively; (c) working environment are safe and hygienic; (d) child labour is banned; (e) wages are adequate to meet the minimum living standard and are paid regularly; (f) management does not bind workers to take excessive work load; (g) no discrimination is practised; (h) regular employment is provided; and (i) harsh or inhumane treatment is prohibited (Mustow 2006). With a combined turnover of over £107b, ETI company members include supermarkets, department stores and stone sourcing companies, fashion retailers, as well as major suppliers to retailers of food and drink, flowers, shoes, clothing, home wear etc. Amongst these members some well known buyers/retailers are Mackays, Madison Hosiery, Marks & Spencer, Marshalls, Monsoon Accessorize, Mothercare, New

Look Retailers, Next Retail, Ruia Group, Rohan Designs, River Island, Sains-bury's, Supremia, Gap Inc etc.

These initiatives are not only standardizing CSR but also developing their management and thereby CSR though voluntary, took the form of quasi-binding responsibility (Utting 2005). They have developed monitoring and verification mechanisms and their institutional application in the global supply chains helps to promote ethical business in broader context. These initiatives, in other way, help to evaluate business enterprises' CSR performances; they have gained necessary acknowledgement from the corporate and civil societies, and supports from international and governmental organizations. The organizations that are creating and nourishing these initiatives have gradually created norms for standardizing the sets of CSR practices for business enterprises. The increasing volume of sub-scription of multi-stake holder codes by business enterprises and the civil society organizations affiliation to these codes have further developed the standardization that can help enterprises to demonstrate their efforts for fulfilling their social, economic, environmental and ethical responsibilities.

The development of CSR standardization has also developed many organiza-tions specialized in diverse initiatives to facilitate entrepreneurs to do business in a more socially acceptable way. These organizations have detailed different social, ethical and environmental standards to evaluate corporate performances in soci-eties as well as to relate business enterprises intensively with their social responsibilities. Table 5.1 below shows the market influence of some CSR stan-dards. This chart is the modified version of Table III prepared by Bendell et al. (2011).

Like these initiatives, there are many other initiatives that have contributed to the development of a number of codes on particular CSR issues and therewith the monitoring and verification procedures. Workplace Code of Conduct and Principle for Monitoring of Fair Labour Association (FLA) has developed internal and independent monitoring procedures to promote labour standards in the workplace in the USA and worldwide apparel industries. Similarly, Clean Cloths Campaign has adopted a code of conduct with a view to improve working environment in the global suppliers' factory premises including garment and sportswear industries (Hu Xiaoyong 2006). The Global Reporting Initiative has provided a framework for reporting on the basis of triple bottom lines which refers to companies' social, economic and environmental impacts. In addition, under the auspices of the United Nations Global Compact, learning and networking processes have been developed for the promotion of CSR practices on the basis of ten principles declared by the Compact.

The synergy of CSR and CG has helped developing the standardization regime. Most of the global business enterprises have acknowledged this development. They exclusively consider some of these initiatives to measure their CSR per-formance. Some of them weed out suppliers from their chains upon the result of performance test based on the evaluation by the CSR standardization organiza-tions. By using multi-stakeholder codes of these organizations, they sort out

Table 5.1 The market influence of selected CSR standards

Standard	Market impact
Multi-stakeholder initiative standards	
4C Association (2004)	Covers 30 % of global coffee production
Fair Labor Association (1998)	Covers 75 % of the branded athletic footwear industry
Fair Wear Foundation (FWF) (1999)	FWF affiliates source from a total of 1,153 factories, with an estimated total of 300,000 workers (growth rate of 60 % in the last three years)
Forest Stewardship Council (1993)	Covers 11 % of global forests used for productive activities
ISO 14001 (1996)	223,149 organizations in 159 countries are certified to ISO 14000
Marine Stewardship Council (1997)	Covers 6 % of global landed fish
SA8000 Standard (1997)	Over 1.4 million workers are employed in over 2,400 SA8000 certified
	facilities in 65 countries, across 66 industrial sectors
Roundtable on Sustainable Palm Oil (2004)	Covers 8 % of global palm oil production
UTZ Certified (1999)	Covers 5 % of global coffee production
Industry association codes	
Business Social Compliance Initiative (BSCI) (2002)	11,200 suppliers audited according to the BSCI code of conduct and 4,000 suppliers trained in nine different countries
International Council of Toy Industries (ICTI) (2004)	75 % of the global toy business is committed to only source from suppliers certified by ICTI in the future
Pharmaceutical supply chain initiative (2007)	Member companies represent at least 45 % of the pharmaceutical industry
Individual company codes	
Nike supplier code of conduct	31 % of the global market for branded athletic footwear; through its supplier code of conduct Nike influences the conditions of more than 800,000 employees in 700 factories in 45 countries
Adidas supplier code of conduct	22 % of the global market for branded athletic footwear; through its supplier code of conduct Adidas influences the conditions of more than 775,000 employees in 1,200 factories in 65 countries

Source UNCTAD (2011)

strategic suppliers to (a) reduce transaction cost; (b) increase profitability; (c) reduce costs as a result of a reduced need to switch suppliers; and to (d) increase competitiveness in the marketplace through increased relationship with the consumers (Goyder and Desmond 2000; Mason 1996).

5.5 Conclusion

The synergy of CSR and CG has transitioned the basis of corporate responsibility from why corporations must be socially responsible to how they can become socially responsible. In the rise of sensitive consumerism, as well as increasing competition for market share, this synergy has made business enterprises more attuned to public, environmental and social needs. Global enterprises/buyers have integrated the ethos of this synergy into their core policy objectives. They tend to ensure that CSR practices are implemented within their supply chains; a demonstrated commitment to CSR helps buyers to secure their long-term profits, brand images and managerial efficiencies. To be competitive they need to be developed in such a way that they can successfully comply with the CSR standards denoted by standardization organizations (Compact 2013); they offset the cost of the gradual incorporation of standardized CSR practices with the benefits of getting extended share of the market. In retrospect to this transition, CSR notions have become more formalized.

References

Adidas Group, Supply Chain http://www.adidasgroup.com/en/sustainability/suppliers_and_workers/default.aspx 25 July 2013.

Alexander, G., & Bucholtz, R. (1978). Corporate social responsibility and stock market performance. *Academy of Management Journal, 21*, 479–486.

Bagi, A., Krabalo, M., & Narani, L. (2004). *An overview of corporate social responsibility in Croatia*. Zagreb: AED.

Bank, B. (2007). *Bnagladesh bank annual report 2006–2007*. Dhaka: Bangladesh Bank.

Bebchuk, L., Cohen, A., & Ferrell, A. (2009). What matters in corporate governance? *Review of Financial Studies, 22*(2), 783.

Becht, M., Bolton, P., & Röell, A. (2003). Corporate governance and control. *Handbook of the Economics of Finance, 1*, 1–109.

Belal, A. R. (2008). Corporate social responsibility reporting in developing countries: The case of Bangladesh. Ashgate Publishing Company.

Bendell, J., Miller, A., & Wortmann, K. (2011). Public policies for scaling corporate responsibility standards: Expending collaborative governance for sustainable development. *Sustainability Accounting, Management and Policy Journal, 2*(2), 263–293.

Bhattacharya, C., & Sen, S. (2004). Doing better at doing good: when, why, and how consumers respond to corporate social initiatives. California Management Review, 47(1), 9–24

Blackett, A. (2000). Global governance, legal pluralism and the decentered state: A labor law critique of codes of corporate conduct. *Indiana Journal of Global Legal Studies, 8*, 401.

Blowfield, M., & Frynas, J. G. (2005). Editorial Setting new agendas: critical perspectives on Corporate Social Responsibility in the developing world. International Affairs, 81(3), 499-513.

Blair, M. (1995). *Ownership and control: Rethinking corporate governance for the twenty-first century*. Washington: Brookings Institution Press.

Bonifant, B., Arnold, M., & Long, F. (1995). Gaining competitive advantage through environmental investments. *Long Range Planning, 28*(6), 128.

Bowman, E., & Haire, M. (1975). A strategic posture towards CSR. *California Management Review, 18*(2), 49–58.

Bradgon, J. H., & Marlin, J. (1972). Is pollution profitable? *Risk Management, 19*(4), 9–18.

Brunsson, N., & Jacobsson, B. (2000). A world of standards.

Cacioppe, R., Forster, N., & Fox, M. (2008). A Survey of Managers' Perceptions of Corporate Ethics and Social Responsibility and Actions that may Affect Companies' Success. Journal of Business Ethics, 82(3), 681–700

Carroll, A. (1999). Corporate social responsibility. *Business and Society, 38*(3), 268.

Commission, E. (2001). *Promoting a European Framework for Corporate Social Responsibility: Green Paper*. Luxembourg: Office for Official Publications of the European Communities.

Commission, E. (2002). Corporate social responsibility: A business contribution to sustainable development. retrieved 7 December,2010, from http://eur-lex.europa.eu/smartapi/cgi/sga_doc?smartapi!celexplus!prod!DocNumber&lg=en&type_doc=COMfinal&an_doc=2002&nu_doc=347.

Compact, G. The ten principles,http://www.unglobalcompact.org/AboutTheGC/TheTen Principles/index.html, 1 June 2013.

Council of Bars and Law Societies in Europe, (2003a). *Corporate Social Responsibility and the Role of the Legal Profession: A Guide for European Lawyers.*

Council of Bars and Law Societies in Europe, (2003b). *Corporate social responsibility and the role of the legal profession: A guide for European lawyers and advising on corporate social responsibility issues.*

Crowther, D., & Capaldi, N. (2008). *The research companion to corporate social responsibility*. Aldershot: Ashgate.

Daily, C., Dalton, D., & Cannella, A, Jr. (2003). Corporate governance: Decades of dialogue and data. *The Academy of Management Review, 28*(3), 371–382.

Davis, K. (1973). The case for and against business assumption of social responsibilities. *Academy of Management Journal, 16*(2), 312–322.

Dechant, K., Altman, B., Downing, R., Keeney, T., Mahoney, M., Swaine, A., et al. (1994). Environmental leadership: from compliance to competitive advantage [and Executive Commentary]. *The Academy of Management Executive (1993–2005), 8*(3), 7–27.

Eisenberg, M. (1982). Modernization of corporate law: An Essay for Bill Cary. *The University of Miami Law Review, 37*, 187.

Elkington, J. (1992). Towards the sustainable corporation: Win-win-win business strategies for sustainable development. *California Management Review, 36*(2), 90–100.

Elkington, J. (1998). Partnerships from cannibals with forks: The triple bottom line of 21st century business. *Environmental Quality Management, 8*(1), 37–51.

Fish 4 Ever, Fish 4 Ever Ethical Policy, http://www.fish4ever.co.uk/static/sustainability.php, 1 June 2013.

Forstater, M., MacGillivray, A., & Raynard, P. (2006). Responsible Trade and Market Access: Opportunities or Obstacles for SMEs in Developing Countries? Vienna: UNIDO.

Freeman, R., & Velamuri, S. (2008). A new approach to CSR: company stakeholder responsibility.

Friedman, M. (2007). The social responsibility of business is to increase its profits. *Corporate Ethics and Corporate Governance*, 173–178.

Frooman, J. (1997). Socially irresponsible and illegal behavior and shareholder wealth. *Business and Society, 36*(3), 221.

GAP, Social Responsibility, http://www.gapinc.com/content/csr/html.html, 1 June 2013.

Garriga, E., & Melé, D. (2004). Corporate social responsibility theories: Mapping the territory. *Journal of Business Ethics, 53*(1), 51–71.

Gill, A. (2008). Corporate governance as social responsibility: A research agenda. *Berkeley Journal of International Law, 26*(452), 462.

Goyder, M., & Desmond, P. (2000). Is Ethical Sourcing Simply a Question of Good-Supply Chain Management? Visions of Ethical Sourcing (Financial Times Prentice Hall, London).

Griffin, J. J., & Mahon, J. F. (1997). The corporate social performance and corporate financial performance debate. *Business and Society, 36*(1), 5.

Gunningham, N., Grabosky, P., & Sinclair, D. (1998). *Smart regulation: Designing environmental policy*. USA: Oxford University Press.

Gawel, A. (2006). Corporate social responsibility: standards and objectives driving corporate initiatives. Pollution Probe.

Hart, O. (1995a). Corporate governance: Some theory and implications. *The Economic Journal, 105*(430), 678–689.

Hart, S. (1995b). A natural-resource-based view of the firm. *Academy of Management Review, 20*(4), 986–1014.

Henderson, D. (2002). *Misguided virtues: False notions of corporate social responsibility*. London: Institute of Economic Affairs.

Holliday, C., Schmidheiny, S., & Watts, P. (2002). *Walking the talk: The business case for sustainable development*. San Francisco: Berrett-Koehler Publishers.

Holliday Jr, C. O., Schmidheiny, S., & Watts, P. (2002). Walking the talk: The business case for sustainable development. Berrett-Koehler Pub.

Hopkins, M. Corporate Social Responsibility: An Issues Paper (May 2004). Available at SSRN:http://ssrn.com/abstract=908181 or http://dx.doi.org/10.2139/ssrn.908181

Hu Xiaoyong, Corporate Codes of Conduct and Labour Related Corporate Social Responsibility: Analyzing the Self Regulatory Mechanisms of Multinational Enterprises and Their Impacts to Developing Countries (2006) The Japan Institute for Labour Policy and Training,http://www.jil.go.jp/profile/documents/Hu.pdf, 23 July 2010.

ISO, Standards, http://www.iso.org/iso/home/standards.htm, 1 June 2013.

Jamali, D. (2008). A stakeholder approach to corporate social responsibility: A fresh perspective into theory and practice. *Journal of Business Ethics, 82*(1), 213–231.

Juholin, E. (2004). For business or the good of all? A Finnish approach to corporate social responsibility. *Corporate Governance, 4*(3), 20–31.

Post, J. E., Lawrence, A. T., & Weber, J. (2002), *Business and society: Corporate strategy, public policy, and ethics with powerweb*. New York: Mcgraw-Hill College.

Just good Business. (2008). *The Economist*, 17 January 2008.

Kakabadse, N. K., Rozuel, C., & Lee-Davies, L. (2005). Corporate social responsibility and stakeholder approach: A conceptual review. *International Journal of Business Governance and Ethics, 1*(4), 277–302.

Kraft, K. L., & Hage, J. (1990). Strategy, social responsibility and implementation. Journal of Business Ethics, 9(1), 11-19.

Kemp, V. (1986). *To Whose profit? Building a sustainable business case*. Surrey: WWF-UK.

Levis, J. (2006). Adoption of corporate social responsibility codes by multinational companies. Journal of Asian Economics, 17(1), 50-55.

Lobel, O. (2004). Setting the agenda for new governance research. *Minnesota Law Review, 89*, 498.

Locke, R., & Romis, M. (2006). Beyond corporate codes of conduct: Work organization and labor standards in two Mexican garment factories. Corporate Social Responsibility Initiative.

Lobel, O. (2005) Interlocking regulatory and industrial relations: The governance of workplace safety.

Margolis, J., & Walsh, J. (2003). Misery loves companies: Rethinking social initiatives by business. *Administrative Science Quarterly, 48*(2), 268–305.

Marshall, A. (1920). *Principles of economics: An introductory volume* (8th ed.). London: Macmillan.

Mason, T. (1996). Getting your suppliers on the team. *Logistics Focus, 4*, 10–12.

Matten, D., & Moon, J. (2007). Pan-European approach. A conceptual framework for understanding CSR. *Corporate Ethics and Corporate Governance*, 179–199.

Mazurkiewicz, P. (2006). CSR implementation guide non-legislative options for the Polish government: WB development communication division and WB ECCU7 Office, The World Bank.

McAdam, R., & Leonard, D. (2003). Corporate social responsibility in a total quality management context: opportunities for sustainable growth. *Corporate Governance, 3*(4), 36–45.

McBarnet, D., Voiculescu, A., & Campbell, T. (2007). *The new corporate accountability: Corporate social responsibility and the law.* Cambridge: Cambridge University Press.

McGuire, J., Sundgren, A., & Schneeweis, T. (1988). Corporate social responsibility and firm financial performance. *Academy of Management Journal*, 854–872.

McWilliams, A., & Siegel, D. (2000). Corporate social responsibility and financial performance: Correlation or misspecification? *Strategic Management Journal, 21*(5), 603–609.

Mikdashi, T., & Leal, W. (2005). Experiences on corporate social responsibility (CSR) implementation in Lebanon: A causal recursive system. *International Journal of Environment and Sustainable Development, 4*(2), 181–192.

Mitchell, L. (2007) The board as a path toward corporate social responsibility.

Mitchell, L. E. (2007b). The Board as a path toward corporate social responsibility. In D. McBarnet, A. Voiculescu, & T. Campbell (Eds.), *The new corporate accountability.* Cambridge: Cambridge University Press.

Mitchell, L., & Diamond, M. (2004). *Corporations, a contemporary approach.* Durham: Carolina Academic Press.

Morgan, B. (2003). The economization of politics: Meta-regulation as a form of nonjudicial legality. *Social and Legal Studies, 12*(4).

Moon, J., & Vogel, D. (2008). Corporate social responsibility, government and civil society.The Oxford handbook of corporate social responsibility, 303-326.

Mustow, S. E. (2006). Procurement of ethical construction products. Proceedings of the ICE Engineering Sustainability, 159(1), 11-21.

Oppenheim, J. M., Bielak, D. and Bonini, S. M. (2007). CEOs on strategy and social issues. The McKinsey Quarterly, 4, 1-8.

Orlitzky, M., Schmidt, F., & Rynes, S. (2003). Corporate social and financial performance: A meta-analysis. *Studies, 24*(3), 403–441.

Palzer, C., & Scheuer, A. (2003). Self-regulation, Co-regulation. *Public-regulation Promote or Protect, 165,* 168.

Parker, C. (2002). *The open corporation: effective self-regulation and democracy.* Cambridge: Cambridge University Press.

Parker, C. (2007). Meta-regulation: legal accountability for corporate social responsibility? In D. McBarnet, A. Voiculescu & T. Campbell (Eds.), *The New Corporate Accountability: Corporate Social Responsibility and the Law.* Cambridge: Cambridge University Press.

Pava, M. L., & Krausz, J. (1996). The association between corporate social-responsibility and financial performance: The paradox of social cost. Journal of Business Ethics, 15(3), 321-357.

Peteraf, M. (1993). The cornerstones of competitive advantage: A resource-based view. *Strategic Management Journal, 14*(3), 179–191.

Porter, M., & Linde, C. (1999). Green and competitive: Ending the stalemate. Journal of Business Administration and Policy Analysis.

Porter, M. E. (1987). From competitive advantage to corporate strategy (Vol. 59). Cambridge, MA: Harvard Business Review.

Porter, M., & Van der Linde, C. (1995). Toward a new conception of the environment-competitiveness relationship. *The Journal of Economic Perspectives, 9*(4), 97–118.

Post, J., Preston, L., & Sachs, S. (2002). Managing the extended enterprise. *California Management Review, 45*(1), 6–28.

Prahalad, C. K. (2004). The blinders of dominant logic. Long Range Planning, 37(2), 171- 179.

Preston, L., & O'Bannon, D. (1997). The corporate social-financial performance relationship. *Business and Society, 36*(4), 419.

Rahim, M. M., & Alam, S. (2013). Convergence of Corporate Social Responsibility and Corporate Governance in Weak Economies: The case of Bangladesh. Journal of Business Ethics, 1-14.

Rahim, M. M., & Wisuttisak, P. (2013). Corporate Social Responsibility–Oriented Compliances and SMEs Access to Global Market: Evidence from Bangladesh. *Journal of Asia-Pacific Business, 14*(1), 58-83.

Rogers, M., & Ryan, R. (2001). The triple bottom line for sustainable community development. *Local Environment, 6*(3), 279–289.

Roman, R. M., Hayibor, S., & Agle, B. R. (1999). The relationship between social and financial performance. *Business and Society, 38*(1), 109.

Samuelson, P. A. (1971). Love that corporation. Mountain Bell Magazine.

Schmidheiny, S. (1992). Changing Course: Executive Summary: a Global Business Perspective on Development and the Environment. MIT press.

Services, Parliamentary Joint Committee on Corporations and Financial Services. (2006). *Corporate responsibility : managing risk and creating value*. Commonwealth of Australia.

Shleifer, A., & Vishny, R. (1997a). A survey of corporate governance. *Journal of Finance, 52*(2), 737–783.

Shleifer, A., & Vishny, R. W. (1997b). A survey of corporate governance. *Journal of Finance, 52*(2), 737–783.

Shrivastava, P. (1996). *Greening business: Profiting the corporation and the environment*. OH: Thomson Executive Press Cincinnati.

Smith, A. (1759). *The Theory of Moral sentiments*.

Standards Australia, Standards and Standardisation, Focus Press, Sydney, 2002.

Stanwick, P. A., & Stanwick, S. D. (1998). The relationship between corporate social performance, and organizational size, financial performance, and environmental performance: An empirical examination. Journal of business ethics, 17(2), 195-204.

Stengel, R. (2009). The responsibility revolution. Time, September, 21, 24-27.

Strategy, C. (2002). The Business case for sustainable development: Making a difference towards the Earth summit 2002 and beyond. *Corporate Environmental Strategy, 9*(3), 226–235.

Sustainability Initiatives, 'Retail'. Available at http://sustainabilityinitiatives.wmwikis.net/Retail#Gap 5 June 2013

Swift, T., Zadek, S., & Institute of Social and Ethical Accountability with the Copenhagen Centre. (2002). *Corporate responsibility and the competitive advantage of nations*: The Copenhagen Centre.

Thévenet, M. (2003). Viewpoint: Global responsibility and individual exemplarity. *Corporate Governance, 3*(3), 114–125.

Tung, C. (2006). The legal implications of CSR: Changing landscape of liability, from http://www.csr-asia.com/CGconference2006/ChrisTung.pdf.

Turnbull, S. (1997). Corporate governance: its scope, concerns and theories. *Corporate Governance, 5*(4), 180–205.

UNCTAD, Promoting standards for responsible investment in value chains. A report to the high-level development working group, Paris, September 2011

Utting, P. (2005). Rethinking business regulation. From Self-Regulation to Social Control, UNRISD.

Valor, C. (2005). Corporate social responsibility and corporate citizenship: Towards corporate accountability. *Business and Society Review, 110*(2), 191–212.

Van Marrewijk, M. (2003). Concepts and definitions of CSR and corporate sustainability: Between agency and communion. *Journal of Business Ethics, 44*(2), 95–105.

Vance, S. (1975). Are socially responsible firms good investment risk? *Management Review, 64*, 18–24.

Vogel, D. (2006). The market for virtue: The potential and limits of corporate social responsibility. Brookings Inst Press.

Vries, H. J. D. (1999). Standards for the nation: Analysis of national standardization organizations. Droit: Universite Rotterdam: 1999.

Waddock, S., & Graves, S. (1997). The corporate social performance-financial performance link. *Strategic Management Journal, 18*(4), 303–319.

Weiser, J., & Zadek, S. (2000). *Conversations with disbelievers: Persuading companies to address social challenges*. Ford Foundation.

Windsor, D. (2006). Corporate social responsibility: Three key approaches. *Journal of Management Studies, 43*(1), 93–114.

When, W., & Respond, H. C. (2004). Doing better at doing good. California management review, 47(1), 10.

Wood, D. (1991). Corporate social performance revisited. *Academy of Management Review, 16*(4), 691–718.

World Business Council for Sustainable Development. (1999). Corporate social responsibility: Meeting changing expectations. World Business Council for Sustainable Development.

Zadek, S. (1999). Stalking sustainability. *Greener Management International*, 21–31.

Chapter 6
The Corporate Declaration Versus Corporate Practice: The Financial Crisis Perspective

Maria Aluchna

Abstract The commencement of the global financial crisis started with the credit crunch on the American sub-prime mortgage market and was followed by the sovereign debt of majority of developed economies which raised a number of questions on its reasons and causes. The scope of the systemic problems as well as the depth of the economic slowdown did post crucial doubts on the regulatory and governance standards on financial markets. This paper proposes an analysis of structural and governance failures which led to the outbreak and development of the credit crunch related to unethical and irresponsible behavior on the part of executives as well as poor corporate governance in listed companies and financial institutions. Pointing at the ethical crisis, it confronts the corporate declaration outlined in the code of conduct/ethics and corporate governance guidelines against the corporate practice. Using the example of investment banks such as Bear Stearns, Lehman Brothers and Goldman Sachs as well as listed companies as AIG and General Motors, the paper traces the most problematic areas of ethics and corporate governance in modern organizations.

6.1 Introduction

The outbreak of the financial crisis which started with the credit crunch on the American sub-prime mortgage market and followed by the sovereign debt of majority of developed economies have exerted significant impact on the economic performance of both countries as well as companies worldwide. The outbreak and

M. Aluchna (✉)
Warsaw School of Economics, Warsaw, Poland
e-mail: maria.aluchna@sgh.waw.pl

A. Yüksel Mermod and S. O. Idowu (eds.), *Corporate Social Responsibility in the Global Business World*, DOI: 10.1007/978-3-642-37620-7_6,
© Springer-Verlag Berlin Heidelberg 2014

the course of the crisis raise questions on its reasons and causes. The scope of the systemic problems as well as the depth of the economic slowdown post crucial doubts on the regulatory and governance standards on financial markets. The prime causes of the crisis may seem odd as the review of corporate governance and public policy literature provides wide range of studies and lists the fundamental recommendations for sound operation and good performance of both companies and countries. These recommendations refer to the corporate bylaws and regulations, board structure, its composition and work, the role of independent directors, the efficient structuring of incentive executive compensation/remuneration in order to motivate top managers to increase the shareholder value, the information policy and investor relations, the corporate relations with the media, stakeholders and other market participants. However, the widely recognized and well researched governance best practice, the emphasis put on the role of efficient monitoring and control over stock market and listed companies as well as the corporate governance ranking tracing positive examples and corporate role models did not prevent major control collapses and failures.

This paper proposes an analysis of structural and governance failures which led to the outbreak and development of the credit crunch related to unethical and irresponsible behavior of executives as well as poor corporate governance in public listed companies and financial institutions. Pointing at the ethical crisis, it confronts the corporate declaration outlined in the code of conduct/ethics and corporate governance guidelines against the corporate practice. Using the example of investment banks such as Bear Stearns, Lehman Brothers and Goldman Sachs as well as listed companies as AIG and General Motors, the paper traces the most problematic areas of ethics and corporate governance in modern organizations. The lack of integrity and strong values, the dominant public respect based on the level of consumption and wealth as well as the prime priority for generating short term profits proved to be the key drivers for inefficiencies in corporate governance. The phantom declaration of ethical standpoint and the lack of real compliance with codes of best practice led to trust crisis on the market and resulted in deterioration of economic performance.

The paper is organized as follows. The first section outlines the outbreak, the course it took and the main results of the financial crisis related to credit crunch on the American sub-prime mortgage market and followed by the sovereign debt of majority of developed economies. The second section using the examples of selected companies and investment banks provides the analysis of the corporate declaration versus corporate practice based on the codes of conduct or code of ethics, respectively and corporate governance best practice, where applicable. The discussion of the corporate declaration versus corporate practice with the reference selected corporate governance criteria is presented in section three which identifies the most significant sources of control inefficiencies and ethical failures of analyzed companies. The final remarks and summary of conducted analysis are delivered in the section on conclusion.

6.2 The Crisis

The long term policy of low interest rates, the easy access to cheap credits, the belief in constant increase of the real estate value and the numerous subprime mortgages sold on the American market faced surge in foreclosures and resulted in severe financial problems and dramatic downturn on the stock market (Posner 2010). The liquidity constrains and the evaporating trust amongst listed companies and financial institutions indicated significant systemic problems and led to credit crunch affecting the global market and resulting in economic recession. The financial crisis officially started with the collapse of Lehman Brothers in September 2008 proved to be of global impact due to the internationalization and integration of financial system (Posner 2010, 40–79). More precisely, the engagement in sophisticated financial instruments of many institutions operating worldwide threatened the stability of global financial system as instruments of different levels of financial risks were grouped into one package and overrated by rating agencies to boost sales (Kansas 2009; Clarke and Chanlat 2009; Posner 2010). The implementation of advanced and complicated financial instruments known as collaterized debt obligations, credit default swaps or mortgage backed securities was driven by the shareholder pressure upon investment banks to quest for higher profitability and better financial indicators (McGee 2010). The outbreak and the course of the financial crisis is attributed to the investment banks' and hedge funds' aggressive high leverage strategy which adopted 30 to 1 investment rate (i.e. borrowing \$30 for every \$1 invested). Although such policy proves to be efficient for profit maximization in the times of prosperity, it causes severe collapse under the condition of economic problems affecting majority of market participants (Kansas 2009; Clarke and Chanlat 2009). Many of these institutions worldwide were widely exposed to toxic subprime mortgages what caused a chain reaction of banks failures and companies collapses. Such a significant impact of the credit crunch is heavily rooted in the increasing phenomenon called as financialization of the global economy, in which financial sector and financial services constitute large proportion of the gross domestic product (Posner 2010).

The causes of the financial sector inefficiencies revealed to be of dramatic power both for companies and financial institutions as well as countries. In sum, the outbreak and the course of the crisis led to:

• The downturn on the stock market—over the peak crisis period of 2008 and 2009 Dow Jones Industrial Average (DJIA) dropped from its record high of 14,164.53 on October 9, 2007 to 7,278.38 on March 20, 2009 (DJIA history). The S&P 500 index lost ca. 45 % over the same period. The DJIA lost 4.4 % (over 500 points) on September 15, 2008 only, when Lehman Brothers admitted it lost liquidity and announced filling for bankruptcy. It was followed by the consequent DJIA drop by 7 % (777.7 points), S&P500 and NASDAQ plummet by ca. 9 % over September 2008 as a result of Representative Council rejecting TARP and it constituted the largest indexes decrease within the last 21 years. The downward trend in 2008 was also visible on other stock markets and accounted from 33 % drop for FTSE, 45 % for DAX and CAC to 62 % for Shanghai (Clarke and Chanlat 2009),

- Severe losses of international banks ranging from over $66 billion for Citigroup, over $44 billion for USB, over $16 billion for RBS, over $1 billion for Commerzbank (banks selected randomly from table 1 in Clarke and Chanlat 2009),
- The value loss of assets managed by pension funds estimated at about $2.3 billion,
- The surge of LIBOR interest rate to 10 base points in August 2007 (Taylor 2009),
- The drop of confidence on the financial market amongst financial institutions and other market participants what affected the credit policy and led to the credit crunch indicated by the plummet in credit activity,
- The economic slowdown or economic recession—the fall of US GDP was estimated at 4 % in 2008–2009, the pace not seen since the 1950s. As noted by Pitman and Ivry (2009) US domestic demand remaining "in decline for five straight quarters, [was] still three months shy of the 1974–75 record, but the pace—down 2.6 % per quarter vs. 1.9 % in the earlier period—is a record-breaker already". Bloomberg report of 2009 stated that $14.5 trillion of value of global companies has been erased since the crisis began (Pitman and Ivry 2009),
- The loss of jobs—estimated at 1.53 million in the US alone (Kansas 2009; Isidore 2008),
- The increase of sovereign expenditures for bailout programs—estimated at over $9 trillion in the case of American economy (Kansas 2009; Pitman and Ivry 2009),
- Global consequences of economic recession indicated by the drop of GDP for developed economies by 2.2 % in 2009 and total collapse of banking system in Iceland.

The national policies targeted at bailouts programs using taxpayers money attempted to rescue financial institutions and listed companies known as too big to fail in order to prevent the whole system from collapse (Sorkin 2010). The national policies delivered quick relief and the short term solution to economic problems. The scale and scope of bailout programs estimated worldwide at nearly $11 trillion in 2008 alone (Clarke and Chanlat 2009) translated themselves into sovereign debt crisis characterized by the increase of bond yields, surge in the fiscal deficits and the public debt. The current sovereign debt crisis demands the necessity for significant austerity programs (cut in public spending and tax increases) to assure for balancing of fiscal budgets and providing countries with liquidity.

6.3 The Corporate Declaration Versus Corporate Practice

6.3.1 Methodology

The paper is based on the analysis of case studies referring to the main corporate documents which provide framework for the ethical dimension of their behavior and corporate governance practice. More precisely, for the purpose of the paper the following documents were analyzed:

- The code of ethics or the codes of conduct,
- Corporate governance best practice documents.

The documents were analyzed in the case of companies which revealed severe ethical and governance failures during the crisis such as Lehman Brothers, Bear Stearns, Goldman Sachs, AIG and General Motors. The main goal of this study is to confront the corporate declaration versus corporate practice with the reference to the fundamental guidelines provided by corporate governance best practice. The widely recognized guidelines include high ethical and moral standards, the responsibility for corporate operation in order to assure for long term sustainable value, the accountability to shareholders and stakeholders. More precisely, corporate governance guidelines cover the following aspects (Monks and Minow 2004):

- Efficient board work adopting separation of CEO and Chairman, providing sufficient number of independent directors and specialized board committees (audit, remuneration, nomination etc.),
- Incentive executive compensation,
- Sound information policy, corporate disclosure and investor relations,
- Active participation of shareholders during shareholder meeting (voice execution).

6.3.2 Findings

6.3.2.1 The Corporate Declaration

The code of ethics/code of conduct which are formulated in majority of large companies prove to be of fundamental importance for corporate operations. Code of ethics referred also to code of conduct or code of business conduct and ethics declare the major philosophical principles and values in organization and function as policy documents defining responsibilities of organizations to their stakeholders (Stevens 2009). The code may play an essential role for company management in strategy formulations, motivation and communication systems and corporate culture. More importantly, the strong ethical values which provide for integrity and accountability are the integral components of sound corporate governance and effective leadership. Thus, the code of ethics while implemented and communicated effectively may contribute to company's strengths and its competitive advantages. The review of code of ethics/conduct documents of analyzed companies indicates that these documents emphasize the importance of values such as trust, responsibility and integrity and praise the fundamental roles of strong customer relations and accountability to shareholders and stakeholders. Lehman Brothers in its five page 2004 code of ethics stated that "(..), integrity and ethical behavior are all the more important because of the trust our clients must place in us". The code addressed the basic topics found in most corporate codes such as conflict of interest, retaliation, stealing, use of proprietary information, non-retaliation, and compliance with laws and fairness and emphasized the importance of trust and strong client relations built over the years (Stevens 2009). More importantly, the high ethical standards were required from all employees of the bank as the code was saying that "ethical business practices entail a clear understanding of right and wrong, and a motivation on the part of our directors and employees to act at all times in a manner of which they can be proud". The 2003 code of business conduct and ethics of Bear Stearns was intended to establish standards that the bank deemed necessary to deter wrongdoing and to promote compliance with governmental laws, rules and regulations and honest and ethical conduct divided into eight sections: accountability for adherence to the code, compliance with applicable laws, rules and regulations, conflicts of interest, corporate opportunities, fair dealing, financial reporting and disclosure, protection and proper use of company assets and confidentiality. The code emphasized the personal accountability of employees and senior executives "for ensuring that their conduct adheres to the letter and the spirit of this Code". Additionally, employees and senior executives were expected to promote ethical conduct and compliance with the laws, rules and regulations that govern the activities of the firm having the affirmative obligation to report any known or suspected violation of the code values. The Goldman Sachs 2005 code of business conduct covered similar aspects addressing the importance of the compliance and reporting, personal conflict of interest, public disclosure, compliance with laws, rules and regulations, corporate opportunities and confidentiality saying that "integrity and honesty are at the heart of our business. We expect our people to maintain high ethical standards in everything they do, both in their work of the firm and in their personal lives". The code of General Motors known as Winning with Integrity (only 2011 version is available) offers according to the introductory sentence the values and guidelines of employee conduct and in five sections covered personal integrity, integrity in the workplace, integrity in the marketplace, integrity in society and communities as well as integrity toward the environment. The code addresses global scope of GM operations, emphasized the deep commitment and outlines policies and obligations that guide the business conduct. Complying with the legal obligations and policies described in the GM guidelines is seen as the imperative of company's operations. According to the code General Motors is "committed to maintaining a culture that promotes the prevention, detection and resolution of misconduct. Each employee has an obligation to report potential misconduct. Examples of misconduct may include fraud, theft, workplace violence, discrimination, harassment, misuse of company resources, conflicts of interest, information breaches, improper accounting controls or purchasing arrangements, and other unethical behaviors". The AIG code of conduct (only the 2010 version is available) presents the core values and principles which reflect on the talents and expertise in order to distinguish AIG on the market. The code is perceived as an integral component of the value proposition brought to customers, employees and all of company's communities. According to the code "AIG expects every employee to collaborate with colleagues throughout the organization, manage risks, comply with all applicable regulations and optimize operational efficiencies". The AIG code consists of six principles covering people (Develop diverse talent. Reward excellence), customer focus (Anticipate their priorities. Exceed their expectations), performance (Be accountable. Manage risks. Deliver AIG's strength), integrity (Work honestly. Enhance AIG's reputation), respect (Value all colleagues. Collaborate with one another) and entrepreneurship (Seize opportunities. Innovate for and with customers).

In sum, the analysis of the key elements of codes of ethics/business conduct (as applicable) in the analyzed companies indicates that the most crucial aspects for corporate operation referring to ethics, responsibility and accountability are covered. It is however important to mention that different studies revealed several systemic or operational shortcomings related to language adopted or communication strategy in place.[1]

Review of the corporate governance guidelines of the analyzed companies reveals declared formal compliance with majority of best practice recommendations addressing the elements crucial from the perspective of efficient monitoring and control. The corporate governance guidelines refer to the board composition and functioning, board director selection, nomination and succession planning, board committee charters, CEO evaluation and board self report, chairman and CEO leadership, executive compensation. The precise breakdown of the corporate governance guidelines of analyzed companies is presented in Table 6.1.

As shown in Table 6.1 corporate governance guidelines covered most important elements addressing key challenges of board work, executive compensation and its contacts with management. Although the documents differed in length and outline (from basic list of key elements for AIG to fancy presentation for Goldman Sachs) they stressed the needs for accountability, commitment and involvement of directors, board evaluation performance and attempt to tie corporate governance guidelines to code of ethics and business conduct.

---

[1] A paragraph on p. 5 about full and fair disclosure is comprised of only three sentences, but the first uses 32 words, the second, 69 words and the third, 56 words (Stevens 2009).

Table 6.1 Areas covered in corporate governance guidelines of analyzed companies

Company	Areas covered in corporate governance guidelines
Lehman Brothers (Based on annual report 2007)	Documents on the website (corporate governance guidelines, code of ethics, charters of audit committee, compensation and benefits committee, nominating and corporate governance committee)
	Board of directors (composition, committees, meetings/sessions, proportion of independent directors, evaluation and report, continuous education, materials from senior management)
	Communicating with the board of directors (information on how to contact the non-management directors, and how to contact the audit committee regarding complaints about accounting, internal accounting controls or auditing matters)
	Certificate of incorporation and by-laws
	Board of directors and committees (composition, voting regulations, directors removal, vacancies in the board, the size of the board)
	CEO and CFO certifications
Bear Stearns	No document available since the company was taken over by JP Morgan. The Annual Report 2006 delivers information on business operation in different market segments and board composition. No data on corporate governance principles is provided
	JP Morgan documents cover widely recognized set corporate governance guidelines.
Goldman Sachs (as of 2011)	Board of directors (independence and oversight, experience & qualifications, engagement and depth of access)
	Director selection and committee structure (accountability, board committees)
	Board oversight (role of the presiding director)
	CEO evaluation
	Succession planning
	Compensation
	Risk management

(continued)

Table 6.1 (continued)

Company	Areas covered in corporate governance guidelines
General motors (as of 2011)	Board mission and responsibilities
	Selection and composition of the board (designation, membership and selection criteria, majority voting in election, director orientation and continuing education)
	Board functioning (selection of the chairman, role of lead director, size, mix of management and independent directors, definition of independence, former CEO board membership, limits on outside board memberships, meeting attendance, retirement age and term limits, board compensation, loans to directors and executives, stock ownership by non-employee directors, assessing board performance, ethics and conflicts of interest, confidentiality)
	Board relationship to senior management (regular attendance of non-directors at board meetings, board access to senior management)
	Meeting procedures (selection of agenda, materials distributed in advance, board presentations)
	Committee matters (committees and their performance evaluation, assignment and rotation of committee members, frequency and length of meetings, agenda)
	Leadership development (formal evaluation of the CEO, succession planning, management development)
AIG (as of 2011)	Roles of board and management
	Board composition (size, skills required, proportion of independent directors)
	The chairman of the board (selection and duties of the chairman)
	Selection of directors (nomination and orientation and continuing education)
	Election, term and retirement of the directors (election and term, voting for directors, director retirement, former CEOs, change in status, board vacancies)
	Board meetings
	The committees of the board (number and types, composition)
	Board responsibilities (business strategy, management succession, evaluating and approving compensation for executives, reviewing and approving significant transactions)
	Expectations of directors (commitment and attendance, participation in meetings, loyalty and ethics, other directorships, contact with management, board interaction with institutional investors and the press, confidentiality)
	Communications with the board of directors
	Evaluating board and committee performance
	Charitable giving
	Political contributions

Source Own compilation based on the materials of analyzed companies

6.4 The Corporate Practice

As presented above all of the analyzed companies formulated code of ethics/
business conducts as well as well corporate governance guidelines. Majority
studies on the reasons of the financial crisis indicate the essential role of aggressive
market policy and shareholder expectations of quarterly results as well as the
pressure for short term profits. However, researchers and practitioners point also at
corporate governance inefficiencies and moral failures as issues contributing to the
financial crisis. The two of the studied companies – Lehman Brothers and Bear
Stearns lost their liquidity due to the extensive involvement in subprime mortgages
financial instruments (Posner 2010, 61–69). Bear Stearns was rescued in a take-
over transaction by JP Morgan for $50 billion. Lehman Brothers collapsed after
158 years of history as result of the drop of its share price to less than $2 after
announcing a $2.8 billion loss in the third quarter of 2008 and declared bankruptcy
on September 15, 2008 what is perceived as the date of the outbreak of credit
crunch (McDonald 2009). The three remaining companies—Goldman Sachs, AIG
and GM—found themselves in severe liquidity problems and were covered by the
government (taxpayers) sponsored Trouble Assets Relief Program (TARP) (Kelly
2009). Table 6.2 presents major corporate governance inefficiencies and ethical
failures of analyzed companies.

Table 6.2 Corporate governance inefficiencies and ethical failures of analyzed companies

Company	Key problems referring to ethics and corporate governance
Lehman Brothers	Poor risk management, extensive involvement in credit derivates based on subprime mortgages
	Insufficient board work, lack of derivatives experts on board
	Excessive executive compensation not tied to corporate performance
	Executives lacking responsibility for the company and its shareholders, self over confidence
	Fraud and misrepresentation
Bear Stearns	Poor risk management, extensive involvement in credit derivates based on subprime mortgages
	Insufficient board work, lack of derivatives experts on board
	Executives lacking responsibility for the company and its shareholders, self over confidence
Goldman Sachs	Excessive executive compensation not tied to corporate performance
	Limited discosure
	Controversies on the board composition
	Unethical practices of consulting services for Greek government as well as ABACUS fund
General Motors	Poor risk management
	Ineffective and irresponsible board
AIG	Poor risk management, extensive involvement in subprime mortgages insurance
	Ineffective and irresponsible board

Source Own compilation based on the materials of analyzed companies

As studies attribute the outbreak of the financial crisis to the corporate governance inefficiencies, the major criticism of control practice in Bear Stearns refers mostly to the poor risk management and the insider dominated board. The poor risk management refers to the excessive involvement in credit derivatives based on subprime mortgage (White Paper 2008). The analysis of the Bear Stearns board reveals that four of the 13 directors were insiders and performed this function for over two decades—James Cayne and Alan Greenberg (both since 1985), Alan Schwartz and Warren Spector (both since 1987). As study shows most of the nine outside directors have been on the board for more than a decade including: Glickman (1985), Harrington and Nickell (both since 1993), Tese (1994), Novelly and Salerno (both since 2002). Only three directors—Williams and Bienen (since 2004) and Goldstein (since 2007) have been on the board for less than five years (Brown 2008). Thus, most of the directors have been together for more than a decade which affected their independence and objectivity as "friendships that arise out of board longevity" led to severe 'structural bias' (Brown 2008; Kelly 2009). Other corporate governance problem referred to the director removal procedure— as put on the corporate website "non management directors are required to submit a letter of resignation to the nominating committee in the event of any significant change in their primary job responsibilities. The nominating committee shall review the director's continuation on the board in light of all circumstances and recommend to the board whether the board should accept such proposed resignation or request that the director continue to serve on the board". Such regulation was interpreted as the possibility of the board to "change a director's duties, force a resignation, and effectively remove them immediately" (Brown 2008). Additional corporate governance shortcoming was rooted in the executive compensation, both excessive in size and inefficient in structure. In 2006 only James Cayne, the CEO and Chairman, received compensation of $33 million, of which $17 million was a cash bonus and a year later he was awarded $38 million while the bank went almost bankrupt and was taken over by JP Morgan. Alan Schwartz, who was then the president, received around $35 million, of which $16 million was a cash bonus. Moreover, executives took home additional pays generated from investment opportunities and limited partnership around the bank (e.g. A. Schwartz earned almost $3 million) (Brown 2008).

The main corporate governance inefficiencies indicated in the case of Lehman Brothers refer to the poor board work heavily rooted in its inadequate composition. As noted by Larcker and Tayan (2010) Lehman Brothers board of directors revealed good practice from a structural standpoint as it had 10 directors, of average age of 68 years old (versus 61 years at the average large corporations). The board complied with the independence requirements (8 directors met the independence standards of the New York Stock Exchange) and revealed sufficient diversity of professional background, including a mix of current and former executives and decent outside board affiliations. The director compensation was based on a mix of pay including a portion of equity (such as restricted stock units and options). However, the board revealed severe shortcomings in terms of composition as none of directors had expertise in financial services or current business experience. Moreover, there were no current CEOs of major public corporations on the board as the former CEOs were into retirement for 12 years on average (Larcker and Tayan 2010). Such a board might have problems in understanding the increasing complexity of financial markets and risk management. The presence of directors with experience in nonprofit organization as well as the membership of a theatrical producer (Roger Berlind) and a former actress who was on the board for 18 years (Dina Merrill) proved not to be very useful in the demanding market conditions. The risk committee which included the mentioned directors with no expertise in risk management and finance (R. Berlindand, D. Merrill) met twice a year and five of its directors were in their 70s and 80s (Gross 2010). The poor performance and inadequate skills of directors resulted in the perception of the board as being a joke' (Gross 2010). The leadership style of the confident CEO was perceived as an additional corporate governance challenge. In 2007 Richard Fuld, the Lehman Brothers CEO, received $34 million ($450 milllion over 10 years) while the bank recorded losses of $10 million with the share price falling down by 95 %. The Lehman collapse was attributed to the fraud and misrepresentation of the factual leverage. The size of assets engaged in credit derivatives based on subprime mortgages was reported with the adoption of the so called repo 105 transaction. The repo 105 transactions which doubled between 2006 and 2008 were conducted at the quarter end at the amounts of $50 billion and were targeted at lowering its leverage (lowering the assets to equity from 13.9 times to 12.1 times) solely for the reporting purposes (Bris-May 2010).

As compared to Bear Stearns and Lehman Brothers the case of Goldman Sachs reveals mostly major shortcomings referring to the limited corporate disclosure, controversial practice of executive compensation and unethical attitude towards clients, shareholders and other market participants (Doria et al. 2010). The analysis of the Goldman Sachs strategy shows that its largest problems affecting the company's reputation as well as performance relate to unethical behavior. The bank not only got involved in hiding Greek debt significantly contributing to the sovereign debt crisis in the euro zone. Goldman Sachs helped the Greek government to borrow billions of dollars in 2001 in order to lower their public debt temporarily solely for reporting purposes in order to meet Maastricht criteria and join the euro zone. Additionally, Goldman Sachs has been recently penalized with the largest in stock market history fine of $500 million for misrepresentation of its CDO related products offered in 2008 (Stempel and Eder 2010; SEC 2010). More precisely, Goldman offered its clients financial products based on subprime mortgages targeted for decline of the market performance (ABACUS scheme) causing losses to clients and business partners (IKB Deutsche Industriebank AG). In effect, the bank was making money on products which were of high risk of default by selling these instruments to its clients without providing full information and disclosing the company own investment strategies. Selling these products the bank itself was interested in the default of the subprime mortgage market and it bet against them. The questioned corporate governance practices at Goldman Sachs also refer to the bank's remuneration policy (Posner 2010, 147–150). In 2007 when Goldman earned a net profit of $11.4 billion, its top 5 executives split

$322 million, while the CEO Lloyd Blankfein took home $70.3 million. In 2008 with the net profit of $2.3 billion, executives resigned from their bonuses, while the CEO pay accounted for $1.1million (owing however still shares worth $570 million). In 2009 the bank earned the net profit of $13.2 billion, while paying out bonuses for its employees of $16.2 billion (Cohan 2011).

The identified problems of AIG which led to severe liquidity problems were also believed to be rooted in corporate governance inefficiencies. Unlike the previous cases the main failure was attributed to poor risk management what led to the extensive involvement in subprime mortgages insurance (Foley 2009). More precisely, according the final report by the government's Financial Crisis Inquiry Commission (FCIC 2011) "**AIG failed and was rescued by the government primarily because its enormous sales of credit default swaps were made without putting up initial collateral, setting aside capital reserves, or hedging its exposure—a profound failure in corporate governance, particularly its risk management practices**". As studies reveal the company continued to make risky investments to boost its short term growth. As a result, it sold insurance (credit default swaps, CDOs) worth billions of dollars based on debt securities backed by wide range of obligations from corporate loans to subprime mortgages to auto loans to credit-card receivables. AIG promised the swaps buyers to pay loses in the case of the debt securities default. Due to the complex nature of CDOs their performance depended on thousands of various loans whose value was hard to determine and difficult to predict (Lenzner 2008). The AIG exaggerated exposure to CDSs stared to be problematic as the sub prime mortgage crisis drove the real estate prices to fall and significantly increased defaults that AIG was supposed to compensate for. The company was accused of misrepresentation of its unreported losses and inflation of profits as "these investments were risks aimed solely at improving the balance sheet and were in complete conflict with the long-term success of the company and investor's money" (Financial Crisis Inquiry Commission 2011). In result, AIG announced a loss of $61.7 billion dollars in the fourth quarter of 2008 and since it was perceived as too big to fail (its collapse would have threaten the stability of the financial system), it was covered by TARP bailout scheme. The public opinion was disappointed by the lack of ethical standpoint of the board of directors whose members joint for a $444,000 spa visit after company participated by the $170 billion dollar bailout. Additionally, AIG paid out $165 million in bonuses to its executives in 2008 alone. Therefore, AIG governance structure and corporate culture is referred to those of Enron and Arthur Andersen.

The corporate governance shortcomings identified in the case of General Motors appeared to have lesser impact on the global economy as compared with the analyzed banks and the largest American insurance company. Yet, the company was nationalized by the US and Canadian governments and joined the bailout program. It turned out that although being the manufacturer of one of the most popular cars in the US and worldwide, the company went bankrupt. The main reasons were rooted in the poor strategic analysis and ignoring the market changes. The GM board of directors did not notice the increasing interests for smaller and more efficient cars (Hill 2009). The studies point at poor strategic performance and structural shortcomings of the board of directors (Finlay 2009). Despite good qualifications of the 13 "independent" directors on the board, eight of them have served with Rick Wagoner, the GM CEO, since 2003 (Macey 2008). The studies on GM board which shocked public opinion debating over the purchase of the new corporate jets fleet while being literally bankrupt was perceived as the poor monitoring passively reacting to executives intensions and strategic directions (Gross 2010). Additionally, observers identified inefficiencies in structuring the executive compensation packages. In 2007 the CEO was rewarded a compensation of almost $16 million (i.e. 64 % increase as compared to 2006) when the company was reporting billion dollar loses of $10.4 billion in 2005, $2 billion in 2006 and $38.7 billion in 2007 (Macey 2008).

6.5 Discussion

The outbreak of financial crisis is attributed to corporate governance failures including inefficiencies of board of directors, inefficiencies in executive compensation packages, inadequate risk management procedures and policies and inefficiencies at the intermediaries and sell side (Kirkpatrick 2009; Isaksson 2009). The main corporate governance shortcomings are presented in Table 6.3.

As presented in Table 6.3 the main shortcomings of corporate governance identified in various studies were also detected in the five analyzed companies. One of the most striking observations derived from the case studies refers to the presence of both corporate governance best practice and code of ethics in all analyzed companies. Therefore, corporate governance failures were not attributed to the lack of know-how and the insufficient access to empirical materials. The control and monitoring inefficiencies related mostly to short term orientation for profit maximization and the lack of fundamental responsibility of executives towards companies and shareholders. The formulation of codes of ethics in the analyzed companies did not lead to implementation of the ethical values in the everyday operation and corporate practice. The norms and values were internalized neither by executives nor by employees. Thus, the codes of conduct and corporate governance documents served simply as phantom declaration which allow for box ticking and the illusory compliance with standards of corporate behavior. The confrontation of corporate declaration and practice demonstrate severe, dramatic gap between that what companies declare for publicity purpose and that what they do pursue in practical dimensions of their activity. The divergence between corporate declaration and practice illustrates the hypocrisy of business and the severe lack of fundamental understanding and needs for ethical and responsible behavior. The messages included in the codes of ethics and the declaration of responsibility and integrity expressed by Bear Stearns, Lehman Brothers and Goldman Sachs proved to be empty declarations formulated solely for the purpose of formal compliance to satisfy shareholders and stakeholders

Table 6.3 Main corporate governance shortcomings

Corporate governance area	Main shortcomings
Board of directors (Gillespie and Zweig 2010)	Lack of sufficient information
	Powerful position of CEO, inefficient leadership
	Drop of trust, negative social perception
	Inadequate board composition—lack of derivative experts, insufficient financial expertise
Executive compensation (Johnson et al. 2009; Kirkpatrick 2009; Bebchuk and Fred 2004; Rost and Osterloh 2009; Clarke and Chanlat 2009)	The lack of incentive function of executive compensation—researchers observed fundamental weaknesses referring to the lack of motivation function (intrinsic vs. extrinsic motivation), maximizing total payoff as the main managerial drive, stock options
	Compensation packages motivated to high risk operations as large portion was paid in cash and structured for short term results
	Growing gap between average CEO compensation (estimated at $18.8 million) and average worker pay from 280 times in 2004 to as much as 520 times in 2008
	Poor work of the board and remuneration committee
	Poor efficiency of independent directors on remuneration committee
Risk management (Kirkpatrick 2009; Clarke and Chanlat 2009; Isaksson 2009)	Inefficient procedures adopted by boards, audit committee and the company management system
	Inefficient procedures referring to operational activity as well as financing policy (value at risk)
	Information asymmetry due to the poor quality of data/materials/documents
Intermediaries and buy side (Kansas 2009; Clapman 2007; Boerner 2008; Clarke and Chanlat 2009)	Wrong practices of rating agencies, financial, analysts and investment funds
	Problematic relationships, conflict of interest, pressure from companies

Source Own compilation based on quoted literature

expectations. Similarly the guidelines provided by corporate governance best practice remained to large extend the phantom declaration as the analysis shows the lack of skilled and experienced board directors, the lack of risk management in place and the lack of efficient executive compensation. The oversight and decision making failure of board of directors is viewed as one of the most problematic and inefficient element of corporate governance system. Board of directors failed not only with the reference to its structural requirements but also and foremost with the reference of theoretical attitude of its directors showing the fundamental lack of responsibility, accountability and integrity (Gillespie and Zweig 2010). The abuse of corporate governance principles affected the quality of control and monitoring over the analyzed companies and eventually led to companies' collapse. In sum, the analysis allows to depict a severe gap between corporate declaration and corporate practice. The declaration not verified by stakeholders or shareholders was (is) not translated into corporate operations. This study may lead to a conclusion that there is a high probability that such patterns are adopted by other companies and refer to other aspects of their activities. The pressure on companies towards compliance with certain guidelines and recommendation results in them undertaking shortcuts – companies formulate declaration, the recommended values are not however implemented in the practical dimensions.

The impact of the financial crisis boosted state intervention, changes in regulation and companies' policies. Newly adopted regulations (e.g. US Dodd-Frank Wall Street Reform and Consumer Protection Act of 2010) and recommendations (e.g. UK Code, EU Green Paper on Corporate Governance) are targeted at improving corporate governance standards and increasing transparency to eliminate severe pathologies. For instance the Dodd-Frank aims at significant reform of executive compensation (e.g. providing for clawbacks, say on pay) and at increasing shareholders participation and exerting of their rights. Another significant result of problems of the divergence of corporate declaration and practice refers to the recent revisions of the code of conduct and updates of corporate governance best practice at GM, AIG and Goldman Sachs. For instance, the Goldman Sachs code of 2011 emphasizes that "No financial incentive or opportunity—regardless of the bottom line—justifies a departure from our values. In fact, loosening our ethical standards in pursuit of business is a betrayal of our duty to clients, shareholders and colleagues and compromises everything we aspire to as a firm". This message seem to address the case of the unethical practice of ABACUS investment scheme as well as trading derivatives by the bank and its hedge funds which proved to be significantly profitable for Goldman Sachs though remaining highly controversial (Wall Street Journal 2010). However, it is too soon to praise for these changes and relate the shift of market regulation and (again) corporate declaration to factual reforms of their practice.

6.6 Conclusion

The outbreak and course of financial crisis are often related to the systemic inefficiencies of the whole financial sector such as practice of rating agencies, the US government housing policy and the Federal Reserve Bank long term policy of low interest rates. Many studies claim that the reasons of the financial crisis are rooted in changes in regulatory regimes which include the introduction of Gramm-Leach-Bliley Act of 1999 to replace Glass-Steagall Act if 1933 (Kansas 2009; Bris-May 2010; Halloran 2010). However, many studies view the crucial role of poor corporate governance in the understanding of the scope and scale of the financial crisis (Larcker and Tayan 2010; White Paper 2008; Stevens 2009; Bris-May 2010). Thus, the outbreak of the financial crisis is attributed to three main systemic shortcomings of corporate governance including institutional failure represented by irresponsible housing policy from the state and banking system, intellectual failure which related to the poor monitoring from the board despite highly recognized directors on board and the moral failure comprising the acceptance of risk taking policy and structuring compensation attached to turnover.

The prime causes of the crisis may seem contradicting the experience and know- how of corporate governance and public policy as the literature provides a wide range of recommendations for sound operation and guidelines for performance of both companies and countries. These recommendations refer to the corporate bylaws and regulations, board structure, its composition and work, the role of independent directors, the efficient structuring of incentive executive compensation in order to motivate top managers for the shareholder value increase, the information policy and investor relations, the corporate relations with media, other market participants and stakeholders. The commonly shared corporate governance best practice, the emphasis put on the role of efficient monitoring and control as well as the expressed requirements for high ethical standards both for financial institutions and listed companies (Boatright 2008) did not prevent from major control failures. What is worse, stock market and corporate governance seem not to have learned from previous ethics failures (McBarnet 2006:35) and frauds indicating a long lasting severe ethical crisis in corporations and financial institutions (Glasbeek 2002; Mitchell 2001; Stewart 1991). Despite efficient law enforcement, compliance with corporate governance best practice and codes of conduct in place, main failures which caused the financial crisis relate to unethical and irresponsible attitude of both public listed companies and financial institutions. The irresponsible behavior of a few exerted severe impact on the global community and global markets. The lack of integrity and strong values, the dominant public respect based on the level of consumption and wealth as well as the prime priority for short term profits prove to be the key drivers for inefficiencies in corporate governance. The phantom declaration of ethical attitude and the lack of true compliance with codes of best practice led to trust crisis on the market and resulted in deterioration of economic performance.

Analyzing the identified corporate governance shortcomings from a wider perspective one may question whether there are any solutions related to business practice or regulation potential which may help improve the control and monitoring standards. Although it is relatively easy to list the required reforms of corporate governance and the need higher ethical standards as well as both for companies as well as for financial institutions, the problem may lay much deeper and refer to the fundamental assumption of market economy and shareholder capitalism. The investor expectations pushing for constant quarter profits and leading to the increase of firm value seem to be at the cornerstone of the crisis. The expectations of higher profits (share price, dividend payout) and demands for increased consumption constitute the fundamentals of shareholder capitalism.

Such a shareholder pressure combined with liberalization on the financial market created new frameworks for structuring executive compensation and aggressive sale policy. At the same time the level of personal wealth and the size of consumption generated at any price was valued more than ethical behavior, integrity and high morale. As long as there is no essential change in value hierarchy and recognized and respected behavior, none of code of ethics declaration or corporate governance guidelines provide significant improvement of corporate behaviors and monitoring standards.

References

AIG. Code of conduct. http://www.aigcorporate.com/corpgovernance/Code_of_Conduct2010/AIGCodeOfConductEng.pdf.

Bear Stearns. Code of business conduct and ethics http://contracts.onecle.com/bear-stearns/ethics-2003-03-26.shtml.

Bebchuk, L., & Fred, J. (2004). *Pay without performance: unfulfilled promise of executive compensation*. Harvard: Harvard University Press.

Boatright, J. (2008). *Ethics in finance*. Oxford: Blackwell Publishing.

Boerner, H. (2008). The capital markets crash of 2008: What kind of regulatory reforms are needed. *Corporate Finance Review, 13*(3), 34–37.

Bris-May A. (2010). The Lehman Brothers case. A corporate governance failure, not a failure of financial markets, International Institute for Management Development. http://www.imd.org/research/challenges/upload/TC039-10PDF.pdf.

Brown R. (2008). Bear Stearns, corporate governance, and the capital markets: The role of the board (part 2). http://www.theracetothebottom.org/independent-directors/bear-stearns-corporate-governance-and-the-capital-markets-th.html.

Clapman, P. (2007). *Committee on fund governance*. Stanford Institutional Investors Forum: Best practice principles.

Clarke T., Chanlat J.F. (2009). Introduction: A new order? The recurring crisis in Anglo-American corporate governance and the increasing impact on European economies and institutions. In T. w Clarke., J. F. Chanlat (Eds.), European corporate governance. Readings and perspectives (pp. 1–42), Routledge: London.

Cohan, W. (2011). *Money and power. How Goldman Sachs came to rule the world*. New York: Doubleday.

DJIA History. http://www.nyse.tv/dow-jones-industrial-average-history-djia.htm.

Doria J., Musselman K., Haskins J. (2010). Ethical issues at Goldman Sachs. http://ssrn.com/abstract=1656514.

Financial Crisis Inquiry Commission (2011). What the financial crisis commission concluded about AIG's failure. http://www.insurancejournal.com/news/national/2011/01/27/182186.htm.

Foley J. (2009). The ultimate cause of AIG's problems, Forbes, 19 March. http://www.forbes.com/fdc/welcome_mjx.shtml.

General motors—winning with integrity. http://investor.gm.com/pdfs/Winning%20With%20Integrity.pdf.

Gillespie, J., & Zweig, D. (2010). *Money for nothing. How the failure of corporate boards is ruining American business and costing us trillions*. New York: Free Press.

Glasbeek, H. (2002). Wealth by stealth. Corporate crime, corporate law and the perversion of democracy. Toronto: Between the Lines.

Goldman Sachs. Code of business conduct. http://www2.goldmansachs.com/investor-relations/corporate-governance/corporate-governance-documents/revise-code-of-conduct.pdf.

Gross, D. (2010). Corporation Killers, interview with J. Gillespie, Newsweek Magazine. http://www.thedailybeast.com/newsweek/2010/02/02/corporation-killers.html.

Halloran, M. (2010) Systemic risks and the Bear Stearns crisis, conference on financial markets: Regaining stability/promoting innovation, Berkley Law School. www.law.berkeley.edu/5302.htm.

Hill, C. (2009). Why did general motors fail?, NY Daily News. http://articles.nydailynews.com/2009-06-01/news/17929088_1_cost-gm-millions-gm-management-princes.

Isaksson, M. (2009). Corporate governance and the financial crisis: Questions and answers, OECD. http://www.oecd.org/document/49/0,3343,en_2649_34813_43063537_1_1_1_1,00.html.

Isidore, C. (2008). It's official: Recession since Dec. '07, CNN Money, December 1. http://money.cnn.com/2008/12/01/news/economy/recession/index.htm.

Johnson S., Ryan H., Tian Y. (2009). Managerial incentives and corporate fraud: The sources of incentives matter. www.ssrn.com/abstract=395960 [21.01.2010].

Kansas, D. (2009). *Guide of the end of Wall Street as we know it.* Nowy Jork: Collins Business.

Kelly, K. (2009). Street fighters. The last 72 hours of Bear Stearns the toughest firm of Wall Street. New York: Portfolio.

Kirkpatrick, G. (2009). The corporate governance lessons from the financial crisis, OCED. http://www.oecd.org/dataoecd/32/1/42229620.pdf [21.01.2010].

Larcker, D., Tayan, B. (2010). Lehman Brothers: Peeking under the board façade, Stanford Graduate School of Business, CGRP-03. www.ssrn.com/abtract=1678044.

Lehman Brothers—code of ethics. http://public.thecorporatelibrary.net/ethics/eth_13734.pdf.

Lenzner, R. (2008). Why wasn't AIG hedged? Forbes. http://www.forbes.com/2008/09/28/croesus-aig-credit- biz-cx_rl_0928croesus.html.

Macey, J. (2008). Holding CEOs accountable; corporate boards are often the last to see what's wrong, Wall Street Journal. http://online.wsj.com/article/SB122878233346989853.html.

McBarnet, B. (2006). Toward ethical compliance. In G. J. Rossouw & A. Sison (Eds.), *Global perspectives on ethics of corporate governance* (pp. 27–38). New York: Plagrave Macmillan.

McDonald, L. (2009). *A colossal failure of common sense. The incredible inside story of collapse of Lehman Brothers.* Ebury Press.

McGee, S. (2010). *Chasing Goldman Sachs.* NowyJork: Crown Business.

Mitchell, L. (2001). *Corporate irresponsibility.* New Haven: Yale University Press.

Monks, R.A., Minow, N. (2004). Corporate governance, Blackwell Publishing.

Pitman, M., Ivry, B. (2009). U.S. taxpayers risk $9.7 trillion on bailout programs. http://www.bloomberg.com/apps/news?pid=washingtonstory&sid=aGq2B3XeGKok.

Posner, R. (2010). *The crisis of capitalist democracy.* London: Harvard University Press.

Rost, K., & Osterloh, M. (2009). Management fashion pay-for-performance for CEOs. *Schmalenbach Business Review, 61*, 119–149.

SEC (2010). Wall Street Reform and Consumer Protection Act,http://www.sec.gov/about/laws/wallstreetreformcpa.pdf

Sorkin, A. R. (2010). *Too big to fail.* London: Penguin Books.

Stempel, J., Eder, S. (2010). Goldman Sachs charged with fraud by SEC. http://www.reuters.com/article/2010/04/16/us-goldman-idUSTRE63F3JX20100416.

Stevens, B. (2009). Corporate ethical codes as strategic documents: An analysis of success and failure. *Electronic Journal of Business Ethics and Organization Studies, 14*(2), 14–20.

Stewart, J. (1991). *Den of thieves.* New York: Touchstone.

Taylor, J. (2009). *Getting off track. How government actions and interventions caused, prolonged and worsened the financial crisis.* Stanford: Hoover Institution Press, Stanford University.

US Bureau of Economic Analysis. http://www.bea.gov/national/nipaweb/TableView.asp?SelectedTable=1&Freq=Qtr&FirstYear=2007&LastYear=2009.

Wall Street Journal (2010). How Goldman profited from subprime meltdown. http://articles.moneycentral.msn.com/.../HowGoldmanProfitedFromSubprimeMeltdown.aspx?page=2.

White Paper (2008). Investment paper is liquid…..until it isn't. The story behind the Bear Stearns case, Fiduciary Vest Investment Strategies. http://www.fiduciaryvest.com/wordpress/wp-content/uploads/2011/03/Bear_StearnsandLiquidity.pdf.

Chapter 7
Corporate Social Responsibility Reporting and Directors' Duties: The Australian Experience

Juliette Overland

Abstract Corporate Social Responsibility (CSR) has the potential to have a significant impact on the conduct of global business. Much has changed since Milton Friedman made the famous and oft-quoted statement that 'there is one and only one social responsibility of business—to use its resources and engage in activities designed to increase its profits' (Friedman 1962). The exponential growth of international trade and business activity, and greater awareness of the impact of corporate behaviour on all aspects of society, has led to an increased global focus on CSR. CSR is not always easy to define, but it is generally based on the notion that corporations should act ethically and aim to do good beyond the minimum requirements of the law (Zerk 2006). The concept of CSR has become a common catch-phrase in recent years. Many businesses now wish to be seen to act in a socially responsible manner and there are increased numbers of interested stakeholders seeking information about corporate activities and the opportunity to influence business practices. Two CSR issues of great significance to business are the public disclosure and reporting of issues that impact on CSR (CSR reporting) and the relationship between CSR and directors' duties, due to the impact that it can have on the corporate decision making process. The issues of CSR reporting and CSR and directors' duties have received prominent attention in Australia in recent times, largely due to public inquiries and reviews addressing the role of CSR in business and the possibility of legislating for CSR. This chapter will review the position in Australia in relation to CSR in this context, looking at the manner in which these issues have been dealt with, for the purpose of offering an example for those in other jurisdictions to consider. Since CSR issues impact and affect businesses internationally, these topics are of global relevance, particularly due to the global reach of transnational corporations.

J. Overland (✉)
University of Sydney Business School, Sydney, Australia
e-mail: juliette.overland@sydney.edu.au

A. Yüksel Mermod and S. O. Idowu (eds.), *Corporate Social Responsibility in the Global Business World*, DOI: 10.1007/978-3-642-37620-7_7,
© Springer-Verlag Berlin Heidelberg 2014

7.1 Introduction

Whilst the term "corporate social responsibility" is now almost common-place, there is some uncertainty as to its true meaning in a business context. In Australia, the Corporations and Markets Advisory Committee (CAMAC) suggests that a company acts socially responsibly if it 'operates in an open and accountable manner, uses its resources for productive ends, complies with relevant regulatory requirements and acknowledges and takes responsibility for the consequences of its actions'. Additionally, it notes that CSR is considered to be 'a balanced approach, under which companies are judged according to their overall economic and other contributions and impacts, including how they manage social and environmental issues relating to their business' (CAMAC 2006).

There has been significant focus in Australia on CSR issues in recent years, particularly issues concerning CSR reporting and directors' duties. Additionally, Australia is in a unique position of having had three separate inquiries since 2005 which have considered CSR in a variety of business contexts—the Parliamentary Joint Committee on Corporations and Financial Services inquiry, the Corporations and Markets Advisory Committee inquiry and the Australian Securities Exchange Corporate Governance Council review.

CSR reporting—the public disclosure and reporting of issues with the potential to impact on CSR—can allow all interested stakeholders to make informed assessments of a company and its behaviours, as well as enabling businesses to positively promote their activities through a variety of mechanisms. However, CSR reporting has the potential to become a significant impost on business if the requirements are onerous or unduly burdensome. The relevance of directors' duties to CSR primarily arises in connection with the interests that are to be considered by a company board in the corporate decision making process, and whether it is appropriate to move from a narrow view in which only the interests of company shareholders are taken into account, to a wider consideration of a much broader group of external stakeholders, with greater potential liability for directors.

This chapter will consider the position in Australia in relation to CSR reporting and directors' duties in this context, particularly focusing on the nature and effect of the current legislative obligations which exist in this area. The outcomes of the various Australian inquiries into CSR issues affecting business will also be reviewed. Where appropriate, comparisons will be drawn with the position in international jurisdictions. The impact of "enlightened self interest" in motivating companies and their management to embrace CSR in business will also be analysed. Thus, this chapter will offer the Australian position as an example on the ways in which these CSR issues are being addressed in a business context.

7.2 CSR Reporting in Australia

When stakeholders are provided with, or otherwise have access to, reliable and current information about a corporation's business activities and practices, those stakeholders are able to make informed judgments about that corporation. It is in this context that CSR reporting becomes relevant. The concept of "triple bottom line" reporting, being the voluntary disclosure by companies of the environmental, social and economic impact of their corporate activities (Elkington 1997) has become popular in recent years and a variety of mechanisms exist to allow companies to engage in this form of reporting if they choose to do so. Triple bottom line reporting relies on the assumption that a corporation's financial success relies not only on its economic sustainability, but also on its social and environmental sustainability (Sarre 2002). However, the primarily voluntary nature of such reporting does result in significant limitations in the nature and content of the information disclosed.

7.2.1 Voluntary CSR Reporting

Corporations that wish to engage in voluntary CSR reporting can choose from many different initiatives which provide frameworks for disclosure—such as the Global Reporting Initiative, the UN Global Compact, the Carbon Disclosure Project and the Global Framework for Climate Risk Disclosure, to name only a few. In this contest, it is useful to consider the findings of the recent KPMG International Survey of Corporate Responsibility Reporting 2011 ("KPMG 2011 Report"). This report indicates that the number of corporations choosing to engage in CSR reporting increases exponentially each year and that, internationally, the Global Reporting Initiative is the most commonly used framework within which to engage in CSR reporting. Indeed, it is reported that 80 % of the 250 largest companies in the world (referred to as the G250) adhere to GRI Sustainability Reporting Guidelines.

The KPMG 2011 Report, whilst a generally positive endorsement of voluntary CSR reporting, does indicate two primary issues of concern with this form of disclosure:

(a) Unlike financial reporting, CSR reporting is largely unregulated; and
(b) On average, only 45 % of the G250 companies that engage in CSR reporting undertake any assurance activities to measure the accuracy of their reporting, with the percentage even lower for small companies.

The Australian position is little different to global trends—57 of the top 100 Australian companies engage in some form of CSR reporting, which is up by 12 % since 2008. However, only 51 % of Australian companies that engage in CSR reporting conduct assurance activities to measure its accuracy.

The voluntary nature of CSR reporting, coupled with a general lack of regulation and the absence of the accuracy assurance, indicates that there are significant limitations to the value which can be placed on this form of disclosure. As a result, it is difficult to use or rely on that information to assess whether a company's business activities and practices are in fact as socially responsible as they might appear to be. Whilst a slowing increasing number and percentage of corporations are choosing to engage in voluntary CSR reporting in accordance with the Global Reporting Initiative and other similar frameworks, there is no obligation for them to do so. Many Australian companies voluntarily choose, independently of any legal obligation, to engage in CSR reporting, and this may occur in a number of ways (CAMAC 2006):

(1) in an annual report;
(2) in independent sustainability reports;
(3) through voluntary reporting initiatives;
(4) through market indices participation; and
(5) through informal communication of their goals and performance.

Thus, a key difficulty arising in connection with CSR reporting in Australia is its ad-hoc and arbitrary character, rendering it difficult to make informed assessments as to the nature of a company's business practices. CSR reporting in Australian risks becoming more of a "public relations" exercise than a true example of information sharing and disclosure. Companies are free to choose not only whether they will engage in CSR reporting, but also the manner in which it will occur, the nature of the information to be provided, and the way in which it will be presented. This may offer too great an opportunity to manipulate information to suit the message a company wishes to project and to provide only "good news" stories. Further, without uniform reporting frameworks and requirements, it is almost impossible to compare Australian companies to determine whether one behaves in a more "socially responsible" manner than another.

7.2.2 Compulsory CSR Reporting

In Australia, whilst there is no truly compulsory form of CSR reporting, there are three primary forms of compulsory public reporting which, ideally, may require disclosure of issues relevant to CSR:

(1) continuous disclosure obligations;
(2) general reporting obligations; and
(3) periodic reporting obligations.

However, as will be demonstrated, to date there has been little utilization of these regimes for the purposes of CSR reporting by Australian companies.

7.2.2.1 Continuous Disclosure

The rules of the Australian Securities Exchange Limited (ASX) require public listed companies to undertake "continuous disclosure" (ASX Listing Rule 3.1). This means that a public listed company must disclose to the ASX 'any information concerning it that a reasonable person would expect to have a material effect on the price or value of the entity's securities'. Once disclosed, the ASX makes the information available to the market. Information is regarded as having a "material effect" on the price of value of securities, if it would be likely to influence investors in deciding whether to acquire or dispose of those securities (Corporations Act 2001 (Cth), s 677).

It is certainly possible that a CSR issue or event could affect a company's share price and therefore require disclosure under the continuous disclosure regime. However, ordinarily, CSR issues are unlikely to be considered to be of such significance that they would have a material effect on the price of securities. Bubna-Litic (2007) notes that on 19 October 2006 Santos Limited notified the ASX under the continuous disclosure regime of an environmental incident which occurred at the Banjar Panji exploration well in East Java. This is the only documented circumstance in which a CSR event, in this case an environmental impact, has been the subject of a report under the continuous disclosure regime in Australia.

7.2.2.2 General Reporting

All Australian companies (other than small proprietary companies) are obliged to lodge annual reports with the local regulator, the Australian Securities and Investments Commission (ASIC). All shareholders must be provided with copies of these reports and they also become publicly available through ASIC. It has also become common practice for listed public companies in Australia to make their annual reports available online for all interested parties to access.

There is no specific obligation to make disclosure about CSR issues in these reports, unless there are direct financial implications for the relevant company. However, the financial report must comply with relevant accounting standards (Corporations Act 2001 (Cth), s 295[2]). An Australian accounting standard, AASB 137 "Provisions, Contingent Liabilities and Contingent Assets", requires companies to make provision in financial accounts for certain contingent liabilities, and these may include CSR issues such as 'penalties or clean-up costs for unlawful environmental damage'. AASB 137 is based on the International accounting standard, IAS37, and it requires companies to make provision in financial accounts for "constructive obligations" to be provided for in financial accounts. Constructive obligations can arise because of undertakings given, policies published, past practices or any such behaviour which creates an expectation that a company will comply with certain obligations it may have taken on. However, such provision is only made where a payment is likely to be made because of such an obligation and the amount of the likely payment can be reliably estimated. It is certainly conceivable that such an obligation could arise, for example, from statements given by a company about its CSR commitments, but if provision in financial accounts is only required where payments are likely and can be estimated, there may be few occasions when such a standard is actually utilized in relation to CSR issues.

Under Australian law, there are particular disclosure obligations for directors in relation to CSR issues such as environmental regulation. Section 299(1)(f) of the *Corporations Act* provides that 'if a company's operations are subject to any particular and significant environmental regulation under a law of the Commonwealth or of a State or Territory, directors must report on the details of the company's performance in relation to environmental regulation'. Ideally companies would disclose details of breaches of environmental laws and licences in their directors' reports (Lyster 2007) but this does not actually appear to occur. A review of recent annual reports indicates that there appears to be a common practice for companies to provide only brief statements in their annual reports without making any substantive disclosure. Directors' reports commonly make statements to the effect that either 'the company's operations are not subject to any particular and significant environmental regulation under any law of the Commonwealth, State or Territory' or 'the company's operations are subject to some significant environmental regulations, but the directors are not aware of any significant breaches during the financial year'.

Australian listed public companies are also obliged to report any information 'that members of the company would reasonably require to make an informed assessment' of:

(a) the operations of the entity;
(b) the financial position of the entity; and
(c) the entity's business strategies and its prospects for future financial years.

Whilst this could conceivably encompass CSR issues, they are not specifically provided for, and disclosure of CSR issues would appear only to be mandated if it would be likely to have a significant impact on the company's operations, financial position, strategies or prospects.

7.2.2.3 Periodic Disclosure

Each listed company in Australia is required to provide an annual review of its operations and activities (ASX Listing Rule 4.10.17). ASX Guidance Note 10, which supplements the Listing Rule, recommends that non-financial information relevant to the company's performance and prospects should be included in the review. This could conceivably include CSR issues, but only to the extent that they may affect the performance and prospects of the company.

Additionally, each listed public company in Australia must also disclose in its annual report the extent to which it has complied with the ASX Corporate Governance Principles and Recommendations (ASX Listing Rule 4.10.3). The ASX Corporate Governance Principles and Recommendations provide a suggested approach to corporate governance for listed corporations, which operates on the basis of "if not, why not?" compliance. A company may choose not to comply with a particular principle or recommendation but, if so, it must explain in its annual report the extent of the failure to comply, and the reasons for this failure.

Of the eight ASX Corporate Governance Principles and Recommendations only two are directly relevant to CSR reporting. Principle 3, to Promote Ethical and Responsible Decision Making, encourages companies to 'establish a code of conduct that considers stakeholders' interests and to report on unethical practices. A review of recent annual report indicates that there is limited disclosure on such topics. Principle 7, to "Recognise and Manage Risk", recommends that 'companies establish a sound system of risk oversight and management and internal control'. Whilst CSR issues may amount to potential material business risks which may materially or significantly impact a company's performance, there is no particular requirement to make disclosure about CSR compliance.

7.2.3 Limitations of Current Compulsory Regimes in Australia

Despite the fact that three different regimes exist in Australia which have relevance to CSR reporting and may require disclosure of issues relevant to CSR, there are significant weaknesses in relation to the application of these regimes:

(1) **continuous disclosure**—as disclosure is only required where the information is likely to have a material effect on a company's share price, many CSR issues which may be relevant to investors, shareholders and other interested parties do not need to be disclosed in the absence of an immediate financial impact.

(2) **general reporting**—as the underlying accounting standards relevant to financial reports make little direct reference to CSR issues, CSR reporting is only required in very limited circumstances where there is direct and easily quantifiable liability. There is also a wide discretion for directors when reporting on CSR issues, and current business practices seems to favour and encourage an approach which provides little in the form of substantive disclosure in relation to CSR.

(3) **periodic reporting**—a review of a company's performance must be included in reporting to the ASX, but it is not compulsory to refer to CSR issues and disclosures are limited to the management of material business risks.

Thus, it can be seen that despite significant numbers of Australian companies embracing voluntary CSR reporting under the Global Reporting Initiative and other similar frameworks, Australian companies have been slow to apply and recognise the applicability of CSR issues to the compulsory forms of disclosure. As will be discussed below, acting in "enlightened self interest" may be the factor which most motivates companies to engage in CSR reporting.

7.3 Directors' Duties and CSR in Australia

In Australia, as in many common law jurisdictions, company directors are required by law to exercise their powers and discharge their duties:

(a) in good faith in the best interests of the company;
(b) for a proper purpose;
(c) in the absence of a conflict of interest;
(d) whilst exercising due care, skill and diligence; and
(e) without allowing the company to engage in insolvent trading.

These directors' duties exist under both the general law as fiduciary duties and under the relevant statute, the Corporations Act 2001 (Cth). The duties are owed, not to any individuals, but to the company itself, and it is in this context that the issue arises as to what "the best interests of the company" represent. Traditionally, the "best interests of the company" have been interpreted narrowly to focus on the interests of shareholders, placing those interests ahead of all others in the corporate decision-making process, and such an approach has become known as the "shareholder primacy" doctrine. When a company is solvent, the interests which the directors must primarily consider are the financial interests of the shareholders as a collective body (see, for example, *Ngurli Ltd v McCann* (1953) 90 CLR 425). Directors need not adopt only a short-term focus, but are entitled to take long-term considerations into account—such as the company's continued future well-being [see, for example, *Provident International Corporation v International Leasing Corporation Ltd* (1969) 1 NSWR 442].

By contrast, CSR recognises that the business activities of corporations affect a great number of stakeholders, not merely company shareholders, and that the interests of all legitimate stakeholders—including employees, customers, suppliers and creditors, as well as local communities, developing nations and even the environment—are deserving of consideration (Horrigan 2002).

Thus, there has been much recent law reform debate in many international jurisdictions as to whether laws relating to directors' duties require significant amendment to better promote and recognize CSR. In Australia, this debate has focused on two key aspects of directors' duties:

(1) whether directors' duties are broad enough to *allow* directors to take into account the interests of legitimate stakeholders other than shareholders; and
(2) whether directors' duties should be reformulated to *require* directors to take into account the interests of those other stakeholders.

Several key issues are relevant in a consideration of CSR and directors' duties in Australia:

(a) the effect of judicial and other pronouncements on directors' duties;
(b) the impact of legislation aimed at protecting particular external interests; and
(c) the relevance of "enlightened self interest".

7.3.1 Pronouncements on Directors' Duties

It is more than four decades since the High Court of Australia (per Barwick CJ, McTiernan and Kitto JJ) stated in the case of *Harlowe's Nominees Pty Ltd v Woodside* (*Lakes Entrance*) *Oil Co NL* (1968) 121 CLR 483, that:

> directors in whom are vested the right and duty of deciding where the company's interests lie and how they are to be served may be concerned with a wide range of practical considerations and their judgment, if exercised in good faith, and not for irrelevant purposes, is not open to review.

Thus, directors are considered to be the best-placed to determine what a company's "best interests" are, so long as they come to that view in good faith (that is, honestly believing it to be in the company's best interests) and without taking into account "irrelevant purposes". A key concern, of course, is whether CSR issues are "irrelevant purposes". How are company directors to balance the profit-seeking concerns of shareholders with the interests of other stakeholders? Are directors entitled, or required, to make decisions which would increase profits at the expense of the wider community? Are they permitted to take action which might benefit the wider community at the expense of greater profits for shareholders?

This conundrum is addressed in one of the few judicial pronouncements on CSR and related issues in Australia in the case of *Woolworths Ltd v Kelly* (1990) 4 ACSR 431, in which Mahoney JA stated that whilst directors may be 'generous' with those parties that the company deals with this is only permissible if 'essentially, it is for the benefit or for the purposes of the company that it do such'.

Long term interests can clearly be balanced against those of the short term—shareholder wealth may be increased as a result of improved corporate business performance and competition, and the long term interests of shareholders can benefit from corporate philanthropy, even though it may seem harmful in the short term (Lumsden and Fridman 2007). The short term loss does not make an action contrary to the company's best interests because of the identifiable future benefit to the company.

Whilst there appears to be some latitude given to company directors to determine what it is the "best interests" of a particular company, there must clearly be a nexus between the resulting action which is taken or decisions which are made and an identifiable benefit for the company. Indeed, company directors may engage in seemingly altruistic activities on behalf of a company, but 'if the altruistic purpose being considered by management cannot be couched in terms of what's good for the corporation, then management will have acted improperly' (Lumsden and Fridman 2007). Thus, whilst directors may 'implement a policy of enlightened self interest on the part of the company' they may not 'be generous with company resources where there is no prospect of commercial advantage to the company' (Austin and Ramsay 2010). Even voluntary ex gratia payments are permissible, so long as the payment is a bona fide transaction, which is reasonably incidental to the carrying on of the company's business, and done for the benefit of and to promote the prosperity of the company (Klein and du Plessis 2005). In the context of charitable donations, it is considered necessary that 'however laudable the object of the donation, discretionary payments of this kind from the funds of shareholders should be undertaken in a transparent and justifiable way with full regard to the interests of shareholders' (Commonwealth of Australia, HIH Royal Commission 2003).

This is in contrast to the position in the United Kingdom which became the first country to introduce a positive obligation on company directors to take into account interests other than those of shareholders. The legislation reformulates the previous duty to act "in the best interests of the company" into a statutory duty for directors to "promote the success of the company". This duty, set out in Section 172 of the *Companies Act* 2006 (UK), obliges company directors to have regard, at least, to the following criteria:

(a) the likely long term consequences of any decision;
(b) the interests of the company's employees;
(c) the need to foster the company business relationship with suppliers, customers and others;
(d) the impact of the company's operations on the community and the environment;
(e) the desirability of the company maintaining a reputation for high standards of business conduct; and
(f) the need to act fairly as between members of the company.

Due to its relatively recent implementation, the impact and scope of this duty are yet to be fully tested in relation to CSR impacts.

Countries with civil rather than common law systems, typically limit the obligations placed on directors by the operation of civil codes. Generally, directors' obligations are directed to the company itself and its shareholders, rather than any external stakeholders. However, some such countries have adopted different corporate governance initiatives, which have the potential to impact on whether a company is more likely to act in a socially responsible manner. For example, a dual board system operates in Germany, with each company having a separate supervisory board and management board—a person cannot be a member of both boards simultaneously. Whilst the management board is responsible for the day-to-day management of the company, the supervisory board is responsible for fundamental decision of policy, and appoints, advises, supervises and dismisses the members of the management board. For companies with more than 500 employees, one third of the positions of the supervisory board must be given to employee representations, and for companies with more than 200 employees, employee representation is increased to 50 % (*German Stock Corporation Act* and the *German Corporate Governance Code* 2005). Whilst employees are only one of many stakeholders, the guarantee of such representation beyond the typical role of executive management is more likely to result in a company making decisions which taken into account the interests of those (and perhaps other) stakeholders.

In Australia, a very practical concern for company directors is one of potential liability or breach of directors' duties. If acting in "the best interests" of the company requires action in the best interests of shareholders as a collective group, is a director potentially in breach of his or her duties when interests of other stakeholders are taken into account? Baxt has suggested that if directors 'are expected to run the activities of their companies with the interests of the community at the forefront of their obligations, then they must have adequate protection in the law' (Baxt 2000 at 42). Without specific authorization, through statute or otherwise, to take into account the interests of other stakeholders, directors may be concerned that they have no "safe harbour" if shareholders were to object to the decision or action. This may mean that some directors are cautious about giving weight to the interests of external stakeholders which may be contrary to the short-term interests of shareholders, and consider that they should give greater weight to shareholders' interests in the decision making process to avoid potential liability.

Additionally, as directors' duties are owed to the company, the company is regarded as the 'proper plaintiff' for any breach of duty. Whilst shareholders may be entitled in some circumstances to bring a derivative action on the company's behalf in respect of a director's breach of duty, external stakeholders have no standing to apply to bring such an action. Again, this may encourage directors to give additional weight to factors more likely to benefit the interests of shareholders over those of other stakeholders. Australian companies may ensure directors who wish to engage in CSR related activities have protection in the company's constitution, which can expressly authorize certain activities—for example, corporate philanthropy or donations (Horrigan 2002). However, Australian companies which use the default constitution contained in the *Corporations Act* (known as the "replaceable rules") receive no such protection, as the replaceable rules do not contain any provision of this nature. This is in contrast to the United States, where "corporate constituency statutes" exist in the majority of states. Such provisions may permit directors to take into account the effects of any action upon wider stakeholders—such as employees, suppliers, customers, communities and others who may have a relevant interest—and empower boards to consider a wide range of interests in the corporate decision making process, although there is no obligation to do so (Orts 1992). Corporate governance guidelines in the United States also provide that whilst a corporation may also allocate '…a reasonable amount of resources to public welfare, humanitarian, educational and philanthropic purposes' and may legitimately '…take into account ethical considerations that are reasonably regarded as appropriate to the responsible conduct of business', even if '…corporate profits and shareholder gain are not thereby enhanced' (American Law Institute 2001). Whilst such activities and considerations are permissible, there is no requirement to engage in such activities or to consider such external matters, but there is protection for directors to legitimately take them into account.

7.3.2 Legislation Protecting Particular Interests

Certain interests of external stakeholders—such as the environment, consumer and employees -are the subject of particular pieces of legislation aimed at protecting those interests. Clearly, where the legislature determines that particular stakeholders are deserving of specific protections these can be imposed as statutory obligations. For example, in Australia, the environment is the subject of the "National Pollutant Inventory" (a set of State-based statutes requiring companies operating industrial facilities to submit annual reports detailing pollutant emissions) from which information is then collected and made available to the public by the relevant department in each Australian State or Territory. Consumers are the subject of the legislation such as *Competition and Consumer Act* 2010 (Cth) which contains a variety of statutory prohibitions aimed at ensuring consumers are not the subject of unfair, unscrupulous or predatory trade practices. Legislation such as the *Fair Work Act* 2009 (Cth) is aimed at protecting and ensuring minimum standards for employed workers. These are examples of particular stakeholder interests deemed worthy of particular legislative protections, not an exhaustive list of such interests. To breach the obligations contained in such statutes is clearly not in the best interests of a company, particularly as it may result in civil or criminal sanctions for the company, the relevant directors, or both. Thus, company directors are obliged, by virtue of these statutes, to consider the particular interests which are the subject of the legislation without the need to determine or demonstrate any discernible interest or resulting benefit to the company.

7.3.3 Enlightened Self Interest

At present, in a strictly legal sense, it is essentially optional for any corporation to choose to act in a socially responsible manner. However, it is becoming increasingly recognised that it may be in the "best interests" of a company for it to be seen to be socially responsible. Even company directors who are inclined to narrowly focus on achieving short-term benefits and profits for existing share-holders cannot afford to completely ignore the interests of other stakeholders. Certain CSR considerations—not exploiting vulnerable workers or disadvantaged communities, and avoiding action which would adversely affect the natural environment—may appear to be at the expense of profits, but can ultimately be in a company's best interests due to the creation of goodwill, an enhanced reputation (or the avoidance of reputational damage) and increased employee morale (Klein and du Plessis 2005). In these situations, the interests of the company (as deter-mined by the interests of the shareholders as a collective group) and the interest of other stakeholders appear to align. Thus, by taking the interests of other stake-holders into account and acting accordingly, directors can be said to be acting in accordance with the "enlightened self interest" of the company.

The concept of enlightened self interest is increasingly relevant in a globalised world, where information is more readily and easily available to a larger and more well-informed audience than ever before. In today's world, information about "socially irresponsible" behaviour and practices of those who run our largest corporations reaches many who, en masse, have the power to influence the future success and viability of those organisations. Thus, many company directors rec-ognise that they should engage, and be seen to engage, with CSR. In order to achieve long term viability, company directors may find themselves all but required to act in a socially responsible manner as a result of external influences. Such influences will include pressure from investors, customer and consumer expectations, market forces and a heightened fear of adverse publicity. Engaging in socially responsible conduct can enhance competitiveness, the quality of pro-ductivity and business reputation, which may have a significant impact on a cor-poration's overall profitability and longevity (De Schutter 2005). Thus, it becomes likely that increasing numbers of companies will act in more "socially responsi-ble" ways over time, even if only because the pursuit of profit will compel them to do so. As more companies take an enlightened self interest approach to business, the interests of external stakeholders are more likely to be considered relevant to corporate decision making and therefore more likely to be embraced as being in a company's best interests.

7.3.4 Limitations of Directors' Duties

It can be seen from the discussion above that there are two primary limitations associated with the current Australian law on directors' duties in the context of CSR:

(a) **no obligation**—company directors have no obligation to consider interests other than those of the company's shareholders when making decision and exercising their powers; and

(b) **Potential liability**—company directors who may wish to take into account other interests have no 'safe harbour' to protect themselves from potential liability for their decisions.

7.4 CSR Inquries and Reviews in Australia

In Australia, as noted above, there have been three major legislative and policy reviews since 2005 which have considered the issues of CSR reporting and directors' duties:

(a) the Parliamentary Joint Committee on Corporations and Financial Services inquiry, which lead to the report "Corporate Responsibility: Managing Risk and Creating Value" in June 2006;
(b) the Corporations and Markets Advisory Committee inquiry, which lead to the report "The Social Responsibility of Corporations" in December 2006; and
(c) the Australian Securities Exchange (ASX) Corporate Governance Council review, which lead to the issue of the Revised Corporate Governance Principles and Recommendations in August 2007. A further revision of the Corporate Governance Principles was released in June 2010.

There has been significant overlap between the topics and focus of these reviews.

7.4.1 Parliamentary Joint Committee on Corporations and Financial Services Inquiry

In July 2005, the Parliamentary Joint Committee on Corporations and Financial Services ("PJCCFS") began an inquiry into "corporate responsibility and triple-bottom-line reporting" and the following CSR issues were amongst those considered:

(a) The extent to which company directors have an existing regard for interests of stakeholders other than shareholders, and the broader community;
(b) The extent to which company directors *should* have regard for the interests of other stakeholders;
(c) The extent to which the current legal framework governing directors' duties encourages or discourages directors from having regard for the interests of other stakeholders;
(d) Whether the law should be amended to require or enable directors to have regard for the interests of other stakeholders; and

(e) Whether alternative mechanisms may enhance consideration of the interests of other stakeholders.

Issues (a) to (d) clearly relate to the issue of directors' duties and CSR and issue (e) included a consideration of CSR reporting. In relation to the directors' duties and CSR, the PJCCFS stated that companies which take an "enlightened self-interest" approach are able to take into account interests of stakeholders other than shareholders, because in is in the interests of company to 'undertake responsible corporate behaviour'—in particular maintaining and improving a company's reputation, the loss of which can result in significant cost to business. As a result, the PJCCFS concluded that there is no need to amend the law concerning directors' duties.

In relation to CSR reporting, the PJCCFS commended companies engaging in this form of reporting but recommended that such reporting should remain voluntary, primarily in order to avoid a "tick-a-box" culture of compliance.

Interestingly, despite recommending no change to the law in relation to CSR issues, the PJCCFS noted that 'by international standards, Australia lags in implementing and reporting on corporate responsibility'. It explained its recommendations on the basis that 'the diverse range of companies and organisations of different sizes and from different sectors mean[s] that it [is] inappropriate to apply a "one-size-fits-all" approach to corporate responsibility'. The PJCCFS also considered that a desire to avoid regulation would naturally encourage companies to improve their performance in relation to CSR, but that legislative intervention might be necessary in the future if Australian companies failed to act "appropriately".

7.4.2 Corporations and Markets Advisory Committee Inquiry

In November 2005, the Corporations and Markets Advisory Committee ("CAMAC") began an inquiry into corporate social responsibility in Australia following a request to do so from the Parliamentary Secretary to the Commonwealth Treasurer. The following CSR issues were amongst those considered:

(a) Should the law be revised to clarify the extent to which directors *may* take into account the interests of stakeholders other than shareholders, and the boarder community, when making corporate decisions?
(b) Should the law be revised to *require* directors to take into account the interests of stakeholders other than shareholders, and the boarder community, when making corporate decisions?
(c) Should the law *require* certain types of companies to report on the social and environmental impacts of their activities?

Issues (a) and (b) clearly relate to directors' duties and CSR and issue (c) to CSR reporting.

In relation to directors' duties and CSR, CAMAC determined that the current legal requirements are sufficiently board to enable directors to take into account a wide variety of interests. Thus, no amendment to the law was recommended.

In relation to CSR reporting, CAMAC determined that there was no need for any additional disclosure or reporting requirements to be implemented. CAMAC came to this position because it considered that existing prescribed reporting requirements and voluntary CSR initiatives were adequate. CAMAC also stated that companies can be sufficiently "encouraged" to engage in and adopt socially and environmentally responsible practices by "light-touch" governmental initiatives and interventions, such as leadership by example, the enunciation of policy objectives, and encouragement through corporate sector consultation. The "enlightened self-interest" approach was also recognised by CAMAC, which noted that many companies already engaging in 'responsible corporate behaviour are being driven by factors that are clearly in the interests of the company'.

7.4.3 Australian Securities Exchange Corporate Governance Council Review

As noted earlier, the ASX has compiled a set of Corporate Governance Principles and Recommendations in respect of which each listed public company in Australia must disclose in its annual report the extent of its compliance with the "best practice" initiatives. The ASX Corporate Governance Principles and Recommendations were first implemented in 2003, and in 2007 the ASX Corporate Governance Council undertook a review to consider possible amendments. One of the issues which the 2007 review considered was whether the ASX Corporate Governance Principles and Recommendations should include some form of compulsory CSR reporting, particularly in the context of "material non-financial risks".

The ASX Corporate Governance Council considered that there is no "systemic failure" in terms of corporate Australia failing to address or respond to issues of sustainability or corporate responsibility and determined that it was not appropriate to adopt compulsory CSR reporting requirements for listed public companies, even in the context of material non-financial risks, as there is no clear "one size fits all" approach or solution.

The ASX released a new version of the ASX Corporate Governance Principles and Recommendations in August 2007 following the review, which has since been superseded by the release of a further updated version in 2010, which makes no further changes in relation to CSR issues.

7.5 Concluding Comments About Global Relevance and Impacts

The increasingly globalised nature of business has had a significant impact on CSR, and vice versa. Increased international availability of information, communications and travel have made it much easier to conduct business globally, but have also lead to greater awareness of international disparities and inequalities. This awareness has in turn resulted in pressure being placed on large companies to act in a more socially responsible manner. A review of the Australian experience in relation to CSR, illustrated through two issues with the potential for a significant impact on business—CSR reporting and directors' duties—highlights the many ambiguities which arise for business globally in connection with CSR. Despite fairly recent reviews into CSR in Australia, there has been little discernable regulatory development in this area. There is no compulsory CSR reporting in Australia, although greater numbers of companies are gradually engaging in various forms of voluntary CSR reporting, mirroring global trends. There are, however, significant limitations to this form of reporting. Directors' duties in Australia still have a relatively narrow focus on the "best interests" of the company, giving most emphasis to the financial interests of shareholders. In the absence of regulation, the "enlightened self interest" approach offers both an inventive for companies to engage with CSR issues and protection for directors who wish to engage with the interests of external stakeholders as part of the corporate decision making process. Bodies such as the Australian Parliamentary Joint Committee on Corporations and Financial Services have suggested that if the desire to avoid regulation does not naturally encourage Australian companies to improve their CSR performance, legislative intervention might occur in the future. Thus, the Australian corporate landscape will no doubt be carefully watched in the future, both nationally and internationally, by corporations, business, regulators and investors alike.

References

American Law Institute. (2001). *Principles of corporate Governance: Analysis and recommendations*. Philadelphia: American Law Institute-American Bar Association, s2.01.
Australian Securities Exchange Corporate Governance Council. (2003–2010). *Corporate Governance principles and recommendations*. Australian stock exchange listing rules.
Austin, R. P., & Ramsay, I. M. (2010). *Ford's principles of corporations law* (14th ed.). London: Lexis Nexis Butterworths.
Baxt, B. (2000). Avoiding the rising floods of criticism: Do directors of certain companies owe a duty to the community?" *Company Director 16*, 42.
Bubna-Litic, K. (2007). Climate change and corporate social responsibility: The intersection of corporate and environmental law. *Environmental and Planning Law Journal 24*, 253.
Commonwealth of Australia, HIH Royal Commission. (2003). *The failure of HIH insurance*.
Corporations Act. (2001). (Cth). Australia.

Corporations and Markets Advisory Committee. (2006). *The social responsibility of corporations*. Sydney: Corporations and Markets Advisory Committee.

De Schutter, O. (2005). The accountability of multinationals for human rights violations in European law. In P. Alston (Ed.), *Non State Actors and Human Rights*. Oxford: Oxford University Press.

Elkington, J. (1997). *Cannibal with forks: The triple bottom line of 21st Century business*. Chichester: Capstone Publishing Limited.

Friedman, M. (1962). *Capitalism and freedom*. Chicago: University of Chicago Press.

German Stock Corporation Act (Atkiengesetz). (2010) The German Co-Determination Act (Mibestimmungsgesetz) and the German Corporate Governance Code (Deutscher Corporate Governance Kodex).

Horrigan, B. (2002). Fault lines in the intersection between corporate Governance and social responsibility. *University of New South Wales Law Journal, 25*, 515.

Klein, E., & du Plessis, J. J. (2005). Corporate donations, the best interest of the company and the proper purpose doctrine. *University of New South Wales Law Journal, 28*, 69.

KPMG. (2011). *International survey of corporate responsibility reporting*. Amsterdam: KPMG International.

Lumsden, A., & Fridman, S. (2007). Corporate social responsibility: The case for a self-regulatory model. *Company and Securities Law Journal, 25*, 147.

Lyster, R. (2007) Chasing down the climate change footprint of the private and public sectors: Forces converge. *Environmental and Planning Law Journal, 24*, 281.

Orts, E. W. (1992). Beyond shareholders: Interpreting corporate constituency statues. *George Washington Law Review, 61*, 14.

Parliamentary Joint Committee. (2006). *Corporate responsibility: Managing risk and creating value*. Canberra: Senate Printing Unit.

Sarre, R. (2002). Responding to corporate collapses: Is there a role for corporate social responsibility?" *Deakin Law Review, 7*, 1.

Wilson, M. (2003). *Corporate sustainability: What is it and where does it come from?* Ivey Business Journal, March-April, 1–5.

Zerk, J. (2006). *Multinationals and corporate social responsibility*. Cambridge: Cambridge University Press.

Part III
Not-for Profit Sector and SMEs

Chapter 8
Social Responsibility: The Italian Case Within Public Administration

Patrizia Torrecchia and Carmela Gulluscio

Abstract This study offers an Italian perspective of the theme of social responsibility and social reporting. Although it is a widely explored field of accounting research, we focus our attention on the Italian case because we believe that this would be the very first step for a broader research that underlines the significant differences between countries which requires exploring different backgrounds and cultures. This study therefore seeks to: (1) Describe the concept of social responsibility regarding the Italian doctrine, in particular in the Public Administration field; (2) Analyze the characteristics of social reporting in two areas of the public administration which operate in the Italian context; (3) Underline the assigned role of stakeholders within the social reporting framework of CSR. Historically non economic or non-financial responsibilities have become more and more important so that the contents of reporting have evolved from the "simple" social relations to natural and immaterial ones. So the evolution of reporting could be seen from social reporting to natural reporting up to intangible reports. We adopt a methodology of research which takes into consideration both theory and practice. In fact, on the one hand we consider the most important Italian literature about the social responsibility topic, and on the other hand we analyze a sample of social reporting mechanisms which are in the Italian domain.

The idea of the paper and Bibliography are due to the common work of the two authors; Points 8.1, 8.3 and 8.4.1 are to be attributed to Patrizia Torrecchia; Points 8.2, 8.4.2 and 8.5 are to be attributed to Carmela Gulluscio.

P. Torrecchia (✉)
Università degli studi di Palermo, Palermo, Italy
e-mail: patrizia.torrecchia@unipa.it

C. Gulluscio
Unitelma Sapienza, Rome, Italy

A. Yüksel Mermod and S. O. Idowu (eds.), *Corporate Social Responsibility in the Global Business World*, DOI: 10.1007/978-3-642-37620-7_8,
© Springer-Verlag Berlin Heidelberg 2014

8.1 Introduction

The debate on the issue of social responsibility is certainly up-to-date. In recent years, the interest around this topic has been gradually growing and numerous areas of public administration have decided to take the path of social responsibility and that have become conscious of its consequences and impacts, including the future effect that their decisions and actions could have on the environment *latu sensu*.

Private companies preceded public sector organizations in identifying the importance and benefits of being socially responsible not just in ethical terms but also in financial and economic terms. It seems that we have taken a new road which leads to a paradigm shift comparing to the past: "honesty is the best practice" and nowadays "people care about social responsibility" (Crowther and Caliyurt 2008).

Social responsibility in fact takes into consideration all the relationships that the organization has with society in general, with the state, customers and suppliers, of course with its workers and citizens and "those groups without whose support the organization would cease to exist" (Freeman 1984, pp. 31–32).

Accountability, *transparency*, and *sustainability* have become an "imperative" for improving organizational performance as they are requested to show concern both for people and for the environment.

This study seeks to illustrate and discuss how social responsibility issues have influenced accounting reports within the public sector. The method we adopt is based on a historiographical research that delineates the evolution of social responsibility in the public context.

We seek to show how the social reporting process produces in practice different "reporting products" according to the different ideas that every organization has about "being socially responsible". Thus we present two case studies which take in consideration two different approaches to social responsibility: the first one sees a social responsibility "translated" into *environmental accounting* as a system of communication to stakeholders that is focused on the environmental impacts of administrative activity; a second one "translated" into a *social reporting* as a system of communication with stakeholders that is focused on the use of a model of reporting based on the quantity and quality of relationship between the administration and the reference group representative of the entire community, which aims to outline a consistent, timely, complete and transparent view of the complex interdependence between the economic, social and political factors inherent in the result of the different decisions.

Finally a critical synthesis of the whole discussion is outlined.

8.2 The Evolution of Social Responsibility in Italy

The subject of social responsibility of companies and its respective reporting originate in the 1930s and were developed, initially, in Germany and in the U.S.A.

The first known social balance was drafted in 1938 by AEG in Germany, while the first theoretical contribution on the issue of social responsibility belongs to Bowen (Bowen 1953).

The Italian doctrine had already developed in those years some theoretical contributions that can be considered as forerunners on this theme. For instance it is worth mentioning the works of Palumbo (Palumbo 1934), who assumed that the objective of maximizing the net profit for the entrepreneur had to be subject to the research of maximization of the benefit for all the components of the company, and Panciera (Panciera 1939), who proposed to differentiate between "revenue balance" (aiming at highlighting the economical result of the accounting period) and the "social functionality balance" (taking into account the economic system where the company operates). Nonetheless, until the end of the 1970s, the issue of social responsibility had a very limited space in the Italian doctrine and use, while it was consolidating in other countries (Germany, France, Great Britain and U.S.A.).

The first social balance was drafted in Italy in 1978 by the group Merloni, who participated in a research project seeking to implement in Italy the basis for the culture of social responsibility. It was an isolated case as, until 1994, no other social balances were drafted in Italy.

During the 1980s an interesting academic debate developed on the themes of social and environmental responsibility, but the actual application of the relevant tools was implemented by the companies only starting from the 1990s. Initially the companies were producing the first assessments. They were mainly companies whose activities had a high environmental impact. In this context, the environmental balances of some oil refineries were produced, followed by the social balance of Agip Petroli.

Almost contemporaries to these first experiences of the Italian companies, the private non profit companies started to produce ethic-social balances.

At the end of the 1990s, also the Public Administration started the process to reach to the social balance. Originally the Local Authorities tested these instruments, followed shortly by health companies and other public companies.

Today the ethic, social and environmental balances are quite wide-spread in the Italian economic context, but it is likely to further expand in the future.

The Italian Public Administration got involved in these issues with some delay compared to not only other countries, but also with national not-for profit organizations. This circumstance could appear singular, considering that the institutional mission of these companies is to satisfy the public needs, pursuing it through the use of resources coming from the community. These characteristics determine the need to communicate in an instant and transparent way the use done of the public resources, the aims fulfilled and the outcome produced. Therefore, if the social balance is an important activity for companies, for the Public Administration it should not be disregarded. In fact companies have as a first aim the creation of economic value, while for Public Administration the creation of economic value is instrumental to the satisfaction of priority social and environmental needs.

The interest of the Italian Public sector for the social responsibility developed in conjunction with some circumstances, as for instance the need to contain the public debt, some major scandals involving the public sector, causing the lack of credibility of these institutions, and as well as the introduction of partnership between public and private sector (Romolini 2007; Hinna 2004).

In our opinion, the delayed interest of the Italian Public Administration towards the social responsibility has two main causes:

- Lack of norms on this subject: the Italian Public Administration, in fact, is imbued with the culture of "obligation", therefore only what is provided for by law is going to be performed;
- The reticence for new elements and lack of consolidated managerial culture.

As just mentioned, the norms on social environmental balance in Italy are few. Among these it is possible to mention:

- Bill n. 1571/1981, which tried to introduce the use of social accounting besides the traditional briefing on the budget. Nevertheless, the bill was never applied;
- Legislative Decree (D. Lgs.) n. 153/1999 forcing the bank establishments to draft the report on the management in two parts: the first as an economic and financial report and the second as a balance on the mission;
- D. Lgs. n. 155/2006 obliging the social enterprises to draft a social balance.

On one hand the cited lack of norms hindered the development of standardized models of accounting, making it difficult to compare the documents produced by the different companies; on the other hand this played a positive role, allowing the companies to develop ingenious models, leaving room for testing and innovation.

8.3 From "Sustainable Development" to "Environmental Accounting" Within the Public Administration

The importance of the relationship between economy and environment, two of the three areas of sustainable development, becomes increasingly evident and with it the need to analyze and measure their impacts. The awareness of this fact has led, among other things, to the development of several new governance methods and tools. Among these, the environmental budget is certainly one of the newer tool in the experience of public administration (ISPRA 2009).

Despite the perceived strategic importance of this tool, there is still no formal arrangement that legitimizes and regulates its adoption and use. As mentioned, the environment has become one of the greatest economic and social priorities. One of the primary targets, pursued in the entire world, is the full integration, protection and environmental restoration through economic and social policies. Hence the need for a new generation of environmental policy whose fundamental paradigm is based on sustainability. All this has had a strong impact on accounting: until few decades ago it was believed that the mere provision of information about financial management was sufficient. Today there is a general advantage which is manifested not only as the sum of the expectations of individuals who have direct dealings with the administration but also as a general interest of the community. Therefore, administrations should adopt a policy of wider communication, which has to be widespread and transparent and that can meet a growing demand for information concerning both the competitive and operating results to management and the social and environmental impacts associated with the provision of administrative activities.

It is necessary to recognize and accept the fact that man depends on nature and can not change the social system to the point of altering the fundamental natural balances. Inevitably, led to an extreme subverting, this would mean extinction for humanity. Environment carries out certain essential functions to the economy and in general for man sustenance as it supplies the natural resources, receives and transforms the waste of the human activity ensuring the survival of mankind. Awareness that natural resources are not infinite led to a kind of turnaround that has led to some rules that are necessary to ensure not only present life forms but also future ones: "Preserving environment meets the needs of the present without compromising the ability of future generations to meet their own needs" (according to the WCED).

Sustainable development implies the adoption of strategies and policies based on a multidimensional approach that will lead to the integration of economic, social and environmental considerations and objectives.

In this sense involvement and public participation assumes a fundamental role because if all parties affected by sustainable development strategies are involved in the design and implementation of them it will be more likely that they are accepted and seen as an opportunity rather than as an imposition.

Historically a first definition of sustainable development appeared during the Conference of the United Nations held in Stockholm in 1972. From that date a series of meetings gave light to the theme of "environment". In an international scene, the first impulse to a "green accounting" came out of the conference held in Rio in 1992 in which was defined the Agenda 21 (work summarizing strategies and actions to promote sustainable development).

Until the eighties, Italy has only resorted to the application of European Directives, and only in recent years it is possible to speak about an Italian Environmental Policy.

Italy has started the implementation of Agenda 21, approved the National Plan for sustainable development with the decision of the CIPE (Interministerial Committee for Economic Planning) of 28th December 1993. Moreover with the environmental protection program excerpt (PSTA) we have a first significant application of new environmental policies to address sustainability.

PSTA provides funding for six projects designed to achieve the Strategic Objective of sustainability in different areas. One of these is the provision of tools to support sustainable development, such as updating the National Plan for Sustainable Development in Implementation of Agenda 21. In 1998, the framework of draft law on the Environmental accounting of the State, Regional and Local Authorities was an important step for Italy towards the introduction of Environmental Accounting as a tool for sustainable development.

The need for legal regulation governing environmental accounting is closely linked to objectives that have prompted some MPs to take an active interest in environmental issues. One of the above targets such as the attempt to bring out those costs referred as "hidden" which are generated by the unconditional use of renewable and un-renewable natural resources, and undisputed cause of damage to the environment and health. Thus the need to allow administrators to have full cognizance of the performances staged in line with government policies in the area. Funding purpose is essentially dictated by the law to bring about the integration of traditional economic and financial documents with the information given by additional documents devoted to defining the objectives of socio-environmental information which must then be able to adequately support policymakers and implement tools for environmental sustainability. Consistent with the purpose of this law there are two fronts:

- establishing the obligation for municipalities, provinces, regions and states to approve with the economic and financial planning documents and also budget documents of the environmental accounting performed as documents relating to the environmental sustainability of development;
- requiring the adoption by municipalities, provinces, regions and states of a system of environmental accounts, namely the collection of information in the context of the national statistical system reflect changes in the texture and natural heritage, the interaction between economy and environment, the cost of prevention, protection and restoration of environment.

The law thus refers not only to the processing of documents by the Government on environmental assessment, it also defines the roles and responsibilities of other institutions in identifying:

- ISTAT as the center of scientific and technical coordination and preparation of environmental accounts,
- APAT as the institute in charge of preparation, organization and validation of environmental information produced and acquired by ARPA;
- ENEA as the institute responsible for the validation of instruments for measurements.

In the annex to the law the statistical tools suitable for processing the accounting requirements is listed:

- NAMEA (National Accounting Matrix Including Environmental Accounts) an array of integrated economic accounts with environmental indicators to describe the interaction between economy and environment;
- SERIEE (Système Européen pour le Rassemblement des Informations Economiques sur l'Environnement) a system of satellite accounts identifying expenditure on the protection of the environment, government, businesses and families;
- A system of sectoral indicators of an environmental pressure system that measures the ratio between natural and social systems in order to define the impact of economic activities on environmental resources.

8.4 Analysis of Some Documents on Environmental and Social Reporting

8.4.1 The Environmental Balance of a Municipality in the Province of Palermo

In this paragraph, we present one of the "translations" or modulation of social responsibility adopted by the Municipality of Corleone, a town in the Province of Palermo (Sicily). ARPA Sicilia (Regional Environmental Protection Agency of Sicily) has signed an understanding charter with the town of Corleone on an experimental basis for the adoption of the environmental balance.

The fundamental objective of environmental reporting is the communication between stakeholders both internal and external. It can be seen as the document by which the Government offices report on its activities for the environment, both in relation to the past (financial statement) and to the future (budget). It has an internal purpose because it is under the scrutiny of all governing bodies of the institution and the elective assembly, but also a purpose of external communication because the groups of stakeholders, including citizens, are the final users. It must therefore be a clear document, prepared in accordance with the principles of responsibility (administration to the citizens-voters) and transparency.

The environmental balance is a new instrument of dialogue between different social actors which become involved in the process of reallocation of resources.

Being accountable means "to measure what the administration have done", that monitor and to account for the results of the policies and activities of the municipality or the Province based on the specific powers given to the Board by law, this process has effects on the system of local governance, because it affects the agreement between the democratically elected local government bodies and groups bearers of legitimate interests that make up the community (Falcioni and Testai 2004). This is the reason why the construction of the environmental balance sheet, and therefore the choice of the parameters of reporting, stakeholder engagement is planned.

The environmental budget is a statement both political and institutional on the environment, built on a database (system of environmental accounts) regarding the environmental and anthropogenic pressures on the environment of the system itself. This document should contain an organized system of environmental accounts (physical and monetary) in relation to the competence of the institution to which it relates. It should be able to show a comparison with the economic and financial planning documents and budgetary and evaluation of environmental impact sectoral policies, undertaken or to be implemented by the body (Tanese 2004). It can be considered one of the forms of the social reporting process, while being in fact limited to a specific sector level, its goal is to make socially responsible the public administration in the first place and then all those involved in the implementation and success of environmental policies. This process is dynamic: the final outcome, i.e. environmental assessment, is used by policymakers to assess actions, interventions and policies and plans and programs, and thus is able to change strategies for the future.

In particular, focusing on Corleone's activity in terms of social responsibility, we present the experimental environmental balance sheet for 2005. It is presented as an accounting document that allows the observance of the actual expenditure for environmental policy of the City, showing source and destination of resources, to relate the ratio of the money provided, committed and paid with a physical indicator for each environmental and financial statement with a series of qualitative information that reclassified data would not allow to capture. The town of Corleone was chosen by the Agency to apply the model because of the typical features both from the perspective of Nature as is an economy that may well represent the whole of Sicily, tied to the agricultural and food industry.

ARPA intended to contribute to the implementation of this accounting tool in public administration through technical and methodological support. After analysis of financial statements conducted by reclassifying the environmental expenditures (both commitments and payments) based on the same accounting areas for the policies adopted, it is possible to identify and reorder what the policy objectives are which the administration has responded to by deciding to devote economic resources. Reclassifying all the accounts of expenditure can highlight the link between the allocation of resources and the purpose that such a destination pursues.

For the analysis of environmental accounting in the town of Corleone, we used the study by CERIECA (Business Research Centre) in Catania, in the context of the technical board between APAT and ARPA, and it is an example that can highlight and achieve a good comparison of economic and environmental performances.

This document is divided into three tables:

- "Environmental allocations and source/funding" (activities and liabilities; investment requirements for current and those of a structural nature);
- "Statement of Environmental Management";
- "Explanatory note".

The first one, the Environmental balance lists the data entry section of the "values of investment (assets)" by destination as we find the multi-year investments in the statement "Environmental allocations and sources/funding" on the *infrastructure* investments but also of *current* investments. For infrastructure investments we intend those actions prepared by the permanent environmental agency for climate protection and the improvement of the environment, while current investments means those maintenance and policy short-term interventions.

The section of "values of source/funding (liabilities)" highlights the necessary financial resources to be allocated to environmental measures. These are divided into internal and external to highlight the financial autonomy and capacity of the institution to meet its commitments with its own resources or through the use of third economies. So it underlines the extent of indebtedness of the institution.

The second document is a statement aimed to analyze the management capacity of local government in the dynamic design that is the basis of the actions to implement environmental strategies. It highlights the efforts and results of operations in the broader process of value creation by ensuring that we integrate both the economic performance and those in the wider environment. In detail, economic performance is assessed by an index called EFG ("indice di efficienza funzionale della gestione" or the index of functional efficiency of the management) which is constructed considering the financial documents included in the estimates of the local authority, beginning with the budget provisions and concludes with the payments. It is given by:

EFG = (Committed/allocated x Paid/Committed)

In this way, on the one hand, it measures the efficiency in planning activities of environmental policies (first ratio), the other by the efficiency in financial processes to complete the various stages of the expenditure (second ratio). To the index of functional efficiency of the management (EFG) is assigned a score value that is synthesized in three ranges: high (A) between 0.81 and 1, medium (M) between 0.46 and 0.80; low (B) between 0 and 0.45. The indicator associated with a value rating can express the capacity of the institution to achieve environmental goals through economic management.

The areas of accountability are: (a) Water; (b) Air; (c) Productive activities; (d) Power management; (e) Waste; (f) Land; (g) Transport and mobility.

This model tries to lead to a full configuration of environmental activities through the use of the rating methodology useful for expressing an "integral value of management" in non-financial and non-physical-technical.

8.4.2 The Social Balance of the Municipality of Turin

The second case study presented on this work is about the first social balance drafted by another local authority: the Municipality of Turin. This is a big city located in the north-west of Italy, with the characteristics of a "metropolitan city". According to the document, the Municipality of Turin, with a total of 13,000 employees, is the biggest company of the city, outnumbering the employees of Fiat. The latter, after the great crisis that struck the automotive industrial sector, has undergone a considerable staff reduction.

The first social balance from the authority here analyzed was drafted in 2003, a period of ferment, when Turin was getting prepared to host the 2006 winter Olympics. The writing of this document was done in cooperation with the University of Turin and the Accountants Association of Turin-Ivrea-Pinerolo, and it was awarded a category prize in the Balance Oscars, an initiative promoted by Fe.R.P.I. (Federazione Relazioni Pubbliche Italiana—Italian Federation for Public Relations).

The choice of drafting a social balance report is connected with the will to provide an instrument for information, understandable not only for experts on balance, but also for all the people interested in knowing the goals planned by the Municipality, the modalities of use of public funds and the results actually achieved.

The social balance of the Municipality of Turin was drafted on the basis of the GBS model (Gruppo di Studio per il Bilancio Sociale—Group of Study for the Social Balance). Academics and professionalists from several countries are part of this Study Group. The Group gathered officially for the first time in 1998 and in 2001 it issued the Principles to Draft the Social Balance. In 2005 a document regarding the social account report in the public sector was produced. The GBS had furthermore identified the minimum content of the social balance.

According to this model the social balance is structured into three parts:

1. Company identity: this section describes the economic and social context where the company operates, its organization, the government system, the mission and company strategy;
2. Creation and distribution of added value: this section provides details on the resources employed in the production process and on the wealth produced, highlighting how the wealth created is distributed among the subjects linked to the company (personnel, other Public Administrations, citizens, companies, non profit sector, credit system, etc.);
3. Social report: in the case of the Municipality of Turin, it underlines the goals planned for 2003, the main stakeholders and the results actually achieved (in qualitative and quantitative terms).

The 2003 social balance includes also some information typically included in the gender balance; starting in 2004 the Municipality of Turin drafted two separate documents: a social balance and a gender balance.

With reference to the company identity, the first part of the document describes the main values pursued by the Municipality of Turin, according to which the authority expressed the will to qualify itself as:

(a) Alpine European metropolis;
(b) City of science, research, technology, education and training;
(c) City caring for the protection of weak and underprivileged people.

For this purpose, the administration needs to get inspiration from values such as:

- Protection of dignity and freedom of people, contrasting any form of discrimination;
- Promotion of the right to work, health, housing, instruction and equal opportunities;
- Engagement in a balanced economic development;
- Support to the family, considered as the fundamental cell of civil society;

- Promotion of social security;
- Integration among different cultures (need particularly felt in the city, subject for some time of significant immigration);
- Protection of environment, nature, animals and removal of the causes of pollution and decay;
- Exploitation of the historical, artistic, environmental and cultural heritage;
- Incentive for the development of associations and voluntary organizations.

Particular attention is given to the explanation of the main expenditure and revenue budget items of the Municipality. The revenues are differentiated according to their origin, and are classified in tributary, extra tributary and transfers. The expenditure is divided in five big sections, corresponding to the activity areas of the local authority. These refer to:

1. Government of territory: this expenditure item is connected to the achievement of large public works, with particular reference to urban planning, recovering of degraded outskirts, environment protection, management of green areas and waste, municipal police and civil defence;
2. Welfare and services to citizens: This expenditure item refers to social, relief and educational services, to residential housing, protection of the right to housing, policies for youth and citizens in general;
3. Promotion of the city for the 2006 winter Olympics and attention to its development in terms city of art, culture and sport;
4. Economic and labour development: this section includes the policies to support the entrepreneurship, commerce and citizens with employment related difficulties;
5. Cost of the Municipality: this last item includes the expenses connected to the management of human resources, finance, IT services.

The second part of the document highlights that in 2003 the Municipality of Turin managed to produce a positive global added value of Euro 604 millions. The results comes from the algebraic sum between the first level added value, obtained as difference between the management revenue (including tributary revenue, transfers, revenue from public services and financial management, etc.) and intermediate management costs (related to the purchase of raw, subsidiary and consumption material, commodities and services, use of third party goods, amortizations of fixed assets), and the results of the financial and extraordinary management and the Municipality joined companies.

After having explained how the global added value is produced, the document points out in which measure this is distributed among the main Municipality stakeholders (personnel, other Public Administrations, credit capital, transfers). Large space is given to the social reporting, highlighting the main expenditure budget items (distinguished between current expenditure and investment expenditure) and showing some relevant management index, among those the financial autonomy, tax autonomy, tributary burden, local pro capita debt and the pro capita assets.

Although the social balance report is drafted in a clear and detailed way, it is possible to point out the three main limits of the document:

- The model of social balance proposed by GBS is that of a final balance. Therefore, although the document shows, for each of the set goals, the pursued target and the results achieved, the comparison between goals and results is possible only through the social balance of account, while a provisional document anticipating, in terms of timing, the drafting of the final balance is missing;
- Although, for each of the set goals, the balance shows the desired results, the main stakeholders and the results actually achieved, the objectives are often defined in quite generic terms. For instance, the goal "increase the number of places available in kindergartens" is identified without a quantification of the planned increase. The definition of the objectives is carried out in qualitative but not quantitative terms, this limiting the possibility to judge, in the final balance, the correspondence between set goals and results achieved;
- As often happens in social balances, the document here examined lingers on the positive results achieved during the year analyzed and only mentions marginally (or omits) the points to improve. Thus the social balance, more than an instrument of accounting and dialogue with the stakeholders, becomes predominantly a document to divulge, pointing out the positive actions performed by the administration during a given period of time.

8.5 Some Conclusions

There are several types of tools for the social account used by the Italian Public administrations. These include (Tanese 2004):

- Annual social balances;
- Mandate balances;
- Environmental balances;
- Gender balances;
- Consolidated group balances;
- Territory balance.

The annual social balance (analyzed in the case study on the Municipality of Turin) is the most often used tool, both in public and private sector. It refers to an administrative year and is linked with the fiscal year balance, but autonomous with reference to the latter. It must focus on several fields of activities of the company drafting it and provides information not only on the output, but also on the company outcomes.

The mandate balance is, instead, a typical instrument of Public Administrations, as it is aimed at providing an account of the activities carried out during the period of the political mandate of a given body.

The environmental balance (analyzed in the case study on the Municipality of Corleone) is formed by an estimate document and by a final balance and provides information (of qualitative and quantitative-monetary type) on the impact of the company's activities on the territory where the company operates.

The gender balance is based on the assumption that the economic policies are not neutral and produce different consequences on men and women, due to the different role they have in society, economy and families. Therefore this balance aims at highlighting the different impact produced by these policies on men and women.

The consolidated balance refers to a group of companies and is drafted by big Public Administrations which have shares in private companies (for instance companies providing local public services).

The territory balance provides a report on the activity carried out by all the public bodies operating in a given geographical area.

As mentioned before, the activity of social account in the Italian Public Administration is quite recent and growing. Today, a widespread culture of social responsibility is missing. It is enough to mention that several public bodies, although issuing social account reports, do not publish them on their websites.

In Italy the factors that led to the adoption of these instruments are different from those which brought to the development of social accounts in other countries. Concerning this, a detailed reconstruction of the development of social accounts in several countries is provided by Hinna (2004). In France this practice developed following the working class turmoil in the 1960s; in Germany the motivating factor was linked to the activities of joint management; in Great Britain to the necessity to protect the environment; in U.S.A. to the request for information coming from the market of capitals. In Italy instead, the necessity for Public Administration to become more accountable is mainly connected to the lack of credibility that followed major political and institutional scandals in 1990s known as "Tangentopoli" and "Mani Pulite" (Clean Hands). In that period some legal investigation in the world of politics and public administration led to the discovery of serious corruption phenomena and illicit financing of political parties. Facing this significant loss of prestige, the public sector felt the need to identify some communications instrument to regain the trust of citizens. The rapid development of social account documents in the Italian Public Administration took place in this context.

The lack of norms and standard schemes on the account tools represented at the same time a hindering and stimulating element for the development of these practices in Italy. On one side, in fact, the lack of a standardized pattern limits the possibility to compare the produced documents, both in space and time (with reference to the other Italian and foreign Public Administration). On the other side, the absence of rules and rigid schemes gave to the companies the freedom to test different ways of producing an account report, thus allowing the development of innovative models that can improve along the time and adapt to the necessity of the companies adopting them.

Although the social account is quite a recent phenomenon in Italy, especially in the public sector, it is reasonable to assume that it will not be just a temporary trend, but that in the next few years it will considerably develop in qualitative and quantitative terms, and become a fully fledged element of the company culture.

Acknowledgments We would like to express our gratitude to all those who gave us the possibility to complete this work. We want to thank all the Staff of the Municipality of Corleone and in particular dott. Sonia Acquado for her kind help in finding the necessary documents and information.

References

Bowen, H. R. (1953). *Social responsibilities of the businessman*. New York: Harper & Brothers.

Corrocher, A. (2005). *Il bilancio sociale. Come realizzarlo nelle aziende profit, nelle organizzazioni non profit, negli enti pubblici*, Milano: Franco Angeli.

Crowther, D., & Caliyurt, K. T. (2008). *Globalization and social responsibility*. Newcastle upon Tyne, UK: Cambridge Scholars Publishing.

Falcioni, F., & Testai, P. (2004). *La comunicazione con gli stakeholder e il bilancio ambientale: un nuovo modello di governance degli enti locali*. APAT Rapporto qualità Ambientale urbana.

Freeman, R. E. (1984). *Strategic management: A stakeholder approach*. Boston: Bitman.

Hinna, L. (2004). *Il bilancio sociale. Scenari, settori e valenze. Modelli di rendicontazione sociale. Gestione responsabile e sviluppo sostenibile. Esperienze europee e casi italiani*. Milano: Il Sole 24 Ore.

ISPRA—Istituto Superiore per la protezione e la ricerca ambientale (2009). *Il Bilancio Ambientale negli Enti Locali. Linee guida, Versione per la sperimentazione*.

Palumbo, P. (1934). *Ragioneria Commerciale*. Palermo: Ciuni.

Panciera, E. (1939). *Riflessi corporativi nell'economia aziendale*. Palermo: Palumbo.

Romolini, A. (2007). *Accountability e bilancio sociale negli enti locali*. Milano: Franco Angeli.

Tanese, A. (2004). *Rendere conto ai cittadini. Il bilancio sociale nelle amministrazioni pubbliche*. Cantieri: Edizioni scientifiche italiane.

www.gruppobilanciosociale.org/

Chapter 9
To the Roots of Entrepreneurial Values: The Relationship with the Territory as a Driver for the Development of Corporate Social Responsibility—An Analysis of the Experiences of Italian SMEs

Del Baldo Mara

Abstract The aim of this study is to propose a reflection on the contribution of small and medium enterprises (SMEs) in spreading the philosophy and practices of governance directed towards Corporate Social Responsibility (CSR) as well as sustainability. The study focuses on the importance of entrepreneurial values as well as on the relationship with the territory, to which the entrepreneurs and SMEs are profoundly rooted. Sharing a system of common values which arises from a whole range of intangible context (social, anthropological, cultural) factors, specific to location, contributes to build a favourable business climate wherein the SMEs, together with other local actors, take part in constructing sustainable company and territory strategies. After presenting the theoretical framework the second section of the paper is developed by way of a qualitative research methodology centered upon the analysis of a sample of SMEs belonging to the Marche region, Italian territory "cradle" of the small-sized company and craft traditions. Using a cognitive approach, the study permits identifying the "roots" of good entrepreneurial practices and to trace the features of a territorial model of socially-responsible orientation based on excellent examples of "convivial enterprises" strongly rooted in their territories.

9.1 Introduction

Within an economic scenario where behavior and strategies of big enterprises are widespread and where developmental processes prevail that are often incapable of giving true answers to the requests of ethical behavior, of local typicality, of better

D. B. Mara (✉)
University of Urbino 'Carlo Bo', Urbino, Italy
e-mail: mara.delbaldo@uniurb.it

A. Yüksel Mermod and S. O. Idowu (eds.), *Corporate Social Responsibility in the Global Business World*, DOI: 10.1007/978-3-642-37620-7_9,
© Springer-Verlag Berlin Heidelberg 2014

thought-out rhythms of life as well as of less rushed and superficial human relationships, the objective of this work is to re-evaluate the role of entrepreneurs and
SMEs (Small and Medium Enterprises), which are profoundly rooted in their
territory of operation and are often considered as being of "minor" relevance.

"Today's international economic scene, marked by grave deviations and failures, requires a profoundly new way of understanding business enterprise. Old
models are disappearing, but promising new ones are taking shape on the horizon"
(Pope Benedict XVI 2009: 62). "Owing to their growth in scale and the need for
more and more capital, it is becoming increasingly rare for enterprises to be in the
hands of a stable director who feels responsible in the long term, not just the short
term, for the life and the results of his company, and it is becoming increasingly
rare for businesses to depend on a single territory" (*Ib.*: 62–63).

In Italy, just as throughout the vast majority of the world, SMEs constitute the
backbone of the socio-economic system and are able to offer both widespread and
little known examples of the ability of fighting the predominant socio-economic
mentality. In the last years national and international literature is turning its
attention to the universe of the SMEs in order to verify and support their role in
contributing to the promotion of forms of sustainable development and of practices
of corporate management and governance aimed at CSR (European Commission
2002; European Union 2004; Spence et al. 2000; Castka et al. 2004; Russo and
Tencati 2006; Luetkenhorst 2004; Matten and Moon 2004; Mandl 2006; Nielsen
and Thomsen 2006). Especially in SMEs, the presence of ethical values of the
entrepreneur represents a fundamental driving force in determining the spreading
of a philosophy of governance and corporate management as well as guiding
towards the adoption of practices and communication tools of CSR and
sustainability.

Such values, besides being linked to personal characteristics of entrepreneurs,
are reinforced by them being profoundly rooted in their socio-economic network
which, in certain local situations, is characterized by the presence of a specific
genius loci.

In light of all this, the research question that orientates the work here is the
following:

> Which values, ethical principles and charisma induce some Italian entrepreneurs,
> embedded to territorial socio-economic systems in which they live and work, to innovative
> paths of development focused on CSR and capable to embed charismatic principle in
> economic life?

The initial proposition at the basis of this study is therefore the following:

P 1. At the heart of the CSR spread throughout SMEs of a certain area, there are
shared values which derive from the culture and the common root which are
passed on and which today translate into the particular missions of companies
"with a soul".

In Italy, whose socio-economic fabric is made up of small companies and
entrepreneurs and their families, there are many zones whose values in terms of
know-how, sense of belonging to a local community, to the same culture, inspire

entrepreneurial behavior. A recent piece of research, which centered on various cases involving Italian SMEs, allowed verifying an important connection between orientation towards sustainability of companies led by entrepreneurs ("champions of CSR") and the sharing of those values typical of their local context (Harvey et al. 1991; Peraro and Vecchiato 2007). Specifically, these values above all spring from the rural culture and from the culture of the Italian cities in Renaissance Humanism which is the heritage of the Civil Economy of historical tradition of the Country (Bruni and Zamagni 2004). In contexts such as these, there are numerous companies, normally small-to-medium sized that—thanks to the entrepreneurial vocation and to the "civil charisms" of those subjects able of leading companies that present themselves as value-based organisations—offer tangible examples of innovative routes of sustainable development which, first and foremost, involve the context of their local territory but not only, since they push themselves to support sustainability projects and actions on a national and international level. These routes are based on the capability of these entrepreneurs/companies to take part (as well as to activate) networks which include several actors: banks, trade associations, unions, local authorities, non-profit organisations, chambers of commerce, etc.

Such entrepreneurs are capable of activating virtuous circuits: charismatic people, who, thanks to their vision, are those who open new frontiers on human need and rights; they communicate with urgency their vision of social life and, later, institutions extend these innovations into social structures.

The second proposition is therefore the following:

P 2. These values, spread among the other main protagonists of the territory (institutions, associations), translate in a particular activism and sensitivity to CSR that operates at a local level and assumes the contents of social responsibility and territorial sustainability (TCSR: Territorial Corporate Social Responsibility).

In order to verify the afore mentioned propositions, this work adopts both a deductive and inductive point of view, which correspond to the main sections of this paper.

In an initial phase, we present a theoretical framework which recalls the currents of study on entrepreneurship and business ethics, placing the values and entrepreneurial trends at the fore. The point of view, then, becomes anthropological in nature and pauses upon the values, reasons, aptitudes of the entrepreneurial figure. A vast amount of literature has investigated its features and, more recently, an interpretation is spreading which re-evaluates the values of the family and family cohesion, grafted onto the company, as well as those values of a particular given place ("*genius loci*"), and of a certain territory (Matacena and Del Baldo 2009).

In a second part, we develop the empirical analysis, by way of presenting multiple company cases, which was directed at Italian entrepreneurs and ("territory" SMEs) working in the Marche region, witnesses to good practices geared towards the common good of the territory and, more generally, to the environment in which they operate.

The aim of this work is, from this point of view, to take the opportunity of giving voice to excellent examples of entrepreneurial spirit and vocation, characterized by cultural and anthropological traits, typical of the culture of the location. These traits typify "spirited businesses" (Jenkins 2006a, b; Lamont 2002), whose economic, as well as human aims, live successfully side by side.

"In recent years a new cosmopolitan class of managers has emerged, who are often answerable only to the shareholders generally consisting of anonymous funds which *de facto* determine their remuneration. By contrast, though, many far-sighted managers today are becoming increasingly aware of the profound links between their enterprise and the territory or territories in which it operates" (Pope Benedict XVI 2009: 63), such that they are multiplying the experiences of those entrepreneurs who possess "strong" values and ethically implied charisma, capable of testifying to a new way of doing business and, putting their particular talents to work, of helping to create a more civil and human society. It is opportune to view these with renewed interest and, perhaps, to "learn" from them.

9.2 Entrepreneurship, Sustainability and CSR: The Role of Values

Before having a professional meaning, entrepreneurship had a human one, since it is an *"actus personae"*, (Giovanni Paolo II 1991: 832–833; Paolo VI 1967: 269–270). The *ethos* and values of entrepreneurship are expressed by way of active aptitudes and refer to typically entrepreneurial attributes: spirit of initiative, creativity, leadership, charisma, enthusiasm, passion, ambition, desire, commitment, responsibility. But, the ethicality of his/her role depends on the moral conscience of the entrepreneur, or rather on the presence of a base strategic and ethically marked orientation transferred to the company. This means reconciling economic function with human conditions, all of which can be done if values and priorities are re-evaluated, and not merely in the sense of arbitrary and personal values, but of "supervalues", which entrepreneurs may become excellent evidence of. These values, can be transferred to companies "with a soul" (Catturi 2006) where economic objectives, and more appropriately human objectives, live side by side successfully.

The recognition of an ethical and social dimension of business activity is founded on a vast corpus of theory and on rich debates involving different academic disciplines: business-economics, management, sociology, anthropology, philosophy (Carrol 1994). Different groups of theories (instrumental, political, integrative and ethical theories) form the core of this literature; they likewise correspond to different approaches, focused on one of the following aspects of the social context: economics, politics, social integration and ethics (Garriga and Melé 2004). Within this corpus of theories (in particular ethical theories), even if they primarily refer to large-scale businesses, one can find interpretations which give importance to the specifics of small businesses and to the role of entrepreneurial values.

The concept of entrepreneurship is one derived from entrepreneur and takes his personal characteristics and the functions and roles carried out by him into account. The attention, placed on the set of motivations and values as well as on existential conditions (the need of achievement theory—McClelland 1965), enlarges to the variables of a social nature leading to different interpretative models (theory of social marginality, Stanworth and Curran 1973). Such approaches strongly put the role of the economic factor, as a driving element of company creation, back into perspective. The entrepreneur is rarely motivated by purely economic factors and he is oriented towards reaping the benefits of his choices (Zamagni 2007) in the long term.

Values and attitudes towards the social context are central factors in the strategic system and are expressed by the vision, the "entrepreneurial formula" (Coda 1985). Values nourish the organisation and enhance the spirit of entrepreneurialism (Lamont 2002). They are like roots, which inspire the strategic orientation and constitute the most important source of identification inside the firm and the primary basis of external legitimization. Values recognizable to human nature ("the system of perennial values": honesty, loyalty, justice, respect for human life—Catturi 2003) forge the "ethical constant of the business management" and represent the premise for "entrepreneurial success".

In SMEs the entrepreneur is both the driver and implementer of values (Hemingway and Maclagan 2004). The process of orientation towards CSR and sustainability is in fact normally promoted by the owner/entrepreneur and depends on his ethical orientation and values (Vyakarnam et al. 1997; Spence and Lozano 2000; Spence and Rutherfoord 2003; Morsing 2006; Molteni et al. 2006; Kvåle and Olsen 2006).[1]

In the light of what has been said, we may state that although the literature on ethics has paid less attention to small firms (Spence 1999) it finds its own matrix in three essential aspects: the influence of the subjective sphere, which in the small firm is maximized, the importance of relating to internal actors and to the external ones, proclaimed by its limited dimension, and the social rooting of the small business and of its creator (Del Baldo 2006a, b).

The "personal" element in SMEs is more contiguous because of the tight framework of interpersonal relations that is held together by the entrepreneur and/ or the family/owner, which stratifies itself inside and outside the firm. The business is nearly always linked to the family, which is essentially composed of a human factor, a civil "cell", over the socio-economic entity.

---

[1] Based on empirical research conducted between 2005 and 2006 on a sample of 51 SMEs from diverse European countries the Authors distinguished three categories of businesses: "the business strategy enterprises", which are making a conscious effort to implement CSR and have adopted CSR as a part of their business strategy; "the intuitive enterprises", which are "doing" CSR without having made a conscious decision to do so—their normal business practices coincide with CSR indicators; "the raison d'être enterprises", which are "doing" CSR because it coincides with their business concept, i.e. the actual business concept is philanthropic" (Kvåle and Olsen 2006: 7).

Secondly, the relational factor is a distinctive aspect of the small business owner and of the small-sized business (Birley 1985) and is the driver of specific strategies not always, nor necessarily aimed at, quantitative development. They diverge from the "biological" models of life cycles of the firm (Churchill and Lewis 1983), and focus instead on the forms of particular developments (qualitative development—Marchini 1995) in an environment in which those centred on an orientation towards CSR and sustainability merge. These relationships are at the base of the concept of "relational goods" (Bruni 2007) that have (and "have to do") with altruism, moral gratification, the "logic of happiness" (Baldarelli 2005), gratuitousness and gifts (Zamagni 1995; Gui and Sugden 2005; Bruni and Porta 2005).

Finally, small and medium entrepreneurs are often active members of a territorial community, of which they represent the "creative soul", to which they are intimately linked and in which they reinvest part of the economic wealth they generated and their energies. They become privileged "witnesses" of CSR thanks to a strong rooting in the socio-economic environment. SMEs—especially "rooted" in their respective region and characterized by long-term, established mechanisms and rules—possess a good starting position for a sustainability strategy as a result of their structure and regional infusion (Leborgne and Lipietz 1991; Storper 1995).

9.3 Socially Oriented Entrepreneurial and "Territorial" Values

The virtuous circle of entrepreneurship and the corporate culture depend on the context of the environment defined in terms of business environment as well as on the presence of selective entrepreneurial policy (Aldrich and Martinez 2001; Minguzzi and Passaro 2000). A favourable business climate, which springs from a system of anthropological, social and positive economic factors, has an influence on the development of the business and favours orientation towards CSR, which finds fertile land in commonly-held values, and sets off a virtuous process that is at the basis of sustainable corporate development as well as the place where the company is rooted.

Liability, identity and sense of belonging to a precise cultural and ethical context, closeness to internal and external networks, flexibility, innovative drive and adaptive competences are attributes of SMEs. Trust is built both on geographical closeness, common history and on joint activities as well (Peredo and Chrisman 2006).

Various studies have highlighted the contribution of CSR in terms of increasing the social capital of SMEs, of participating in the construction of the common good (Thomson and Smith 1991; Spence and Schmidpeter 2003), of contributing to the sustainability of specific territories.

That which has been said explains the development of peculiar approaches to CSR, centred on a logic of SME involvement in networks or based on membership in specific districts (Molteni et al. 2006; Battaglia et al. 2006; Ørskov 2006; Kromminga and Dresewski 2006). The participation of the SME in networks characterized by the presence of a plurality of actors, both public (local organisations, chambers of commerce, universities and research centres) and private (trade associations, non-profit organisations, credit institutions, professional orders), facilitates the implementation of actions and programmes of socially-oriented development of SMEs and of the local environment/specific geographical area in which they are inserted (Fugazza et al. 2006; Lepoutre 2006; Maaß 2006).

Thus, when there is a common aim to improve the quality of life that ties together individuals and organisations belonging to the same territory, it is possible to introduce the notion of Social Responsibility of the Territory. No longer is responsibility solely the realm of the individual firm, which is called to put itself in relation to the collective, but rather it is the whole community, the territory, which comes to be conceptualized as an *unicum*. Social responsibility of the territory is founded on the rediscovery of shared values that the territory's economic, social and institutional actors know how to reinforce, thanks to solid networks of relationships.

However, it is important to underline that this approach can be applied only in specific social and economic contexts where all local actors have absorbed a common culture that spreads in mutual values with respect to the way business is run.

The concept of culture reminds to beliefs, norms, traditions and attitudes that drive the behavior of individuals and organisations belonging to a definite community (Schein 1990). In literature there are many research about the relations between culture and management (Hofstede 1980) but just a few investigate the impact of culture on corporate social performance. Ringov and Zollo (2007) interesting contribution offers empirical evidence to test the assumption that corporations' socially responsible behavior is influenced by specific dimension of the cultural context in their home country. Those results are consistent with the findings of the report on European SMEs and social and environmental responsibility showing a highest percentage of SMEs sustainable-oriented in those Nordic Countries (i.e. Finland, Denmark, Ireland, Norway, The Netherlands and Sweden) notably characterized by a more "feminine" and a low "power-distance" culture.

Thus, in our opinion, to better understand the phenomenon it is not sufficient to consider the cultural dimensions at a national level, but one should consider also the different local culture that exist in the same Country. That is the case of Italy where CSR attitude is not equally distributed in the different Italian regions (Perrini et al. 2006). As literature poses (Becattini 1979) in Italy there are some territories characterized by the presence of relational environmental between local actors sharing a collective identity arising from the past of the region where they live (Bagnasco 1977; Braudel 1979; Putnam 1993). That is, in our opinion, the rationale why the Marche—along with other Italian territories such as Tuscany and the Veneto—offers an interesting laboratory to study not only the extent of CSR, but also Social Responsibility of the Territory.

9.4 An Analysis of the Experiences of "Local" Italian SMEs

9.4.1 Research Methodology

The study was developed according to a qualitative approach and a case study methodology (Yin 1994) in order to pinpointing the internal factors (organisational structures, internal micro-processes, attitudes, points of view, perceptions) that, together with the corporate characteristics (size, sector, age of the business, etc.) and the general contextual factors (economic, political, cultural, etc.) are able to explain the orientation towards CSR and sustainability (Adams 2002) of entrepreneurs and SMEs, and to "capture" the diverse manifestations of CSR in SMEs as well as for indicating best practices and suggesting criteria for further action (Craig 2003).

The study was centered on the analysis of ten Marche SMEs (multiple case study approach) enrolled in Confindustria (the main association of Italian industrial companies) and belonging to industrial and service sectors that represent the entrepreneurial and economic fabric of the region. In the choice of enterprises, we considered the "cohesive" and "multi-certified" Italian SMEs typology (Molteni and Lucchini 2004; Unioncamere 2003).[2]

The analysis was based on information collected in the period January-May 2010 through in-depth semi-structured interviews to entrepreneurs/managers (founder/successor, managing director, general manager), direct observations during companies visits, participation to workshops, congresses and focus groups, and access to internal documentary sources.

Case studies allow researchers to use different types of evidence and to triangulate their findings. The scope of the triangulated approach was to make use of different advantages and strengths offered by the various method of data collection (primary and secondary data).

Primary data were based on information acquired from several in-depth semi-structured interviews with entrepreneurs and managers. In January 2010 we held the first exploratory interviews with each company's managing director or entrepreneurs to determine their willingness and compatibility for this study. Since this initial phase was satisfactory, we proceeded to the second phase – interviewing the management or entrepreneurial team. The interviews were semistructured in manner, with a set list of questions designed to elicit discussion. The face-to-face interviews (two for each interlocutors, lasting an average of one hours each) were aimed at 40 people. All the interviews were tape-recorded, transcribed and analyzed. Field notes and informal conversations complemented the taped interviews.

---

[2] Molteni and Lucchini (2004) identify a typology of orientations among Italian firms, based on two coordinates (intensity of the phenomenon—i.e. the socially responsible behavior—and qualitative aspects linked to the practice and to corporate behavior): cohesive firms, multi-certified, aware, able to be mobilised, skeptical.

The first interview was conducted according to a narration approach; the second interview (conducted in structural form) had the aim of focusing upon the mission, the governance, the accountability and upon the stakeholders commitment and the relationship with the local community.

The primary data were then combined (and supplemented) with secondary data gathered through direct observation during visits to the company and through the analysis of documentary sources from the firm's websites, relations, and other internal documents.

The interviews with the managers, the entrepreneurs, and other internal and esternal stakeholders (i.e. family members, employees, suppliers) became particularly useful for identifying these actors' common values. Also useful was the rich documentation provided by the firms, such as their social reports, statement of values, historical-celebratory publications, journal and newspaper articles and company newspapers. Direct observations in the firms offered the possibility of comparing the results of the interviews with the reality inside the business. We observed the interactions (with internal and external stakeholders) of the entrepreneurs and managers in the company as well as their relational approach in congresses, forum, workshops, and conferences.

9.4.2 Results

All the companies follow strategies of social responsibility with an adhesion to CSR codes, adopt processes of social and environmental certification, regularly publish social and environmental reports, have obtained recognitions/awards for their robust activities of social responsibility and carry out ample and significant of initiatives of social responsibility both on the national and international level. In short, these aspects refer to the following declinations: presence of a framework of ethically-connoted values, shared by the leaders of the firm and diffuse throughout the organisation; realisation and promotion of CSR actions and strategies as well as sustainability; development of systems of accountability.

Specifically, the analysis focuses on the following aspects:

1. the solid ethical and moral base, whose roots come from a sense of civility and rural tradition that was influenced by shared religious principles, personal and family values, transmitted by entrepreneurs across personal relations in the business, and passed down by their agricultural forefathers;
2. the strong sense of community membership as well as a true desire to "attract" and to "infect". In these companies "conviviality" is manifested in the creation of CSR oriented networks and partnerships.

Below, the results of the study relative to these two aspects are summarised.

With reference to the map of orientations towards CSR most of the ten companies possess the characteristics of "cohesive" and "multi-certified" firms (Molteni and Lucchini 2004).

In the "cohesive" group of companies, the areas of engagement and the forms of communication of CSR are systematic and creative, and manifest themselves in a variety of forms:

- involvement, valorization and formation of employees;
- transparency in processes and in the modes of governance, presence of formal and informal instruments, and procedures for internal and external informative disclosure;
- manufacture of products of social and environmental merit;
- extensive collaboration with the local community (donations, sponsorships, promotion and production directed to projects of social, cultural, environmental, etc. merit);
- relationships with non-profit organizations and associations;
- stable and durable collaboration with clients, providers, and financial partners;
- attention to the global environment, across the activation of procedures and programs of environmental protection and of quality of life (recycling trash, reduction of emissions, saving energy, etc.).

In the so-called multi-certified firms, the orientation is more focused on procedural aspects. The typical forms are found in their client offerings and in their requests to their own suppliers for ethical, social and environmental guarantees (green purchasing – ISO and Vision certification, quality of products, etc.). However, they appear to be dynamic companies, since they are multiplying their areas of engagement towards CSR, researching more structured forms of communication (projects to implement their social and environmental reports), implementing modifications to their system of government and multiplying the front of engagement and dialogue with stakeholders.

9.4.3 Core Values Inherited from the Family and Rural Culture

The first aspect that emerged from relates to the existence of a mission connoted by a strong system of values (ethical, moral, social, as well as economic). Those core values are inherited from the family and rural culture and they inspires a corporate culture oriented towards CSR and sustainability, that is the practical implementation of the company's ethos. Values common to entrepreneurs are: diligence, labour, equity, trust, honesty, simplicity, integrity, parsimony, sense of family, team spirit, enthusiasm, energy, responsibility, communicative nature. Such values are widespread and shared by the internal and external stakeholders. With their personal commitment and engagement, they represent "the first best practices". Purpose, vision and values are constantly reinforced through culture and processes and continuously communicated throughout the organisation and beyond. The entrepreneurs are also strongly involved in the well-being of the local community.

For the reason of highlighting these aspects, some passages taken from interviews of entrepreneurs and managers are as follow provided.

> Values sustain actions, that are positive and responsible generate a type of development
> that respects humans and the environment. Without values one cannot go far. Values are
> the identity of the group: they provide a common language, they give strength to our
> businesses and guide them as they adapt to the market. Our intangible values are imag-
> ination (to know how to create), energy (to achieve our dreams), responsibility (for the air
> we breathe, the land we walk on, the resources that we utilize, the trust that we gain).
> Values at the foundation of agrarian culture are "tigna" ("obstinacy"—literally a
> "ringworm"), desire, dedication to one's work, parsimony, the sense of one's limits, the
> sense of the family as the nucleus of solidarity, responsibility. There exists a parallel
> between the industrialist and the agriculturalist. From the agrarian culture we have
> learned: the importance of traditional values, the transmission of trust with a handshake;
> the habit of working in seasonal uncertainty (E. Loccioni, president of Loccioni Group,
> entrepreneur of the year 2007; Ernst & Young Award for Quality of life; recognition
> "Olivettiano businessman of the year 2008; Sodalitas Social Award 2005 finalist for the
> "metalmezzadro" project in the knowledge-based business").

> From the very beginning I have felt welcome, like a part of the family, and I've been
> given the trust necessary to grow. I've done, and I continued to do, my best to personally
> embrace those same values and to experience the company as a communal good, recog-
> nizing the entrepreneurial spirit that I've had the good fortune to know (…) Our founders
> have swiftly climbed the ladder of needs, transforming them into values to construct a
> reality that produces the best aspects of life and security for the future. (…) Values
> constitute the firm's Culture and, therefore, have their own value, their own richness. They
> are their own intangible goods, which strengthen faith and certainty in the business (T.
> Dominici, Managing director of BoxMarche, winner Italian "Oscar di Bilancio" (Balance
> Award 2007).

> Our cardinal values are tradition, innovation, quality, passion, social responsibility,
> respect for nature and human resources. The experience of Faam testifies that market
> challenges can be won only if one competes through values. Our working environment
> expresses the passions, valorises relationships, and communicates quickly to a territory
> attentive to traditions, towards which it nurtures a sentimental bond (F. Vitali, President of
> FAAM Group).

> *"Wood has always been part of my life. Since I was a child, I built toys using pieces of
> wood that were lying around my house. When I was 13 years old I started my first job as a
> carver of wooden furniture. But the passion for processing this material can be traced to my
> family and family business' history, which in the small town of Belvedere Fogliense, in the
> workshop under the house, since the 1940s built accordions. I started to build the first
> "Pinocchio" in wood and other games that made me dream as I was a child. Our products,
> our company transmit strong and authentic intangible values. Our products can transmit
> dreams, poems. They try to bring a fairytale world into people's homes. Our "mission" is to
> convey the emotions that underlie the creation of each article: the love for tradition and the
> importance of being a little children, always leaving room for imagination. The recovery of
> our craft tradition, strong values and simplicity of a bygone time stays alive and is renewed
> every day in our creations"* (Francesco Bartolucci, founder of Bartolucci S.r.l.).

9.4.4 Convivial Enterprises: Companies "with a Soul"

The centrality of CSR with respect to the development of these firms allows one to
connote them as "spirited business", high-performing companies where competitive success grows out of their commitment to values and to the human spirit.

"Spirited businesses", in other words, are "companies with a soul": they have a character, their own personality, which is the fruit of the values and principles founded in their mission and translated into their governance. The firms are conceptualised as "narrative identity", that, in fact, every day tells a story that traces its origins from the traditions of the entrepreneurs and territory. A type of "art" lives within these companies, reconciling economic objectives and humane ones. The profiles of "convivial enterprises" (Balloni and Trupia 2005) correspond to a business "way of being" in which one can view the co-penetration of the two drivers of socially-oriented governance: discipline and commitment: the former is formalised and codified, the latter is informal, emergent and value-based (Minoja and Romano 2006).

> There are three ways of being a leader: through price, through technology, through intimacy. This is our way. My greatest satisfaction is when I see others happy (R. Forni, General Manager of Della Rovere).
>
> The value of BoxMarche's products is measured by a profound harmony with all of our 'travel companions' who smile, suffer, and live within the company. With the passion that we put into this partnership, we will obtain significant results even in the global context, which doesn't mean only internationally, but also "in the family". A friendship that is transformed into a partnership. And this is beautiful (BoxMarche, letter from the Managing director, Global Report 2007).
>
> Perhaps it's a little presumptuous, but we love to define ourselves as the agents of civilization. The small entrepreneur is a builder (of systems, of men, of wealth); he relates himself to the world, to his clients, to his community; he lives his passions, hopes, dreams, plans. The enterprise has a soul and it has those intangible assets linked to the spirit and to the dignity of the person (T. Dominici, Managing director of BoxMarche).
>
> *"He who has the economic power must be the one most responsible. We are certain that CSR grows stakeholder value, social consensus, economic value, originating more trust and understanding and the best transparency to governance. In this sense, what's central is the example top management sets"* (Giorgio Arvizzigno, Director of Product Development, Quality Control and Social Responsibility TVS).
>
> *"The company acts as an interpreter of social and environmental concerns, making good of its own job, generating profit in a responsible way with respect to its economic partners, its community and its environment"* (Paolini Fiorella, entrepreneur (successor), President Young Industrial Group Confindustria Pesaro-Urbino).
>
> *"In thirty years of life, only two employees were fired. We do not give employees any time card; but they [come to us] themselves to show the number of hours worked"* (Francesco Bartolucci, founder of Bartolucci Srl.).
>
> *"In 2008 and 2009, a period of economic crisis, two banks competed for our financing and a bank loan manager has written a nice letter first and then paid us a visit. Such behavior is increasingly rare today".* (M.G. Stocchi, founder's wife, Bartolucci Srl).

9.4.5 The Link with the Local Context: Embeddedness and Social Cohesion of SMEs

"Conviviality" is a manifestation of an attitude to improve relationships and the territory itself. This last aspect refers to the active involvement of the enterprise in local development, because business' success goes alongside with the surrounding local context. One of the principle motivations of these entrepreneurs is the desire to do something useful for their own community. This is because the histories of their businesses have always been founded on "passion" rather than merely on pure mathematical sums. The effort of the companies in advancing best practices of CSR is nourished by the will and desire to testify to and understand best practices adhering to multiple occasions of exchange, comparison and partnerships and performing the role of stimulators and catalyzers (Collins and Porras 1991). Embeddedness, intended as a sense of belonging and co-participation bringing about a territorial community, represents the "strong" element of the network assets they activate. Rootedness constitutes one of the principle drivers for the development of CSR and sustainability that are raised in "identity" contexts and is at the core of the process of formation of cultural, ethical, visionary and responsible networks, based on a nucleus of common cultural characteristics and on a shared ethical orientation. Such networks—which are the translation of social forms based on personal relations between individuals linked in relationships such as friendship, family, esteem, faith, wherein the logic of reciprocity lives—are rich in intangible resources, set within the fabric of relationships, and in themselves actualize the exchange of "social goods" (Niccolini 2008). They are activated by communicating internal values to the broader external world. Such processes of externalization favor the aggregation and reinforcement of links in an inter-organisational and complementary point of view and the creation of macro-culture.

Analysis of this aspect (proposition 2), underlines the centrality of the "sense of belonging to a specific territorial context" as the fruit of anthropological, social and cultural roots. An examination of the socio-economic contexts of Marche territory, formed predominantly by SMEs, and which attempts to understand the essence of the people and their history, allows us to more closely view an entrepreneurial system constructed on solid principles. It also allows us to discover an indirect but important protagonist: the territory of Marche.

Within the studies that have analysed the processes of industrialisation diffuse in Central-North-Eastern Italy—where the Marche region lies—some have identified factors such as the culture, history, institutions, beliefs and communal convictions, as a sort of *humus* of the intangible assets or social capabilities of the context, difficult to define and to quantify (Cipolla 1990), that correspond to a *genius loci*, connected to a particular place. The aforesaid "convivial enterprises" plunge their roots into a territorial model based on "holy agriculture"—the agrarian culture embraced profound values that were based on Christian doctrine—(Fuà and Zacchia 1983) that has characterised the Marche region from the first half of the 1800 s to the post-WWII era.

The best practices of socially-oriented Marche SMEs contribute to a model of territorial development that progresses in this particular socio-economic context. The territory thus becomes the place in which avenues of sustainable development can be concretely constructed and a terrain on which reciprocal approaches can be forged. Socially-oriented "local governance" is made possible by an integrated representation of social, economic and institutional communal feeling, and activates new mechanisms of participation and planning. The model of sustainable development that appeals to the territory's businesses depends on the capacity of the whole productive, associative, entrepreneurial and institutional world to act and to be made to act in socially-responsible ways.

For the reason of highlighting this aspect, below a summary of the thoughts of the entrepreneurs interviewed is as follow provided. Almost always does reference to the importance of common "roots" and belonging to a territory which they owe much to and to which they give much back, come through.

> We have an emotional ties to the territory. We want to use our abilities to sustain the local economy. Our activities are not only business choices. Our ability, though we are a small firm compared to other companies, is to weave threads (through the determination to follow the "dream" of an enterprise and of the environment in which it is inserted); it is to pull thread (through cohesion and collaboration inside and outside the firm) and to stretch thread (through the motivation that feeds creativity, understanding, sensibility, the capacity to listen) of a network. A network made, first and foremost, by Men (T. Dominici, Managing director of BoxMarche).

> What's important is the passion you do things with. This is the principle that over the years allowed us to grow, to arrive at certain finishing lines we never contemplated at the outset of our business, without ever having reneged on our identity, without ever having forgotten where we come from, where we live (G. Bini of Lordflex).

> We have the privilege of working in this territory and we have never once thought about moving. We want our competence to be used to support the local economy. We have an affective link with the territory, and the historic centre of the Varnelli distillery, in the small mountain village of Pievebovigliana (Sibillini Mountains) is a distinctive element. Girolamo Varnelli (our founder) was convinced of the identification of the company with the territory. He also stood firmly rooted here, even when it was more convenient to look down the coast for a more agreeable movement of people and goods (O. Varnelli, Chief Executive of Varnelli Distillery).

> With our work, we don't want to go and just sell a product, we want to sell ourselves. We want to send an important message, to transmit a philosophy. We want to create a culture in this territory and of this territory: a sense of responsibility as a cause and not an effect of situations. We're not saints; we just carry out our obligations. We're not better than others; we're just different (F. Vitali, President of Gruppo FAAM).

> My grandfather Gino lived and worked in this rustic place. He transmitted his love and passion for our land to me. Our original business was born from this love. Nature is a heritage resource that must be safeguarded, and it's important to do so now. This is the environmentally friendly philosophy which has encouraged us from the very beginning in the preservative renovation of the Cà Virginia structure, deciding to equip it with a photovoltaic, solar—thermal and geothermal—system, the largest in the Marche region (G. Rossi, Managing director of Cà Virginia, Country House & Wellness, Green Community area).

> *"Our bank is leveraged on one attitude: proximity, which is physical, relational, family-oriented, oriented to our associates, to the personalization of products and services. That means identifying oneself with the local economy, starting from the region and having the capacity to render it aprotagonist. The components of board of directors are exponents in the areas in which BCC operates and it has committed itself on its own honor to create social values for its associates and for the community." (Luigi D'annibale, General Manager BCC Gradara).*

9.5 Conclusions and Implications

The study proposes a reflection upon the importance of entrepreneurial and business values, shared and reinforced throughout given areas, with reference to the proclaiming of CSR and orientation towards sustainability of the SME by way of paths "rooted" within the local contexts. Deductive and inductive analysis is aimed at supporting the role of small and medium-sized businesses in providing examples of, and "driving," real means of good governance—many of which truly spring from that family-based world of capitalism, often criticized—, which hosts precious testimonies.

Empirical analysis carried out on a sample of Italian SMEs, CSR-oriented and belonging to the Marche region, strengthens the propositions posed as basis for the study. The social strategy of the enterprises observed is based on an effective government of systems of relations within the firm whose principal actor is the owner-entrepreneur/manager. The successful entrepreneur always appears to be the one who helps rediscover values, and who is capable of creating solid rapports and "true" relationships with interlocutors. The case studies are examples of how entrepreneurs thanks to their particular "way of being and of doing business" promote cultural reorientation, helping others to unlearn the bad habits inspired by "turbo-capitalism" (Matacena and Del Baldo 2009) and to valorise humanity, relationships, and the territory in which they do business. They show themselves to be capable of influencing and molding the socio-economic terrain from which they come. In sum, this emerges from the richness and the appeal of their own virtuous examples, capable of calling others to imitate those virtues". A solid ethical framework depends both on entrepreneurs' personal values as well as on a synthesis of socio-cultural and anthropological, environmental factors. This so called *genius loci* characterises the given territorial area, such as Marche, marked by a proliferation of local systems of production formed predominantly by small businesses.

The possible pathway of territorial CSR based on the culture of doing "good" in the local context, may offer to be a possible alternative to the often, unfortunately, short-sighted "turbo-capitalism" of the major transnational companies (Matacena 2008), which are not rooted in the area where they are located and "nomadic" in their character. The model of "gentle capitalism" centred around "territorial" SMEs, which can be found in the business contexts under discussion, leans on the construction of a large consensus both within and external to the company, as well as on an environment which is neither restraint or limitation, rather it is an opportunity. An actor in the foreground can therefore be identified, in that industrial world made up of "minor" companies, often less visible since it is scattered and fragmented, and sees the territory as a resource and is studded with virtuous situations, which with their own daily effort to bet on a brighter future, on knowledge and on territory, defend and make the most of not just the economy, but also the environment and landscape, the cultural, historic and artistic heritage of a country. "Convivial" companies, experienced as common good, do not limit themselves to being hidden champions, rather they offer the chance to inspire the world in another manner. "In the era of globalization, economic activity can no longer leave aside gratuitousness, which disseminates and nourishes solidarity and responsibility for justice and the common good in its various subjects and actors" (Pope Benedict XVI 2009: 60).

Perhaps it is opportune to bet on this way of doing business in the era of globalization, where, paradoxically, competition seems to be destined to be played out on the excellence of individual and local areas. Here is the starting line for building new economically-sustainable development itineraries, which preserves territorial structures and vocations.

9.6 Limitations and Further Research

Focusing attention on entrepreneurial values, on social capital and on the root-edness of SMEs, the study allows us to generate the hypothesis that SMEs' CSR orientation and strategies are influenced by both the firms and the entrepreneurs' values structure, and their embeddedness in the local socio-economic contexts to which they belong and in which they are inserted.

However, despite providing some additional contributions to the current liter-ature on CSR and SMEs, this study has a number of limitations some of which could be overcome at later stages of the research.

Firstly, we mention that the limitations are mainly related to the fact that the empirical study is qualitative in nature and based on the analysis of a multiple case-studies. Thus, the results cannot be generalized and cannot be considered exhaustive.

More research is needed in the future. A more profound understanding requires an even deeper qualitative analysis that is broadened by a quantitative analysis. The question remains whether it is possible to extend these findings to a broader sample (analytic generalization) across different Italian local contexts, starting with SMEs belonging to the same region (Marches) and extending across other regions and even other countries. This would necessitate a detailed investigation into how the socio-economic environments influence entrepreneurial and SMEs' values. In addition, it can collect data on the similarities and differences in firms' values frameworks that come from different cultural factors. As far as the reflections matured during the course of this study are concerned, future research may attempt to critically evaluate this model by turning our attention to regions both geographically and culturally close to the Marche and to local national and international contexts characterised by widespread entrepreneurship, in order to identify and to analyze, in a comparative way, the cultural, anthropological, social variables which make up the values context. Furthermore, the analysis could be extended to SMEs belonging to other regions, characterized by different socio-economic, cultural and anthropological contexts (i.e. regions in the South or Northern Italy). In this way it would be possible to verify if and how several factors of context, more or less favourable (i.e. the presence of large companies and large urban areas) impact on the development of CSR, social capital and embeddedness.

Possible research developments could also derive from a quantitative analysis. The qualitative study could then be accompanied by quantitative research aimed at verifying the hypothesis drawn from the propositions.

At the same time, other successful cases need to be considered, but conversely, a number of "cases of failure" need to be analysed to verify the validity of the propositions. Future research should focus on testing the suggested hypothesis, with the scope of providing a foundation to the model of development centered on the best practices of territorial and convivial SMEs.

Lastly, this paper argues that SMEs' social capital and embeddedness stems from their strong identification with a shared heritage of cultural values at the local level, but there are no distinct criteria for measuring these factors. Hence, further research must address the operationalization of social capital with a set of variables that may affect responsible behaviour, such as religiosity, family business, community culture and incentives.

Nevertheless, it is hoped that the study presented here has marked a step towards better understanding the centrality of a place's culture, of which territorial companies are expression and constitutes a useful starting point for future reflections on the possibility that the relationship existing between the culture of a territory and the entrepreneurial values expressed within it is predicated on CSR-oriented strategies. Consequently, it is useful to reflect on the possibility that these experiences, even in their specificity, can offer an original contribution and enrich the literature on SMEs' role in promoting forms of genuine stakeholders management and innovative pathways to sustainability in a world that need a profound cultural renewal, starting from values and relations.

References

Adams, C. (2002). Internal organizational factors influencing corporate social and ethical reporting: Beyond current theorising. *Accounting, Auditing and Accountability Journal, 47*(15), 223–250.

Aldrich, H. E., & Martinez, M. A. (2001). Many are called but few are chosen: An evolutionary perspective for the study of entrepreneurship. *Entrepreneurship Theory & Practice, 25*(4), 41–56.

Bagnasco, A. (1977). *Tre Italie: La problematica territoriale dello sviluppo italiano.* Bologna: Il Mulino.

Baldarelli, M. G. (2005). *Le aziende eticamente orientate. Mission, Governance e Accountability.* Bologna: Clueb.

Balloni, V., & Trupia, P. (Eds.) (2005). *Origine, caratteristiche e sviluppo dell'imprenditorialità nelle Valli dell'Esino e del Misa.* Ancona: Ed. Conerografia.

Battaglia, M., Campi, S., Frey, M., & Iraldo, F. (2006). A 'Cluster' Approach for the Promotion of CSR among SMEs. Paper Presented at the *EABIS/CBS International Conference,* Copenhagen: Copenhagen Business School, 26 October.

Becattini, G. (1979). *Mercato e forze sociali: il distretto industriale*. Bologna: Il Mulino.

Benedict, X. V. I. (2009). *Caritas in Veritate*. Città del Vaticano: Libreria Editrice Vaticana.

Birley, S. (1985). The role of networks in the entrepreneurial process. *Journal of Business Venturing, 1*(1), 107–118.

Braudel, F. (1979). *Civiltà materiale, economia e capitalismo (secolo XV-XVIII)* (Vol. III). Torino: Einaudi.

Bruni, L. (2007). *La ferita dell'altro. Economia e relazioni umane*. Trento: Il Margine.

Bruni, L., & Porta, P. L. (Eds.). (2005). *Happiness and Economics*. Oxford: Oxford University Press.

Bruni, L., & Zamagni, S. (2004). *Economia civile*. Bologna: Il Mulino.

Carrol, A. B. (1994). Social Issues in Management Research. *Business and Society, 33*(1), 5–25.

Castka, P., Balzarova, M. A., Bomber, C. J., & Sharp, J. M. (2004). How can SMEs effectively implement the CSR agenda? A UK case study perspective. *Corporate Social Responsibility and Environmental Management, 11*(3), 140–149.

Catturi, G. (2003). Valori etici e principi economici: equilibrio possibile. *Studi e Note di Economia, 3*, 7–37.

Catturi, G. (2006). Potere aziendale e responsabilità socio-politica. In G. Rusconi & M. Dorigatti (Eds.), *Impresa e responsabilità sociale*. Milano: Franco Angeli.

Churchill, N. V., & Lewis, V. L. (1983). The Five Stages of Small Business Growth. *Harvard Business Review, 61*(3), 30–50.

Cipolla, C. M. (1990). *Storia economica dell'Europa pre-industriale*. Bologna: Il Mulino.

Coda, V. (1985). Valori imprenditoriali e successo dell'impresa. *Finanza, Marketing e Produzione, 2*, 23–56.

Collins, J., & Porras, J. I. (1991). Organizational vision and visionary organizations. *California Management Review Fall, 34*(1), 30–52.

Craig, S. N. (2003). Corporate social responsibility: Whether or how. *California Management Review, 45*(4), 52–76.

Del Baldo, M. (2006a). Piccoli imprenditori e piccole imprese socialmente responsabili. In University of Padua (Ed.) *Scritti in onore di Isa Marchini*. Milano: Franco Angeli, 329–353.

Del Baldo, M. (2006b). SMEs and corporate social responsibility. Some evidences from an empirical research. In Proceedings of the Emerging Issues in International Accounting & Business Conference 2006, vol. 1. Padua: University of Padua, July 20–22, 314–343.

European Commission. (2002). *European SMEs and social and environmental responsibility', 7th observatory of european SMEs, 4*. Belgium: Enterprise Publications.

European Union (2004). *European Multistakeholder Forum on CSR: Report of the Round Table on Fostering CSR among SMEs. EC: Brussels,* final version 3 May 2005, 1–26.

Fuà, G., & Zacchia, C. (Eds.). (1983). *Industrializzazione senza fratture*. Bologna: Il Mulino.

Fugazza, S., Pandini, L., Gostner von Stefenelli, C., & Equalitas. (2006). Interreg 3A Project. A Model for the Development of Corporate Social Responsibility in the Province of Bolzano. Paper Presented at the *EABIS/CBS International Conference*, Copenhagen: Copenhagen Business School, 26 October.

Garriga, E., & Melé, D. (2004). Corporate Social Responsibility Theories: Mapping the Territory. *Journal of Business Ethics, 53*(1), 51–71.

Giovanni Paolo, I. I. (1991). *Centesimus Annus*. Città del Vaticano: Libreria Editrice Vaticana.

Gui, B., & Sugden, R. (2005). *Economics and social interactions. Accounting for interpersonal relations*. Cambridge: Cambridge University Press.

Harvey, B., Van Luijk, H., & Corbetta, G. (1991). *Market morality and company size*. London: Kluwer.

Hemingway, C. A., & Maclagan, P. W. (2004). Managers' Personal Values as Drivers of Corporate Social Responsibility. *Journal of Business Ethics, 50*(1), 33–44.

Hofstede, G. (1980). *Culture's Consequences. International Differences in Work-related Values*. London: Sage Publications.

Jenkins, H. (2006a). A 'Business opportunity' model of corporate social responsibility for small and medium sized enterprises. Paper Presented at the EABIS/CBS International Conference,Copenhagen: Copenhagen Business School, 26 October.

Jenkins, H. (2006b). Small business champions for corporate social responsibility. *Journal of Business Ethics, 67*(3), 241–256.

Kromminga, P., & Dresewski, F. (2006). Promoting CSR Among SMEs: Experiences from Germany. Paper Presented at the EABIS/CBS International Conference, Copenhagen: Copenhagen Business School, 26 October.

Kvåle, G., & Olsen, T. S. (2006). Variations in CSR in SMEs in five European countries. Paper Presented at the EABIS/CBS International Conference, Copenhagen: Copenhagen Business School, 26 October.

Lamont, G. (2002). *The spirited business: Success stories of soul friendly companies.* London: Hoddes and Stoughton.

Leborgne, D., & Lipietz, A. (1991). Two social strategies in the production of new industrial spaces. In G. Benko & M. Dunford (Eds.), *Industrial Change and Regional Development: The Transformation of New Industrial Spaces.* London: Pinter Publisher-Belhaven Press, 27–49.

Lepoutre, J. (2006). Capabilities for effectively executing socially responsible strategies in small businesses. Paper Presented at the EABIS/CBS International Conference, Copenhagen: Copenhagen Business School, 26 October.

Luetkenhorst, W. (2004). Corporate social responsibility and the development Agenda - the case for actively involving small and medium enterprises. *Intereconomics, Review of European Economic Policy, 39*(3), 157–166.

Maaß, F. (2006). Integrating corporate citizenship into corporate strategy: Empirical evidence on SMEs in Germany. Paper Presented at the EABIS/CBS International Conference, Copenhagen: Copenhagen Business School, 26 October.

Mandl, I. (2006). CSR and Competitiveness—European SMEs Good Practice. Paper Presented at the EABIS/CBS International Conference.Copenhagen: Copenhagen Business School, 26 October.

Marchini, I. (1995). *Il governo della piccola impresa. vol. II—La gestione strategica.* Genova: Aspi/Ins-Edit.

Matacena, A. (2008). *Responsabilità sociale delle imprese e accountability: alcune glosse.* Rimini: Diapason.

Matacena, A., & Del Baldo, M. D. (Eds.). (2009). *Responsabilità sociale d'impresa e territorio. L'esperienza delle piccole e medie imprese marchigiane.* Milano: Franco Angeli.

Matten, D., & Moon, J. (2004). Implicit and explicit CSR. A conceptual framework to understand CSR in Europe. ICCSR Research paper series, 29.

McClelland, D. C. (1965). Need of achievement and entrepreneurship. A longitudinal study. *Journal of Personality and Social Psychology, 1*, 89–92.

Minguzzi, A., & Passaro, R. (2000). The network of relationship between the economic environment and the entrepreneurial culture in small firms. *Journal of Business Venturing, 16*(2), 181–207.

Minoja, M., & Romano, G. (2006). Managing Turnaround with Responsible Entrepreneurship: the Kendrion Case. Paper presented at the EABIS/CBS International Conference, Copenhagen: Copenhagen Business School, 26 October.

Molteni, M., & Lucchini, M. (2004). *I modelli di responsabilità sociale nelle imprese italiane.* Milano: Franco Angeli.

Molteni, M., Antoldi, F., & Todisco, A. (2006). SMEs and corporate social responsibility: An empirical survey in Italian industrial district. Paper Presented at the EABIS/CBS International Conference, Copenhagen: Copenhagen Business School, 26 October.

Molteni, M., Pedrini, M., & Bertolini, S. (2006b). *La responsabilità sociale nelle aziende familiari italiane.* Milano: Aidaf, ISVI.

Morsing, M. (2006). Drivers of corporate social responsibility in SMEs. Paper Presented at the EABIS/CBS International Conference, Copenhagen: Copenhagen Business School, 26 October.

Niccolini, F. (2008). *Responsabilità sociale e competenze organizzative distintive*. Pisa: Edizioni ETS.

Nielsen, A. E., & Thomsen, C. (2006). CSR in small and medium sized enterprises (SME's): A holistic and strategic approach to the communication with the stakeholders. Paper Presented at the EABIS/CBS International Conference, Copenhagen: Copenhagen Business School, 26 October.

Ørskov, E. (2006). Green Network—a Showcase for Working with CSR in SMEs. Paper Presented at the EABIS/CBS International Conference, Copenhagen: Copenhagen Business School, 26 October.

Paolo VI (1967). *Populorum Progressio*. Bologna: Centro Ed. Dehoniane.

Peraro, F., & Vecchiato, G. (2007). *Responsabilità sociale del territorio. Manuale operativo di sviluppo sostenibile e best practices*. Milano: Franco Angeli.

Peredo, A. M., & Chrisman, J. (2006). Towards a theory of community-based enterprise. *Academy of Management Review, 31*(2), 309–328.

Perrini, F., Pogutz, S., & Tencati, A. (2006). Corporate social responsibility in Italy: State of the art. *Journal of Business Strategies, 23*(1), 65–91.

Putnam, R. D. (1993). *Making democracy work. Civic tradition in modern Italy*. Princeton: Princeton University Press.

Ringov, D., & Zollo, M. (2007). Corporate responsibility from a socio-institutional perspective. The impact of national culture on corporate social performance. *Corporate Governance, 7*(4), 476–485.

Russo, A., & Tencati, A. (2006). Formal vs Informal CSR strategies. The case of Italian SMEs. Paper Presented at the EABIS/CBS International Conference, Copenhagen: Copenhagen Business School, 26 October.

Schein, E. (1990). *Cultura d'azienda e leadership*. Milano: Guerini e Associati.

Spence, L. J. (1999). Does size matter? The state of the art in small business ethics. *Business Ethics: A European Review, 8*(3), 163–174.

Spence, L. J., & Lozano, J. F. (2000). Communicating about ethics with small firms: Experiences from the U.K. and Spain. *Journal of Business Ethics, 47*(1), 43–53.

Spence, L. J., & Rutherfoord, R. (2003). Small business and empirical perspectives in business ethics. *Journal of Business Ethics, 47*(1), 1–5.

Spence, L. J., & Schmidpeter, R. (2003). SMEs, social capital and the common good. *Journal of Business Ethics, 45*(1/2), 93–108.

Spence, L. J., Jeurissen, R., & Rutherfoord, R. (2000). Small business and the environment in the UK and the Netherlands: Toward stakeholder cooperation. *Business Ethics Quarterly, 10*(4), 945–965.

Stanworth, J., & Curran, J. (1973). *Management Motivation in Smaller Business*. Aldershot: Gower Press.

Storper, M. (1995). The resurgence of regional economics, Ten years later: The region as a nexus of Intraded Interdepencies. *European Urban and Regional Studies, 2*, 191–221.

Thomson, J. K., & Smith, H. L. (1991). Social responsibility and small business: Suggestion for research. *Journal of Small Business Management, 29*, 30–44.

Vyakarnam, S., Bailey, A., Myers, A., & Burnett, D. (1997). Towards an understanding of ethical behaviour in small firms. *Journal of Business Ethics, 16*(15), 1625–1636.

Unioncamere. (2003). Models of corporate social responsibility in Italy. Executive Summary. Rome: Italian Union of Chambers of Commerce, Industry, Craft and Agriculture.

Yin, R. K. (1994). *Case study research: Design and methods* (2nd ed.). Thousand Oaks: Sage.

Zamagni, S. (Ed.). (1995). *The economics of altruism*. Hants: E. Elgar.

Zamagni, S. (2007). *L'economia del bene comune*. Roma: Città Nuova.

Author Biography

Mara Del Baldo is Assistant Professor of Small Business Management. Moreover she teaches Financial Accounting at the Department of Economics, Society and Politics, University of Urbino "Carlo Bo", (Italy). Her main research interests are in small business economics and management with particular focus on Corporate Social Responsibility and small entrepreneurs/SMEs' business ethics; entrepreneurial values and attitudes as drivers for the diffusion and implementing of CSR and sustainability in SMEs; SMEs strategies of qualitative development; networking processes and networking strategies for the development of SMEs and on Social and Environamental Accounting (SEAR). She is currently involved in diverse researches and projects on those topics. She is member of European Council for Small Business (ECSB); Centre for Social and Environmental Accounting Research (CSEAR), University of St Andrews, Scotland; EBEN Italia (European Business Ethics Network) and Editorial Board Member of journals (International Journal Piccola Impresa/Small Business; International Journal of Society Systems Science; Journal of Business Administration Research (JBAR); International Journal of Business and Management) as well as reviewer for different international journals. She published in Italian and foreign journals as well as in national and international conferences proceedings

Chapter 10
Social Responsibility and Health Care Public Sector: Some Notes on the Concept of "Value"

Patrizia Torrecchia and Carmela Gulluscio

Abstract This chapter outlines the concept of *value* specifically within the context of public sector. Starting from the literature, it defines a *new* concept of value that better fits with the public sector organizations characteristics. In doing this it proposes a shift on the established doctrine for making the expectations of multiple stakeholders converge. Firstly, basic framework of the characteristics of public health agencies is made; secondly, the identification of the main stakeholders of public health agencies and their expectations towards these institutions; and finally a definition of health value, intended as a specification of the concept of "public value" in the context of public health organizations.

10.1 Introduction

The literature has produced several studies to identify the main objectives of the different organizations. The prevailing doctrine identifies this goal in *creating* and *delivering* value. Therefore, the essential condition for an organization to operate sustainably is to create a higher value than the one of the utilities consumed during the production process. Although the discovery of the value as the ultimate goal of every organization is widely accepted in the academic setting, over time this figure has been designed and defined in various ways.

The idea of the paper and Bibliography are due to the common work of the two authors; Points 10.1, 10.2 and 10.3 are to be attributed to Patrizia Torrecchia; Points 10.4, 10.5 and 10.6 are to be attributed to Carmela Gulluscio.

P. Torrecchia
Università degli studi di Palermo, Palermo, Italy

C. Gulluscio (⊠)
Unitelma Sapienza, Rome, Italy
e-mail: carmela.gulluscio@unitelma.it

A. Yüksel Mermod and S. O. Idowu (eds.), *Corporate Social Responsibility in the Global Business World*, DOI: 10.1007/978-3-642-37620-7_10,
© Springer-Verlag Berlin Heidelberg 2014

Traditionally, in the perspective of creating value, the attention was focused on the *economic value*, considered as excess of revenues over costs. The value, therefore, was identified in the profit, to be distributed to shareholders. The consistency of performance is a necessary condition for investors to maintain their capital investment, allowing, thus, the survival time in the company. The attention to the prevailing perspective of the owner has, for some time, showed the obvious limitation that it neglects to consider that public companies are entities to which the expectations of multiple stakeholders converge. Thus, the stakeholder theory has been spread, and the accepted idea is that the company's goal to create value and its fair distribution among the various stakeholders is the basis for being accountable.

First of all, an organization for being social accountable has to contemplate a concept of value which cannot be limited only to shareholders. Thus it must be interpreted in a "multidimensional" approach, in order to take into account the various subjects to which the value itself must be distributed. The identification and measurement of the produced value is a complex process for the public organizations.

In such companies, the concept of value (and its consequent social responsible being) is attributable to the degree (qualitative and quantitative) of matching the needs of the community managed. This implies the use of non-monetary tools. In this context, it is important to consider the theories of public value (Moore 1997). Assuming that the creation and distribution of value is a common goal to all types of organizations, the methodology we use in this study starts from outlining the characteristics of public health agencies; then highlights the expectations of the various key stakeholders; and finally defines a particular configuration of value to public health agencies, which is the *health value*.

This chapter is structured in three parts:

(1) a basic framework of the characteristics of public health agencies;
(2) the identification of the main stakeholders of public health agencies and their expectations towards these institutions;
(3) a definition of *health value*, intended as a specification of the concept of "public value" in the context of public health organizations.

10.2 Preliminary Framework for Public Health Care Organizations

To correctly frame the phenomenon from an accounting point of view, it may be useful to take a three-part division of "sectors" of the economy as a function of transaction costs with a view specifically neo-institutional, represented by a relationship that binds *Enterprise Market* (first sector), *Government Bureaucracy* (second sector) and the *Non Profit of the Clan* (third sector). Given their distinctive factors in relation to the nature and purpose of the transaction, the public health organizations can be positioned in the second field.

In consideration of the difficulty in delineating "pure" forms of transactions, it could be considered more appropriate to look at this report in light of the prevalence of a transaction type over the others. Thus, in our case, the reference context is characterized by the presence of prevailing exchange bureaucratic whose related goods and services are provided by entities of a public nature.

This leads to important consequences in the context of the institutional set by the competent level of government and how to achieve the same instrument. At this point we need to calibrate the criteria traditionally inspired by a business area to achieve an appropriate generalization that can be adapted to our type of administration. Thus, the well-known criterion of economy in the long run, understood as a continuing trend of income, it becomes kind of a more general criterion of economic viability.

Going back, in fact, the relationship that saw our companies included in the above mentioned second sector, and assuming the prevalence of bureaucratic trade, does not seem appropriate to bring economic sustainability concepts typical of the first sector (companies) that are resolved in a traditional relation as follows:

Revenues > Expenses

In the second sector, in fact, the above translates into the following relationship of sustainability:[1]

Grants > Transfer payments + use of grants

In our case, for this particular class of companies, we find no financial transfers payable and therefore the previous report is simplified compared to the more general referring to the entire industry to shrink II, with reference to the institutional management of healthcare organizations the following:

Grants > Use of grants

Starting from this fundamental relationship, and not from the traditional cost-benefit gap here simply misleading, characteristics of the administration in question are derived later in the flow before moving to the analysis of the most critical aspects that present accounting and budgetary assumptions and indicated existing regulatory system.

Considering the semiotic nature of accounting, it is necessary at this point to outline what the flow characteristic of the class of companies concerned, which articulate its specific content in a semantic, syntactic and pragmatic in relation to objects, respectively, means and ends.

---

[1] See Costa (2005, p. 36). This report is not in itself sufficient to determine the "economic sustainability" mentioned above, since it must be accompanied by the presence of other objectives of public economics that here not worth calling. Then the merits of the terminology used to define the typical income and expenses of the public sector, there is a clear reminder of accounting for some classic Italian and, in particular, at D'Ippolito for the category of "consumi di erogazione".

As a preliminary, therefore, from the signification of the resources administered by the companies before moving to the syntactic representation through surveys, to conclude with pragmatic communication of information to stakeholders.

We focus in particular on the distinction between capital flows and balance sheet. Regarding the first, emphasizes the importance of "value added" as a net flow that shows the remuneration of all the prime factors of production.

As for capital flows is not necessary to distinguish between those who come "from" and those who go "for" the companies in question.

The streams that come from companies in this environment and spill reporting find their maximum expression in end-user satisfaction, and for companies in health care means the same.

The streams that flow on the reference companies and therefore come from within the report relate to all the positive and negative variations caused for example by the attention of citizens in the prevention, road links with the emergency room, administrative efficiency etc.

It now seeks to clarify how the notes phases of acquisition, modification and disposal of public health resources companies specify the ways of manifestation of the points of intersection between the business system of reference and the environmental report.

In the first phase they typically acquire resources through transfers attributable essentially to "contributions by financial year" and to "quote for the contributions over the financial year" thus affecting movements in financial resources without there being any consideration in other resources.

In the second phase, companies typically change the relationships between resources.

Finally in the third stage, companies typically give resources first acquired and then transformed through provision of proper health services and also "accessories".

10.3 The Need of a Shift in the Concept of Value

The downturn of the economy has underlined the weaknesses of traditional accounting approaches reopening the important issue of the relationships between accounting and information systems which is strongly linked to reporting.

When we refer to accounting in the public sector we have to take in consideration also the complex political and financial control processes occurring at various levels of public administration.

This chapter stems from the desire to deepen the theme of reporting for public health administrations considering the transformation process over the last two decades that seems to have given them, in form and substance, a real new face.

This issue is particularly interesting because the public nature of this class of entities makes them more directly "permeable" to the economic, social and especially political context.

The general innovative trend, involving the public administration in general, has influenced legislation in order to lead to adoption of accounting management tools and broad sense most suitable to improve the performance of the administrations in question.

Although the original objective, and in itself more than legitimate, was to make more understandable—and close to the public sector—concepts such as efficiency, effectiveness and economy, however, following the issuance of the D. Lgs. 502/92 and subsequent modifications and additions, it appears that while equal attention to economic-financial value that is prevailing in some ways ends in itself, with the consequence of distorting the true extent of the rules adopted. In particular, the need to compress spending, albeit justified by the serious deficit situation of public health has often resulted in the "aggressive" pursuit of the goals with results that often went in the direction contrary to the purpose of the principal administrations, ultimately manifesting itself in the form of a depletion in the quality of services provided.

In fact, the need to contain expenses has often led to forget that these results should be achieved not as ultimate goals, but rather instrumental, which are essential conditions for the attainment of the goal and priority imperative of protecting the "right to health".

In this context, talk of economy in administrative activities does not mean distorting the health and unlikely to sacrifice the imperatives of profit; it means, however, recognizing that the expenditure restraint and the adoption of a more rational use of resources are an unavoidable necessity, whose non-compliance could jeopardize the ability of the health system to pursue its institutional goals of protecting the health and wellbeing.

Moreover, the above objective can not be achieved with tools that are resolved in the simple prescription of formal obligations to respect because they can not produce the expected change if their application is preceded and accompanied by a much more profound and problematic internalization process of the new principles and new logic. In the present case then is whether these "new" principles and these "new" are actually logical "transmigration" from the field traditionally private to public. And not because these principles are considered "outsiders" to the world of the public but because they are often translated into tools that typically belong to private companies, not pandered to the needs of the public, in a "warpin" of public disorder and physiology (alleged) private.

In this sense, we think about the need of a shift in the concept of value. Not more a value linked only to *shareholders* but a wider value which considers other aspects and subjects. As it will be explained in the following sections.

10.4 Stakeholders of Reference in Public Health Administration

The most recent trends of business economics doctrine agree that all types of organizations, both public and private, profit and no profit, pursue a common objective: the creation of value and its fair distribution among the stakeholders.

As compared with the past, a new awareness took shape: in order to get the approval of stakeholders and improve the survival probability of the organization, it is not sufficient to create value in favor of just one category of subjects (usually the equity holders). This value should meet the needs of several stakeholders that are able to influence the success of the company and its ability to survive.

Assuming that there is a common goal to all types of organizations, that is the creation and distribution of value, this paper develops the *hypothesis* that it is necessary to determine the characteristics of this value peculiar to the public health administrations.

The paper presumes that the value acquires specific features depending on the stakeholders having expectations in the organization. Therefore, the characteristics of the overall value generated by a public health administration may present some differentiating elements as compared with the value characteristics the stake-holders expect from an organization operating in another sector.

The *objective* of this paper is to seek a value configuration, determined with specific reference to the system of public companies (reference is made therefore to the concept of *public value*), with particular attention to the health sector. This configuration of value is referred to as *health value*.

To build up this definition it is necessary to previously determine the key elements according to which the several stakeholders attribute to the obtained utilities a superior value as compared with the utilities used during the production process. Thus, an attempt is made to detect some "dimensions" of the *health value*, each of them matching with the expectations of a specific category of stakeholders.

Firstly it is necessary to determine the stakeholders of reference for the public health administrations. Among them, the privileged stakeholders are selected and their expectations are pivotal for the health governance strategic and operational choices. Therefore, the health administrations seek to steer their behaviors towards the creation of a value able to sufficiently satisfy the subjects qualified as stakeholders.

As a result, a definition of *health value* is proposed, formed by as many "areas of value" as the main expectations of the privileged stakeholders are. For that reason, the definition of the health value should be multidimensional, as it has to take into account the distinct expectations of the different stakeholders.[2]

---

[2] Therefore, the value can be defined as "sharing of multiple interests, expecting an adequate satisfaction (Bergamaschi 2009). In this sense, the creation of value is meant as the adoption of government choices and managerial and organizational practices allowing to obtain, over time, results with a value superior to that of goods and services necessary for their production" (Bergamaschi 2009).

The detection and measurement of the value produced is a process presenting elements of complexity for the public administrations, as they do not sell out their production against a payment at market price, but instead provide free performances (or at political prices, that do not allow to cover the costs sustained to produce the goods and services provided). Therefore, public administrations cannot autonomously replenish the resources used during the productive process; this replenishment can take place through tax revenues or transfers from other public bodies. Anyway, this does not mean that the public health administrations did not create any significant value for the administered community.

Consequently these forms of replenishment are not able to represent the value that users attribute to goods and services provided. While in for-profit companies the year income is a valid indicator of the value produced or destroyed, for public administrations this value is much more difficult to determine, as monetary paybacks are not always present for acquisition of productive factors and for the selling of goods and services produced.

In these companies the concept of value is linked to the degree (qualitative and quantitative) of satisfaction of the needs of the administered society. This implies the necessity to carry out measurements without using the monetary meter.

In this context, theories on the public value are formulated (Moore 1995; Valotti 2005). According to Moore, the public value is represented by the satisfaction of the citizens and community needs.[3]

For this purpose, it is necessary to determine which are the stakeholders of the public health administrations with the aim of understanding what the value constitutes for them. In general, the *health value* can be identified with the adoption of strategic choices and operational interventions enabling to improve the health conditions (and welfare broadly speaking) of the society, where the value created is bigger than the resources used during the production process.

More specifically, it is important to identify the main types of stakeholders of the public health administrations and their needs. Only in this way it will be possible to build up a comprehensive definition of *health value*. The main stakeholders of the public health organizations include:

1. Citizens;
2. Health and non health personnel;
3. Subjects operating according to agreements with the health agency;
4. Other public administrations;
5. Suppliers;
6. University and other research centers;
7. Trade Unions;

---

[3] The author affirms that:

(a) Public value focuses on the objectives established by public political authorities and also on community expectations;
(b) The evaluation of public value is not limited to the short-term but necessarily it should be in a long-term perspective (Moore 2003).

8. Professional associations;
9. Voluntary associations;
10. Media.

The above listed subjects' expectations will not be analyzed in depth for concision, in order to directly determine the privileged stakeholders among them. The privileged stakeholders can influence more deeply the strategic and operative choices of the public health administrations. They are:

- Citizens;
- Governance body of the health organization and other public administrations (especially the superior public administration defining the objectives and managing the health agencies funding);
- Human resources.

The subjects above are qualified as holders of privileged (or preeminent) interests. Their main expectation can be determined and consequently some of the elements that contribute to the creation of value can be identified. It is believed that citizens are primarily interested in:

- Performance of health service able to satisfy their health necessities;
- Fair consistency between the costs related to the funding of the health services (taxes, prescription charges, etc.) and the related benefits.

The governance body of the health organizations is composed by a coalition of politicians (linked to the superior public administration of reference) and technicians (part of the top management). Its main interests are:

- Presence of appropriate economic and financial equilibriums that are key conditions for the survival of the organization;
- Ability of the health administration to achieve the strategic objectives.

Human resources are principally interested in:

- Proportional remuneration to the quality and quantity of work provided;
- Occupational health and safety;
- Possibility of career improvement;
- Stimulating, gratifying and involving work atmosphere.

10.5 A Wider Definition of Value for Public Health Organizations

According to the considerations elaborated above, the privileged stakeholders and their expectation towards health administrations were determined. Therefore the *health value* can be defined as *the satisfaction of (expressed or latent) health needs of single individuals or the community, respecting the objectives established by the public planning (national, regional, etc.), timely, in comfort conditions, without waste of resources, maintaining the conditions of economic, financial and capital balance, with the parallel social balance, enhancing the intellectual capital and guaranteeing the knowledge development and improvement in the medical and health sector.*

The definition of *health value* is manifold, as it takes into account different types of stakeholders and several needs to satisfy.

It is worth elaborating a few remarks on the different elements composing the definition of the *health value* proposed. Firstly the definition refers to the health need that should be interpreted in a broad sense.[4] This is a multifaceted[5] concept that assumes multiple activities, having reference to prevention, diagnosis, care and rehabilitation. This results contemporaneously into (Marinò 2001):

(1) Individual care performances (more or less complex);
(2) Collective performances, where the individual share of use cannot be identified (for instance the prevention services).

This need may vary, as it modifies depending on several elements (cultural level of the population, life standards, etc.). Moreover it is potentially unlimited. Therefore, with a limited quantity of resources, it is necessary to define upstream the health levels to guarantee.

In the proposed definition reference is made to the satisfaction of both the *expressed* and *latent* health need. This implies that the health administrations are requested to perform services following specific requests of users but should also be able to perform services not specifically requested, in order to contribute to the overall improvement of the health state of the community (for example: preventive screening promoted by the health organizations in favor of specific subjects categories).

An additional element of the proposed definition is the *respect of the objectives established by public planning (national, regional, etc.)*, this implying a case of *internal effectiveness*.

The *timely* satisfaction of the health need and *in comfort conditions* determines on the other hand an element of *external effectiveness*, connected with the quality of the service performed.[6]

---

[4] The World Health Organization (WHO) defines the health as the "state of physical, psychic and social wellbeing and not simply the absence of sickness or infirmity".

[5] "The objective of the public intervention in the health sector is to reduce any suffering, prolonging and improving the quality of life. Several studies had to cope with the difficulty to reach satisfying levels of knowledge regarding the health state of the population; these difficulties are linked to the high uncertainty of defined relations between interventions and health conditions, in the great differentiation that the same pathology may assume, in the space and time that elapse between intervention and measuring of the outcome. It should not be disregarded that the health state is not only a consequence of health interventions, but also and not marginally, of other elements as environment, life and self-control conditions of individuals". (Anselmi and Saita 2002).

[6] Reference is made to the necessity to guarantee timely and patient-friendly services in addition to welcoming and accessible structures.

The reference to the *absence of resources waste* implicitly refers to good conditions of *efficiency*.

Moreover, the maintenance of conditions of *economic and financial balance*, which are all elements that can be highlighted through the traditional financial statement data, is a necessary (but not sufficient condition) condition to guarantee the survival of the organization.

The proposed definition refers furthermore to the concept of *social balance*. This concept assumes first of all the presence of *social effectiveness*. The latter can be considered as *external effectiveness*,[7] which is the ability of the organization to perform services that meet the needs of the community (in a quantitative and qualitative way). In this specific case, the social balance is achieved when the community attributes to the health performances a higher utility as compared to the resources (taxes, prescription charges, etc.) that are required to guarantee the performances of the services themselves.

The concept of social balance is extremely difficult to be quantified. It should be taken into account that:

• Whereas it is not particularly problematic to measure the inputs in the production process (resources collected from the community), it is much more difficult to attribute a value to the health outputs and outcomes;
• Due to the needs of equalization, redistribution and to the presence of individual and collective demand services, the subjects that contribute to the funding of the health system are not necessarily the same (in identity and quantity) who benefit of the services provided.

Moreover the *health value* assumes the presence of an *organizational environment* favorable to the satisfaction of the *intellectual capital* expectations. This is a detail of particular relevance in any organization and to a greater extent, in the health administrations, where the relationship with patients is a key variable for the performances effectiveness and perceived quality. The approach here proposed presumes that the attention for the intellectual capital is linked to the analysis of the employed leadership style. It is known that the leadership style (causal variable) impacts on employees' level of satisfaction (intercurrent variable) and ultimately on the overall administration's performance (resulting variable). It is assumed that in public health administrations, that are subject to frequent turnover at the management level, the overall *health value* is influenced by the leadership style adopted and by the related organizational environment.

The proposed definition assumes that the ability of the administration to develop knowledge, competences and skills to guarantee *progress in the medical and health field* has an influence on the *health value*. In conclusion, the research

---

[7] According to the business economics doctrine, there is distinction between managerial effectiveness and social effectiveness. The managerial effectiveness refers to the "assessment on the qualitative and quantitative suitability of the service provided compared to the objectives" whereas the social effectiveness refers to the "modification of need driven by the offer of services". (Farneti et al. 1996).

and scientific knowledge (and consequently the medical and technical knowledge) impact on the *health value* enabling an improvement of citizens' and community care conditions and health. Public health administrations can provide a twofold contribution to the medical and health development:

(a) Directly, through research activity;
(b) Indirectly, with the updating and personnel retraining on research outcomes of other institutions.

10.6 Conclusions

This chapter tried to provide a definition of the overall value produced by public health administrations, analyzing the expectation of the main stakeholders and the contribution of these institutions for their fulfillment. This value configuration was called *health value*.

Through an analysis of the aspects composing this value, it appeared that the traditional economic and financial elements are only a part of the utilities that the public health administrations produce. The large part of this value cannot be expressed through data translated in monetary terms. For instance, the *health value* strongly depends on the effectiveness of health protection activities: this can be submitted to a qualitative evaluation whereas it is very difficult to quantify it.

The *health value* is composed of many elements that cannot be measured through the traditional accounting data, this enabling to express an assessment of the administration performance much broader than the one produced by financial statement data (forecast and actual amounts).

The concept of social responsibility shares some common points with the definition of health value. According to the definition proposed by the European Commission, the *corporate social responsibility* (CSR) is "a concept whereby companies integrate social and environmental concerns in their business operations and in their interaction with their stakeholders on a voluntary basis".

This definition, that specifically refers to private profit-making companies, is similar to the approach called *public sector social responsibility*, that is increasingly involving public administrations. Recently, public organizations introduced important innovation elements in accounting and financial disclosure, mainly with reference to the following aspects (Pollifroni 2007):

(a) Harmonization, at international level, of financial and accounting systems;
(b) Inclusion of additional elements (strategic planning and management control), once used almost exclusively in private companies, into the traditional financial statement;
(c) Adaptation in public administration of corporate social responsibility instruments, created in the private context.

The implementation of the public sector social responsibility logic implied several important modifications to the information system of these organizations, mainly in the following two aspects (Pollifroni 2007):

(a) Limitation of discretionary in accounting the achieved results;
(b) Enlargement of the disclosure in advantage of all the stakeholders of reference.

In the same way to move towards the *health value* logic implies focusing on elements of the produced value that are not limited to economic-financial aspects (highlighted by the traditional accounting approach). Thus the discretionary accounting is limited and some basic management elements of a certain importance for the stakeholders have to be provided. Therefore, the choice on the information to be provided is not left on the total discretion of financial statement drafters, but is bound to the main stakeholders needs of knowledge.

The implementation of the *health value*, as essential objective for all the public health administrations, presumes:

• to monitor all its key elements;
• to provide to all the stakeholders information on the administration ability to create value in several areas, corresponding to their expectations;
• to determine areas of value where to carry on improvement interventions in the future.

According to the authors of this chapter, an entity that creates value for each category of stakeholders of reference is to be considered as socially responsible, as it generates a utility to the advantage of all the stakeholders.

With specific reference to public health administrations, the seven areas that constitute the *health value* are mandatory for them to be considered as socially responsible. Several instruments supporting the public sector social responsibility (for instance: social accounts, mandate account, etc.) should enable to highlight the seven areas of the *health value*.

As previously stated, some of these areas are not included in the traditional financial statement documents. Their inclusion would increase and improve the public health administrations accountability and transparency. The proposed definition of *health value* could constitute a support to public health organizations for the build up and adoption of public sector social responsibility practices. This helps to identify:

• the elements to be tackled in order for the public health authority to create value for the stakeholders;
• which types of information should be added to the traditional financial statement, in order to provide factual answers to the stakeholders with reference to their requirements.

The concept of *health value* could therefore constitute a principle of reference to build up documents supporting the public sector social responsibility (for instance social balance). The *health value* can indicate the areas of information to be implemented (should the health administration not provide such information yet), strengthened and improved, in order to enhance the mandatory financial statement with additional voluntary information. Furthermore, the overall analysis of all the information on the *health value* could enable to formulate a general assessment on the administration ability to create value for all its stakeholders. Thus the performances assessment could be carried on:

- individually, for each area of value (for instance with reference to the economic situation, the financial situation, the contribution provided to medical knowledge, care and prevention effectiveness, etc.);
- on the whole, for all the areas composing the *health value*.

References

Anselmi, L., Saita, M. (eds.) (2002). *La gestione manageriale e strategica nelle aziende sanitarie.* L'evoluzione del sistema sanitario nella prospettiva federale, Il Sole 24 Ore, Milano.

Bergamaschi, M. (2009). *Creazione del valore e organizzazione in sanità.* Milano: McGraw-Hill.

Costa, M. (2005). *Le aziende di formazione professionale.* Profili sistematici e determinazioni di ragioneria, Torino: Giappichelli.

Farneti, G., Mazzara, L., & Savioli, G. (1996). *Il sistema degli indicatori negli enti locali.* Torino: Giappichelli.

Marinò, L. (2001). *Dinamiche competitive ed equilibrio economico nelle aziende sanitarie.* Milano: Giuffrè.

Moore, M. H. (1995). *Creating public value: strategic management in government.* Cambridge: Harvard University Press.

Moore, M.H. (1997). *Creating public value: strategic management in government.* Cambridge: Harvard University Press.

Moore, M.H. (2003). *La creazione di valore pubblico.* Guerini e Associati, edizione italiana a cura di Sinatra A., Milano

Pollifroni, M. (2007). *Public sector social responsibility.* Strumenti di rendicontazione etico-sociale per l'azienda pubblica. Giuffrè, Milano.

Valotti, G. (2005). *Management pubblico.* Temi per il cambiamento. Egea, Milano.

Part IV
Ethics, Morality and CSR in Corporations

Chapter 11
The Two Walmarts

Phillip Gordon

Abstract Walmart has gained a significant reputation as both a sustainable business and a proponent of, and leader in, sustainability. But Walmart seems to be two companies: one which can embrace sustainability outside itself, in its supply chain, and one which does not embrace CSR inside itself, towards employees and the communities where it does business. Walmart's culture of cost containment creates the two Walmarts, one which can do outward facing sustainability activities and the other which is incapable of doing inward facing sustainability.

11.1 Introduction

If we use the Triple Bottom Line (Savitz and Weber 2006) as the definition of a complete, integrated CSR framework, then a for profit company, in addition to the obvious need to make a Profit, must also pay attention to and do something about People and Planet. Of course, no CSR activity, including simple corporate donations, should be denigrated, but the ideal CSR framework would include People and Planet.

Planet is, in general, an external facing CSR concern, involving activities which often don't require a company to make changes in their internal facing policies, procedures, processes, and culture. This aspect of CSR is often called Sustainability (Werther and Chandler 2006), although some think that sustainability embraces all of CSR, and companies sometimes use the term synonymously with CSR. Companies can make changes to products and services, save energy, buy

P. Gordon (✉)
Lokey Graduate School of Business, Mills College, UC-Berkeley, Norwegian School of Management, Berkeley, USA
e-mail: ucgordon@gmail.com

A. Yüksel Mermod and S. O. Idowu (eds.), *Corporate Social Responsibility in the Global Business World*, DOI: 10.1007/978-3-642-37620-7_11,
© Springer-Verlag Berlin Heidelberg 2014

carbon offsets, adhere to and advocate for environmental standards, and do a wide variety of other activities to benefit the environment.

The external facing changes required by Planet activities might require some, usually minor, changes to policies, procedures, and processes, but generally not to the culture, since they can be implemented through standard management decision making, and are not viewed as cultural changes. In fact, in some companies, they are used as "window dressing," and are noted as such by external parties (TerraChoice 2007).

People activities, on the other hand, can include, among other things, actions in benefit of employees and communities where business takes place, and therefore often require changes to internal facing policies, procedures, processes, changing, to a greater or lesser extent, the corporate culture.

> [Culture is] a set of basic assumptions–invented, discovered, or developed by a given group as it learns to cope with its problems of external adaptation and internal integration–that has worked well enough to be considered valid, and therefore, to be taught to new members as the correct way to perceive, think and feel in relation to those problems (Schein 1985).

Culture, in other words, both defines and limits what a company sees, thinks, and does. Despite the fact that business schools, management consultants, and the media portray business people as rational machines, they are still human, and exist in a culture, which can affect their decisions and even prevent action.

> I came to see, in my time at IBM, that culture isn't just one aspect of the game; it is the game. Lew Gerstner, former Chairman of the Board and CEO, IBM (Seidman 2007).

> There is nothing more difficult to carry out, nor more doubtful of success, nor more dangerous to handle, than to initiate a new order of things. For the reformer has enemies in all who profit from the old order... (Machiavelli 1532).

Changing culture is extremely difficult because it first requires that a company realize it has a culture, and then take steps to change it (Cox 2008). Changing culture requires changing "behaviours, beliefs, social interactions and nature of decision making" (Charan 2006). The changes will almost invariably meet with resistance, both passive and active, because employees have a vested interest in the old culture, since it defines who they are and what they do (Want 2003; Cox 2008). This sort of profound change often fails, and many times barely gets off the ground or is simply not even attempted (Kotter 1995).

Even companies in a crisis, where cultural change is seen to be necessary, may fail to carry out the cultural transformation (Kotter 1995).

This article will show that Walmart, because of its culture, seems split into two companies, one capable of leading edge Planet activities and the other incapable of changing to allow it to aggressively and successfully address People issues; where the culture of the "second" Walmart in fact appears to drive it to carry out extensive anti-People activities.

11.2 Planet and Walmart

Walmart is a striking example of a company which has not only been able to carry out a complex set of Planet-related CSR activities, but to become a world leader in Sustainability (Hume 2011). All it took was one person, Jib Ellison, a consultant, persuading Walmart's then CEO, H. Lee Scott Jr., that Sustainability eliminated waste, and therefore saved money.

Studies by a Walmart management team and Ellison's consulting company had identified high-impact areas, most of which would result from actions by suppliers, which would also, not incidentally, save Walmart money (Stanford Graduate School of Business, revised 6 December 2010).

Scott announced Walmart's sustainability strategy in October 2005 in the first company-wide broadcast. Walmart would significantly reduce its impact on the environment, guided by three goals: (1) use 100 % renewable energy; (2) create zero waste; (3) sell products that sustain resources and the environment (Stanford Graduate School of Business, revised 6 December 2010).

Ellison demonstrated the possible savings by suggesting a reduction in the packaging for one product, toy trucks, reducing costs by millions of dollars. Walmart followed up by reducing packaging in many product lines, saving an estimated $3.4 billion a year, as well as greatly reducing cardboard trash.

Internal changes were minimized: rather than creating a major sustainability group, Walmart added sustainability to existing jobs (Stanford Graduate School of Business, revised 6 December 2010). Although this helped insure that sustainability was seen as a core activity, it also fit with Walmart's culture, since it was simply another cost-cutting activity, and everyone at Walmart was already responsible for that.

The one major cultural change resulting from Walmart's sustainability initiative was the decision to reach out aggressively for advice and collaboration, something that had never happened on that scale before as Walmart's insular culture had kept it from seeking advice on operations (Stanford Graduate School of Business, revised 6 December 2010).

Walmart has expanded its Sustainability activities by requiring suppliers to do things like provide double-strength laundry detergent, and ending the sale of incandescent bulbs in favor of compact fluorescents.

In 2009 Walmart initiated a Sustainability Index (SI—Fact Sheet, ND) for every product it sells, becoming a world leader in eco-efficient products, and providing a measure which can be used not only by Walmart for its products, but by consumers, other companies, and by organizations which promote and monitor Sustainable products. As part of the SI efforts, Walmart is partnering with universities to create a global database of product cradle-grave lifecycle information.

In association with the Index, Walmart is requiring a Supplier Sustainability Assessment (SSA), starting in July 2009 with 15 questions and expanding to a full survey (15 Questions for Suppliers, ND). Suppliers as well as their products will be scored, and although the SSA is not mandatory, it is obvious that suppliers will feel pressured to respond as well as to improve their scores.

Even before the SI and SSA, Walmart in 2008 announced a major initiative in China, a Sustainability Summit. The intention was to "drive innovation and sustainable business practices throughout our company and those of our suppliers and is focused on three objectives:

- Build a world-class, high-value sustainable supply chain;
- Sell sustainable products in China and around the world; and
- Become the best-in-class sustainable retailer in China." (Sustainability Summit 2008)

One of the main reasons why Walmart has concentrated on Planet-related activities relates both to its business model and its culture: cost savings gained through its supply chain. For example, Walmart expects to save $12 billion by 2013 by reducing packaging by 5 % from 2006 levels (Bonini and Görner 2011).

Walmart also benefitted from its Sustainability activities by improving its image and tying into an interest in the environment on the part of many of the women who are its primary customers.

Unfortunately, Walmart's culture, which requires it to grow, can conflict with its Planet-related activities: since launching its campaign in 2005, its store footage, which among other things requires materials and energy, has grown 168 million square feet in the US, and the number of stores outside the US has grown by almost 3,000. (Mitchell 2011)

While Walmart has saved about 1.5 million metric tons of CO_2 each year in its stores built before 2006, its stores generates about 3.5–3.9 million metric tons each year, and its purchases of renewable energy constitute less than 2 % of its total electricity use (Mitchell 2011).

In China especially, Walmart has slowed or stopped its Planet activities, and its cost cutting requirements have driven a number of its major suppliers to use "shadow" manufacturers, whose operations generate significant amounts of pollution (Kroll and Jones 2012). This is a major problem because the 30,000 Chinese factories in Walmart's supply chain produce an estimated 70 % of the products it sells (Kroll and Jones 2012).

Despite the fact that Walmart had to be pushed into Sustainability through assaults on its image, and through lobbying, it did not have to change its basic culture, since one of the main tenets of that culture is low prices—saving money allows Walmart to keep prices low.

In addition, the vast majority of its Sustainability activities are outward-facing, requiring suppliers to make changes to their policies, procedures, and processes, something which is another core aspect of Walmart's culture as the company has always pressured suppliers for lower costs.

Campaign contributions are one telling indication that Walmart, for all its Planet-related activities and statements, has not changed it culture:

Since 2005, nearly 60 % of the $3.9 million Walmart has given to members of Congress went to lawmakers whose lifetime scores on the League of Conservation Voters' National Environmental Scorecard indicate they vote against the environment most of the time. More than 40 % of its donations went to lawmakers who vote against the environment at least 80 % of the time. (Institute for Local Self-Reliance 2012).

11.3 People and Walmart

With its cost-containment business model and culture, the cost of internal-facing CSR activities, which is required by the majority of People-oriented activities, would be a major stumbling block for Walmart, while at the same time it would be difficult for executives to understand where any savings or benefits might come from, since that is the primary way they measure all activities.

Since the Walmart culture is so focused on costs, and although they don't like negative publicity related to People issues, it is difficult for the company to undertake substantial People-related CSR activities. In fact, Walmart has responded to People-related issues in a way consistent with its culture, through attempts to refute its critics and offer positive publicity, a low cost effort which requires no internal-facing changes (Briones 2009).

Some of the People-related issues are a direct result of Walmart's cost conscious culture, such as managers forcing employees to work off the clock, requiring associates to skip lunch and short breaks, and tampering with time and wage records. By 2008 the company was facing 80 different lawsuits on these labor-related issues. (Wal-Mart Watch 2008)

Human Rights Watch in New York and the Clean Clothes Campaign in Europe have both pointed out that, in its effort to create a more ethical supply chain, a Planet-related activity, Walmart has actually promoted worker benefits and rights in other countries that it opposes in US unions (Birchall 2007).

The male-dominated Walmart culture also resulted in significant gender dis-crimination, including the largest class action suit in history, which was rejected in 2011 by the US Supreme Court (Wade 2011). In some ways, gender discrimination is also a result of the cost saving aspects of Walmart culture, as it allows the company to save money on a significant part of their labor force. The drive to keep costs down has also led Walmart to strongly resist unionization of its work force (Briones 2009).

Other People-related issues come from Walmart's significant impact on local communities and their small businesses. Studies have shown that some small towns lose up to 47 % of their retail trade within 10 years after a Walmart opens (Stone 1997; Mitchell 2007). Resistance to Walmart has been strong in rural communities across the US, and even in major cities like Chicago (Warren 2010), and in places like India, where small businesses serve many communities without major retailers (Bajaj 2011).

One reason Chicago might have been resistant to Walmart is a study which showed that opening of a Walmart on the West Side of Chicago in 2006 led to the closure of about one-quarter of the businesses within a four-mile radius. Businesses within close proximity of Walmart had a 40 % chance of closing. The probability of going out of business fell 6 % with each mile away from Walmart. These closures eliminated the equivalent of 300 full-time jobs, about as many Walmart added to the area (Davis et al. 2009).

A recent study has also shown that Walmart (along with other "big box" businesses) has a detrimental effect on the health of communities, with higher mortality, obesity, and diabetes where there are fewer small businesses (Blancharda et al. 2011).

Walmart's purchasing power regarding groceries—one-third of all food dollars are spent at Walmart and it is the largest buyer of American agricultural products—affects not only communities, but the entire agriculture industry, pushing it towards consolidation and industrialization (Food & Water Watch 2012).

Walmart's purchasing power has also led to loss of American jobs as major suppliers have been forced to move production offshore to meet Walmart's demand for lower prices, affecting the entire US economy and those communities where the plants were closed (Food & Water Watch 2012).

In 2010, labor unions and farmers accused Walmart of using its purchasing power to keep food costs artificially low (Bliss and Forden 2010). Given both its opposition to labor unions and its cultural obsession with lowering costs, this accusation would appear to have some credence.

Walmart has had other effects on local communities, also consistent with its cost-conscious culture, including aggressive attempts to lower its local taxes (Drucker 2007). They used accounting firms to gather ideas, issuing a letter to those firms in 2001:

> Wal-Mart is requesting your proposal(s) for professional tax advice and related implementation services in connection with minimization of state income taxes in the following states: Arizona, California, Florida, Illinois, Indiana, Michigan, Minnesota, and Pennsylvania.

These activities led to Walmart's paying, on average, "taxes at a rate equal to about half of the average statutory state rate over the past decade (1997–2007), according to an analysis of the company's regulatory filings by Standard & Poor's Compustat (Drucker 2007)."

One scheme, involving real estate trusts, in partnership with accounting firm Ernst & Young, led to a challenge by North Carolina.

Walmart has had additional negative effects on the local and state level through systematic attempts to lower its property taxes (Mattera et al. 2007). It is estimated that Walmart has challenged its assessments at more than 1000 stores, often in multiple years. In addition, a complete count reveals that 40 % of its distribution centers filed an assessment challenge, despite the fact that in many cases they were built because of property tax abatements granted by localities. Walmart's win rate for these challenges is about 50 %, due to active opposition by local authorities. All this activity is, of course, consistent with Walmart's cost-cutting culture.

Other community effects of Walmart include lowering the ability of families to move out of poverty. U.S. counties that had more Walmart stores in 1987 had a higher poverty rate in 1999 than did counties that started the period with fewer or no Walmart stores. Counties that added Walmart stores between 1987 and 1998 experienced higher poverty rates and greater usage of food stamps than counties where Walmart did not build, all other things being equal (Goetz and Swaminathan 2006).

Walmart has a major effect on employment in those communities where it operates.

A 2007 analysis suggested that, for every new retail job created by Walmart, 1.4 jobs are lost as existing businesses downsize or close. The study also found that the arrival of a Walmart store reduces total county-wide retail payroll by an average of about $1.2 million (Neumark et al. 2007).

Not surprisingly, the profound community effects of Walmart appear to decrease what sociologists call "social capital," the glue that holds communities together, including such things as voter participation and active community organizations (Goetz and Rupasingha 2006). Communities that gained a Walmart had fewer non-profit groups and social capital-generating associations (such as churches, political organizations, and business groups) per capita than those that did not. Walmart's presence also depressed civic participation and is associated with lower voter turnout.

At the state level, Walmart jobs contribute significantly to a demand for social services because they do not pay a living wage. For example, one study showed that California taxpayers were spending $86 million a year providing healthcare and other public assistance to the state's 44,000 Walmart employees (Institute for Industrial Relations 2004). The same study showed that Walmart workers earn 31 % less than the average for workers at large retail companies and require 39 % more in public assistance.

Nationwide, this effect of Walmart's low salaries (http://www.glassdoor.com/Salary/Walmart-Salaries-E715.htm, as of 15 Feb 2012.) on demand for social services leads to the average Walmart employee requiring $2,100 per year in public assistance, including Sect. 8 housing vouchers, reduced-cost lunches for dependent children, health care programs, and tax credits for the working poor (Democratic Staff of the House Committee on Education and the Workforce 2004).

An average Walmart associate, as of 2012, makes $8.85/hour, according to the Website glassdoor. As of 2011, about 900,000 Walmart workers, or 65 % of its U. S. workforce, are paid less than $12 an hour. More than one-fifth earn less than $9 an hour. Overall, Walmart's hourly workers earn 12.4 % less than retail workers as a whole (UC-Berkeley Center for Labor Research and Education 2011).

Walmart also appears to have a dampening effect on other retail salaries throughout the local area. Not only did Walmart lower average wage rates, but "every new Walmart in a county reduced the combined or aggregate earnings of retail workers by around 1.5 %. The study concluded that, nationally, workers lost $3.4 billion in earnings in 2000 (Dube et al. 2007).

One other effect of Walmart on local and state communities is that it takes advantage of a tax law that lets it retain some of the sales taxes it collects, allowing it to take in about $1 billion a year. In addition, it receives sales tax rebates or funding part of its projects with sales tax increment financing from states, which amounted to $130 million over a decade (Mattera and McIlvaine 2008). Walmart is not the only retailer to take advantage of these tax benefits, but since it is the largest, it gets the most.

Again, this tax harvesting is simply an outgrowth of its cost-cutting culture, as well as, of course, the constant battle of states to attract retailers for jobs. Nationally, 244 Walmart stores and distribution centers in 35 states have received state and local development subsidies totaling just over $1 billion (Mattera et al. 2004).

Walmart tends to address People-related issues through cash contributions and donations from local stores for such things as disaster relief, which is consistent with its culture: contributions require no internal facing changes, generate positive publicity, and can also be tax deductible (Briones 2009).

Walmart has done some non-contribution People-related activities, but those are mostly ones which are external-facing, and could be considered extension of its Sustainability activities. For example, they announced that in 2012 they will reduce the fat, sugar, and sodium levels in a number of private-label foods, will note healthy foods throughout their stores, and will work to lower the prices of healthy foods (Weise 2012).

Walmart has made strides towards providing health care for its employees. In a 2008 speech by then CEO Lee Scott, it was noted that "nearly 93 %" of associates had health care, compared to an average of 82 % of all US workers. This does not indicate, however, the quality of the health care plans provided, or the amounts paid by employees for those plans—one study outlines the out-of-pocket costs, coverage limitations, and eligibility requirements for the retailer's health insurance plan, and compiles information on what various states are spending to provide Medicaid to uninsured Walmart employees and their children (Bernhardt et al. 2005).

And a 2005 internal Walmart memo reports that only 48 % of the company's employees are enrolled in its insurance plan, compared to an average of 68 % for national employers. Excessive out-of-pocket costs, including expensive premiums and high deductibles, are to blame: "Our coverage is expensive for low-income families, and Walmart has a significant percentage of Associates and their children on public assistance." Employees enrolled in Walmart's insurance plan spend an average of 8 % of their income on health care, nearly twice the national average. Almost 40 % spend more than 16 % of their income, a crippling cost for workers who earn less than $20,000 a year on average. The EVP author of the memo recommended a strategy that included dissuading unhealthy people from working at Walmart, and increasing part-time workers who do not get benefits (Chambers 2005).

Consistent with its cost-cutting culture, and in apparent contradiction to its CEO's concern with employee health care, Walmart has made attempts to claw back health care outlays from employees, making use of a little-noticed clause in their health plans regarding payments from multiple sources, including damage awards, a legal provision called "subrogation (Fuhrmans 2007)." In one case, where an employee was brain-damaged and confined to a wheelchair as a result of a collision with a truck, Walmart demanded and was awarded by the courts, $417,000 that was to be used for her care. It should be noted that Walmart is not the only company using subrogation against their employees.

In China, where many thousands of workers produce for Walmart, poor work conditions exist in the many shadow factories:

> In 2009, the advocacy group China Labor Watch obtained documents from a Walmart packaging supplier on how to hide or adjust safety and environmental records; how workers should lie to auditors about wages, benefits, and working hours; and how to conceal a shadow factory. Another investigation by the group uncovered forced overtime, phony pay stubs, poor living conditions, and the use of hazardous chemicals at a Walmart shoe factory. (Kroll and Jones 2012).

11.4 Can Walmart Change its Culture?

Walmart, even if it desired to, would find it difficult, if not impossible, to change its culture in order to do more People-oriented activities. Cost consciousness is at the core of Walmart's business model, and is ingrained in its culture, leading to the many anti-People activities cited above. In addition, low prices are the primary way that Walmart competes.

For Walmart, then, changing its culture might mean becoming something else, which is no easier for an organization than it is for a person. It could, it is true, become less predatory in regard to tax benefits and associate salaries, while retaining its culture, but that would affect its competitiveness.

Thus, there is no simple solution for Walmart's anti-People activities as long as its existence depends on remaining cost-competitive.

References

Bajaj, V. (2011). Wal-Mart Debate Rages in India, NY Times, 5 Dec 2011.
Bernhardt, A., Chaddha, A., McGrath, S. (2005). What do we know about Wal-Mart? Brennan Center for Justice, Aug 2005.
Birchall, J. (2007). Charity towards trades unions begins: but not at home. Financial Times, 10 Sep 2007.
Blancharda, T. C., Tolbertb, C., & Mencken, C. (2011). The health and wealth of US counties: how the small business environment impacts alternative measures of development. *Cambridge Journal of Regions, Economy Society, 5*(1), 149–162.

Bliss, J., & Forden, S. (2010). Wal-Mart Targeted by Labor Union, Farmers on Antitrust Claims, Bloomberg, 14 Sep 2010, www.bloomberg.com/news/print/2010-09-14/wal-mart-accused-by-labor-union-farmers-of-suppressing-agriculture-prices.html.

Bonini, S., & Görner, S. (2011). The Business of Sustainability. McKinsey & Company.

Briones, R. (2009). Did Wal-Mart Wake Up?: how strategic management handled Wal-Mart's reputation. Case study submitted for the Arthur W. Page Society Case Study Competition.

Reviewing and Revising Wal-Mart's Benefits Strategy, Memo to the Wal-Mart Board of Directors from Susan Chambers, Wal-Mart EVP for benefits, Oct 2005.

Charan, R. (2006). Home Depot's Blueprint for culture change. *Harvard Business Review*.

Cox, V. (2008). What is organizational culture and how can you change it? iProCon HCM Insight, May 2008.

Davis, J., Merriman, D., Samayoa, L., Flanagan, B., Baiman, R., Persky J. (2009). The Impact of an Urban Wal-Mart Store on Area Businesses. Center for Urban Research and Learning, Loyola University, Dec 2009.

Democratic Staff of the House Committee on Education and the Workforce (2004). Everyday low wages: The hidden price we all pay for Wal-Mart, Feb 2004.

Drucker, J. (2007). Inside Wal-Mart's Bid To Slash State Taxes. *Wall Street Journal*.

Dube, A., Lester, T.W., Eidlin, B. (2007). A downward push: the impact of Wal-Mart stores on retail wages and benefits. UC-Berkeley Center for Labor Research and Education, Dec 2007.

Food & Water Watch (2012). Why Walmart Can't Fix the Food System, Feb 2012.

Fuhrmans, V. (2007). Accident victims face grab for legal winnings. *Wall Street Journal*.

Goetz, S., Swaminathan, H. (2006). Wal-Mart and county-wide poverty. *Social Science Quarterly*.

Goetz, S.J., Rupasingha, A. (2006). Wal-Mart and social capital. *American Journal of Agricultural Economics*.

Hume, E. (2011) Force of Nature. Harper Business.

Institute for Industrial Relations (2004). Hidden cost of Wal-Mart jobs. UC-Berkeley, Aug 2004.

Institute for Self-Reliance (2012). Top 10 ways Walmart fails on sustainability, Apr 2012.

Kotter, J.P. (1995). Leading change: Why transformation efforts fail. *Harvard Business Review*.

Kroll, A., Jones, M. (2012). Are Walmart's Chinese factories as bad as Apple's? Mar/Apr 2012.

Machiavelli, N. (1532). The Prince.

Mattera, P., Purinton, A., McCourt, J., Hoffer, D., Greenwood, S., Talanker, A. (2004). Shopping for subsidies: How wal-mart uses taxpayer money to finance its never-ending growth. Good Jobs First, May 2004.

Mattera, P., Walter, K., Blain, J.F., Ruddick, C. (2007). Rolling back property tax payments: How Wal-Mart short-changes schools and other public services by challenging its property tax assessments. Good Jobs First, Oct 2007.

Mattera, P., McIlvaine, L. (2008). Skimming the sales Tax: How Wal-Mart and other big retailers (Legally) keep a cut of the taxes we pay on everyday purchases. Good Jobs First, Nov 2008.

Mitchell, S. (2007). *Big-Box Swindle: The true cost of mega-retailers and the fight for America's independent businesses*. Boston: Beacon Press.

Mitchell, S. (2011). Walmart by the numbers: Green vs. Growth, Grist.org, 7 Nov 2011 http://grist.org/business-technology/2011-11-07-walmart-by-the-numbers-green-vs-growth/.

Neumark, D., Zhang, J., Ciccarella, S. (2007). The effects of Wal-Mart on local labor markets. IZA discussion paper No. 2545, Jan 2007.

Savitz, AW., Weber, K. (2006). *The triple bottom line*. San Francisco, CA: Jossey-Bass.

Schein, E.H. (1985). *Organizational culture and leadership*. Francisco, CA: Jossey-Bass.

Seidman, D. (2007). *How: Why how we do anything means everything*, Expanded Edition. New York: Wiley.

Stanford Graduate School of Business (2010). Walmart's sustainability strategy (A), case OIT-71. 17 Apr 2007, revised 6 Dec 2010.

Stone, K.E. (1997). Impact of the Wal-Mart phenomenon on rural communities. In *Proceedings: Increasing Understanding of Public Problems and Policies*.

TerraChoice Environmental Marketing Inc (2007). The "Six Sins of Greenwashing": A study of environmental claims in North American consumer markets Nov 2007.

UC-Berkeley Center for Labor Research and Education (2011). Living wage policies and big-box retail: how a higher wage standard would impact Wal-Mart workers and shoppers, Apr 2011.

Sustainable Product Index: Fact Sheet, Wal-Mart, ND   http://news.walmart.com/news-archive/2009/07/16/walmart-announces-sustainable-product-index

Sustainability Product Index: 15 Questions for Suppliers, Wal-Mart, ND   http://news.walmart.com/news-archive/2009/07/16/walmart-announces-sustainable-product-index

Sustainability Summit (2008). Beijing http://walmartstores.com/Sustainability/8685.aspx.

Remarks as Prepared for Lee Scott, CEO and President of Wal-Mart Stores, Inc. (2008). The Company of the Future, Wal-Mart U.S. Year Beginning Meeting January 23, 2008 http://www.walmartfacts.com/articles/5625.aspx.

Wal-Mart Watch (2008). Issues: Labor Relations.

Wade, L. (2011). The data behind the Walmart gender discrimiination lawsuit. Sociological Images, posted 20 Jun, at 11:00 am http://thesocietypages.org/socimages/2011/06/20/the-data-behind-the-walmart-not-yet-class-action-lawsuit/.

Want, J. (2003). Corporate culture: Illuminating the Black Hole. *Journal of Bus Strategy*, Jul/Aug 2003.

Warren, J. (2010). How Wal-Mart Won Chicago. Business Week 19 Jul 2010.

Weise, K. (2012). Wal-Mart: A new label for healthy food. Bloomberg Business Week, 13-19 Feb 2012.

Werther, W.B. Jr., & Chandler, D. (2006). *Strategic corporate social responsibility: Stakeholders in a global environment* (pp. 7). Beverley Hills, CA: Sage Publications.

Chapter 12
Cultural Heritage and Women: The Case of Beypazari

Melike Kaplan and Zuhal Yonca Odabas

Abstract This study builds upon the data acquired in a fieldwork made in Ankara's Beypazari County between the months of April and May 2012. The point of departure of the study is the locomotive role of women, who produce and sell traditional hand labor products for commercial purposes, in the revival of cultural tourism in Beypazari county and, therefore, in the publicity of the county in general. The fieldwork was shaped by face-to-face interviews with women who produce and sell intergenerationally transmitted homemade food, jewelery and hand loomed products and by observations, made in Beypazari County center which is a lively touristic place where traditional hand labor products are being sold to tourists. The study seeks to present an evaluation from the perspective of *women* who are the producers of items that could be described as cultural heritage.

12.1 Introduction

Beypazarı County is located in an area 99 km northwest of Ankara. It has a congested structure in the center with two- and three-storey buildings. Due to its location and to the fact that traditional architecture is under protection, new settlements are located in the periphery of the old city, especially, on the road that connects the county with the capital city. Tourism in Beypazari has been revived through the pioneering role of Mansur Yavaş who has served as the Mayor between 1999 and 2008. Today, Beypazari has 3,500 houses of which 500 have been renovated, 20 religious structures, and a historical bazaar with 600 shops (Yavaş 2006, 6).

Z. Y. Odabas (✉)
Ataturk University, Ankra, Turkey
e-mail: yoncaodabas@yahoo.com

M. Kaplan
Ankara University, Ankra, Turkey

A. Yüksel Mermod and S. O. Idowu (eds.), *Corporate Social Responsibility in the Global Business World*, DOI: 10.1007/978-3-642-37620-7_12,
© Springer-Verlag Berlin Heidelberg 2014

In the 1990s, Beypazari started a *regional economic development* process, with the initiative of local government, through a project which was designed to enable renovation of houses with regional attributes, similar to *listed buildings*, is European countries. The start of this project stimulated some other activities in the county and led to significant increases in the number of incoming tourists. Even though this initiative in Beypazari had a single objective, other sectors were also positively affected by the process. Development initiative in Beypazari accelerated as the public started realizing the resources the county has. The process started with the leadership of the local government and progressed with the help of the university, the private sector, and the NGOs and the county's economic livelihood became remarkable in recent years (Altınkaya Özmen 2007, 95–96).

In addition to its traditional architecture, the most important aspect of Beypazarı tourism today is shopping (Kara 2011; Takano 2008). Yet, previous studies made in Beypazari paid little or no attention to the women; to the *producers* of traditional products which remain the principal elements of shopping. Cultural heritage, being transmitted from one generation to another through traditions, is re-evaluated in this study with a special emphasis on women.

Apart from Beypazari's being a source suitable for cultural tourism such as archaeological relics, thermal waters, eco-tourism, and agriculture, today the most preferred type of tourism is the "heritage tourism" which originates from traditional architecture of the past and folklore and presents these via museums, architecture, clothing, and nutrition (Christou 2005, 5–8). This new fact that is called *heritage* or *cultural* tourism can also be found within the urbanization-related discussions of neo-liberal policies. Üçer et al. (2008) emphasize this when they note that, in a globalizing world, culture needs to be capitalized as an element of the economic competition among countries. Therefore, hybrid formations within which the local and global meet come into existence. This process through which culture becomes a commodity can be understood in four stages (Günay 2008): the shift from cultural assets to cultural heritage, the shift from regeneration-led conservation to conservation-led regeneration, the shift from state-governance to entrepreneurial governance, and the shift from citizens to users. These may imply that the importance of the local is ignored and that the development policy is pursued under the hegemony of large-scale capitalists and media. On the other hand, it can be said that cultural tourism in Turkey has had a path that is different from these practices. As noted by Günay (2008), these practices that essentially are for protection and related with museums include the meeting of historical, cultural, and architectural elements with economic and functional potentials. In this context, Beypazarı may be seen as an important model.

An example of the commercialization of traditional products, that is, the commoditization of culture, in Beypazarı is *the Living Museum*. Established as a private enterprise in an old Beypazarı mansion, the Living Museum has a perspective that attaches importance to the interaction between exhibited items and visitors in the transmission of cultural elements across generations. That a high proportion of museum personnel are women shows the effectiveness of women's social capital in cultural transmission. The storyteller grandmother who tells fairytales originated in the county and the women who melt lead and pour it into cold water to putatively break evil spells give life to the museum.

12.2 Cultural Heritage

According to the European Union's predictions, cultural heritage will affect societies' living standards in the 21st century's global conditions just as the economy does. In fact, in some reports of the European Union, it was noted that cultural heritage is not only a moral or spiritual value for contemporary societies but also a unique economic resource, and tourism's importance in transforming cultural heritage into economic return is emphasized (Tahir 2007).

Though for many, tourism is solely about travel, entertainment, and resting, the number of those who participate in touristic activities to "meet with different cultures" is not low. Not only natural structure but also historical and cultural attributes play a role in the decision of where to travel. Intangible traditional heritage, in addition to traditionally produced tangibles, is among the cultural attributes that are of interest to tourists (Şahin 2009, 57). With the adoption of the **Convention for the Safeguarding of the Intangible Cultural Heritage** in UNESCO's 32nd General Conference in October 17, 2003, it became apparent that the concept of "cultural heritage" has a very rich area of usage. In the definitions given in the second article of the *Convention*, "*intangible cultural heritage* means the practices, representations, expressions, knowledge, skills (as well as the instruments, objects, artefacts and cultural spaces associated therewith) that communities, groups, and, in some cases, individuals recognize as part of their cultural heritage. This intangible cultural heritage, transmitted from generation to generation, is constantly recreated by communities and groups in response to their environment, their interaction with nature and their history, and provides them with a sense of identity and continuity, thus promoting respect for cultural diversity and human creativity" (Oğuz 2009, 167).

The domains in which cultural heritage is especially manifested include, among others, "the oral traditions and expressions of which language is a vehicle of the intangible cultural heritage, performing arts, social practices, rituals and festive events, knowledge and practices concerning nature and the universe, and traditional craftsmanship" (Oğuz 2009, 168). One can count traditional products of Beypazarı in this context, but the multifaceted nature of women's contribution to cultural heritage should also be emphasized. Trademarked homemade foods such as *güveç*, *yaprak dolması*, *ev eriştesi*, *Beypazarı kurusu*, and *baklava*, hand loom products, and embroidery work on silver and gold called *telkari*, all labeled by producer women "specific to us" as a part of their cultural heritage, can be interpreted within this classification. Similarly, *the International Festival of Beypazarı and Region*, the 13th of which has been held this year, can be regarded as an example of rituals and festive events, i.e. the vehicles of the transmission of heritage according to the Convention's definitions mentioned above.

Tradition is a part of culture, and the research over traditions contributes to the analysis of society in many respects. As emphasized by (Shils and Edward 2003, 108), traditions do not recreate themselves independently. Only the knowledge of living, knowing and desiring "people" can be applied to life, and what makes this knowledge "traditional" is its re-enactability and changeability. The transmitters of traditional knowledge are in the meantime the carriers of tradition. Women, with their place in the family and their fundamental function in child rearing, play a key role in carrying traditions and traditional applications. Women, whose two fundamental social identities are "wife" and "mother", assume more duties than men do in intergenerational cultural transmission. The fundamental roles and tasks that women undertake in child rearing via their *motherhood identity* strengthen the women's function in "the transmission of tradition." Numerous studies show that the creators and the transmitters of tradition are in general women (Acar-Savran and Tura Demiryontan 2008; Özçelik 2002; Gürsoy 1994).

12.3 Women in Beypazarı and Tourism

Activities of women who actively regenerate and commercialize material culture are in general focused on jewelery, hand loom, and homemade food, and it is not misleading to claim that these activities, in general, are fostered by women's social capital originating from their traditional roles.

The concept of "inequality" can, for analytical purposes, be approached under four headings. Due to (1) social class differences, (2) ethnic origin and racial diversity, (3) reflections of sex in social life, i.e. gender, and (4) the adverse situations the elderly face with, the concept implies that not all groups of society are in equal positions and that people in lower socio-economic layers and in minority groups, women, and the elderly remain disadvantageous against various problems. Development policies that take this discrimination into account target the empowerment of these disadvantageous groups and the sustainability of this empowerment. Within this context, it should be noted that the development initiative in Beypazarı has been planned under the direction of such targets. The declaration of the mayor of the time, Mansur Yavaş, in the line of "You produce, and I will buy all if you cannot sell." helped producer women to avoid uncertainty and directed them to start production.

12.3.1 Jewelry

One of the women interviewed—a producer and seller of jewelery and a mother of three stated that her purpose of being in the sector is *to obtain a material return*. That her daughters help her in making the jewelry demonstrates that there exists knowledge transmission from one generation to another. Another woman who also produces and sells jewelery and transmits knowledge emphasized that she taught this job to her daughter-in-law. However, her statement that she will do this until she finds a permanent job (to gain access to health services and social security) shows that she produces and sells jewelery primarily to make money. Almost all sellers in the open bazaar are women whereas those who sell in shops are mostly men. The only man who sells in the open bazaar stated that he does so because his wife, who actually produces the items, was ill at the time of the study. Additionally, it is remarkable, in the context of intergenerational transmission, that there are young girls who are majoring in university degrees in jewelry design in their departments and participating in kirmesses held in big cities. A look at the jewelry suggests that designs are in general popular and modern, instead of being "traditional", and similar to the contemporary models that one can find in big city shops.

12.3.2 Hand Loom and Other Textile Products with Traditional Patterns

There are three people in Beypazari who make prints on hand loomed products, two women and one man. In Beypazari, the one who wants to produce hand loomed products and sell them on stands has to obtain permission from the municipal authority. Besides, no one other than the producer can sell these products on stands. The municipal authority supports the production of hand loomed items and subsidizes it. Hand loomed items in Beypazari include the traditional dress for women called *bürgü*, table clothing, and various casual dresses. In general, the patterns used in these hand loomed products are inspired from Beypazarı houses and their distinctive architecture.

In addition to these, one can also see that some mass-produced textile products inspired by traditional patterns are being sold in open bazaars by women. One of these women stated that her husband supports her but mostly in financial matters. This situation can be read more in the line of the encouragement of women's participation in the labor force as an economic resource than the rise of womanhood consciousness. In general, it is not misleading to claim that the situation is similar for all interviewed women.

12.3.3 Homemade Food

Among the food products produced and sold in Beypazari, regional dishes such as *yaprak dolması*, *baklava*, *ev erİştesi*, *tarhana*, and *Beypazarı kurusu* come first. Carrot and its side products such as *cezerye*, carrot juice and Turkish delight are among the other food products sold in Beypazarı. Women are very active especially in the making of *yaprak dolması*, *baklava*, and *ev erişitesi*. The statement by one of the women who sells homemade food in a shop that she and some other women who make food for weddings do this for monetary purposes shows that women's role is central to *the marketing of tradition*. Woman who is the representer and the creator of tradition takes stage in the marketing as well. It is remarkable that entrepreneurs, producers, sellers, and buyers are women. It should also be noted that women very actively participate in the recycling process.

12.4 Culture Tourism and Folklorism

The content of folklore, a field of science defined as the recording of the public life by the ones concerned about the decline or the deterioration of tradition (in terms of folklorists) and of "authentic" values (as a result of the Industrial Revolution), expanded in subsequent centuries. That folklore products are now being created and diffused through platforms other than the traditional media such as radio, TV, and the Internet, that tradition is used in commercial spaces, and that there exist some interventions to tradition lead to new terms in folklore research such as *imitation of tradition*, *invention of tradition*, *marketing of tradition*, and *intervention to tradition*. That tourism activities in general focus on cultural heritage and especially on tradition naturally leads to new relations such as tourism-culture and tourism-tradition. The usage of traditional values in tourism activities, in particular, seem to be interpreted with the term *folklorism* in the sense of tradition utilized outside of its natural space (Şahin 2009, 51). The popularized and prominent "traditional products" of Beypazarı tourism can be evaluated within this context.

Considering that the term of culture covers a large area and at the end is about people, it is rather difficult to define culture tourism. In summary, culture tourism has two aspects (Pekin 2011, 150):

1. Cultural heritage (those belonging to past)
2. Living culture

    (a) Traditions, customs, folklore, religious beliefs, culinary, etc.
    (b) Contemporary cultural products, performing arts, outcome of all creative cultural industries

Culture tourism is an understanding of tourism that presents (1) natural and historical wealth, (2) cultural activities and contemporary art, (3) the output of culture industries, and (4) some socio-economic facts as touristic products to travelers. It covers not only the historical one but also the contemporary (Pekin 2011, 150–151). Pekin (2011) includes all cultural products such as "*all natural and cultural heritage, whether it is abstract or not, craftsmanship, ethnography, botanics, flora and fauna, folklore, traditional and contemporary lifestyle, culinary, drinking, etc.*" in this definition.

Building upon this classification, the handmade products by women in Bey-pazarı can be interpreted, the first and the foremost, as a tradition-custom part of living culture and secondarily in the area of folklore. Additionally, especially the food and the hand loomed products satisfy the definition of cultural heritage. For re-vitalization and re-generation, conceptualized as "the re-invention of tradition", can be achieved only by sustaining the traditions. Though change includes tendencies such as transformation and the adoption of innovations, women play the biggest role in the recreation of tradition.

Regina Bendix, who claims that "folklorism" is to cut off the folklore products from their context and to use them in larger areas, points to the facts that (1) the term *neofolklorism* was used instead of folklorism in France and Russia before 1960, neofolklorism meaning the adaptation of folklore products to progressed forms of music, art, and literature, (2) the term attributed to Hans Moser in Germany corresponds to situations such as that of a folk dance played for tourists with commercial purposes, and (3) the term is used in different meanings in different parts of Europe (Bendix 1997). Products made by women in Beypazarı are not different than a folk dance played for commercial purposes with respect to the context of usage. These products can be interpreted as *reinvented forms of tradition* presented to tourists for commercial purposes.

Viewed within the perspective of the relation between tourism and tradition, tourism opens new ways of travel for visitors with the help of tradition and tradition reaches a larger audience with the help of tourism. Emphasizing the importance of traditional products used in tourism for folklore research, Şahin (2009, 53–54) argues that taking out of the traditional from its natural environment and using it for various purposes such as tourism inevitably lead to some changes in the structure and the presentation forms of traditional products. It can be said that this is the case for traditional products sold to tourists in Beypazarı.

12.5 Conclusion

Initiatives in Beypazari can be seen as an example of the dissolution of the sharp distinction between the practical needs and roles of women, e.g. domestic duties, and the strategical needs and roles. In other words, it can be observed from this county's experience that the public space is being mixed with the private one.

A woman, being let out of the "home", obtains an "identity" that makes her sells wares in bazaars. Though the first stimulant was the intervention of local government, positive outcomes in time led more women to participate in the initiative.

The transformation in Beypazari with respect to tourism not only caused women to become economically stronger but also led to improvements in women's social status. In Günay's (2008) study, it is stated that, before 2000, it is not approved for a woman to go out alone. Today, however, women are visible in the public space.

It is seen that, in Beypazari, the local government and especially the mayor as a local leader played significant roles in the regional economic development initiative and in the process continuing today. The support of the university, the private sector, and the NGOs along with the local government were important in the improvement of the initiative. That institutional structure in regional scale is underdeveloped in Turkey and that sector—and region-specific programs cannot be implemented are true for Beypazari as well as other regions. In cultural and social sphere, on the other hand, it can be said that the regularly held festival and festive events contribute to the publicity of the county. Since the contribution of the transformation in the county to the cultural and social life is not reflected to the space as physical infrastructure, however, the development pace of cultural and social life remains slow (Altınkaya Özmen 2007, 95–96).

One of the most important issues in regional economic development is institutional structure. Those women producer in Beypazarı do not have institutional ties which result in them being disadvantaged in terms of sustainability of the production of traditional products. Despite the support of the local government, the women producer cannot act as a unified body. The prime target for these women is not the publicity of Beypazari but mostly the commercial gain originating from homemade food, jewelery, and hand loomed products. Thus, it is not plausible to think that there exists a common ground for *cooperation* for these women in this context.

In the process by which traditional products become touristic "commodities", the products made at home by women lose their attribute of being "traditional." The reason is that what is "for sale" is not the traditional one once it becomes available for sale; it is the "recreation" of the tradition in different forms and for different purposes. To conclude, a very important outcome of change and social transformation in Beypazari is that the women's role in the recreation and the marketing of tradition once again becomes clear.

References

Acar-Savran, G., & Tura Demiryontan, N. (2008). *Kadının Görünmeyen Emeği*. İstanbul: Maddeci Bir Feminizm Üzerine. Yordam Kitap.

Altınkaya Özmen C. (2007). Yerel Ekonomik Kalkınma Girişimi ve Etkileri: Beypazarı Örneği. Yüksek Lisans Tezi. Gazi Üniversitesi Fen Bilimleri Enstitüsü Şehir ve Bölge Planlama Anabilim Dalı.

Bendix, R. (1997). *"Folklorismus/Folklorism", folklore: an encyclopedia of bliefs, customs, tales, music, and art* (pp. 337–339). Santa-Barbara: ABC-CLIO.

Christou E. (2005). Heritage and cultural tourism: a marketing-focused approach. In M. Sigala, D. Leslie (Ed.) *International cultural tourism*. (pp 3–15). Oxford: Elsevier.

Gürsoy A. (1994). Traditional practices affecting the health of women and children. The basics of maternal and child health. İstanbul: İstanbul University Institute of Child Health-Unicef Turkey Health Education Directorate of Turkish Ministry of Health.

Kara, Ç. (2011). Turistik Ticari Halkbilimsel Ürünler ve Beypazarı, Milli Folklor, Year: 23 Number: 89, (pp 54-65). Ankara: Geleneksel Yayınları.

Oğuz, Ö. (2009). *Somut Olmayan Kültürel Miras Nedir?*. Ankara: Geleneksel Yayınları.

Adak, N. Ö. (2002). *Sağlık Sosyolojisi, Kadın ve Kentleşme*. İstanbul: Birey Yayıncılık.

Pekin, F. (2011). *Çözüm: Kültür Turizmi*. İletişim Yayınları: Turizm ve Kültür Politikaları. İstanbul.

Shils E (2003). "Gelenek". *Doğu Batı* - Düşünce Dergisi. Year: 7, Number: 25. (pp. 101–135). Ankara: Doğu Batı Yayınları.

Şahin H. İ. (2009). Dalyan ve Köyceğiz Çevresinde Gelenek, Turizm ve Folklorizm. Milli Folklor, Year: 21 Number: 82. (pp. 50-58). Ankara: Geleneksel yayınları.

Tahir M. (2007). Cultural tourism and the opportunities for presentation of the ethno cultural heritage. (online: vasil7penchev.files.wordpress.com*).

Takano A. (2008). Türkiye'de Turizm ve Kültür: Beypazarı'nda Turizm Gelişme Sürecinde Yerli Halk İle Turist Yabancılar Arasındaki Etkileşim Üzerine Etnolojik Bir İnceleme. Yüksek Lisans Tezi. Ankara Üniversitesi Sosyal Bilimler Enstitüsü Halkbilim Anabilim Dalı.

Üçer A., Gürer N., Sat N. A. (2008) Cultural tourism as a tool for sustainity local values: beypazarı case, paper presented at NIE-SEAGA conference—sustainability and southeast Asia, Singapore.

Yavaş M. (2006). Kentsel Dönüşüme Bir Örnek: Beypazarı. Geçmişten Geleceğe Yerel Kimlik (online: http://www.tarihikentler-birligi.org. Number: 8).

.

Chapter 13
The Challenges of a Peruvian Inclusive State

Vanina A. Farber

Abstract The objective of this chapter is to reflect on the specific challenges that the Peruvian state faces to become an inclusive State. It assesses the important role that the private sector can play, through corporate social responsibility and private public partnerships in realising the goal. For that purpose, various dimensions of social inclusion are analyzed in direct connection to the economic, social, political and cultural rights of each citizen. Urgent measures are described and analyzed in section two. Subsequently, section three presents some ideas on medium and long term policies, mainly education and the labor market issues. Section four includes some structural traits (informality, decentralization, discrimination) which constrained public policy options. The current challenge of establishing an Inclusive State in Peru is clearly to move from the rhetoric of social inclusion to a functional design and practice of collaborative governance and social responsibility.

13.1 Introduction

Throughout history, scholars and laymen have tried to define "State". Territory, population, law, bureaucracy, monopoly of force, external recognition… all these recurring elements of the most popular definitions undoubtedly facilitate the comprehension of that "philanthropic ogre"—in the words of the brilliant analogy drawn by Octavio Paz. The title of this work portrays the disproportionate size of state bureaucracy and the evil derived from the extension of socialism and Marxist ideologies in many Latin American countries during that historical period. The Ogre-State is perverse and deleterious, although social benefits accrued from its philanthropy with regard to the extension of education, health and labor rights to the majority of the population.

V. A. Farber (✉)
Graduate Business School, Universidad del Pacifico,
Av. Salaverry 2020, Lima 11, Lima, Peru
e-mail: farber_va@up.edu.pe

A. Yüksel Mermod and S. O. Idowu (eds.), *Corporate Social Responsibility in the Global Business World*, DOI: 10.1007/978-3-642-37620-7_13,
© Springer-Verlag Berlin Heidelberg 2014

One specific definition, as old as current, highlights a further fundamental, albeit sometimes forgotten, issue. Hugo Grotius, Dutch legal scholar and poet of the seventeenth century, claimed that the State is a "perfect body of free men, united together in order to enjoy rights and the common good." If a portion of these "united free men"—citizens—may not enforce their rights or if individual benefits prevail over public interest, then that perfect body we call State is severely affected. In other words, a State which is not oriented towards social inclusion is an imperfect State.

This analysis of the State focused on rights is, today, paramount for the contemporary Peruvian reality. In a context of growth and democratic stability, with savings and investment capacity, it is essential that the Peruvian State be regarded and employed as a means towards inclusion, in lieu of a tool of exclusion, without undermining its economic foundations at the same time. This new framework implies a quest for a State with public managers rather than beaurocrats pursuing public value (O'Flynn 2007).

Therefore, those who, at certain points in time, have State may capitalize on and enhance the resources of this astounding machinery in order to enable citizens to exercise their rights, thus working towards that elusive goal we call "social cohesion". Social cohesion is a European concept which has only recently been introduced into Latin American political discussion. ECLAC defined social cohesion as "the dialectic between instituted social inclusion and exclusion mechanisms and the responses, perceptions and attitudes of citizens towards the way these mechanisms operate." (ECLAC 2007: 18). Put differently, there is social cohesion when the gaps in the access to welfare by the different sectors of the population are bridged and when these sectors feel included in their own society.

Scholarly debates on the models of State and the funding of public policies which favor inclusion have recently multiplied, largely due to the 2008–2009 major international crisis, demographic changes in global population and the rapid growth of emerging economies. These discussions give rise to several questions and two certainties: (1) equitable and sustainable development requires the participation of a State able to redistribute and include; and (2) the welfare State, such as we knew it in developed countries in the last five or six decades, must evolve in order to continue guaranteeing social cohesion and inclusion. The role of the State actively promoting corporate social responsibilidy (CSR) initiatives also has sparked much attention as a way incorporating the private sector in the fight for sustainable development and social inclusion.

These concepts reflect, on the one hand, the exhaustion of models exclusively oriented towards the market proposed during the last decades of the last century, generically named the "Washington Consensus". On the other hand, they show that the State must streamline its traditional mainstays—education, health and pensions,—enhancing, in turn, coverage against other social risks related, for instance, to unemployment and poverty. In this respect, a stimulating idea is that of a "dynamizing State", defined as a structure for a more effective and efficient allocation of resources aimed at dynamizing economic and social players. This dynamization leads to an active citizenry, where each individual has the same opportunities to enhance their skills and exercise their rights freely. This dynamizing State creates the conditions necessary for inclusion: the philanthropic ogre becomes a just teacher, able to stimulate the skills of the people, fostering and facilitating full participation respecting the rules of the game. Obviously, the analysis conducted in the State of Peru cannot be a carbon copy of those in Europe or the United States. Nonetheless, the idea of a State able to dynamize social and economic players in furtherance of citizenry and inclusive development is alluring inasmuch as it allows, in a certain manner, to overcome regressive discussions over the relation between the public and private spheres. As many Latin American countries, Peru has gone through and suffered the adoption of policies wavering between the authoritarian control of the State and the *laissez faire* doctrine. It is high time to acknowledge that the State has a role to perform in social and economic development, but that this role must be stimulating, not oppressing.

Nevertheless, including and generating social cohesion is far from being a simple task, as revealed by Latin American history. Inclusion arises when the war against poverty and, especially, inequality is waged successfully. It should not be forgotten that one of the most distinctive traits of Latin America, in general, and Peru, in particular, is the gross inequality of income, exacerbated by racial, sexual or age discrimination. Thus, this chapter will especially focus on the prominence of social policies in the matter of inclusion, without disregarding the economic and labor policies that enable their support and implementation.

13.2 Urgent Measures Towards Inclusion

The reduction of poverty, inequality and exclusion are long-term goals, but discriminated and highly vulnerable persons cannot wait. Therefore, social inclusion policies must provide urgent answers to go along with the structural change processes unfolded in the economy, society and culture, which are, by definition, slow and complex.

During the past decades, Latin America has developed multiple tested cash transfer programs for the poorest families. The original idea, prompted from Brazil, was embodied by virtually every country in the region with the support of international financial organizations such as the World Bank. These programs are significant since not only do they result in an increase in available income for families (which addresses a pressing need for resources), but also force families to adopt specific behavioral patterns in terms of the health, education and labor of their members, especially of children at school age. This constitutes an attempt to solve some of the structural causes of the inequality of opportunities which determines the "intergenerational transmission" of poverty, such as the lack of access to education or health issues.

In Peru, the National Program for the Direct Support of the Poor ("Juntos"), created in 2005, falls within this category. "Juntos" provides assistance to almost half a million homes, including over a million children under the age of 14.

Nowadays, there are over 8.5 million persons aged between 0 and 14 in Peru, 2.7 million (32 %) of which, projecting national averages, are below the poverty threshold. "Juntos" reaches, therefore, over a third of the entire potentially target population, which represents a remarkable yet still insufficient attainment.

As many other tested transfer programs, "Juntos" faces a series of challenges related to the management of subsidies, the control of joint responsibility and the equilibrium between the demand for services it entails and the existing supply of the country. It is often difficult to know whether the "correct" family is receiving funds in geographical areas where there persists a serious problem of registration and documentation (especially with regard to minors) or in the informal sectors of the economy, where the actual amount of income of each household is unknown. Delivering resources is also difficult due to the low banking degree, distances and communication problems, particularly in isolated areas. It is sometimes impossible to know with certainty whether the children have had the required medical check-ups and whether they regularly attend school.

Finally, these programs increase the demand for educational and health services that the existing public infrastructure may not usually meet. In some cases, there are no sanitary posts or schools at a reasonable distance, or there is a lack of human resources or of the inputs necessary for health and educational care.

Notwithstanding its problems, this type of initiative perfectly illustrates the difference between the "philanthropic ogre" and a dynamizing State. Social programs and policies may no longer be deemed mere counters for the provision of resources or services to the most needed portion of the population for no consideration at all. Said differently, people who receive assistance must adopt "active" behavioral patterns in connection with their own wellbeing and development. These patterns may be related to health care or the education of children, to communal organization to co-manage programs (as in the case of the Wawa Wasi), to professional training or the active search of employment. In short, programs aim at creating more dynamic, organized and "empowered" citizens in the quest for their own development, an effective means, if executed correctly, for the attainment of social inclusion. The theoretical framework behind this idea is that of Kooiman's (2005) *interactive governance*. The interactive perspective on governance (Kooiman 2008) proposes that societies are made up of large numbers of actors constrained or enabled by structures (culture, legislation and material possibilities among others). This view proposes not a one-dimensional participation of the government as the only agent but an interaction with the governed in the context of the societal system.

The purpose of these reflections is not to conduct a global assessment on Peru's current social policy. It is true that most programs aimed at reducing poverty or any of its symptoms—undernourishment, food insecurity, inadequate housing, diseases, domestic violence, lack of access to basic services—apply the philosophy described in the preceding paragraph, especially those administered by the Ministry of Women and Social Development. But it is also true that all of them may be improved in order to create "positive" incentives towards a non-traumatizing classification of the beneficiary families and "negative" incentives towards the perpetuation of dependence on assistance. In this regard, it will be necessary to periodically review the amounts offered—in the case of cash transfers, —the requirements for qualification, the maximum term of assistance, the consideration requested, control and follow-up mechanisms, the systematic assessment of the resulting impact and externalities, among other issues related to the administration of these programs. It will also be paramount to seek synergies, economies of scale and greater coordination among programs in order to guarantee that the State efficiently administers the social tools available—considering that this is a further trait of the dynamizing State, in contrast with the old philanthropic ogre. The key is, for instance, the existence of a sole register or cadastre of beneficiary families receiving assistance which is realistic and complete and updated periodically, as a basis for delivery, follow-up and control systems. In this respect, before Peru lies still a long way ahead.

The second urgent measure towards inclusion through income is the raise of minimum wage. In Peru, the benefits of a measure of this nature would extend basically to the formal sector of the economy and to salaried workers, but still, they are significant. The ILO Global Wage Report 2010/2011 (2010a) argues that wage policies—including the promotion of collective bargaining and reasonable minimum wage—can make a direct contribution towards the sustainability of economic and social models, since they increase the share of working families—especially those obtaining low wages—on national income, thereby decreasing inequality indexes. Interestingly, many countries reacted to the recent international financial crisis by raising minimum wage, as part of the countercyclical policies oriented towards the consolidation of aggregate domestic demand. And this reaction enabled a swifter, less traumatic escape from the crisis. In the case of Peru, even within a growth cycle (though with decreasing rates), a minimum wage policy agreed upon by employers, workers and the government represents an interesting alternative to foster the economic inclusion of lower-income salaried workers.

Finally, it is imperative to guarantee a greater extension of social protection, especially with regard to health and pensions, so that an increasing portion of the population may reap the benefits of these policies. Even though there has been evident progress in coverage indicators during the past years, virtually two thirds of the population of this country is somehow unprotected. Efforts in this field must be focused, in the short term, on the most vulnerable groups, especially older and disabled persons. Women deserve special consideration, mainly because a large portion of their work is performed within the informal economy or is disregarded when they reach pensionable age—for instance, housework or reproduction work.

The United Nations initiative for the establishment of a basic social protection floor is an interesting frame of reference for the current Peruvian situation, since it merges the guarantee of income provided by transfer programs with the "classic" concept of social security in health care and pensions. This floor is based on four goals: (1) the entire population has access to a set of basic health care services; (2) all families with children receive income equal to or exceeding the poverty threshold through the transfer of financial or material resources, for the purpose of providing access to essential nutrition, education and health goods and services; (3) every working person who does not receive sufficient income in the labor market has a secured income through social transfers that enables them to acquire basic goods and services; and (4) the entire population of older and disabled persons receives guaranteed income at least at the poverty threshold level. This social protection floor must be in fitting with the conditions of each country, which must define what is deemed "basic health care", as well as determine the poverty threshold.

A system with these characteristics creates a virtuous development cycle in which investment made in connection with the basic floor translates into a healthier and more educated population, which can thus obtain better paid jobs within the formal sector of the economy, which in turn results in increased fiscal revenue—collected through taxes—which may be reinvested in social programs. By including, the State dynamizes citizens, creating future conditions for the maintenance of its inclusion policies.

13.3 Medium Term Goals: Decent Labour and Education

Even if social programs, including cash transfer programs, extend over time and become actual institutions, they must be deemed mere partial solutions to a highly complex problem. Medically speaking, these programs provide palliative care for the symptoms of a disease that is deeply rooted in matters related to the insufficiency of public services provision systems (education, health care, social protection), as well as of the production-business sphere, in achieving greater equality of opportunities in terms of access to basic conditions for inclusion, particularly education and decent work. The immediate solution provided by these programs, however, should not be underestimated, since—as mentioned above—it is aimed at a population sector for which "medium and long term" is far afield.

Education is, definitely, the means of socialization and inclusion par excellence. It must be conceived as a continued process, throughout the cycle of life, even though it is unquestionable that its incidence is much higher during childhood and youth. Education has improved considerably in the past decade, as evidenced by the steady increase in the rates of enrollment in initial, primary and secondary education. Illiteracy levels are low, below 4 % of the population. This has led the United Nations Development Programme to state in 2008 that the generalization of primary education in Peru has almost been accomplished.

Nevertheless, there are significant gaps between these indicators considering, in particular, the place of residence of children and the income level of their families. In short, the level of education in the rural areas of Peru and among the poorest families is deeply distressing. Let us consider just one indicator by way of example: the national average of the percentage of children aged 11 who complete primary school at that age amounts to approximately 65 %, but this proportion climbs up to over 74 % in urban areas and to 77.4 % if only Lima Metropolitan Area is considered, while it drops to less than 50 % in rural areas.

Even more distressing is the quality of education. Between the 65 countries subject to the examinations administered by the Programme for International

Student Assessment (PISA) in 2009, Peru ranked 62nd in reading comprehension, 60th in mathematics literacy and 63rd in sciences, an overwhelmingly negative situation even in contrast with other participating Latin American countries (OECD 2010). These results—albeit questionable and questioned indeed—are the symptoms of a serious problem of quality in the educational systems which needs to be addressed.

Although education is a service that may be provided by private parties, the State must be able to guarantee this basic public service en its entire territory and for its entire population, throughout the cycle of life of the people. Equality of opportunities and inclusion through education may only be attained if the State guarantees coverage and quality, preventing the educational system from segmenting into a private subsystem with (relatively) high standards, accessible to the rich, and a low-quality public subsystem, accessible to the poor.

This task is not an easy one: even countries with a stronger tradition of quality public educational systems in the region, such as Argentina or Brazil, have been experiencing significant setbacks in this field since the 1990s. But this does not release the Peruvian State from the need to undertake a substantial reform of its educational system, considering both medium and long term, that consolidates some of the improvements achieved during the past five years, especially with regard to teacher training and the professionalization of teaching studies.

This reform must direct the focus towards education in rural areas, guaranteeing bilingualism, on the basis of adequate infrastructure and materials and teachers sufficiently trained for this situation. It must find a way to increase enrollment in initial education and even foster educational centers for children aged 0–3, since early stimulation is one of the keys to subsequent success in learning. This reform must also comprise higher levels—secondary school and higher education–enhancing professional, vocational and technical training systems in order to adapt them to the needs of the labor market and of undergraduate and graduate education. In furtherance of greater degrees of equality, scholarship systems for lower-income students must be promoted at all levels.

Last but not least, it is essential to further the professionalization of teaching studies, guaranteeing adequate salaries and decent working conditions for teachers throughout the country. In order for these changes to be effective, public spending in education must be steadily increased in keeping with the growth of the product, until achieving –at least– the average level prevailing in Latin America.

In addition to fostering socialization, education prepares persons to effectively enter the labor world. At an adult age, employment is the means for social integration par excellence. However, not every type of employment has this function: if a person wants to work but cannot find a job, or if they only find short-term jobs, or jobs which entail extensive working hours, under poor conditions, for a poor salary, threatening their health or risking death, they will most probably not feel integrated into the society they live in.

The same holds true if they lose their job and unexpectedly find themselves utterly defenseless, with the bare opportunity of resorting to the charity of their families or membership groups, if they are fortunate enough.

This is the idea underlying the concept of "decent work" coined by the International Labour Organization (ILO) in 1999. The concept of decent work was introduced by the ILO's Director-General, Juan Somavía, from Chile, in his report on the 87th International Labour Conference, held in 1999. This idea was subsequently translated into an agenda or work program. Specific indicators were developed to measure decent work and several reports were drafted with regard to the policies necessary to generate decent work. It basically means having opportunities for productive jobs, which provide a decent income, safety at the workplace and social protection for families. Decent work entails projections of personal development and social integration, free expression of opinions and free organization and participation of the working person in all decisions affecting their life. It further entails equality of opportunities and treatment, without any kind of discrimination.

The labor market situation in Peru, considering the "number" of jobs and their quality, is far from perfect. A recent study conducted by Gamero (2011) analyzes this phenomenon on the basis of basic indicators (the existence of an employment contract, salaries exceeding minimum wage) and supplementary indicators (working weeks of less than 48 h, health and pension insurance) of decent work. The study found that, in 2009, only 8.2 % of the economically active population of the country—mainly salaried workers employed by medium or large companies and the public sector—had jobs that could fall under this category. The concept and measure of decent work should not be mistaken for the idea of "adequate employment" arising from the Permanent Employment Surveys conducted by the INEI, which basically considers the population working 35 weekly hours or more and receiving income above the minimum consumption basket and those working less than 35 weekly hours who do not desire to work more. The proportion of adequately employed persons in Lima Metropolitan Area during the first quarter of 2011 accounts for 52 % of the economically active population (INEI 2011: 2).

Employment results, in Peru and most countries of the world, essentially from private economic activity. The relevance of the State in the generation of decent work is not related, thus, to its capacity as employer—an important albeit decreasing role in terms of quantity—but to its capacity to dynamize the economy, generate an adequate environment for the development of business, guarantee the existence of reasonable, common rules, guarantee adequate levels of inspection and control and, in every instance, guarantee social dialogue with the active participation of employers and workers organizations.

In this regard, it is crucial that the State introduces active policies oriented towards the labor market to facilitate the connection between labor supply and demand—for instance, through employment services,—in order to enhance labor force training—professional training—and promote the creation of new jobs through subsidies to hiring or the promotion of the creation of new companies and the expansion of existing ones (including access to credit). As to labor regulations, it is essential to find a balance between the necessary levels of security so that male and female workers may truly enjoy their labor rights and of flexibility so that the cost of hiring entailed to companies does not discourage the generation of employment. Such balance may only be attained through social dialogue, which must be enhanced and respected (thus the prominence of an institution such as the Peruvian Council of Labor and Employment Promotion).

These policies must give special consideration to the young portion of the population that suffers from unemployment and poor working conditions to a greater extent than the adult population. It is essential that technical and vocational systems be adjusted and adapted to provide competencies adequate to the most dynamic professions in the market. It would also be effective to develop specific, active programs to enable young persons to obtain their first job under decent working conditions, for example by means of some kind of subsidy or tax advantage.

In turn, it is necessary to give special consideration to the situation of women in the field of employment, enhancing their progressive incorporation into the formal labor market. To this end, in addition to the measures described above, the State must introduce measures that facilitate the harmonization of family and work life and severely punish all types of sexual discrimination, including unequal pay for equal work.

Finally, the State has the moral and practical responsibility of guaranteeing the incorporation of disabled persons into the labor market. This entails the simultaneous implementation of several actions at the abovementioned fronts, from the adaptation of infrastructure (for example, in technical training centers) to the development of regulations, including—of course—the development of active employment policies aimed at this sector of the population.

13.4 The Challenges of the Peruvian Reality: Informality, Decentralisation and Discrimination

The above paragraphs have outlined the main guidelines of what could constitute a "roadmap" towards an inclusive State in Peru, with short—and medium-term measures. It is, actually, an idealized portray, a vision that may be difficult to materialize in the current reality of this country, considering specific challenges posed by the social, economic and cultural structures comprising it.

The first remarkable characteristic of this reality is the size of what could be called the "informal economy"—or, generically, informality—, that is, legal economic activities invisible to the Treasury Department or undeclared before the government. In a broad sense, informal economy comprises productive units which do not pay taxes (the informal sector) and undeclared employment in "formal" companies (informal employment). This is a worldwide phenomenon, but it is more patent in developing countries and is of particular relevance in the case of Peru. According to the statistics prepared by the ILO, 76.2 % of male workers and 65.5 % of female workers in Peru (excluding the agricultural sector) fall into the category of informal employment. Over two million persons are informally employed in companies of the formal economy (ILO 2011).

Informality in Peru is neither a new situation nor a current reaction to the crisis: it is a structural trait of the economy and culture of the country. Efforts to address this issue have been multiple and persistent; legislative, political and administrative efforts have been made by the government and the organizations of civil society. The truth is that, despite it all, the outcome achieved in terms of formalization has been and continues to be poor.

The inclusive and dynamizing state must continue pursuing all measures to attack the roots of informality, making greater progress in terms of: (1) bureaucracy simplicity and reduction of the formalization cost; (2) tax, business (for instance, the possibility of public sector acquisitions) and services incentives (training, assistance, technology, commercialization); (3) mass information campaigns on the advantages of formality; and (4) inspection and sanctions upon failure to comply with the regulations in force. The State must further promote the creation of micro and small businesses in the formal sector as well as the formalization of existing ones, introducing the appropriate measures to guarantee—as far as possible—their sustainability in time and compliance with labor regulations for its male and female workers.

Anyhow, this will not suffice; therefore, the State will also have to consider alternatives and additional measures. A first alternative would be to consolidate its presence throughout its territory and extend inclusion programs and services to the entire population, particularly including social policies and the awarding of property. There is a strong proven correlation between informality and poverty; thus, the war against poverty will indirectly contribute to the reduction of informality. Furthermore, as stated in the introduction, social cohesion also entails the feeling of being part of a community, which must be encouraged by the State.

A second possible alternative is related to the promotion of self-organization in informal sectors, including the possibility of a certain degree of unionization. This may facilitate negotiation with multiple productive units—occasionally consisting of a sole person—which would otherwise be lengthy, if not impossible.

In the third place, it will be necessary to thoroughly characterize this phenomenon, by economic sector and geographical area, since the needs of the parties involved vary significantly. The reality of a Puno cab driver differs substantially from that of the owner of a small plot devoted to agricultural production in Piura. The detailed analysis must lead to the adjustment of the pertaining policies and the enhancement of employment administration public systems aimed at connecting labor demand and supply, as well as professional training supply.

Geographical and cultural diversity is a second characteristic of the Peruvian reality that will affect inclusion policies. This statement leads to the analysis of two major political trends that, undoubtedly, are closely related to the outcome of employment and social programs and policies necessary to generate cohesion: decentralization and the struggle against discrimination.

Since the last decade, decentralization has been a State policy in Peru, focused on the progressive transfer of competencies and resources of public administration.

In a country with a strong centralization tradition, this task is not always easy, neither in the political nor in the economic arena. Beyond any value judgments that could be made on the outcome of the decentralization process during the past years, reference should be made to certain potentialities and challenges it poses to the inclusive and dynamizing State.

With regard to potentialities, decentralization obviously contributes to draw the administration and the citizenry together. Two-way relationships—services provided by the State to citizens, and demands of citizens to the State—are much more fluid and allow the implementation of social, educational, economic and labor policies and programs more appropriate to the specific conditions of the population. In turn, efficient decentralization based on sound territorial planning may facilitate the consolidation of economic "clusters" and integrated value chains that enhance local economic development. From a social standpoint, this may encourage settlement processes within the territory, buffering migration flows and incorporating remote or marginalized areas into the advance of progress. From the standpoint of the centralized State, decentralization furthers administrative relief and constitutes an additional element of control.

However, disorderly decentralization also entails risks in terms of territorial inclusion and cohesion. The most significant among them is the risk associated with unequal progress of certain areas on account of privileged access to natural, human or technology resources, which may give rise to inter-territorial conflicts and threats of secession, in addition to boosting internal migration flows that affect demography dynamics. Uncontrolled decentralization may similarly bring about clientelistic relationships between politically prevailing elites in a given territory and its inhabitants; such circumstances may lead to an everlasting tenure in office, to caudillism or to corruption practices which are clearly undesirable from the standpoint of social cohesion and inclusion.

A decentralization policy shall, therefore, maximize all positive effects and elude all risks in terms of territorial integration; to that end, coordinate actions from the governments at the local, regional and central levels are essential. In that sense, resource reallocation mechanisms should be in place and managed by the central Government following clear, agreed rules of the game, including those applicable to mining fees. In a legislative context with only one house of Congress and without representation of the different regions, as is the case of Peru, some kind of high-level political coordination mechanisms should be consolidated to enable the formulation of shared policies. The transfer of powers and accountabilities to local governments should similarly transpire through the management of social programs, for instance, by delegating on local level authorities supervision and monitoring roles with respect to joint accountabilities, wherever possible.

The State as a whole shall ensure that each level is furnished with the necessary resources to perform their corresponding tasks and all levels have the necessary training to do so. In a decentralized country, an inclusive State is the result of territorial solidarity, and guarantees equal opportunities regardless of the environment, whether sylvan, coastal or montane.

Peruvian territories show a rich tapestry of both natural and cultural diversity. Such diversity has often been the source of discrimination by reason of ethnic or racial origin. The situation of indigenous people and those of African descent in the country still shows the remnants of such discrimination, and pose an extremely important and specific challenge to social inclusion policies. Inter-cultural dialogue, deep respect for the rights of indigenous people in accordance with international conventions and provisions—all of which have been ratified by Peru-; the enactment of laws aimed at guaranteeing early consultations prior to undertaking exploitation activities in their territories; adequately planned, quality bilingual education; the promotion of relevant, culturally appropriate economic activities; the development of particular justice systems; severe sanctions against discrimination of any kind… all such elements should be inherent in the actions of an inclusive State, in the understanding that diversity is an element to enrich rather than threaten social cohesion.

Gender discrimination—in Peru, in the rest of Latin America and in many other places throughout the world—should also be eradicated, in the sphere of education—where school enrollment and attendance levels already show gender equality-, as well as in employment—where there are still significant differences in terms of wages, tasks and in accessibility to managerial positions—and in political representation positions—where there is still ample room for improvement. An inclusive State should support women empowerment so as to overcome some barriers to inclusion which still stand.

For example, and in connection with social programs, an interesting point to further is the implementation of strategies whereby women receive the funds from the State for their households, as such procedures enhance self-esteem, award recognition and offer a specific position of authority. Moreover, these additional resources have proven to be more likely devoted to fostering the families' development needs—namely: nourishment, health care, education—if managed by women.

At a the macro level, as already explained, it is important to formulate policies and take steps to encourage the joint responsibility of both men and women in household care and in typically reproductive tasks, which enables a more thorough insertion of women into the labor market under equal conditions. Measures such as paternity leave, the establishment of day-care centers and the expansion of initial schooling levels—both in terms of duration and coverage-, innovative labor organization schemes—including telework-, are some of the alternatives an inclusive State should especially contemplate. A gender approach focused in reconciliation is by no means a marginal note of social inclusion: it is at its core.

13.5 Finance Inclusion

One of the underpinning concerns evidenced in various topics of the above account lies on the finances of public inclusion policies relative to the benefits they generate. In other words: inclusion cannot become a phagocytic child engulfing its own father, that is, the State, by consuming every available resource without producing anything in return. Conversely, inclusion should contribute to budget sustainability, hence the relevance of the notion of State as a dynamistic agent driving the economy, society and individuals.

Basically, investment in social policy requires fiscal resources. In the case of Peru, the relation between tax pressure and product was by 2007 approximately 17 %, nearly two points lower than the Latin American average and lagged far behind those of countries such as Uruguay, Argentina and Brazil, which are close to 25, 30 and 35 %, respectively (ECLAC 2009). Even though it is difficult to compare taxpaying levels between countries due to the different tax structures and expenditure patterns, the above figures are illustrative in that there is a margin for maneuvering and improvement, which necessarily implies an increase in tax collection. The imperative increase in public expenditure implicit in inclusion policies should not necessarily involve a significant reduction of fiscal surplus if the margin for maneuvering is used.

Taxation policy should consider, however, the need to set tax rates at reasonable levels so as to dynamize the economy, such dynamism being a key factor to achieve inclusion through employment. This goal requires careful and detailed analysis of the payment and contribution capacity of the various sectors, in order to establish special taxes and define optimum tax types to increase revenues obtained through general taxes. A key element of such policy should lie on the strengthening of tax administration, so that collection levels increase thanks to a reduction of tax avoidance and evasion rates, which are really high in Peru.

Reforms of the tax regime to better balance direct and indirect taxes and to maximize redistribution effects of taxes are essential elements in an inclusive State. The fact that inequalities before and after tax are similar in Peru and in Latin American countries at large, is illustrative in that the economic and political system tends to exclude rather than include, and to fragment rather than unite, thus undermining the country's very foundations. The large number of social conflicts is a reflex of such reality, which can be changed by an inclusive, dynamistic State.

Finance for inclusion can also be partly private. This should not be seen as a surrender of responsibilities by the State, nor used by the administration as a means to avoid compliance with its own mandate; in contrast, it should be deemed a creative alternative to improve the finance and execution of specific policy actions in the social context. Oon (2004). Shows how the British government has been a major driver of the institutionalization of CSR in the UK. The success came in part from the view that governments cannot manage contemporary social and economic challenges alone. The establishment of public—private partnerships (PPP) to provide a number of services and distribute public goods is a worldwide trend which is becoming consolidated and proves useful in making the social role of businesses more and better viewed. A growing number of businesses of all sizes devote resources to to create a positive impact in society through CSR initiatives. The State may support this trend by implementing specific policies by focusing it, at least partly, on sectors, geographies and priorities considered essential to boost social inclusion, fostering PPP and socially responsible corporate behavior. As word a caution on these type of initiatives Richter (2004) mentions that it is important to ensure that public interests remain at the center of all financial relationships between the public and private sectors. Successful PPP require careful policy reflection on the positive and possible negative impacts of the interactions.

The role of the inclusive State as the ultimate guardian of the public interest should extend to promoting CSR with a clear previous reflection of what is the specific purpose of the private sector intervention and how it stays focus on the public interest. The State through its public administration can play different roles enhancing CSR private initiatives:

1. Promotion and awareness-raising role: defining strategies and programs for CSR training, information and dissemination. Initiatives like CSR promotion and awareness-raising campaigns aimed at distinguishing good from bad business practices should be promoted.
2. Regulatory role: even if CSR is voluntary from a business standpoint, it could/ must be supported by an adequate public policy framework that fosters thinking about the triple bottom line. Attention must be drawn to international CSR regulations already in place, especially those issued by the United Nations and the International Labor Organization. To become a reality, the regulatory role must be complemented with the right supervision and control to dissuaded business from producing a negative impact on society. At the same time, right behavior and compliance should be rewarded.
3. Policy-making role: Public administrations can affect businesses' market behavior by changing short term incentives. In this regard, the role of the public administration in public contracts, public investment and project financing presents an opportunity to include CSR criteria in the selection of partners. Public procurement rules, understood not only in light of economic criteria, can promote the incorporation of social, environmental and ethical in compliance with social and environmental laws, and international conventions.

CSR is not a matter reserved purely to the business arena but, rather, a discussion as to what kind of society one wishes to build. In this regard, an inclusive State, responsible for sustainable development and the fair management of society, cannot stay away from the development of CSR, neither in form nor in substance. Peru has the possibility in the current context to lead such process by bridging the distance between the public and private sector. This alliance has the potential create in the Peruvian context a real "collaborative governance" (Zadek 2006) that could foster social inclusion but at the same time serve as a means of managing political and economic risks associated with high societal expectations faced by Ollanta's office.

13.6 Almost Concluding: A Leap Towards Inclusion

The foregoing considerations offer some ideas on the way a dynamistic State may create inclusion, enabling the giant leap Peru needs to make. The past failure of the State in allocating resources and enforcing rules to effectively secure public goods (Zadek 2006) can be the source of a new collaborative governance view towards social inclusion. For that purpose, various dimensions of inclusion have been analyzed, in direct connection to the economic, social, political and cultural rights of each citizen. Urgent measures have been described and analyzed, with a varying level of thoroughness, in regard to social and cash transfer programs, minimum wage and the establishment of a threshold for universal protection; subsequently, some ideas were put forward for medium and long term policies, essentially in the realms of education and the labor market, which may boost inclusion. All of the above was presented as an attempt to adjust the proposals to the Peruvian context and some of its structural traits (informality, decentralization, discrimination) and to highlight the necessary availability of resources in order to finance inclusion policies.

Policies should be broad, universal and addressed at the whole population, but in any case they require specific adjustments to put the sectors which are currently excluded high on the priority order. In some cases, they are women. In other cases, the young. Almost invariably, people with disabilities. Specific measures are similarly required with respect to indigenous people and people with African descent. An inclusive State should be able to develop both general and focused policies, to reach specific groups coordinately, while avoiding duplication and addressing the particular needs of each individual.

The current challenge of establishing an Inclusive State in Peru is clearly to move from the rhetoric of social inclusion to functional design and practice of collaborative governance and social responsibility. Future research on *on the ground* applications is muchly needed as well as the underlying conceptual framework about dynamics of interaction between the civil society, public and private sectors to build an inclusive State.

The Peruvian State has yet to meet all the necessary characteristics to be considered inclusive and dynamistic. Sometimes, its parts still remind of the philanthropic ogre of the 1970's and 1980's. However, the country is changing. Change should be deepened by future administrations, regardless of their political orientation, for inclusion is neither a left-wing nor a right-wing banner: it is a moral duty and an economic priority to any society aspiring to call itself civilized.

References

ECLAC (2007). *Social Cohesion: Inclusion and a sense of belonging in Latin America and the Caribbean* Santiago de Chile: Economic Commission for Latin America and the Caribbean.

Gamero Requena, J. (2011). Trabajo decente en el Perú: una medición al 2009. Niveles de Trabajo decente en función a un set de indicadores básicos. Electronic version available at: http://es.scribd.com/doc/55553410/TRABAJO-DECENTE-2009.

ILO (2010a). *Global wage report 2010/2011. Wage policies in times of crisis.* Geneva, Switzerland: International Labour Organization.

ILO (2011). Statistical update on employment in the informal economy. Available at: http://www.ilo.org/wcmsp5/groups/public/@dgreports/@integration/@stat/documents/presentation/wcms_157467.pdf.

INEI (2011). Situación del Mercado Laboral en Lima Metropolitana. Informe técnico 06, junio de 2011. Viewed at http://www.inei.gob.pe/web/BoletinFlotante.asp?file=12651.pdf.

Kooiman, J. (2008). Interactive governance and governability: an introduction. *The Journal of Transdisciplinary Environmental Studies, 7*(1), 2–11.

Kooiman, J., Bavinck, M., Jentoft, S., & Pullin, R. (Eds.). (2005). *Fish for life.* Amsterdam: Amsterdam University Press.

O'Flynn, J. (2007). From new public management to public value: paradigmatic change and managerial implications. *The Australian Journal of Public Administration. 66* (3), 353–366.

OECD (2010). *PISA 2009 results: what students know and can do–student performance in reading, mathematics and science* (vol I). http://dx.doi.org/10.1787/9789264091450-en.

Richter, J. (2004). Public–private partnerships for health: a trend with no alternatives? *Development, 47*(2), 43–48.

Zadek, S. (2006). The logic of collaborative governance: corporate social responsibility, accountability, and the social contract, Corporate Social Responsibility. Initiative Working Paper 17, J. F. Kennedy School of Givernment, Harvard University, pp. 1-30.

Chapter 14
Dynamics Behind the 'Moral Corruption' of the Financial System

Özlem Arzu Azer

Abstract The first phase of transformation of the world economic system was realized at the beginning of the 1980s. These were years in which neo-liberalist politics had been widening all over the world due to the Washington Consensus. Decreasing role of government as one of the most important principle of Consensus played a very important role to establish the New World Order. The New World Order as a system of global governance that institutionalizes cooperation (Slaughter in A new world order, Princeton University Press, Princeton, p. 15, 2004). The decreasing role of government means decreasing the effect of 'wealth government.' Privatizations increased at high rate particularly in the Post Cold War era. The New World Order required the transformation of society. This transformation of society was realized from year to year since the 1980s. In the Post Cold War era, there had been change in paradigms in terms of political as well as change in the structure of production. This era can be assumed to be the second phase of transformation. In the 1990s, some big financial firms which were assumed to be free from the problem of liquidation (banktrupcy), went bankcrupt. The moral erosion of the financial system became evident. The mechanism behind the moral erosion was versatile. The components of the balance sheet and delibrate disinformation to increase the value of firms and consequently shareholder value were part of the problem. In the second part, auditing firms which approved the finaancial statements were vigorously scrutinized. And the most important part was the mechanism which allows and/or directs CEOs and executives to act in such a corrupt and irresponsible way.

Ö. A. Azer (✉)
Kadir Has University, Selimpaşa, İstanbul, Turkey
e-mail: mularoz@gmail.com

A. Yüksel Mermod and S. O. Idowu (eds.), *Corporate Social Responsibility in the Global Business World*, DOI: 10.1007/978-3-642-37620-7_14,
© Springer-Verlag Berlin Heidelberg 2014

14.1 Introduction

Neo-liberal policies have spread and been adopted around the world with the Washington Consensus, which was initially implemented in 1980 particularly by the Thatcher government in the United Kingdom and by Reagan in the United States. The Washington Consensus is used as a synonym with Neoliberalism which protected the sovereignty for about 25 years, in relation to the political and technocratic structure it consists (Chang and Grabel 2005, p. 29). By means of the Consensus, the main principals of which have been determined as deregulation and downsizing the state, liberalization has created an acceleration in the finance market. However, as the deregulation and technological developments have accelerated the finance market, structural reforms in the same line and the liberalized financial markets have caused an increase in financial vulnerabilities. It is observed that in economies where current deficit is tried to be closed by means of portfolio investment financial vulnerability increases even further and in economies where risk factor is available, it is higher.

The end of the Cold War with collapse of the Soviet Union, following the fall of the Berlin Wall in 1989, have accelerated this process where deregulation based mechanism widened its domain and financial vulnerability increased.

The purpose of this chapter is to analyze the fraud-based mechanism and the moral corruption in the finance industry arisen in line with the developments in the finance markets and the economic and social transformations of the 21st Century. The aim of this chapter is to analyze dynamics behind 'moral corruption' of financial system which seems one of the biggest reason of the 2008 crisis.

This chapter tries to answer the following questions:

1. What are the roots of the fraud-based mechanism?
2. Why is the fraud-based mechanism so effective in the finance sector?
3. What are legal base of this mechanism?

In this context, the first part of the chapter will deal with the social transformation that lay in the core, while the second part will focus on the developments in the finance market on the axis of deregulation, the third part will set forth the factors causing moral corruption in the finance market and finally the fourth part will analyze the case of the ENRON company.

14.2 Social Transformation Within the Core of the Global World

In the world of the 1980s, while financial and political transformation was underway on one hand, on the other one social transformation took place through the path leading from 'conventionalism to post-modernism'. The social transformation occurred in the post-modern world, and the world where the borders of supra-national capital were removed with the spread of the liberalization policies on the axis of the Washington Consensus of the 1980s, fall of the Berlin Wall in 1989 and the following cessation of the Cold War, also lie on the foundation of the global crisis of the 21st Century.

While the concept of globalization intended for the utopia of a world state without any borders, since it was probable to experience some social-borne problems during the phases of establishing the technical infrastructure of such a state and implementing the rules, also a social transformation was needed as well as the transformation of the capital. Removal of borders by means of globalization does not only accelerate the movements human and physical capital and trade of goods and services, it also brings about social transformation.

In this frame, transformation of the society takes place within the core of the new world order. That is because of the fact that, institutional and hypothetical changes not adopted by the society will set forth various risks, in terms of their application. Embracement of such changes by the society will enable the new world order to function in an unrestricted and smooth way, thus will play a substantial role in bringing a supranational quality to international capital.

The individual, who takes the advantage of the direct and indirect benefits of globalization, is the best implementer of the law of 'marginal benefits' of the consumption society trying to keep up with the monetary and physical movements. Congruency between individual maximization and social maximization gradually looses its applicability in the global world. When the individual finds its own happiness, freedom and more importantly its belonging within the concept of 'global citizen', its social responsibilities fall into background. The individual expressing itself with the quality of being a 'global citizen', alienates from the society it has lived in, and desires to carry its individual maximization to the highest point possible. In turn, societies where such individuals constitute the majority, social maximization looses its importance.

Along with the changes in value judgments, the concept of transforming the society is complemented with the areas of emotional satisfaction shifting from the feelings and humane sharing to a platform, where materiality is increased by numeric values. As happiness, within this transformation process, is achieved by means of 'material', which is accepted as the criterion of wealth, any way and particularly the fastest way, leading to this will be admissible. Society engineering that will create the new values to replace traditions is needed for realizing social transformation.

Having the most important role in getting new life styles adopted, the media acts as an intermediary to a world where individuals prove their existence in a world of brands and embrace the cultural values and different lifestyles symbolized by these brands. A rapid transition from the traditions, which reflect cultural values, to the future that implies brands and the life styles symbolized by brands is underway and social transformation is carried out. And it is the human factor that plays the most important role for this fraud-based system of irregularity to function.

The 'laisser-faire, laissez-passer/let them do, let them pass' philosophy constituting the basis of liberalism, have found place for itself this time in the individual's dreams of 'wealth'. Especially in the light of the neoliberal policies initially implemented in the 1980s and rapidly extended ever since, the 'free' and 'liberal' individual has become nothing but a slave to the material. In other words, while 'freedom' is defined as one living its life as it desires and 'investing in the material' as the necessity of being a consumption society, with the 'humane values' lost on the other hand individuals become slaves of consumption rather than becoming free.

In this world where individual interests come before social interests, a model of 'leisurely individuals' emerges, who perceives its existence with the material values it possesses in a setting where it is that easy to readily buy and sell all kinds of materials.

The leisure class Veblen defines in his 'Theory of the Leisure Class', will doubtlessly be the best supporter and implementer of liberal policies, enhance its life standard with a consumption happiness and the increases in its material values, yet when it loses its material values it will not be able to perceive its own existence and will never comprehend the complexity of existence.

Veblen states that courage will manifest itself in the barbarian's world through fraud and pressure. The pillage culture Veblen defines virtually depicts the world society of the 21st Century (Veblen 2005 [1899], p. 176):

> Aggression (violence) and cunningness, these two barbarous features constitute the pillage culture. Both of these features express a self-regarding mentality, even if being in the narrow meaning. Both serve the interests of the individuals aiming for unearned success. Both feed on the material culture. However, neither have a contribution to the communal living.

14.3 Finance Market Developments in the Axis of Deregulation

The period following the end of the Cold War proved to be an important milestone, particularly for the movement rate and the 'money capital', the barriers of which have been removed as from the 1980s, and with that a platform where the rules of the new world are determined and where the limitations and barriers before the movement of money are dismissed, has been established.

Integration of technological advancements with finance has carried along the developments in finance market into a new phase and with the legalization of deregulation money movements have been accelerated and financial globalization has been carried out. According to Castells (2005, pp. 131–132), the global interdependence of finance markets has emerged with five fundamental matters of fact:

1. The fact that in many countries finance sector is not subject to legal regulations and deregulation of extraterritorial transactions,
2. Development of technologic infrastructure,
3. Complex derivative products increase the instability of the global finance networks,
4. Speculative capital movements becoming the tools of financial instability,
5. And the capability of market rating agencies such as Standard&Poor and Moody's to influence the market with the ratings they give.

In the process of financial globalization, accepted as the milestone of money capital getting ahead of trade of goods, the barriers before the capital movements and control mechanisms have been removed, and while the financial system based on deregulation has constituted the basis of the finance-borne crises, it also set the stage for moral corruption.

The two most important factors that facilitate liquidity in capital markets are international financial liberalization and deregulation, which eventually paved the way for foreign private borrowing (Jomo 2005). While capital movements, which are also referred to as portfolio movements, affect economic data in a positive way in the countries they are transferred to, they bear a major risk since their retrievals in a short period of time is always possible.

Within this process it is observed that 'portfolio investments', rather than direct foreign capital investments, come into prominence and rapidly flow into developing countries. Developing countries have adopted these speculation-oriented portfolio movements as the means to close their current deficits, and even enacted legal regulations with the intention of attracting such money movements to them. In this process where the control mechanism is no longer in used and money movements have gained speed in line with the technological developments, in a deregulated and uncontrolled setting financial crises have occurred successively: 1994–1995 Tequila Crisis in Mexico, 1997 South East Asian Crisis started in Thailand, 1998 Russian Crisis, 1999 Argentinean Crisis and 2001 Turkey Crisis. The 1990s have accompanied rapid growth on one hand, and the crises with domino effect on the other.

Among the most important causes of the witnessed global financial crises are the facilitation of the deregulated and uncontrolled movement of capital, the newly created derivative products in the world finance system being more and more involved by the economic system and their volume reaching to an immeasurable magnitude in a setting that lacked a control mechanism.

While the neoliberal policies spread rapidly in the 1980s, the derivative markets constituted in parallel to the capital movements developed and gained liquidity in line with the technological developments have become an important factor of the money creation mechanism. The mechanism created with the development of derivative markets has gained an important function for 'money capital'. In this period where consumption shifted from being the 'means' to being the 'ends', it transformed into a market that incites consumption and that creates funds (Fig. 14.1).

While in 1980 new ways of hedging such as option and futures emerged in the finance markets, which developed rapidly since the 1970s, high volume realization of derivative products have been observed since the 1990s.

According to the Credit Derivatives Market Report of the British Bankers Association, while the value of the global credit derivative markets was USD 180 million in 1996, it is believed to have reached USD 33 trillion in 2008.

Global Credit Derivatives Market, USD bn.

	1996	1998	1999	2000	2001	2002	2003	2004	2006	2008 (est)
▫Years	180	350	586	893	1189	1952	3548	5021	20207	33120

Fig. 14.1 Global credit derivatives market, *source* British Banking Association, Credit Derivatives Report 2006, http://www.bba.org.uk/publications/entry/bba-credit-derivatives-report-2006/books-reports-subscriptions/

On the basis of this substantial rate of increase in the derivative markets lies the 'leverage' factor. Derivatives generate leverage that can increase liquidity or the effective money supply throughout the financial system and increasing leverage and liquidity results by rise in asset prices and creates price bubbles (Gerding 2011, p. 102).

Being the invention of financial engineering, asset-backed securities and other derivative products increase the liquidity in the market on one hand, while on the other hand they have a function that increases asset prices and create, in a sense, a bubble effect. Another aspect of the matter is that, a mechanism to which the risks are transferred by packaging the subprime credits of the financial institutions, and thus increasing their risk appetites has been established. It is obvious that such a mechanism will increase the risks of moral corruption in the finance sector.

14.4 Moral Corruption of Financial System

In this part of the chapter, the factors that create moral corruption in the finance sector will be set forth. It is essential to carry out the necessary regulations in the system by analyzing the factors causing moral corruption, and to establish a mechanism that will ensure the control and measurement of the derivative markets functioning as leverage. As Pettifor mentioned, there is a big necessity to examine the ethics underlying bankruptcy, the need to periodically correct imbalances and the ethics of money-creation itself (Pettifor 2006, p. 127).

The factors constituting risk of moral corruption have been examined under six headings. These are:

1. deregulation as one of the main principles of the Washington Consensus,
2. state incentives and protectionism that increase systemic risk,
3. securitization of the low quality credits and the derivative markets that diversified and grew particularly after the 1990s,
4. the problem of asymmetric information,
5. human nature and effect of wealth in the context of social transformation that is imperative for the functioning of this system based on irregularity and deregulation,
6. finally the new wage/compensation system adopted particularly in the United States for senior managers/CEOs.

14.5 Deregulation

One of the most important principles of the Washington Consensus, the principals of which were determined in 1978, was deregulation.

The fact that there is no mechanism measuring the high volume of the derivative markets, diversified with new products particularly from the 1990s, has been manifested with the latest global crisis. Certainly, the only problem was not the inability to measure the value of the derivative products that realized with such a substantial volume and marketed virtually all around the world. During the crisis it was unfolded that, these derivative products that have several names and are dealt off the balance sheet, do not in fact constitute a security for those who regard these as tools of investment. Majority of the giant financial institutions which put these derivative products into the market while not having security for the investors, have been either saved with government assistance or nationalized. The fact that there is no 'security' for the products monitored off the balance sheet was a result of the deregulation mechanism established by the system. Toffler (1996, p. 16) had emphasized the inadequacy of national regulatory mechanism over supra-national economic reality in the new world.

Some structural changes lie under the roots of the finance system based on deregulation. Many important deregulation decisions have been listed by Skidelsky (2009, p. 7) as follows:

1. The repeal in 1999 of the Glass-Steagal Act, which came into force in 1933 and prohibited banks to deal in capital markets,
2. the decision by the Clinton administration not to regulate credit-default swaps,
3. the 2004 decision by the US Securities and Exchange Commission to allow banks to increase their leverage ratios from 10:1 to 30:1.

The first one of the three decisions Slidelsky refer to as deregulation laws is the Glass-Steagal Act (or the Banking Act of 1933), which separated investment and commercial banking from each other. Stiglitz (2004, p. 88) points out that the annulment of the Glass-Steagal Act has created new conflicts of interest, and that stronger legal regulations that will solve the growing conflicts of interests are necessary.

The Glass-Steagal Act 1933 which had brought in measures to regulate banking, was repealed with the Gramm-Leach-Bliley Act, or the Financial Services Modernization Act of 1999, with which the essentials of deregulation has been determined. However, it is clear that the first steps of deregulation were being gradually taken since the 1980s, before the Gramm-Leach-Bliley Act of 1999, with the Depository Institutions Deregulation and Monetary Control Act 1980 and Reigle-Neal Interstate Banking and Branching Efficiency Act of 1994. By this way, in an environment of fierce competition a system that guarantees grant of credit to anyone who applies for it has been established (Minton 2008, p. 2).

With the Depository Institutions Deregulation and Monetary Control Act 1980, the capacity of the FED to determine the interest rate on deposits were removed, the banks were left free to act on this matter, the saving deposits insurance fund of the US banks and credit unions was raised from USD 40.000 to USD 100.000 and the banks were allowed to consolidate. As for the Reigle-Neal Interstate Banking and Branching Efficiency Act 1994, it removed the restrictions over the shoulders of the banks and granted them the capacity to operate on an interstates basis. And finally, the Gramm-Leach-Bliley Act 1999 has removed all the restrictions brought in with the Glass-Steagal Act 1933 and entitled the banks to deal with non-banking activities. This act opened the gates of consolidation to banks, insurance companies, investment banks and capital market companies (US Government Public Law 106–102 Nov 12th, 1999).

Eichengreen asserts that, since the annulment of the Glass-Steagal Act diminished the capitals of the banks in investment companies, investment companies had to find new business channels such as 'originating and distributing' complex derivative securities, and consequently, in order to maintain their profitabilities, they funded themselves from the money markets by using even more leverages (Eichengreen 2008).

14.6 State Incentives and Protectionism

The policies and implementations increasing the vulnerability in the finance sector and causing financial crisis that create domino effect, also increase 'systemic risk' by serving as model to the other financial institutions in the sector. The policies implemented by the state take the first place among the causes increasing systemic risk.

This rapid development in the derivative markets and its articulation into the money market have gained the 'intermediary organizations' a new function.

With intermediaries as Freddie Mac and Fannie Mae being incentivized by the government in the United States, the scene for a rapid increase in the 'mortgage-based credits' was set. With such incentive of the state, financial institutions have abandoned their selective and cautious approaches during the phase of credit evaluation, and adopted highly risk-taking and growth-oriented approaches. This change in the mentalities of the financial institutions, adopted with the confidence in the state to save them in case of bankruptcy, have caused the emergence of the moral corruption in the finance sector (Acharya 2009).

Besides these incentivising mechanisms of the state, also the policies it implements for the sake of maintaining the system constitute an important cause of the moral corruption and increase the systemic risk. Saving deposits insurance funds and similar supports of the state, enables the financial institutions to know that they will be saved and take higher risks. This risk-increasing effect of state support on the financial institutions is also among the causes of the moral corruption of the finance sector (Nier 2009). The rescue operations of the FED in the United States have caused injustice by burdening the costs of these rescue operations on the shoulders of the public through taxes, it has also strengthened the belief that the rescue operations witnessed in the past will be repeated also in the future and consequently increased the risk appetites of financial institutions and caused systemic risk to increase.

The systemic risk of liquidity has grown rapidly by means of the policies followed by the FED since 2001, globalization and disintermediation (Perotti 2010). As Perotti mentioned, the privileges granted in 2005, with the pressure of the banking lobby, to the creditors and promoters of derivative products in the United States and Europe, have enabled creditors to give more credit by reducing their respective risks and securing their credits, and served as a cost-reducing factor from the viewpoints of the burrowers.

14.7 Derivative Markets and the Securitization of the Subprime Credits

While the mortgage credits in the United States are classified within three different risk classes as Prime, Alternative-A and Subprime, the securities based on the mortgages backing such credits are separated according to their respective risk-income groups and securitized as Collateralized Debt Obligations (CDOs). Since the combination and securitization of different risk groups under the item title CDO also covers subprime credits, this transaction bears a high level of risk. The mechanism that packages and transfers risks has not only become a money creation mechanism, but it also had an effect that accelerated consumption.

While the financial institutions have found a new instrument to transfer credit risk and subprime credits by securitizing mortgage-backed credit risks, a new money creation mechanism has been established. By expediting the mechanism of subprime credit assignment, securitization has created a bubble effect in the real estate market. Securitization subprime credits constitutes another aspect of the moral corruption (Dell'Ariccia et al. 2008). Financial institutions transfer their risks through securitizing their highly risky credits and in this way minimize their risks and increase their earnings from derivative markets (Jacobs 2009). The mechanism that exacerbates financial vulnerability, gains from speculation and overvaluation.

With their 'asset-backed funds', 'stock markets', 'secondary markets', 'credit risk swaps' and other similar varieties, derivative markets function through increasing the value of money, without actually creating any added value by production. The values of the movable and immovable assets, which are only virtual values when not turned into cash, decrease and even fully evaporate during crises.

In these markets when an asset is not sold, its worth is nothing more than a fictitious value. While this fictitious value creates a 'sense of wealth' in the individuals during increasing periods and encourages consumption, as it was seen in the latest world crisis, the total evaporation of the asset is also possible.

In such a setting where assets can be evaporated instantly, the values of the assets melt down with the price decreases and at this point the individuals have to face the true colors of their 'senses of wealth'. At this time, the mechanism of supra-income consumption starts to function in the reverse direction and while consumption recedes, also recessions and shrinkages are observed.

While the values of the assets purchased by individuals with lower incomes than the values, by means of the credit mechanisms, rapidly diminish, the individuals can not be confident on the fate of their incomes.

Considering the matter from this aspect, it is clear that a mechanism finding its place within the expression 'Casino Capitalism' is in question (Strange 1986). According to Strange, the instabilities and fluctuations in the markets may cause economic collapses. Within this frame, it can be asserted that, by their natures, derivative markets cause fluctuations and instability in markets.

14.8 Asymmetric Information

Pursuant to the Washington Consensus and in line with the technologic developments, capital movements have become liberalized and deregulated since from the 1980s. Following this milestone, derivative markets have developed rapidly and with the newly created products a new market, absent from the control of a body, has been established. This new market functions through the aforementioned assets gaining value based on the asset-backed securities.

In the next phase it is observed that the assets cease to be 'commodities' so to say, and become merely instruments of the market that have no material value as the 'composite index', or become the transfer of risk as in credit risk swaps. The products promoted in the market as structured funds find their values with the fluctuations of the assets on definite periods or the indexes they are dealt with, rather than being index-linked with the value increases of the assets. While promoting the structured funds, based on the fluctuations between a definite range of value of a certain commodity such as petrol, as well as focusing on a level of composite index, the investors are not provided with full information and consequently misguided. Also the high ratings given by the rating agencies to securities including low-quality credits where risks are transferred, constitute a setting of asymmetric information for the investors and create a moral corruption by not reflecting the real risk.

These products promoted in the setting of asymmetric information as a whole carry a certain quality of betting, and as a marketing policy the investors are usually misled by not being provided with complete information and in this way these products are rendered marketable. The 'asymmetric information' conditions the investors are an important cause of the moral corruption in the financial market. The fact that the investors do not fully know the components of the product they invest in, that they are provided with false and/or lacking information, negate the possibility for them to be aware of the risk level they are in.

Within the process of the global crisis started in late 2007 in the United States, it has been witnessed that the monetary assets of many wealthy people have evaporated. Casino capitalism has shown that as it is possible to earn big substantial amounts of money in a very short period, it is also possible that all of them can be evaporated in an instant.

While the derivative markets based on commodity prices, indexes or the securitization of credit risk, grow in an uncontrolled and deregulated way, with the prevailing of asymmetric information conditions moral corruptions in the finance sector have been made possible.

14.9 Human Nature and the Effect of Wealth

While the dreams of becoming homeowners, not only of the middle income citizens of the United States but also of those who are included in the low income group have been realized through the 'mortgage backed long term credits' they get, the construction sector has grown and house prices have increased in line with the increasing demand. This increase in house prices has created a 'virtual wealth', and the 'illusion of increasing prosperity' created by the price increase has encouraged individuals to spend more than their incomes.

Besides the consumption increasing effect of the 'sense of wealth' on the individuals, the social transformation required by liberalism and the phenomenon of 'achievable sweet life' and 'perfect woman/man' created by the media either through the movie industry or commercials have dragged individuals into a world they do not belong. Being more beautiful, purchasing more with less income and reaching the dreams of tomorrow from today have been made possible by means of instruments such as credit cards and personal loans. In this way, credit cards and other credit types within the scope of personal loans function to create money and contribute to financial growth.

As for the most important factor underlying financial growth, it is surely the human factor, besides the credit cards, consumer loans, car loans, mortgage-based loans and the other types under the roof of the personal loans with the derivative markets that rapidly developed after 1980 taking the first place. The term human factor here refers to the human nature that connects happiness with materiality through the 'virtual sense of wealth'.

In the presence of the sense of 'wealth' and materiality-based peace, the personal crediting instruments are not widely used in order to enable individuals to spend more than their incomes for realizing this sense of 'wealth'. With the diversification of the mechanisms of money creation, it has been made possible to spend unguaranteed, unearned and nonexistent money and the world has been turned into a huge market.

Examining the human factor underlying growth from the moral aspect reveals a human model acting as per the Machiavellian philosophy. While contributing to the financial growth at the same time this new human model also constitutes an equal threat against the financial growth. In order to obtain status in the developing global world and to get its share from the prosperity and wealth of the new century, the new human model has to adapt its value justifications and reason of existence to the new world order.

On the other hand, the development of the derivative markets as another type of money creation mechanism and the increase in possessed monetary values in line with the increase in the prices of the assets create the 'sense of wealth' and in periods of increase of immovable values, that can not be turned into cash in reality, cause higher levels of consumption.

14.10 The New Wage/Compensation System

The changes in the wage systems particularly in the United States, constitutes one of the most important moral corruption laying under the 2007 Global Crisis, the effects of which can still be seen. In the mechanism where the wages and compensations are paid to senior managers and the CEOs as the shares of the companies they work in, the real purpose is to increase the share values of the companies in question, rather than to increase commercial profitability. In line with this, senior managers and CEOs securing their incomes in an index-linked way with the market value of the shares by taking high risks creates the risk of moral corruption within the system (Acharya 2009).

From the viewpoint of such managers and CEOs, even the utilization of fraudulent techniques for increasing the values of the company shares may be deemed acceptable as long as they are not detected, and a more prosperous and prestigious life can be attained in this way. Fraudulent methods, accounting frauds, balance sheet makeup, omitting, not reporting or turning a blind eye on the problems by supervising companies, or even presenting a false positive opinion for the sake of increasing the values of the shares have become common practices. Price increases and marketing techniques based on misguiding the investors are now the realities of the new world.

The seeds of a future where honesty has sunk into oblivion along with the traditions, and where particularly the educated young adults consider the fastest ways to become rich acceptable, even if such ways may strain the limits of morality, have been planted.

The ENRON Company, having gone bankrupt by late 2001, constitutes the best example on how this new wage/compensation mechanism creates moral corruption. The analysis of the bankruptcy of the ENRON Company is also important in terms of manifesting the magnitude of the moral corruption in the financial sector.

14.11 Fraudulent System: The Case of ENRON

In the 21st century, the bankruptcies of many financial organizations in developed countries, which had been believed to be very well managed and could never go bankrupt, have been witnessed. In fact, the initial confusion caused by the bankruptcy of a company that had been believed to be invulnerable has been experienced in late 2001, with the bankruptcy of the Houston based Enron Company, which was originally founded as a pipe line company and later intermediated energy and electric sales. The fact that the Enron Company has gone bankrupt although being included in the top 500 companies ranking of Forbes and Fortune for years, has also raised questions on the reliability of the relative auditing company Arthur Andersen. In fact, the truths faced with the bankruptcy of Enron Company have drawn the attentions to the significance of the 'human' factor and the moral corruption in the financial sector.

Two substantially important concepts are encountered while trying to answer the question, 'Being among the top rankings of the fastest growing companies and the seventh largest company in the United States, how could Enron go bankrupt?'.

1. First is the scaling of the 'laisser faire, laissez passer' philosophy down to human level. This can be further explained by explaining another change: The new system of payments for the managers.

New payment systems have been developed for the senior managers and CEOs. As a new way of payment, giving out the shares of the companies to the managers as their wages, or in other words rendering them shareholders, was initially implemented and rapidly spread in the 2000s, and particularly in developed countries. While this payment system made the key managers shareholders, it also brought along a motivation focused on the value increase of the company's share.

With this system, the managers will be more powerful and of higher status, only if the value of the shares can be increased. For this reason, the motivation to increase the share value of the companies has gotten ahead of the target of enhancing the profitability of the company, which in turn has rendered all unethical and illegal ways intended to increase share value, such as spreading inaccurate information, balance sheet makeup and accounting frauds applicable.

Now that the purpose is set as to increase the share values of companies, the methods utilized for this are not inquired and the investors are misguided with methods such as fraudulent accounting technics and showing the sales higher than they actually are (Krugman 2004).

In fact, the winning culture of the new world can be deemed as 'civilized barbarism'. The 'plundering culture' is spread either by gaining more strength and power by misguiding others or by being a consumption society at the highest possible level.

Right at this point, we face the fact of the commodification of human being who measures everything with money. The fact that becoming wealthier in the shortest possible way is now set as the target and all relative ways are tried for achieving this, has caused the humane values to transform, and materiality has started to come before morality. The acceptability of all ways that will bring in prosperity and wealth in a setting where morality is no longer applicable, has dragged individuals to a ground where they get used to unethical actions and deem honesty worthless. The individual trying all unethical ways to improve its personal wealth has an important function in the growth factors. The individual that does anything and disregards morality can now be rich in a short way and contributes with its such unethical behavior pattern to financial growth.

2. As it was the case in the Enron example, multiple bankruptcies will be witnessed in such an environment where the real increases in profitabilities of the companies are masked with the ever widening unethical behaviors, if also the auditing companies do not carry out their duties properly. As implied, the case of Enron did not end only with the bankruptcy of Enron but also with the bankruptcy of the relative auditing company Arthur Andersan, and made it clear that in the new order no company can be reliable. Krugman characterized the companies of the 1990s that grew by means of fraudulent methods as 'corporate pillagers'.

While accounting fraud, fictitious sales transactions and spreading inaccurate information have become the common tactics of the companies to increase their share values, the blind eyes of the auditing companies on the actual statuses and frauds have become one of the financial realities of the century. In this way a new world has been created where fraudulent increases of share values come before the targets and concerns to increase commercial profitability and where the key executives can achieve what they want with unethical actions.

However, it is the law of the nature that all fraud-based accounts and actions will eventually be revealed for any reason. That is to say that, when the gears of the fraud-based mechanism broke down, the collapse of the whole mechanism will be in question. In fact, the breakdown of the gears of the mechanism is not a consequence, but something that will happen by the very nature of the mechanism. Right at this point, new gears, or in other words new markets, are needed for the mechanism to keep on functioning. These new markets do not only constitute a new field for the commodity trade buy also a field from in which the money will be marketed and new investor candidates will be drawn into the casino capitalism.

These new markets will eventually achieve financial growth and thus will provide the grounds on which the capital can be restructured.

The rules of order of the new world, where supra-national capital dominate the natural resources and trade routes of the world and where new markets are created by facilitating these with the mental and cultural changes of the societies, are defined through 'deregulations'.

14.12 Conclusion

The setting of neoliberal rules which initially started to spread in the 1980s has created a sui generis human model, besides paving the way for financial and political changes. On the basis of the 1978 Washington Consensus, which is accepted as the constitution of this new order, lay 'liberalization' and 'deregulation'.

The most prominent characteristic of the 2008 Global Financial Crisis that distinguishes it from the other crises is the social transformation enabling working of the fraud-based system and the deregulation-based financial system. In the finance sector that has rapidly grown ever since the 1970s, derivative markets, as the invention of finance engineering on the axis of technological developments and deregulation, have gained speed. With the 2008 Global Crisis, it has been revealed that these high volume markets can not be measured. The uncontrolled and unaudited developments in the money markets, the rate of the money movements based on technology, the illusions of 'prosperity' and 'wealth' created by means of the new instruments of money creation and the new life styles and consumption constantly being promoted by the media are among the dynamics of the global crisis of the new century.

Being the result of such dynamics of the new century, moral corruption created by the system lays on the basis of the financial crises experienced as from the early 1990s. While deregulation policies are at the core of the mechanisms that created the moral corruption in the financial sector, with the incentives and supports granted by the states, the risk appetites of financial institutions have increased, systemic risks have grown rapidly as the consequence of rescue operations and by feeling the security provided by the states financial institutions no longer hesitate to increase their risks. Another matter that causes moral corruption, is the setting of asymmetric information created by the financial institutions using the derivative markets as the mechanisms to transfer their risks and provide imperfect information while promoting their derivative products. In an environment of asymmetric information, the level of the risks being taken can not be acknowledged, and great losses occur due to the resulting wrong decisions.

In the United States and in some other developed countries, a new payment mechanism, where the wages and compensations of senior managers and CEOs are connected to the shares of their companies, has been established. With this mechanism where the income of the senior managers and CEOs are index-linked with the market value of the shares, the main purpose has shifted from improving the profitability of the company to increasing the share value of the company. Adopting methods such as balance sheet makeup and accounting fraud for the sake of increasing share values has constituted a system based on fraud. And on the basis of the fraudulent mechanism lays social transformation. Indeed, since such a mechanism would not function if the generally accepted moral values remain unchanged, all values and morality are being questioned and the conditions where winning through fraud will be deemed natural is being created.

The inability to negate the moral corruption in the financial system is the foreteller of more severe and wider crises. On the other hand, in an environment where the rules of deregulation are not changed, moral corruption will maintain its existence.

References

Acharya, V., Philippon, T., Richardson, M., & Roubini, N. (2009). The financial crisis of 2007–2009: Causes and remedies. *Financial Markets, Institutions and Instruments, 18*(2), 89–137.

Castells, M. (2005). *The information age: Economy, society and culture, vol 1: The rise of the network society* (p. 131, 132). Istanbul: Istanbul Bilgi Üniversitesi Yayınları.

Chang, H. J., & Grabel, I. (2005). *Kalkınma Yeniden: Alternatif İktisat Politikaları El Kitabı* (1st ed.). Ankara: İmge Kitabevi Yayınları.

Dell'Ariccia, G., Igan, D., & Laeven, L. (2008). *Credit booms and lending standards: Evidence from the subprime mortgage market*. CEPR Discussion Paper No. DP6683.

Eichengreen, B. (2008). *The anatomy of the financial crisis*. VoxEU, http://www.voxeu.org/index.php?q=node/1684http://www.voxeu.org.

Gerding, E. F. (2011). Credit derivatives, leverage and financial Regulation's missing macroeconomic dimension. *Berkeley Business Law Journal, 8*, 102.

Jacobs, B. I. (2009). Tumbling tower of babel: Subprime securitization and the credit crisis. *Financial Analysis Journal, CFA Institute, 65*(2), 17–30.

Jomo, K.S. (24 Sept 2005). *Globalisation for whom? A world for all* (p. 3). IDEAs, http://www.ideas.org.

Krugman, P. (2004). *The great unraveling* (p. 112). Canada: CSA Global.

Minton, M. (2008). *The community reinvestment act's harmful legacy, how it hampers access to credit* (p. 2). Competitive Enterprise Institute, No. 132.

Nier, E. (2009). *Financial stability frameworks and the role of central banks: Lessons from the crisis* (1–64). IMF Working Paper, WP/09/70.

Perotti, E. (2010). *Systemic liquidity risk and banktruptcy exceptions* (p. 1). Center for Economic Policy Research, Policy Insight No. 52.

Pettifor, A. (2006). *The coming first world debt crisis* (p. 127). Basingstoke: Palgrave Macmillan.

Slaughter, A. M. (2004). *A new world order* (p. 15). Princeton: Princeton University Press.

Stiglitz, J. E. (2004). *The roaring nineties* (p. 88). Canada: CSA Global.

Skidelsky, R. (2009). *Keynes: The Return of the Master*. (p. 6, 7). New York: Publicaffairs.

Toffler, A.(1996). Eco-spazm. *Insan*, p. 16.

US Government Printing Office. (1999, November 12). Public Law 106-102-Gramm-Leach-Bliley Act, http://www.gpo.gov/fdsys/pkg/PLAW-106publ102/content-detail.html.

Veblen, T. (2005). *Aylak Sınıfın Teorisi* (p. 176). İstanbul: Babil Yayınları.

Chapter 15
The Responsibilities of Corporations: An Analytical Appraisal

Abubakar Sadiq Kasum

Abstract The concern for this study is about the long-drawn-out CSR argument, which was observed to have been controversial, because the responsibilities of businesses are rarely critically analyzed. The study, therefore, appraises the responsibilities of businesses based on a strictly just and fair relationship with all the stakeholders. So that corporations are only and 'strictly expected' to do what is right and fair at all times—being ethical. The study suggests that corporate responsibilities can be classified from three guises namely primary (which are about a business's survival in its market and industry), secondary (which is about its responsibilities as a corporate citizen) and tertiary (this in effect is discretionary and is about its moral obligations to society and its stakeholders). The study observes that all corporate responsibilities, except philanthropy, can be and should be discharged by corporations and that this will only mean doing the right things which have been argued to be good for business. The study is also of the opinion that if corporations are fair especially with, measure and value as they relate to price, philanthropy will rarely be possible and may even be unnecessary. The study, therefore, concludes that rather than cutting corners in terms of their charitable obligations, corporations should be compelled to do what is right and to act fairly in their dealings with stakeholders.

15.1 Introduction

Corporate Social Responsibility (CSR) discourse is mature and rich. It is, however, important to note that CSR discourse is still a work in progress, as intellectuals continue to strive towards the best society, while identifying the best of roles for

A. S. Kasum (✉)
University of Ilorin, Ilorin, Nigeria
e-mail: abubakarsk@yahoo.com

A. Yüksel Mermod and S. O. Idowu (eds.), *Corporate Social Responsibility in the Global Business World*, DOI: 10.1007/978-3-642-37620-7_15,
© Springer-Verlag Berlin Heidelberg 2014

the business sector in society. According to Votaw's (1973) the term "social responsibility", is a brilliant one; it means something, but not always the same thing to everybody. To some it conveys the idea of legal responsibility or liability; to others it means socially responsible behaviour in an ethical sense; still to others, the meaning transmitted is that of "responsible for, in a causal mode; many simply equate it with a charitable contribution". In line with these, various roles have been ascribed to the business sector, in the name of CSR. While to some sector of society a business is only expected to concern itself with making the best profits for its owners, the other extreme believes "A corporation's stakeholder constituents ... extend far beyond the traditional confines of shareholders, employees, managers, consumers and investors" (Brammer and Millington 2003) and want businesses to distribute a reasonable proportion of their profits for good causes.

The two extremes together with the various middle grounds, no doubt, provide justifications for their stance and all the ideologies are probably capable of being accommodated. It is the belief of this study that the current state of CSR discourse demands negotiation. Stakeholders outside the organizations and corporate watchdogs and the civil society are placed in a position where issues and areas where there are differences can be negotiated with the companies not to be too profit oriented but to consider also other stakeholders who are directly or indirectly affected by their actions. This is not a good situation, as it places businesses in a better bargaining position in any societal contract to be agreed.

This study considers a situation where nobody goes with a bowl in hand begging for CSR or a situation that gives the corporation the opportunity to stop a scenario where stakeholders and corporate watchdogs and the civil society are compelling managers to violate the terms of their fiduciary duties to use owners' resources for things which are non value adding to providers of capital. Based on the statement of Friedman (1970) that "The only social responsibility of business managers is to maximize profits while complying with the rules of the game", we argue that strict compliance with societal-embedded and legal contractual agreements, is enough for CSR and corporations may not even be able to do more than that. It is a state of the world where the business sector is only expected to do what is objectively their responsibility and those responsibilities are fulfilled completely and nothing less than 'strictly completely' Fisher (2004). Similarly, Munilla and Miles (2005), argue that the compliance perspective of society should not go to the extent of coercion perspective but where compliance is voluntary and total.

15.2 The Concept of Corporate Social Responsibility

Scholars have defined CSR in different ways. According to Whitehouse (2006), definitions of CSR range from the ... "view of the one and only social responsibility of business being "to use its resources and engage in activities designed to increase its profits so long as it stays within the rules of the game" to the "conception which encourages companies to obey the law, be profitable, be ethical, and be a good corporate citizen". The school of taught that business enterprises are "being concerned with CSR only to the extent that it contributes to the aim of business, which is the creation of long-term value for the owners of the business" is referred to as the profit approach. The school of taught at the other end suggests "that organizations are not only accountable to their shareholders but should also balance a multiplicity of stakeholders interests that can affect or are affected by the achievement of an organization's objectives" is referred to as stakeholder approach (Marrewijk 2003).

Most of the definitions of CSR encourage companies to be good corporate citizens. According to Fisher (2004), "Corporate social responsibility is defined as an obligation of the organization to act in ways that serve both its own interests and the interests of its many external stakeholders". "Organizations have a social responsibility to protect and enhance society in which they operate" (Fisher 2004). Epistien (1987) sees social responsibility as "…achieving outcomes from organizational decisions concerning specific issues or problems which have beneficial rather than adverse effects upon pertinent corporate stakeholders". In a similar tone, Strike et al. (2006) have defined CSR as "the set of corporate actions that positively affect an identifiable social stakeholder's interests and do not violate the legitimate claims of another identifiable social stakeholder (in the long run)". Marrewijk (2003) simply put CSR as "more humane, more ethical and a more transparent way of doing business". Although with different degrees of freedom for corporations, these scholars believe, that an organization is not only about its positive actions on its owners but on all its stakeholders.

15.3 Responsibilities of Business

CSR discourse provides extensive literature on the responsibilities of business. Quazi and O'Brien (2000), in describing CSR, have identified the classical, socio-economic, modern and philanthropic views of CSR. Under the classical view, the business is concerned with making profit for its owners. Business responsibility expands to basic social demands under the socio-economic point of view, while the modern view embraces "the broader matrix of society…and includes the stakeholders view noted earlier" (Quazi and O'Brien 2000). The philanthropic view, according to Quazi and O'Brien (2000), expands the responsibilities of business to include charitable activities. In relating social responsibility to ethics, Fisher (2004) stated that the "most widely supported view, is that there are four dimensions of corporate social responsibility: economic, legal, ethical and philanthropic". "The pyramid places economic responsibilities at the foundation and moving up the pyramid are legal, ethical and philanthropic responsibilities" (Fisher 2004).

Robbins et al. (2000:183) identify four stages of social responsibility, based on stakeholders' categories. Business at first is responsible only to stockholders, at stage two, to the stockholders and employees, at stage three stakeholders in the specific environment are added and at the final stage society as a whole is included

(Robbins et. al. 2000). Munilla and Miles (2005) put forward continuums of the responsibilities of business. The continuums include the Social Responsibility Continuum that emphasizes compliance perspective, under which corporations are expected to meet legal and ethical requirements only. Others are the strategic perspective where corporations change their business models to include CSR strategies that create economic returns for stockholders and the forced perspective where corporations are pressured by various entities to go beyond compliance or strategic interests and expend resources to all stakeholders, which may not be in the best interest of the stockholders. Unlike the previous scholars, Munilla and Miles (2005) place Legal and Ethical responsibilities above Economic responsibilities.

15.4 Appraisal of Corporate Responsibilities

According to Maignan (2001), businesses must maximize profits; Control their production costs strictly; Plan for their long-term success; Always improve economic performance; Ensure that their employees act within the standards defined by the law; Refrain from putting aside their contractual obligations; Refrain from bending the law even it this helps improve performance. Always submit to the principles defined by the regulatory system; Permit ethical concerns to negatively affect economic performance; Ensure that the respect of ethical principles has priority over economic performance; be committed to well-defined ethics principles. Avoid compromising ethical standards in order to achieve corporate goals; Help solve social problems. Participate in the management of public affairs; allocate some of their resources to philanthropic activities; Play a role in our society that goes beyond the mere generation of profits. Soh and Markus (1995) similarly appraise the responsibilities organizations and state that organizations could be viewed as rational, goal-seeking entities; successful goal accomplishment is the appropriate measure of performance for this view. According to Soh and Markus (1995), it may also be viewed as a coalition of power constituencies (team production theory); the measure of performance appropriate for this view is the degree of satisfaction of the constituents such as employees and customers. Finally, it could be viewed as entities "involved in a bargaining relationship with their surroundings" (communitarian theory); performance here will be measured in the organization's ability to garner scarce resources and productively turn them into valued outputs. This study, therefore, identifies the real and practical duties that a corporation can be expected to discharge. Corporations' responsibilities will include:

- To produce and sell goods/render services, at a price,
- To produce/render adequate quality and quantity of goods and services, respectively,
- To (adequately) reward employees and other inputs of production,
- To make profit for owners,

- Management of the impacts of business on environment,
- To pay taxes and other levies of government,
- To comply with all relevant regulations and standards,
- Healthy competition/rivalry, and
- Philanthropy.

Although CSR has been intelligently broken down and ranked to, include Economic, Legal, Ethical and Philanthropic responsibilities. This study hereby, reviews this analysis for the purpose of the intended line of argument by holistically looking at the implication of corporate activities.

There are responsibilities that are part of live of business. Businesses must fulfill these responsibilities; otherwise, the business does not exist. From the above list, those responsibilities include:

- To produce and/or sell goods/render services, at a price,
- To (adequately) reward employees and other inputs of production, and
- To make profit for owners.

According to Quazi and O'Brien (2000), '...social responsibility of business is a single dimensional activity in which business has the only responsibility of supplying goods and services to society at a profit...' A corporation must either be offering goods or services to customers, if not, it is not a business, because the purposes of any venture is either good or service or both. To produce or render services is always at a cost to the corporation and the costs must be met. Lastly, all investors expect benefits and in fact, the purposes of investment are the benefits, be it return or appreciation. All of these are basic for business, none of it could be left out, and because of these, we refer to them here as '**primary**' because they are '**ordinary/fundamental**' responsibilities of a corporation. The responsibilities are delivered to the primary stakeholders and according to Whitehouse (2006) these stakeholders are the shareholders, investors, employees, customers, and supplier.

Because the corporation is a part of the community, some responsibilities are required by law and otherwise imposed on it. Those responsibilities are by right demanded of corporations and the corporations either fulfill the responsibilities or exit that community. These responsibilities, therefore, become necessary, but if not demanded by the community, the corporation can continue to operate. They include:

- Management of the impacts of business on the environment,
- To pay taxes and other levies of government,
- To comply with all relevant regulations and standards.

The existence of the corporation in the community where the corporation operates may bring about changes to human beings, animals, land, waters, air and plants in the community. If the existence of a corporation reduces the quality or quantity of any of the above or other components of the environment, the corporation must, as a matter of obligation, restore or compensate for it. This is because the corporation directly caused the situation. Without their operations the reduced state of the environment will not be. According to Kasum (2010), "organisations that cause harm to the environment should be made to pay an amount in tax apart from the general corporation tax in respect of the degradation they have directly caused". In addition, "research shows that consumers prefer to purchase products from and invest in shares of those companies caring for the environment and maintaining good citizenship behavior" (Quazi and O'Brien 2000).

The activities of governments are, usually, financed through taxation. It is usually a joint decision of citizens; including business owners and every individual, that corporate citizens must pay taxes, except by exemptions of the Law. Standardization involves inspection, assurance and certification services that are aimed at regulating business, enforcing contracts and assurance for acceptable social and environmental behavior expectations (Blair, Williams and Lin 2008). According to Russell (2007), standards that are applicable to and are expected to be complied with are either 'de facto' standards (that became standards through market activities), voluntary consensus standard (that are set by committees and association) or 'de jure' standards (that are mandated by the government). Therefore, corporations in a standardized/regulated environment must comply with standards and other similar regulations, except in some instances, the 'de facto' standards. Although the items mentioned above are not the purposes of business, they are unavoidably incidental to doing business and should not be negotiable. Going by their importance, this study classifies them as '**secondary**' because they are '**civic and/or legal**' responsibilities of corporations.

The items left in our list noted previously include:

- To produce/render adequate quality and quantity of goods and services, respectively,
- Healthy competition/rivalry, and
- Philanthropy.

These items we refer to as '**Tertiary**' responsibilities, because they can be '**discretionary**' and a matter of '**moral and ethics**'. Looking at the items, it is possible that the quality of goods and services may be standardized or regulated, it is rear that the quantities are standardized or regulated but quality with reference to price. According to Roe (2001), "when much of a nation's industry is monopolistically organized, maximizing shareholders' wealth would maximize the monopolists' profits, induce firms to produce fewer goods than society could potentially produce and motivate firms to raise price to consumers beyond that which is necessary to produce the goods". It is a responsibility that corporation produce, within their capacity, as much as the consumers can buy. It is also moral and fair that the price charged is that which is necessary to produce the goods, so that those weaknesses of consumers are not capitalized on to in order to over-price the good.

It is expected that a corporation should conduct its activities in a manner that other businesses are not undermined. The business environment is a competitive one and undermining another business may be advantageous to a business, which makes it part of the competition. Healthy competition is, therefore, advisable only to the extent of the benefit in return, against the cost of unhealthy rivalry. Philanthropic giving is separately discussed in the next section.

15.5 Corporate Philanthropy

The primary responsibilities of business are fundamental and are necessary for business survival. The secondary responsibilities too are not avoidable. Discharging the responsibilities is only doing the right thing. "Non-compliance', however, 'is also costly in term of fines…" (Quazi and O'Brien 2000). It is fair and beneficial to corporations that the tertiary items are discharged. Philanthropy is controversial because it is difficult to prove that it is fair to give owners' profit out in charity. Philanthropy thus is the only responsibility that is up for negotiation.

According to Brammer and Millington (2005), motivations for firms making philanthropic donations include demonstrating 'their social responsiveness to the communities in which they operate… and as an activity that stimulates goodwill towards companies within those communities'. According to them, philanthropic donations may, therefore, serve both the needs of communities, and enhance the long-run financial performance of the firm. In fact, what was then the understanding of CSR was much more about philanthropic giving (Whitehouse 2006). In similar manner, Minow (1999) stated that "companies should evaluate their charitable contributions exclusively in terms of documentable benefits to shareholders' value and consider charitable contributions a part of the company's advertising and marketing expenditures", therefore "companies which make higher levels of philanthropic expenditures have better reputations" (Brammer and Millington 2005). Corporations, therefore, select charities in areas that are related to their businesses (Whitehouse 2006).

A brief survey of financial statements of 28 out of the 218 listed companies on the Nigeria Stock Exchange shows that 23 of the companies provided CSR information with only 19 disclosing it under the heading of CSR. All the 23 reported philanthropic giving (named: financial support, provision of fund, donation and sponsorship) and only 7 out of the 23 provided other CSR information in addition to philanthropic giving. Only 2 out of the non philanthropic CSR are to correct environmental impacts. These show that philanthropy could be said to be the most understood form of CSR by Nigerian companies.

15.6 Discussion

This study is of the opinion that doing what is right and not less than right, with a bit of fairness takes care of all that is expected of corporations as their responsibilities. The study is of the view that all responsibilities of business except for philanthropy is taken care of by these. This view also supports Munilla and Miles' (2005) continuums of the responsibilities of business that gave primary importance to legal and ethical responsibilities. In essence, all responsibilities of corporation are mandatory apart from charitable giving.

According to Brammer and Millington (2005), "discretionary aspects of social responsibility, including corporate donations, may not be in the financial interests of organizations". "We cannot and must not expect formal organizations, or their representatives acting in their official capacities, to be honest, courageous, considerate, sympathetic, or to have any kind of moral integrity" (Soares 2003). However, while engaging in activities that increases owners profits, corporations can stay "within the rules of the game, which is to say, engage in open and free competition without deception or fraud" (Fisher 2004) to do what is right always and be fair. Added to some established findings that charitable giving in most cases is to the extent that they are related and beneficial to the philanthropic corporation, corporations should be obliged to always do the right things and be fair, but not to necessarily include charity. "The company that is viable economically through its good use of financial, social and environmental resources may not be good for society. If the company then distributes some of its wealth through philanthropy, it does not necessarily make the company socially responsible" (Whitehouse 2005). These will imply that all the responsibilities; primary, secondary and tertiary should be obligatory except for philanthropic giving.

A critical evaluation of philanthropy (if corporations apply the principle of fairness) will suggest that philanthropy is not practicable. It is fair that investors receive returns adequate for their interests; it is fair that customers pay the price necessary to produce the goods. Given that costs of inputs are adequately remunerated, a fair price will leave a return around the market rate, which should be adequate for investors as their return. If charitable donations are given at this stage, the investors will be remunerated at less than an adequate rate of return. This is not likely to be acceptable and the investors can change to other corporations in the market. If, on the other hand, philanthropic giving is made and investors still receives adequate return, it only means that a super-profit (profit over and above market rate/cost of investment) has been made. The most likely source of super-profit is pricing over and above that which is necessary to produce the goods. This last possible state is then equal to collecting with the left hand in the first instance and giving part of or, at most, same back, but calling it charity.

15.7 Conclusion

According to Wilmot (2001), "... a responsible corporation is one that behaves well—wisely, prudently and morally". It is, therefore, pertinent that we recognize that it will be difficult to ask corporation not to be prudent or not to act wisely. Furthermore, it is not necessary that we ask or negotiate for charities from businesses; they are not for that purpose. However, "everyone is in a competitive market and if companies reputations start to suffer because they are not doing what they should be doing then investors and customers will go elsewhere" (Whitehouse 2005). It will thus not be too much to ask corporations to do what is right and to act fairly.

In this study, we identified that CSR is a concept that is defined, as expecting organization to be responsible to owners only at one end and to be responsible to society as a whole at the other. CSR component include economic, legal, ethical and philanthropic responsibilities, while another author provided for stages of responsibilities to only the stockholders; then the stockholders and employees; followed by the stage where stakeholders in the specific environment are added and the final stage that society as a whole is included. Economic responsibility used to be ranked highest but the recent position is that legal and ethical responsibilities come before economic responsibilities.

This study went further to appraise the practical responsibilities of corporation and came up with three categories of corporate responsibilities that include:

- Primary responsibilities (ordinary and fundamental to survival as a going concern)
- Secondary responsibilities (mandatory, civic responsibilities for corporations as citizens)
- Tertiary responsibilities (discretionary, for ethical and moral reasons).

The place and nature of philanthropy was, also, appraised. The study observed that charity is allotted top priority as a CSR. Nigerian companies were observed to place high priority on philanthropy as CSR and majority of the companies have only philanthropic giving as CSR. Philanthropy, according to literature, is against proprietary purpose of business, therefore, corporations usually engage in philanthropy for the benefits to corporations; that is for strategic reasons.

The study, based on the revelations, finally argued that philanthropy should not be demanded or negotiated from corporations. Rather, corporations should be made to do the right things by discharging all corporate responsibilities and to act fairly. This is supported by the fact that philanthropy is in fact, on most occasions, beneficial to the benevolent corporations and the fact that it is not practicable by a truly fair corporation.

References

Blair, M. M., Williams C. A. & Lin L. (2008). The Role of standardization, certification and assurance services in global business. *Comparative Research in Law and Political Economics Research Paper No 12/2008,* www.ssrn.com. Retrieved in February 2009.

Brammer, S., & Millington, A. (2003). The effect of stakeholder preferences, organizational structure and industry type on corporate community involvement. *Journal of Business Ethics,* 45(3), 213–226. http://www.jstor.org/stable/25075067. Accessed: October 2010.

Brammer, S., & Millington, A. (2005). Corporate reputation and philanthropy: an empirical analysis. *Journal of Business Ethics*, 61(1), 29–44. http://www.jstor.org/stable/25123599. Accessed Sept 2010.

Epstein, E. M. (1987). The corporate social policy process: beyond business ethics, corporate responsibility, and corporate social responsiveness. *California Management Review, 29*(3), 99–114.

Fisher, J. (2004). Social responsibility and ethics: clarifying the concepts. *Journal of Business Ethics*, 52(4), 391–400. http://www.jstor.org/stable/25123269. Accessed Oct 2010.

FFriedman, M. (1970). Social responsibility of business is to increase its profit', The New York Times Magazine. http://www.umich.edu/ ~ thecore/doc/Friedman.pdf. Accessed Sep 2010.

Kasum, A. S. (2010). Environmental degradation problems caused by human activities in Nigeria: enforced vs voluntary solution. *International Journal of Banking, Accounting and Finance, 2*(3), 245–260.

Maignan, I (2001). Consumers' perceptions of corporate social responsibilities: a cross-cultural comparison. *Journal of Business Ethics*, 30(1), 57–72. http://www.jstor.org/stable/25074480. Accessed Octs 2010.

Marrewijk, M. V. (2003). Concepts and definitions of CSR and corporate sustainability: between agency and communion. *Journal of Business Ethics*, 44(2/3), 95–105. http://www.jstor.org/stable/25075020. Accessed: September 2010.

Minow, N. (1999). Corporate charity an oxymoron? *The Business Lawyer, 54*(3), 997–1005.

Munilla, L. and M. P. Miles, M. P. (2005), 'The Corporate Social Responsibility Continuum as a Component of Stake holder Theory', *Business and Society Review*, 110(4), 371-387.

Quazi, A. M. & O'Brien, D. (2000). An empirical test of a cross-national model of corporate social responsibility, *Journal of Business Ethics*, 25(1), 33–51. http://www.jstor.org/stable/25074298. Accessed Sept 2010.

Robbins, S. P., Bergman, R., Stagg, I., & Coulter, M. (2000). *Management* (2nd ed.). Sydney: Prentice Hall.

Roe, M. J. (2001). The shareholder wealth maximization norm and industrial organization. *University of Pennsylvania Law Review*, 2063–2081, www.ssrn.com, Retrieved in Nov 2008.

Russell A. L. (2007). The America system: a schumpeterian history of standardization. Progress on Point Release 14.4. The Progress and Freedom Foundation. Washington.

Soares, C. (2003). Corporate versus individual moral responsibility. *Journal of Business Ethics*, 46(2), 143–150. http://www.jstor.org/stable/25075096. Accessed Sept 2010.

Soh, C. & Markus M. L. (1995). How it create business value: a process theory synthesis. In G. Ariav (Ed.), *Proceedings of the 16th International Conference on Information System, Amsterdam*, December, 10–13.

Strike, V. M., Gao, J. & Bansal, P. (2006). Being good while being bad: social responsibility and the international diversification of USFirms', *Journal of International Business Studies*, 37(6), 850–862. http://www.jstor.org/stable/4540388. Accessed Oct 2010.

Votaw, D. (1973). Genius becomes rare. In D. Votaw & S. P. Sethi (Eds.), *The corporate dilemma: traditional values versus contemporary problems*. Englewood Cliffs: Prentice Hall.

Whitehouse, L. (2006). Corporate social responsibility: views from the frontline. *Journal of Business Ethics*, 63(3), 279–296. http://www.jstor.org/stable/25123709. Accessed Sept 2010.

Wilmot, S (2001). Corporate moral responsibility: what can we infer from our understanding of organisations? *Journal of Business Ethics*, 30(2): 161–169 http://www.jstor.org/stable/25074488. Accessed Sept 2010.

Chapter 16
Success in Philanthropic Corporate Social Responsibility: The Case of Turkey

İrem Eren-Erdoğmuş, Emine Çobanoğlu and Burcu Öğüt

Abstract Corporate Social Responsibility (CSR) is about a firm's activities in its social, economic and environmental performance—its triple bottom line. CSR has received considerable attention due to changing consumer expectations and failure of governments to solve many social problems. One of the concentrations in CSR is on philanthropic responsibilities, which supports that a company should assist projects that will enhance community's quality of life (Lantos, 2001). Philanthropy is used as a means of public relations in order to promote company's image or brand through cause-related marketing or other types of sponsorships. Every philanthropic CSR initiative has to be planned taking into consideration the stakeholders, company, and context. Stakeholder expectations and perceptions vary from culture to culture, from country to country, and current topics of interest or happenings in that specific environment. The aim of this paper is to draw evidence from CSR practices in an emerging market, Turkey, to shed light on some types of local philanthropic CSR activities that have gained acceptance, appreciation, and sometimes criticism of the society; so that, companies willing to initiate philanthropic CSR projects in emerging markets are inspired in the process. Two cases were selected, Sabancı Holding, and Borusan Holding. Both companies are well-known, leading conglomerates of the country, are considered by the public and the business world among the leaders of CSR in Turkey. Sabancı Holding was included in the study to provide a positive example since the holding's chairwoman, Güler Sabancı, was recently awarded "The Clinton Global Citizen" due to her contributions to the welfare of the women and young girls in Turkey. Borusan Holding, on the other hand, was included in the study since it recently suffered public criticisms due to the "supposedly" discriminatory acts in handling their sponsorship contract (Başörtüsü 2011). While the CSR projects contributed to Sabancı's image in a positive way, Borusan's image was negatively affected. In topic selection, Sabancı Holding spared its resources on areas that are

İ. Eren-Erdoğmuş (✉) · E. Çobanoğlu · B. Öğüt
Marmara University, Istanbul, Turkey
e-mail: ireme@marmara.edu.tr

A. Yüksel Mermod and S. O. Idowu (eds.), *Corporate Social Responsibility in the Global Business World*, DOI: 10.1007/978-3-642-37620-7_16,
© Springer-Verlag Berlin Heidelberg 2014

more pressing as needs of the general society such as education and welfare of the underprivileged in society. The CSR topics of Sabancı were accepted and embraced more by the masses, and Sabancı and Güler Sabancı got awareness, popularity, liking, and preference of the public for their CSR activities. Borusan Holding, on the other hand, apart from its support for education, focused on projects that attract the attention of the elitist minority in the country such as motorsports and Western classical music. When one small mistake on in one of these niche CSR activities occurred, criticism of the masses, even though they were not part of the target market, was raised in traditional and social media, punishing Borusan for missing out facts related to certain sensitive issues in Turkey. Overall, the results of the study show that the topics that are accepted by the general public are the "safe" way to reach effective CSR solutions. Of course, niche areas should not be neglected. As these niche areas are selected, besides the primary target markets of the brands, the interest and feelings of the general public should also be taken into account. A delicate balance is needed for observing the reflections of every act in the mass market.

16.1 Introduction

Corporate Social Responsibility (CSR), a firm's activities and status related to its perceived or societal stakeholder obligations (Brown and Dacin 1997), received serious attention in order to respond to changing consumer expectations and failure of governments to solve many social problems (Smith 2003). There is no consensus on the definition of corporate social responsibility and its extent. To some it means legal responsibility, to some it means socially responsible behaviors in an ethical manner, to some others it means being responsible for in a causal mode, many others see it as charitable donations and still, some others describe it as a mere synonym of legitimacy. The companies realized the mutual benefits and outcomes of CSR and involved in strategic planning to implement successful CSR projects, and inform the consumers and society about their CSR activities (Hohnen 2007). CSR is seen as a vehicle to establish good relationships with the public, support brand image and corporate reputation, improve employee commitment, and create positive impact in the marketplace (Godfrey 2005; Lou and Bhattacharya 2006; Ali et al. 2010; Bronn and Vrioni 2001; Vlachos et al. 2009; Porter and Kramer 2002).

One of the concentrations in CSR is on philanthropic responsibilities, which has received a significant attention in recent years. Philanthropic CSR, which makes the company a good corporate citizen (Wulfson 2001), says that a company should assist performing arts, participate in voluntary and charitable activities, provide assistance to educational institutions, and support projects that will enhance community's quality of life (Lantos 2001). Some CSR activities are requirements for the companies such as fulfilling economic and legal obligations, however, philanthropic responsibilities are social contributions that are voluntary. Thus, these are considered to be the least important among the rest of social responsibilities (Carroll 1991), but also the most visible way of a company to help society and gain appreciation in return. That's why philanthropic responsibilities of the firms will be the focus of this study.

Philanthropy is used as a means of public relations in order to promote company's image or brand through cause-related marketing or other types of sponsorships (Kotler and Lee 2006). One of the methods that companies can use is corporate cause promotions, whereby a company provides funds, goods and services in order to increase awareness, support and participation in a social cause. Another type of philanthropic responsibility is cause-related marketing, in which a company promises to donate a percentage or a fixed amount of its product sales for a social cause. In corporate social marketing, on the other hand, a company supports a campaign that aims to change the attitude regarding health, security, environment and social wellbeing. When a company directly supports a cause or a non-profit organization by donations, cash, goods and services, then it is engaged in corporate philanthropy. Community volunteering is another alternative philanthropic act that a company can do by encouraging its employees, agents and suppliers to donate their time and effort in order to support social causes and non-profit organizations. Finally, a company can run business practices and investments voluntarily that increase social welfare and protect environment, what is called socially responsible business practice (Kotler and Lee 2006).

It is vital to strategically plan and implement any philanthropic project in order to be successful. Philanthropic CSR can be conceptualized as the degree of fit between the society's expectations of the company action and company mission, objectives, resources (Maignan et al. 2005; Hohnen 2007) and what a firm's managers consider to be legitimate societal demands (Zenisek 1979). Thus, every philanthropic CSR initiative has to be planned taking into consideration the stakeholders, company, and context. The stakeholder opinion and nature is a matter of significant managerial interest since companies seek to receive their approval and support (Maignan et al. 2005). It is also essential to evaluate the context and events in which companies operate since they can affect both implementation and also perception of the stakeholders (O'Riordan and Fairbass 2008). Stakeholder expectations and perceptions vary from culture to culture, from country to country, and current topics of interest or happenings in that specific environment. For example, CSR in developing countries has become a topic of interest, in recognition of the fact that context matters and the peculiarities of stakeholders in emerging markets (Kolk and Lenfant 2010).

Emerging market countries are gaining importance in the world trade every year, and are described as key locations for world trade growth. These markets, however, present both opportunities and also unique challenges embedded in their nature, what makes it hard for the multinational companies (MNCs) to import the "Western-style marketing" to compete in these markets. Emerging markets differ from advanced markets on dimensions such as political and economic uncertainty, low resources, price sensitivity, informal economies, weaker infrastructures, and reliance on social contracts (Auklah et al. 2000; Wright et al. 2005; de Soto 2000; BCG Report 2011). Strategies that work in the developed markets do not work in emerging markets (Dawar and Chattopadhyay 2002). To be accepted, and appreciated in emerging market settings, companies need to create social value or become locally embedded in the social infrastructure (London and Hart 2004). There is the pressure to create more inclusive capitalism for companies working in emerging markets (Hart and Christensen 2002). Thus, working on solutions based upon leveraging existing social, economic, and environmental capital of the emerging markets requires differentiated and specialized philanthropic CSR projects that differ from those in advanced nations.

The aim of this paper is to draw evidence from CSR practices in an emerging market and shed light on the types of local philanthropic CSR activities that have gained acceptance, appreciation, and sometimes criticism of the society; so that, companies willing to initiate philanthropic CSR projects in emerging markets are guided in the process. Turkey provides a good case to study emerging markets since the country is described within the MIST group of countries, the next tier of large emerging economies, at about 1 % of global GDP each, with a large population and market (After BRIC comes MIST 2011). The country is also an attractive destination for foreign direct investment (FDI), eager to join European Union, pushing economic reforms, with a regulated banking system, and enjoying a young population (Emerging Markets: Beyond the Big Four 2005).

16.2 Philanthrophic CSR in Turkey

Turkey has a rich and significant philanthropic history dated back to the Ottoman era, when the "waqf" (foundation) was the premier institutional mechanism for philanthropic provision of public services. Waqfs are common form of philanthropy in the Islamic tradition. Giving, as a part of the Islamic religion, was reflected in the business life of the country since those times (Ararat and Göcenoğlu 2008). However, even though the philanthropic CSR concept in Turkey dated back to the Ottoman period, the country lived a long period of stagnation in CSR activities until the recent years due to economic downturns and political instabilities.

The structured CSR activities in Turkey started in the last 30 years. Philanthropists who were also the founding leaders of the family-owned holding companies like Vehbi Koc, Kadir Has, İzzet Baysal, Hacı Ömer Sabancı, and Asım Kocabıyık were the pioneers in the community development via their donations to hospitals, schools and museums (Turkey Corporate Social Responsibility Baseline Report 2010). Most holdings in Turkey have provisions to donate a percentage of their net profits to foundations set up by their founding families. The drivers behind this phenomenon can be related to the need for gaining legitimacy and social acceptance for the relatively new wealth, in a country where the duality of income levels is disturbing (Ararat and Göcenoğlu 2008). The decreasing role of the state in the economy, political stabilization and the increasing GDP growth for the last three decades led many companies to engage in intensive CSR actions. The increased association with international bodies, events, developments and campaigns was another factor that helped to establish consciousness for CSR in Turkey. Additionally, the increasing number of MNCs, that followed the procedures of their home country, promoted CSR policies, and set the CSR standards in the Turkish market (Ararat 2008). Finally, the awareness and interest of the Turkish citizens in social responsibility projects increased after the Izmit earthquake in 1999. This catastrophe proved that the governments alone was not efficient in such incidents and that everybody should do something, so civil organizations, companies and NGOs started to take more responsibilities and actions (Turkey Corporate Social Responsibility Baseline Report 2010).

Capital Magazine, a national monthly business magazine, in corporation with GfK research company, have been publishing a yearly report "The Leaders of Corporate Social Responsibility" since 2005. The report of 2010 shows that 60 % of the public's most admired CSR projects were the ones on education (Leaders of Corporate Social Responsibility 2010). Another study in 2009 also proved that the expectations of the society from the companies were to develop projects to support education in Turkey (Turkey Corporate Social Responsibility Baseline Report 2010). As the interest of the society in CSR increased, Kelgökmen (2010) stated that 75 % of the Turkish society wanted that social responsibility projects should be announced effectively.

16.3 Methodology

The aim of this research is to provide a guideline to companies that want to apply CSR initiative in an emerging market setting in order to differentiate themselves and create positive image in the minds and hearts of emerging market consumers. Taking into consideration the purpose of the study, a qualitative case study approach is preferred since the research considers processes such as topic selection, and implementation of the CSR initiative rather than outcomes (Ghauri and Gronhaug 2010; Yin 2003). CSR projects are considered as essential to promote the image of the company and its brands since in emerging markets, inclusive capitalism is a requirement of the society (Hart and Christensen 2002). However, it is important to choose an appropriate subject, plan the CSR process, and implement the CSR plan effectively. CSR can boost the image of the company as much as it can damage it unless it is run appropriately. Considering these issues, the case selection was based on providing positive and negative perceptions of CSR initiatives in the public's eyes. Two cases were selected, the Sabancı Holding, and the Borusan Holding. Both of the holdings are well-known CSR leaders according to Capital Magazine's study. The Sabancı Holding was included in the study to provide a positive example since the holding's chairwoman, Güler Sabancı, was recently awarded "The Clinton Global Citizen" due to her contributions to the welfare of the women and young girls in Turkey (Güler Sabancı'ya Küresel Vatandaşlık Ödülü 2011). The "Fifth Philanthropic Seminar" held by the Sabancı Foundation (http://www.sabancivakfi.org/sayfa/nesilden-nesile-hayirseverlik-2), also found reflections in the eyes of the public in 2011, improving the Sabancı and Güler Sabancı image. The Borusan Holding, on the other hand, was included in the study since it recently suffered public criticisms due to the "supposedly" discriminatory acts in handling their sponsorship contract (Başörtüsü BMW'nin Kimyasını Bozdu 2011). While the CSR projects contributed to Sabancı's image in a positive way, Borusan's image was negatively affected.

16.4 The Case of Sabanci Holding

Sabancı Holding is one of Turkey's leading industrial and financial conglomerates, which had been founded by Hacı Ömer Sabancı in 1967. The mission of the holding is to manage a competitive strategic portfolio with sustainable growth potential to create value for all of its stakeholders. The holding has controlling interests in 11 companies that enjoy leading positions in their respective sectors which include financial services, energy, cement, retail, tire, tire reinforcement materials and automotive. They currently operate in 18 countries and market their products in various regions in Europe, the Middle East, Asia, North Africa and North and South America. Having generated significant value and know how in Turkey, the holding companies further extended their operations into the global market especially through joint ventures. Sabancı Holding's multinational business partners include such prominent companies as Ageas, Aviva, Bridgestone, Carrefour, Citigroup, Dia, Heidelberg Cement, Hilton International, International Paper, Mitsubishi Motor Co., Philip Morris and Verbund. In 2010, the consolidated revenue of Sabancı Holding was US$ 13.0 billion with an EBITDA of US$ 3.0 billion (Hacı Ömer Sabancı Holding Annual Report 2010).

16.4.1 Glancing at the Philanthropic CSR Initiatives

Hacı Ömer Sabancı's sons set up the Haci Omer Sabanci Foundation (the Sabanci Foundation) in 1974 to continue his philosophy of life, "to share what they have gained from this land with its people." (Hacı Ömer Sabancı Holding Annual Report 2010). The Sabancı family members view social responsibility as an unchangeable core component of the holding's management approach to respect and build proximity with people (Uslu 2012). According to a "2010 Leaders of Corporate Social Responsibility" research of the Capital Magazine with GfK research company, Sabancı Holding ranked 1st from the consumers' perpective, and ranked

3h from management perspective and Güler Sabancı ranked 1st among the CSR leaders both from the consumers' and also the managers' eyes.

The Foundation programs and investments have the mission "to promote social development and awareness among current and future generations by supporting initiatives that impact and create lasting change in people's lives" (www.sabancivakfi.org). In addition to its existing investments in health, education, scholarships, awards, arts and culture, the Foundation also created new programs that focus directly on "women", "youth" and "the disabled". Over the past 36 years, the Foundation has built almost 120 institutions in 78 residential areas across Turkey, specifically schools, student dormitories, health facilities, cultural centers, sports facilities, libraries, teacher centers, social facilities, museums and the Sabancı University. The income base of the Foundation, was sustained mainly through donations from family members, the Sabancı Group companies and the revenue generated by its own assets, making the Sabancı Foundation one of the largest foundations in Turkey. The foundation is a member of the Turkish Third Sector Foundation (TÜSEV), the European Foundation Center (EFC), the Council on Foundations (COF) and the European Consortium of Foundations on Human Rights and Disability (Hacı Ömer Sabancı Holding Annual Report 2010). In 2006, the Sabancı Foundation also entered into a partnership with the United Nations agencies in Turkey and the Ministry of Interior Affairs to support the United Nations Joint Program to Promote and Protect the Human Rights of Women and Female Children in six pilot cities (Global Giving Matters 2011).

The Sabancı Group considers the success of its companies with regard to social responsibility activities as a significant criterion for evaluating overall company performance. All of its executives and employees, starting with Güler Sabancı, undertake accountability for carrying out CSR activities (Uslu 2012). As the Financial Times put it, "Güler Sabancı is more than a chairwoman of one of Turkey's largest corporations. She is also an important force in the country's political, social and cultural life." In 2010, Sabancı ranked the third business-woman in Financial Times' list of "2010 The Top Businesswomen around the world." In 2009, Spain's Deputy Prime Minister honored Güler Sabancı with the Spanish Order of Civil Merit, "Encomienda de Numero" in a ceremony organized in the name of King Juan Carlos. Again, in 2009, Güler Sabancı was awarded "The 2009 Raymond Georis Prize for Innovative Philanthropy" by the Council of European Union. In 2011, Güler Sabancı also received the Clinton Global Citizen Award (en.wikipedia.org/wiki/G%C3%BCler_Sabanc%C4%B1), reflecting her interest in philanthropy. The Sabancı Foundation with the leadership of Güler Sabancı makes the final decision on CSR initiatives by taking into consideration the demand of the stakeholders, the society in general, and the other partner NGOs (Uslu 2012).

The holding persuades the government and media participation in its CSR projects. Even celebrities want to join and be a part of projects. CSR activities realized by the Foundation are shared with the public via annual reports, press releases, press conferences, and the corporate website (Uslu 2012). Güler Sabancı also personally leads some of the projects herself and acts as the face of the initiative. In an interview (Global Giving Matters 2011), as the spokesperson of a unique TV program, that was launched by the Foundation in 2010, called Turkey's Changemakers, she claimed that, "I personally was the spokesperson for this program, what promoted the visibility of the issue of women and their needs in the eyes of the public…. I think it is extremely important to promote role models and good examples to mobilize more people to get involved in social issues."

Since 1990s, the Sabancı Foundation started to identify the country's most pressing needs through research; and the priority issues included education, employment, reproductive health, and violence against women. Thus, the Sabanci Group has been supporting the society through CSR projects addressing these issues (Uslu 2012). First of all, the Sabanci Foundation aims to enable social inclusion by promoting a social and economic environment in which women, youth and persons with disabilities have access and equal opportunities to actively participate in society. Some of the projects, they hold within this frame for women include "Turkey's Changemakers" TV Program, United Nations Joint Program to Promote and Protect the Human Rights of Women and Girls, Grant Program for Multidimensional Women's Empowerment, the Child Brides: Victims Of Destructive Traditions And Patriarchic Heritage, and lending their support to the most recalled CSR Project in Turkey, "Daddy, Send Me to School" Project, which is supported by Çağdaş Yaşamı Destekleme Derneği/Association of Supporting Contemporary Life. The Foundation also supports young people by helping them raise their voice, and ideas through programs such as Voice of the Unheard, I Saw I Heard I Know, and Local Democracy Academies For Effective Social Partici-pation. Moreover, the Foundation lent their support to the disabled people for a very long time. Some of the projects under this initiative include Prevention Of Discrimination Against Persons With Disabilities Platform, Conscious Families, Unimpeded Kids, Service For Persons With Disabilities and Job For Women And Youth, Economic Integration and Employment of Visually Impaired People To Business, and Removing Barriers. In total, the Foundation has 40 educational institutions, 19 dormitories, and 17 teachers' centers. Each year, more than 1,300 students—including 380 new students- benefited from the Sabancı Foundation Scholarships. Since its establishment, more than 33,000 students have obtained scholarships (Hacı Ömer Sabancı Holding Annual Report 2010).

The Foundation is also active in supporting cultural and arts activities as well; supporting annual events, the Turkish Folk Dance Competition and the Sabancı International Adana Theater Festival, and commencing support for the Mehtap Ar Children's Theater to make drama more accessible to children. From the start, 2,000 performances gave almost 400,000 children a chance to watch theater for the first time in their lives in 35 provinces. The Ankara International Music Festival with almost 350 artists and the Metropolis Antique City excavation were also supported through the Foundation's Arts and Culture program. In 2009, the Foundation began supporting the National Youth Symphony Orchestra, consisting of 93 musicians studying at conservatories in Turkey. Besides lending their sup-port to various organizations and events, the Foundation also opened up the

Sabancı Museum in 2002 in order to exhibit and share with the public the numerous collections of the Sabancı family, host international exhibitions, conferences, meetings, concerts, and create its own art education programs. Similarly, in 2009 the Sakıp Sabancı Mardin City Museum opened up together with the Dilek Sabancı Art Gallery in the city of Mardin. Finally, the Foundation also owns 32 cultural and social facilities, and 5 sports facilities (Hacı Ömer Sabancı Holding Annual Report 2010).

16.5 The Case of Borusan Holding

Borusan, founded by the Kocabıyık Family in 1944, is a conglomerate with a business to business focus operating in 8 countries. The areas of operation of Borusan Group comprise of manufacturing of steel pipes, cold rolled coils, galvanized coils and metal sheets, exclusive sales and after sales service of BMW, Mini, Land Rover and Aston Martin vehicles and car rental services, exclusive sales and after sales service of Caterpillar, earthmoving equipment and power systems in Turkey and in Central Asia (Azerbaijan, Georgia, Kazakhstan, Kyrgyzstan) and Iran, providing integrated logistic services, manufacturing of engine valves for the automotive industry, generation and wholesaling of electricity. The growth strategy is partnerships or exclusive distribution agreements with well known world brands like Arcelor Mittal, Caterpillar, BMW, Land Rover, and Mini. The consolidated revenue in 2010 is 3,5 billion USD (Borusan Holding Annual Report 2011).

The objective of Borusan is sustainable growth by doing the job well, to be a good corporate citizen and, to the best of their abilities, fulfill their responsibilities to the environment, society and nation (Uğur 2010). In order to reach this objective, Borusan defines a unique management approach that they call as the "Borusan Way". "The Borusan Way" encompasses such ideals as respecting the environment while growing as a company, contributing to society, respecting human rights and working efficiently. These principles are the same ones listed in the United Nations Global Compact agreement", which is signed by Borusan in 2006 (Erimez 2008).

16.5.1 Glancing at the Philanthropic CSR Initiatives

Borusan participates in short and long run social responsibility projects. According to "Corporate Social Responsibility" research of the Capital Magazine and GFK research company, Borusan is not in the top 20 list from the consumers' perpective, but ranks 9th from management perspective and Asım Kocabıyık, the founder of Borusan Holding ranks 7th among the CSR leaders. When the CSR programs of Borusan are considered, it is observed that Asım Kocabıyık is the main initiator and the promoter of these projects. Embracing his motivation and aim, Board of Directors of Borusan Holding is the decision-maker for important social responsibility projects and every project must be approved by the Board. Employees are encouraged to make suggestions and participate in social projects. Suggestions from other stakeholders besides the employees are also encouraged. After the approval of the board of directors, department of corporate communication takes part where they organize details, make plans, initiate employees and arrange budgets. To measure the effect of projects done, research companies monitor the corporate reputation periodically and report to the holding (Cömert 2011).

Borusan adopts the mission of contributing "to create economical welfare of society" and "to the development of Turkey, and its international promotion", overall "giving back to the community with which it does business" (www.borusan.com). Thus Borusan accepted the responsibility of helping society in areas where the government falls short. In fulfilling its social responsibilities, Borusan Kocabıyık Foundation supports cultural and artistic activities and puts signature under various sponsorships. Moreover, Borusan has global objectives as "to provide the best living standards for each individual, to decrease the consumption of natural resources and to offer a quality of life without consuming the future." (borusan.com.tr). Borusan invests in CSR projects for the general welfare of the community related to culture, art and education (www.borusan.com.tr/BorusanSurdurulebilirlik/default.aspx 2011).

The projects related to education are Borusan Asım Kocabıyık Anadolu Teknik Lisesi/Technical High school (Beylikdüzü, İstanbul), Borusan Otomotiv Zehra Nurhan Kocabıyık İlköğretim Okulu/Primary School (Avcılar, İstanbul), Asım ve Nurhan Kocabıyık Öğretmenevi/Teachers' House (Avcılar, İstanbul), Asım Kocabıyık Meslek Yüksek Okulu/Vocational School (Kocaeli Üniversitesi), Asım Kocabıyık Meslek Yüksek Okulu/Vocational School (Uludağ Üniversitesi) and two dormitories in Kocaeli Üniversitesi. Moreover, the Foundation continues to support many schools by providing equipments, renovating conference rooms and libraries. Also successful students with limited financial resources are awarded with scholarships. Currently, 150 promising students are receiving scholarships from the Foundation with a supportive agreement with Türkiye Eğitim Gönüllüleri Vakfı/Educational Volunteers Foundation of Turkey. 100 girls are sent to school in the east part of Turkey under the campaign "Daddy, Send Me to School" (www.borusan.com).

For art and culture, Borusan aims to develop the notion of art and raise new talents through their CSR projects which can be listed as The Borusan Philharmonic Orchestra, Borusan String Quartet, Children's Choir and The Music Library. Another project by Borusan is the Contemporary Art Museum of Perili Köşk which displays and shares the contemporary arts collection of Asım Kocabıyık and the office buildings of Borusan to wider audiences. The collection is settled in Perili Köşk which is still the conglomerate's central office near Bosporus. Another mission of the museum is supporting the exhibition program with educational programs and academic discussions for all age groups, and thus to contribute to Turkey's artistic and cultural environment.

The Borusan Holding established the Ephesus Foundation, with an aim to contribute in protection, reservation, the culture development and international promotion of the ancient Ephesus city. The main mission is generating funds and continuing promotional activities to introduce Ephesus to the world. Some of the Foundation's activities are providing financial support for upcoming excavations and the museum, contributing to the shortening of the time period of the excavations in the ancient city, developing plans and projects towards conducting the excavation works under local and international experts' guidance (borusan.com.tr).

Finally, Borusan is also contributing to the society by its sponsorships for different projects to promote and attract public attention to certain issues. Borusan was the sponsor of the projects "Istanbul 2010 European Capital of Culture". Also they started to a project called "TEMA–BORUSAN Afyonkarahisar- Sinanpaşa-Güney, Düzağaç ve Tokuşlar Beldeleri ile Kınık ve Karacaören Köyleri Kırsal Kalkınma Projesi/Rural Areas Improvement Project". Moreover, Borusan is the sponsor of Borusan Otomotiv Motorsport. The objective of this sponsorship is to encourage the development of motorsports in Turkey, and to contribute to the global image of Turkey in this field (Okyay 2011).

16.6 Borusan Breaks Hearts in Motorsports Sponsorship

One of these motorsports sponsorships became a major problem, the after effects of which is to be further observed on the image of Borusan (Görgülü 2012). As a sponsor of motorsports in Turkey, Borusan was also the sponsor of Turkish Woman Rally Champion Burcu Çetinkaya. Borusan agreed in principle to give the champion rally driver grant and the right to use two MINI Coopers. The sponsorship deal was meant to be valid for one year. Three months later, Çetinkaya began to host a TV program on automobiles on Kanal 24/Channel 24 of Turkey together with the reporter of the conservative Yeni Şafak daily newspaper, Merve Sena Kılıç, a woman with a headscarf. An interview with Çetinkaya and Kılıç published on December 21, 2011 in Hürriyet daily newspaper featured photographs of Kılıç and Çetinkaya driving the MINI Cooper. Çetinkaya received a warning from Borusan Holding MINI Brand Manager Hakan Bayülgen. "We have seen your photos in the press with the MINI and a woman wearing a headscarf. This has created an image problem for us. BMW general headquarters do not want this," Bayülgen told Çetinkaya. Moreover, he added that the Holding was disturbed by Çetinkaya's "religious" image. Several days after this warning, Borusan cancelled the sponsorship deal with Çetinkaya, citing economic problems.

"Our attitude is never specifically against the use of headscarves. We would have acted the same way if there had been the use of a political emblem. This is an issue to keep the brand an equal distance from all and prevent it from being identified with any specific political view, party, logo, religious movement or other movements," Bayülgen said. He claimed that the cancellation of the sponsorship deal with Çetinkaya was due to financial restrictions. By this approach, Bayülgen drew an analogy between politics and scarf which lead him to submit his resignation from the company (Yıldırımkaya 2011).

As these statements took place in the press, and social media, there were criticisms to Borusan in regard to their view of ethics and stressing that Borusan was discriminating people based on scarves and contradicted with itself about the "properly implemented Human Rights" subject. Kılıç said she had difficulty in understanding the company's concerns about its image. She stressed "This company does not care about its image when women with headscarves buy automobiles from them, but they voice such concerns when a woman with headscarf tests their automobile on a TV program" (Borusan cancels sponsorship allegedly over company image concerns 2011).

After arousal of the issue, the chairman of the executive board of Borusan, Eşref Biryıldız, denied these accusations stating that the reason of the refusal of the sponsorship is not related to any beliefs or lifestyles of people. He also mentioned that in last eight months the company had already given 5 cars to Merve Sena Kılıç that are under distribution of Borusan. (Yıldırımkaya 2011). Later, Borusan announced that sponsorship deal was not officially made with Çetinkaya, so it is not possible to talk about a cancellation. Borusan cited financial concerns for not going ahead with a sponsorship deal with the famous rally driver. The company also said remarks by Bayülgen "that have been inappropriate" do not reflect the views of either Borusan Automotive or BMW or the Borusan Group. "Borusan has never had a discriminatory stance or practice on the basis of religion, language, belief or ethnicity, and it will never have such a stance or attitude," added Borusan's statement. Finally the company CEO, Agah Uğur attended to a press conference and clarified all the misunderstanding with relevant proof statements also mentioning that the explanation of the earlier brand director was inacceptable (Uğur 2011).

16.7 Discussion

The two companies, the Sabancı and Borusan Holdings are well-known, leading conglomerates of the country, with some changes in their target market concentrations. The Borusan Holding is more focused on the business to business markets, whereas the Sabancı Holding has more diversified target markets focusing on both consumer/mass market and also business markets with the different companies under its portfolio. Both of them run their CSR activities under their foundations. The outcomes in the CSR are consistent with their target markets. The Borusan Holding is well appreciated among the managers as a company with business to business focus, whereas the Sabancı Holding is well known by both the managers and the public as a company with more diversified areas of operation according to the leaders of the CSR research conducted in Turkey.

Both holdings focus on CSR activities, related to education, art and culture. Education is an issue of primary importance in the Turkish context, especially the girls' education. As the UNICEF statistics indicate, roughly a million girls of primary-school age are not going to school in Turkey. In primarily the southeast provinces, more than 50 % of girls between six and 14 years of age are unschooled (Zahir 2006). Moreover, the public considers education as the most important issue in CSR (Leaders of Corporate Social Responsibility 2010). Thus, it can be claimed that both of the holdings made the right topic selection, by focusing on a topic of importance in the context and stakeholders' perspective. When compared though, the Sabancı Holding stands out in its support for education, especially the education of young girls and women due to the budget allocated and the variety of CSR activities followed. The benefits are shared by the masses and returned as awards to its chairwoman.

Art and culture are also prominent issues for Turkey, since there is a great potential for growth and investment of arts and culture in the country, but in the meanwhile there is still a need for funding and support (Bulut and Yumrukaya 2009) to focus on areas where government support is not satisfactory. Therefore, the holdings are righteous in their decision to support arts and culture. Both have museums, and fund organizations and events related to arts and culture. The differences lay in the fact that the Borusan Holding is more "elitist" in the topic selection focusing on Western classical music which is not yet assimilated by the masses, while the Sabancı Holding is engaged in more traditional forms of art and culture like music festivals, theater, and folk dance.

Finally, educating and integrating the disabled to daily life is one of the major CSR topics supported by the Sabancı Holding. Considering that 12.29 % of the Turkish population is disabled; 36 % of the disabled is undereducated; and nearly 80 % is unemployed, supporting the disabled is another major social issue of the country (Türkiye Özürlüler Araştırması/Turkey Disabled People Research 2002). The Sabancı Holding establishes differentiation in its CSR initiatives by penetrating to different regions of the country to educate and integrate the disabled.

As the Sabancı Holding selects CSR topics that are accepted and embraced more by the masses, the Borusan Holding focuses some of its CSR initiatives on niche areas. However, as Sabancı and Güler Sabancı get awareness, popularity, liking, and preference of the public for their CSR activites, Borusan, focusing on niches, does not attract the attention, interest, awareness and appreciation of the general public. On the other hand, when there is a problem in the implementation process of the CSR activities, criticism of the masses is raised in traditional and social media, punishing Borusan for missing out facts related to certain sensitive issues in Turkey. Even though motorsports, and rally racing are not common areas of interest of the public, general repercussions were expressed in media when the Borusan Holding decided to cancel its sponsorship of the woman rally champion when she appeared as a spokesperson together with a woman reporter with a headscarf on TV. The Borusan Holding hurt the feelings of the religious and conservative mass of the Turkish society, which has increased in number and social and political influence in the country (Çarkoğlu and Kalaycıoğlu 2009) while it was trying to protect the brand image of the brands under its portfolio.

16.8 Conclusion

The two cases point out the importance of topic selection in CSR especially in emerging markets. Low resources, and weaker infrastructures in emerging markets are the major problems that have to be resolved. Each emerging market has its own social issue priorities which cannot be fully resolved by government investment and intervention. CSR projects seem to a solution. The companies should take into priorities into consideration in their CSR decision making process. The topics that are accepted by the general public are the "safe" way to reach effective CSR solutions as the cases under the scrutiny of this research show. Of course, niche areas should not be neglected. As these niche areas are selected, besides the primary target markets of the brands, the interest and feelings of the general public should also be taken into account. General public is aware of, follow and judge the CSR activities of companies. Doing "good", taking responsibility in company's environment is important but at the same time very sensitive. A delicate balance is needed for observing the reflections of every act in the mass market.

References

After BRIC comes MIST, the acronym Turkey would certainly welcome. (2011). The guardian. Retrieved from: http://www.guardian.co.uk/global-development/poverty-matters/2011/feb/01/emerging-economies-turkey-jim-oneill, January, 09, 2012.

Ali, I., Rehman, K. U., Yılmaz, A. K., Nazır, S., & Ali, J. F. (2010). Effects of corporate social responsibility on consumer retention in cellular industry of Pakistan. *African Journal of Business Management, 4*, 475–485.

Ararat, M. & Göcenoğlu, C. (2008), Drivers for sustainable corporate social responsibility, case of Turkey." Retrieved from: http://gocenoglu.net/CSRTurkeyMDF5.pdf, January, 16, 2012.

Ararat, M. (2008). A development perspective for corporate social responsibility: case of Turkey. *Corporate Governance, 8*(3), 271–286.

Auklah, P. S., Kotabe, M., & Teegen, H. (2000). Export strategies and performance of firms from emerging economies: evidence from Brazil, Chile, and Mexico. *Academy of Management Journal, 43*(3), 342–361.

Başörtüsü BMW'nin Kimyasını Bozdu. (2011). *Star Gazetesi*, Retrieved from: http://www.stargazete.com/guncel/borusan-yobazligi-haber-409890.htm, January, 16, 2012.

BCG Report (2011). Companies on the move rising stars from rapidely developing economies are reshaping global industries. *2011 BCG Global Challengers*, Retrieved from: http://www.bcg.com/documents/file70055.pdf, on January, 16, 2012.

Borusan cancels sponsorship allegedly over company image concerns (2011). *Today's Zaman*. Retrieved from: http://www.todayszaman.com/newsDetail_getNewsById.action?newsId=267001, January, 13, 2012.

Bronn, P. S., & Vrioni, A. B. (2001). Corporate social responsibility and cause related marketing: an overview. *International Journal of Advertising, 20*, 207–222.

Brown, T. J., & Dacin, P. A. (1997). The company and the product: corporate associations and consumer product responses. *Journal of Marketing, 61*(1), 68–84.

Bulut, D., & Yumrukaya, C. B. (2009). Corporate social responsibility in culture and art. *Management of Environmental Quality: An International Journal, 20*(3), 311–320.

Carroll, A. (1991). The pyramid of corporate social responsibility: toward the moral management of organizational stakeholders. *Business Horizons*, 39–48.

Cömert, S. (2011). Unpublished Interview with Ms. Seyhan Cömert, Communications Managers at Borusan Lojistik, December 2011.

Corporate Social Responsibility Association (2010). Turkey corporate social responsibility baseline report 2010. Retrieved from: http://www.undp.org.tr/publicationsDocuments/CSR_Report_en.pdf, January, 09, 2012.

Dawar, N., & Chattopadhyay, A. (2002). Rethinking marketing programs for emerging markets. *Long Range Planning, 32*, 457–474.

Çarkoğlu, A., & Kalaycıoğlu, E. (2009). *The rising tide of conservatism in Turkey*. New York: Palgrave MacMillan.

de Soto, H. (2000). *The mystery of capital: why capitalism triumphs in the west and fails everywhere else*. New York: Basic Books.

Emerging Markets: Beyond the Big Four. (2006). *Business Week*. Retrieved from: http://www.businessweek.com/magazine/content/05_52/b3965450.htm, January, 09, 2012.

Erimez, E. (2008). Borusan sustainability report (2008). Retrieved from: www.borusan.com.tr/BorusanSurdurulebilirlik/sustainability.pdf, January, 13, 2012.

Ghauri, P. N., & Gronhaug, K. (2010). *Research methods in business studies: a practical guide* (4th ed.). London: Prentice Hall.

Global Giving Matters (2011). Güler Sabanci sets a new course for turkish philantropy issue 43. Retrieved from: www.synergos.org/globalgivingmatters/archives/ggm201102.pdf, January, 16, 2012.

Godfrey, P. (2005). The relationship between corporate philanthropy and shareholder wealth: a risk management perspective. *Academy of Management Review, 30*(4), 777–799.

Görgülü, G. (2012). *Başörtülü marka, başörtüsüz marka*, Retrieved from: http://www.dunya.com/basortulu-marka,-basortusuz-marka-143831yy.htm, January, 20, 2012.

Güler Sabancı'ya Küresel Vatandaşlık Ödülü (2011). *Habertürk Ekonomi*, Retrieved from: http://ekonomi.haberturk.com/makro-ekonomi/haber/670368-guler-sabanciya-clinton-kuresel-vatandaslik-odulu, January, 16, 2012.

Hacı Ömer Sabancı Holding Annual Report (2010). Retrieved from: http://www.sabanci.com/pdf/2010tr/sa_fr_2010_tr.pdf, January, 15, 2012.

Hart, S. L., & Christensen, C. M. (2002). The great leap: driving innovation from the base of the pyramid. *Sloan Management Review, 44*(1), 51–56.

Hohnen, P. (2007). Corporate social responsibility: an implementation guide for business. International Institute for Sustainable Development.

Kelgökmen, D. (2010). İşletmelerin Kurumsal Sosyal Sorumluluk Düzeylerinin Belirlenmesine Yönelik bir Literatür Taraması. *Ege Academic Review, 10*(1), 303–318.

Kolk, A., & Lenfant, F. (2010). MNC reporting on CSR and conflict in Central Africa. *Journal of Business Ethics, 93*, 241–255.

Kotler, P., & Lee, N. (2006). *Kurumsal Sosyal Sorumluluk, 2*. Baskı: KApital Medya Hizmetleri.

Lantos, G. (2001). The boundaries of strategic corporate social responsibility. *Journal of Consumer Marketing, 18*(7), 595–630.

Leaders of Corporate Social Responsibility, (2010), *Capital Magazine*, Source: http://www.capital.com.tr/haber.aspx?HBR_KOD=5871, August, 11, 2010.

London, T. & Hart, S.L. (2004). Reinventing strategies for emerging markets: beyond the transnational model. *Journal of International Business Studies*, 1–21.

Luo, X., & Bhattacharya, C. B. (2006). Corporate social responsibility, customer satisfaction, and market value. *Journal of Marketing, 70*, 1–18.

Maignan, I., Ferrel, O. C., & Derrel, L. (2005). A stakeholder model for implementing social responsibility in marketing. *European Journal of Marketing, 39*(9–10), 956–977.

O'Riordan, L., & Fairbass, J. (2008). Corporate social responsibility (CSR): models and theories in stakeholder dialogue. *Journal of Business Ethics, 83*, 745–758.

Okyay. (2011). Borusan otomotiv motorsports 2011 sponsorluk sunumu. Retrieved from: http://www.kaanonder.com/images/2011SponsorSunum.pdf, January, 15, 2012.

Porter, M. & Kramer, M. (2002). The Competitive Advantage of Corporate Philanthropy. *Harvard Business Review*, December: 5–16.

Smith, C. (2003). Corporate social responsibility: whether or how? *California Management Review, 45*(4), 52–76.

Uğur, A. (2010) The borusan way and our 2010 targets. Retrieved from: http://www.borusan.com.tr/BorusanSurdurulebilirlik/messagefromtheCEO.aspx January, 13, 2012.

Uğur, A. (2011). Borusan holdİng ceo'su Agah Uğur'un basin toplantisi konuşma metni. Retrieved from: http://www.borusan.com.tr/tr/BasinOdasi/BorusanHoldingBultenleri.aspx? PageName=BorusanHoldingCeosuAgahUgurunBasinToplantisiKonusmaMetni, January, 13, 2012.

Uslu, E. (2012). Interview. Sabancı Vakfı Kurumsal İletişim Sorumlusu.

Vlachos, P.A., Tsamakos, A., Vrechopoulos, A.P., & Avramidis, P.K (2009). *Journal of the Academy of Marketing Science*, 37: 170–180.

Wright, M., Filatotchev, I., Hoskisson, R. E., & Peng, M. W. (2005). Strategy research in emerging economies: challenging the collective wisdom. *Journal of Management Studies, 42*(1), 1–33.

Wulfson, M. (2001). The ethics of corporate social responsibility and philanthropic ventures. *Journal of Business Ethics, 29*, 135–145.

Yıldırımkaya, G. (2011). Borusan türbanlı test sürüşü nedeniyle sponsorluğu iptal etti iddiası tartışılıyor. *Haber Türk*, Retrieved from http://www.haberturk.com/yazarlar/gulin-yildirim kaya/701408-borusan-turbanli-test-surusu-nedeniyle-sponsorlugu-iptal-etti-iddiasi-tartisiliyor January, 13, 2012.

Yin, R. K. (2003). *Case Study Research, Design and Methods*. London: Sage Publications.

Zahir, F. (2006). Winning the gender gap war in Turkey. Retrieved from: http://www.ungei.org/infobycountry/turkey_895.html, January, 16, 2012.

Zenisek, T. (1979). Corporate social responsibility: a conceptualization based on organizational literature. *Academy of Management Review, 4*(3), 359–368.

Part V
CSR in Education and Socially Responsible Investment

Chapter 17
Fostering Management Education for Professional Integrity: The Case of the Centre for Economic and Managerial Sciences, University of Guadalajara, Mexico

José G. Vargas-Hernández

Abstract This chapter seeks to analyze professional integrity as an improvement concept to the actual values and virtues and meaning managerial capabilities and attitudes to assume any professional task. This chapter analyzes a case of management education for professional integrity at the University Centre for Economic and Managerial Sciences, University of Guadalajara. The research method employed is the ethnographic, documental and life's history, complemented with field work supported by in-depth interviews and analyzed using a comparative method. The outcomes of the research on the application of management education demonstrate that the drama of economic efficiency is centred on a dysfunctional professional integrity. This chapter provides a sound professional philosophy that empowers professionals to act with integrity, increases the probability for long-term success and professional fulfilment. The results provide also the basis to develop a code of conduct and regulation policies to sustain management education for professional integrity which, can positively impact on business culture through influencing the behaviour of key actors.

17.1 Introduction

Professional integrity has been explained as an improvement concept to the actual values and virtues as meaningful managerial capabilities and attitudes to assume any professional task. The objective of this chapter is to analyze the importance of professional integrity as the improvement concept and ethics in the development of professionals in administration and management sciences. The chapter also

J. G. Vargas-Hernández (✉)
University Center for Economic and Managerial Sciences,
University of Guadalajara, Guadalajara, Mexico
e-mail: jvargas2006@gmail.com

A. Yüksel Mermod and S. O. Idowu (eds.), *Corporate Social Responsibility in the Global Business World*, DOI: 10.1007/978-3-642-37620-7_17,
© Springer-Verlag Berlin Heidelberg 2014

pretends to present some suggestions of ethical and integrity program based in professional integrity that can lead the manager to a more ethical and humanistic practice based on a case at University Centre for Economic and Managerial Sciences, University of Guadalajara.

Economic and political conditions of the globalization processes carry with them the elements toward the multinational integration which implies a higher professional competitiveness. Professionals have to be prepared for a global market constrained by time and resources for their basic developments. Thus, there is a need for optimizing the resources applied to the development of the new professionals. The most important change facing the new demands of education is the task of personal and professional integrity formation for the performance of citizenship and productive capabilities. Llano (1997) makes reference to a divorce between professional formation and the real labor market as the product of non-existent but necessary synchronization, between the graduated professionals from Universities and technological institutes and the requirements of employers that have resulted to be devastating for the social responsibility that the organizations must fulfil.

The manager's success in the provision of services to individuals and society depends to a certain extent in the degree of knowledge, skills and experiences obtained in the classroom and the professional performance. Moreover, it depends of the achieved level of personal qualities development that distinguishes him/her as an individual, such as the professional integrity, independence, ethics, and so forth (AICPA 1980: 16). There is a peremptory need to recover credibility, integrity and respect in the management profession through a truth reconstruction of the ethical and integrity fundamentals. Professional formation and development in management sciences conducted in Universities must specify the required behaviours for the professional integrity. The formation of professional integrity at University programs, more than the added value must be the inherent value expected to grant to the organizations and society as a whole.

17.2 Notion of Integrity

Integrity is important to build a good society, a reason that makes necessary to define with precision the origin and sense of the term. Adler and Bird (1988) and Srivastva et al. (1988) describe integrity with an emphasis on congruence, consistency, morality, universality and concern for others. Kerr (1988: 126–127) lists the Ten Commandments of Executive Integrity. Covey (1992) describes integrity as honestly matching words and feelings with thoughts and actions for the good of others. A key component of integrity is the consistency between actions and words. Integrity is defined by the Webster's New World Dictionary (1994) as: "(1) the quality or state of being complete; unbroken condition; wholeness; entirety; (2) the quality or state of being unimpaired; perfect condition; soundness; and (3) the quality or state of being of sound moral principle; uprightness, honesty, and sincerity". Integrity is a state or condition of being whole, complete, unbroken, unimpaired, sound, perfect condition.

The word integrity suggest the wholeness of the person in such a way that can be said that person with integrity are whole as human beings. The term integrity refers to honesty, playing by the rules and not necessarily following the rules, which means setting aside in situations where people may be victimized. Becker (1998) conceptually distinguishes integrity from honesty and fairness. However, the empirical research conducted by Hooijberg and Lane (2005) shows those managers and their direct reports, peers, and bosses do not distinguish integrity from honesty and fairness. Integrity in the context of other values that are in the eye of the beholder is an implicit model to evaluate the meaning of integrity (Jensen 2009; Jensen, Granger and Erhard 2010). Becker (1998) found no standard definition of integrity because it is treated as synonymous with other values such as honesty and fairness, which makes very difficult to measure it.

Integrity means honesty or stating what one really thinks even if the honest person runs the risk of hurting relationships and getting the organization in trouble. The condition of integrity must emerge at the heart of the person, people and organizations as the distinctive seal in all actions, decisions, determinations, etc. Simons (1999) defines Behavioural Integrity (BI) as the perceived degree of congruence between the values expressed by words and those expressed through action. Integrity is primarily a formal relation one has to oneself. Integrity refers to the wholeness, intactness or purity of a thing, meanings that are sometimes, applied to people (Cox et al. 2005).

> What is it to be a person of integrity? Ordinary discourse about integrity involves two fundamental intuitions: first, that integrity is primarily a formal relation one has to oneself or between parts or aspects of one's self; and second, that integrity is connected in an important way to acting morally, in other words, there are some substantive or normative constraints on what it is to act with integrity. How these two intuitions can be incorporated into a consistent theory of integrity is not obvious, and most accounts of integrity tend to focus on one of these intuitions to the detriment of the other. (Cox et al. 2005).

Erhard et al. (2010) combine the two intuitions of integrity developed by Cox et al. (2005), the second becoming a logical implication of the first, in one consistent theory. Integrity is the integration of self, the maintenance of identity and standing for something. Personal integrity, defined as honouring one's word, becomes predictable with first-hand reliable and accurate information (Erhard et al. 2007). Integrity is the base to trust to people because it guarantees the subject consistency in making decisions and in how he/she relates to others. Trust and ethics are terms related to the concept of integrity. Integrity is a guarantee of being ready to repair any threat to honesty. Integrity is defined as honouring one's word in a positive model developed by Erhard et al. (2008) revealing the causal link between integrity and performance. There is not a consistent and validated framework of integrity. Erhard et al. (2010) define integrity as: *a state or condition of being whole, complete, unbroken, unimpaired, sound, perfect condition.* Personal integrity has to do with the wholeness and completeness of that person's word. Personal integrity is one of the personal qualities. The Oxford Dictionary

(2011) defines integrity as "the quality of being honest and having strong moral principles", "the state of being whole and undivided".

Integrity has different meanings to different respondents. Integrity is for an individual, group, or organization as honouring one's word.

At an individual level, integrity is the matter of that person's word "being whole and complete". Personal integrity has to do with the wholeness and completeness of that person's word (Erhard et al. 2010). A person's word may consist of what is said, known, expected, is said is so, stands for, and the social moral, group ethical and governmental legal standards. Integrity is a matter of a human entity's word being whole and complete. One's word is not a matter of being obligated or not, being willing or not willing to fulfil the expectations of others. To be a person of integrity is honouring one's word and not a matter of keeping one's word. Simons (2002) defines integrity as keeping one's word. Honouring one's word is defined by Erhard et al. (2010) as keeping or not keeping the word on time when it is impossible, saying to everyone impacted if the conditions are not met and cleaning up any consequences.

Keeping the word is doing what it is said will be done and on time. Keeping the word is doing what it is known to do and doing the way it was meant to be done, and on time, unless it has been said it would no so doing what others expect to be done. It is congruent to define integrity to the capability to rationalize without interest's influences or particular sensations. Even if it has been never said it would not be done, and doing it on time, unless it has been said it would not been done and it has been made expectations of others clear to them by making explicit requests being willing to held accountable when it is asserted something that others would accept the evidence on the issue as valid.

Considered as a positive phenomenon, independent of normative value judgments, integrity is defined as honouring one's word. Honouring the one's word to oneself provides a solid foundation for self discipline as a way to maintain one whole and complete as a person that empowers him/her to deal with the matter with integrity. One may create trust by others when honouring one's word although fails to *keep* one's word. Honouring the word maintains integrity when it is not possible or appropriate to keep the word or to choose not to keep the word. The concept of integrity as Honouring One's Word includes a way to maintain integrity when one is for any reason not going to keep one's word. Integrity is a guarantee of being ready to repair any threat to honesty. However, for Kaizer and Hogan (2010), integrity is a moral attribution that we place on the behaviour of another person, in such a way that integrity is in the eyes of the beholder rather than consistency of that person's words and actions.

Argyris (1991) contends that people consistently act inconsistently; unaware of the contradiction between the way they think they are acting and the way they really act. Simons (1999) argues that behavioural integrity is the perceived degree of congruence between the values expressed by words and those expressed through action that he terms "wordaction". However, while keeping the words is not always possible, honouring the word, and thus, to be a person of integrity, whole and complete, is always possible. Honouring one's word when failing to keep it provides a behaviour that can generate substantial benefits. It is the interpretation of one's body, emotions and thoughts in the own words that are said, which ultimately defines who is one is for self.

Authenticity means being and acting consistent with which you hold yourself out to be for others, and who you hold yourself to be for yourself. Being authentic is "being willing to discover, confront, and tell the truth about your in authenticities" (Erhard et al. 2009). Argyris (1991) argues that "people consistently act inconsistently; unaware of the contradiction between their espoused theory and their theory-in-use, between the way they think they are acting, and the way they really act".

For a group or organizational entity, Erhard et al. (2010) define integrity as that group's or organization's word being whole and complete. Organizational integrity as any human system is an organization that honours whole and complete its word to its members and to outsiders. Respondents refuse to answer questions related to identify integrity issues and behaviours of managers lacking integrity besides the difficulties to observe and rate them.

Honouring one's word to another creates a whole and complete relationship. One's word is constituted by what literally one person says in words, in the "speaking" of his/her actions and in what these actions say to others. Being in-integrity leaves one person whole and complete outside or inside the relationship with other person who may be out-of integrity. Shakespeare (1914) said, "This above all: to thine own self be true, it must follow, as the night the day, Thou can't not be false to any man". When one is true to one's word, which is being true to one's self, one cannot be but true to any man. Being in-integrity allows one person to continue to be effective and workable in the relationship with other or others.

The terms integrity, morality, ethics, and legality are confused by the common usage. Morality, ethics and legality exist in a normative realm of virtues while integrity exists in a positive real. Erhard et al. (2010: 1) distinguish the domain of integrity "as the objective state or condition of an object, system, person, group, or organizational entity". Integrity is within the positive realm and its domain is one of the objective state or condition. The virtue phenomena of morality and ethics are related to integrity as a positive phenomenon.

The Oxford Dictionary (2011) defines morals as "standards of behaviour or beliefs concerning what is and is not acceptable to do". Morality exists in the social virtue domain in the normative realm. Morality is the generally accepted standards of what is desirable and undesirable; of right and wrong conduct, and what is considered by that society as good behaviour and what is considered bad behaviour of a person, group, or entity. Integrity cannot be falsified because it is, by its own nature, the truthiness, what avoids the fragmentation of persons and the cracking down of moral strengthens.

The Oxford Dictionary (2011) defines ethics as "moral principles that govern a person's or group's behavior" (Sic). Ethics refers to the set of values and behaviours defined by society as desirable in such a way that any action can be judged as "good or bad" (Pojman 1995). Ethics exists in the group virtue domain in the normative realm. Ethics is defined as in a given group (the benefits of inclusion in which group a person, sub-group, or entity enjoys), ethics is the agreed on standards of what is desirable and undesirable; of right and wrong conduct; of what is considered by that group as good and bad behavior of a person, sub-group, or entity that is a member of the group, and may include defined bases for discipline, including exclusion.

Integrity as the condition of being whole and complete is a necessary condition for workability. Workability is defined as the state or condition that constitutes the available opportunity for something or somebody or a group or an organization to function, operate or behave to produce an intended outcome, i.e., to be effective; or the state or condition that determines the opportunity set from which someone or a group or an organization can choose outcomes, or design or construct for outcomes (Erhard et al. 2010). The resultant level of workability determines the available opportunity set for superior performance. Integrity provides access for superior performance and competitive advantage for individuals, groups, organizations, and societies. Erhard et al. (2010) conclude that the way in which integrity is defined for individuals, groups and organizations reveals the impact of integrity on workability and trustworthiness, and consequently on performance.

Variations in personal behaviour depending on situations may be interpreted as lack of integrity. Lack of integrity is compatible with a multiplicity of interests that are in collision among each other. Lack of integrity implies a gap between what is said and what is thought, between what is considered a proper conduct and what is finally done, between what is morally fair and what it appears to result from pressure of circumstances. The lack of integrity goes beyond and has effects far away the sphere of the specific activity in each organization, even impact the society's rules of the game. Personal as well as professional integrity in firms declines more and more in an environment of global economy, leading to a decrease in performance.

Moral and ethical values may guide human action and interactions shaping professional integrity and determining performance. Professional integrity derives its substance from the fundamental goals or mission of the profession (McDowell 2010).

Legality exists in governmental virtue domain in the normative realm. Legality is defined as the system of laws and regulations of right and wrong behaviour that are enforceable by the state (federal, state, or local governmental body in the U.S.) through the exercise of its policing powers and judicial process, with the threat and use of penalties, including its monopoly on the right to use physical violence.

Honouring the standards of the three virtue phenomena of morality, ethics and legality and its relationships with performance, including being complete as a person and the quality of life, raises the likelihood to shape human behaviour.

17.3 Professional Integrity

One of the first documents that treat on professional integrity is the Hippocratic Oath. The thesis behind is that professionals have to aspire to excellence. Personal integrity is directly related to professional integrity. Personal integrity and professional integrity are generally interdependent and compatible. Professional integrity is related to, but different from personal integrity. Professional integrity is an attribute although philosophically the term integrity relates to general character. Professional integrity derives its substance from the fundamental goals or mission of the profession (McDowell 2010) Professional integrity is sustained on the principle of moral integrity and ethical principles centred in transparency, honesty, sincerity, moral consciousness, loyalty, truthiness and reality in the functions performed adhered to legality. Professional integrity is the set of principles and commitments to improve the results of the manager's activities, to maximize autonomy, to create relationships characterized by integrity, the ethical practice, social justice and team work.

Different aspects of professional integrity are derived from the basic functions of each profession. The professional integrity includes the role-specific obligations and responsibilities of a particular profession. Well-established professions often spell out and stand on the role-specific principles of professional integrity. Professional integrity derives its substance from the mission and fundamental goals of the profession. Where the stakes for society are so high, professional integrity must be first over personal loyalties of friendships. Professional integrity is based on value integrity first, service before self, and excellence in all that we do. When a professional commits himself/herself to "integrity first" is that he or she understands the importance of both personal integrity and professional integrity, and through his/her efforts to keep them compatible, he or she best provides the crucial professional functions and activities to the society.

A clash between personal integrity and professional integrity leads to integrity dilemmas which are present in some situations such as for example a professional refuse to participate on moral grounds because it is not morally obligatory even though it is legally permitted. In any professional role it may be possible to live up to high standards of competence and conduct but not to sustain professional integrity outside the professional realm and context by living entirely different, opposed, conflicting or contradictory moral values in private life. It reveals a direct conflict between personal integrity and professional integrity. Culpable incompetence is clearly violation of professional integrity.

At the times when professional integrity is most valuable, there is an excuse to avoid the obligation to be in integrity. To be in professional integrity when it is most valuable to others, means to bear the costs. Professional integrity may be sacrificed to avoid some costs imposed on others, such as to protect institutional reputation. Based on integrity, it is build the personal reputation, and also as an extension the institutional reputation, when these are liberated according to the integrity criteria. The value of good reputation has been manifested several times in management. With violations of the public trust by actions of authority are serious breaches of professional integrity. When the stakes are so high in a profession, the breach of professional integrity could be devastating to society. Mayor challenges to professional integrity are the misuse of science, research and evidence in policymaking (McDowell 2010).

The concept of professional integrity is separated from normative concepts to understand it as a "purely positive phenomenon that plays a foundational role" in economic performance. The issue of competence is directly relevant to professional integrity. The duties of competent professionals can be carried out by professional practices, functions and actions constrained by moral, ethical and legal restraints on professional integrity. "Ethical implies conformity with an elaborated, ideal code of moral principles, sometimes, specifically, with the code of a particular profession" (*Webster's New World Dictionary*).

The codes of conduct support the profession's conception of professional integrity. A code of professional ethics (Hernández, Silvestri, and Álvarez, 2007) allows to norm a more ethical and humanistic professional practice and the commitment with individuals and society, the actions that must be guided not only by the speculation but for the necessity to act with justice, responsibility, discretion, honesty, etc. A myopic vision of professional integrity and ethic is reduced to a catalogue of things that are good and that are bad, and that there are not considered under a wider vision as the set of principles that serve to the human beings to achieve perfection and plenitude which is an arduous task. Changes on environment and the actual life can originate the loss of a clear vision of the limits between the honest and what is not, where it finishes the dignity and where begins the non dignity and what are the moral principles that must rule professional behaviour.

Professional integrity is formed by social responsibility and some other social elements that professionals inherit to maintain high standards of competence and conduct in the entire full range of professional activities and not just for themselves. Professional integrity has as an effect a major consistency of one person on himself/herself and produces greater social cohesion. Honest members of society strengthen the links of the structure and make advancements toward the own end, the common good. Professional integrity involves competences shared by all members of the profession and joint responsibilities for conduct. Integrity in communication is the pillar in trusting interpersonal networks building as a condition for the cooperation among human beings.

17.4 Professionalism

Professionalism has integrity as the essential and defining element. Professionalism is an ethical movement defined by essential elements of professional good will and good doing and reflects on values, actions and curricular implications. Professionalism as an aspect of a person's life is an attribute of integrity.

17.5 Managerial Integrity

Organizational activities include regular issues of professional managerial integrity (Thompson et al. 2008) Professional management integrity is defined as a "leadership competency and measures it using co-worker ratings of observed ethical behavior" (Sic). Professional managers displaying integrity are more concerned about the welfare of others (Brown and Trevino 2006). Managerial integrity acknowledges responsiveness among one another, receptivity and creative efforts to understand other's perspectives while at the same time articulating their own (Levinson 1988: 318).

Perceived managerial integrity is central to managers—stakeholder's relations as it is for leaders in the role of leader–follower relations, although it is questionable as to what extent integrity is important for various stakeholders. A manager would like to be able to look at themselves as someone who has integrity, is fair and honest. Kerr (1988) argues about the difference between the conceptual work on integrity and the realities faced by management practitioners. Kerr truly explored the meaning of integrity for real managers. As Kerr (1988: 138) states that the author's prescriptions about how to behave with ethics and integrity, were far away from the managerial practice in everyday organizational life. When the mistakes and incompetency of managers are buried instead of being exposed and removed from their practice, the managerial authorities fall short of their responsibilities to the mission and goals of the profession. Managers act with integrity to stay true to themselves (Levinson 1988: 268).

The environment under which the role of management takes place include managerial integrity, honesty and in safeguarding the integrity of the management system. Trust may create a "transformation in relational logic" which produces differential interaction effects for personal and professional integrity trust and capability trust (Bigley, G., & McAllister, D. (2002). *Transformations in Relational Logic: How Types of Supervisory Trust Interact to Predict Subordinate OCB*. Unpublished manuscript. University of Washington) in professionals. Professional managers must have high integrity in order to be trusted by other stakeholders, as leaders by followers. There are negative as well as the positive effects on public managerial integrity caused by the introduction of businesslike methods in the public service Kolthoff et al. (2003). However, global perceptions of supervisor integrity are a function of discrete, and primarily destructive, supervisor behaviours (Craig and Gustafson 1998, p. 134).

Moral philosophers agreed that integrity is linked to personality psychology and also Allport (1937) recognized this connection which can be measured directly through integrity testing. In organizational life, managerial integrity and other related competencies can be measured and evaluated through structured interviews, background checks, assessment centres, and other methods such as high-fidelity simulations and strategically designed assessment exercises that are other more valid and reliable methods for measuring integrity. Little effort has been made to link ethical theory to management behaviour Fritzche and Becker (1984: 166).

Becker (1998: 159) suggests obtaining assessments of integrity from supervisors or peers because integrity tests invoke social desirability responses with an emphasis on action. One important instrument to assess managerial integrity is the Diamond of Managerial Integrity model was developed by Kaptein (2003) to assess and improve the integrity of managers.

Leslie and Fleenor (1998) reported 24 popular assessment instruments that are similar in content to other competency instruments used by organizations that were compared and analyzed by Kaiser and Hogan (2010) who found several weaknesses centred on the lack of clarification of the integrity domain. Moreover, the instruments define low integrity by the absence of high integrity rather than by the presence of devious behaviours, and were found used for rating the integrity of managers only focusing on the positive desirable integrity construct but not on a lack of integrity or unethical behaviour. Minor breaches of integrity are not rated as violations against serious violations of integrity that are usually covert.

However, Kaiser and Hogan (2010) measure managerial integrity framed by personality theory to identify the integrity of managers, drawing on the concepts of reputation and the influence of "weak" situations on the expression of dark-side tendencies. According to Kaiser and Hogan (2010) self assessments of managerial integrity are dubious sources of information because the manipulation and deceit of persons lacking integrity. Managers who lack integrity hardly recognize themselves as that and observers may identify questionable integrity behaviours of managers. Thus, subordinates are likely to be a prime and the best source of information about the personal and professional integrity of managers (Brown and Trevino 2006). Kaiser and Hogan (2010) found that competency ratings do not identify managers with integrity issues. Ratings of an integrity competency are heavily skewed favouring managers who receive high ratings for integrity and are unlikely to identify managerial misconduct. Respondents refuse to answer questions related to identify integrity issues and behaviours of managers lacking integrity besides the difficulties to observe and rate them.

Firms may be concerned with effectively preventing declines in managerial integrity. Erhard et al. (2007) assume that the decision of a firm to appoint a previous CEO, relies to a greater extent on firm-specific information on personal and professional integrity. In the case of the integrity of the previous CEO, firms promote an insider and hire an outsider in the case of a former dishonest CEO. However, it is not enough to be trusted in terms of managerial integrity to predict OCB.

Ratings of managerial integrity always favour managers and rarely identify the ones who may lack integrity. Kaiser and Hogan (2010) contend that competency ratings are unlikely to identify managerial integrity issues. They propose an alternative method, referred as the dubious reputation approach, to identify managers with potential integrity problems focusing on the lower level of the integrity, not relying on ratings of observed behaviour but estimating the likelihood those managerial engagements in unethical behaviours. Ratings focused on the undesirable behaviours of the integrity domain of managers may identify their integrity problems. The dubious reputation approach involves personal integrity evaluations of the dark side of managers' personalities. This method proves to identify and assess levels of managerial integrity and effective competency.

The epitome of the dubious reputation method developed by Kaiser and Hogan (2010) is the Perceived Leader Integrity Scale (PLIS) developed by Craig and Gustafson (1998) which identifies low integrity of managers. An empirical research conducted by Kaiser and Hogan (2010) found that the PLIS yielded variability and higher incidence of low scores of managerial integrity than the integrity competency scale. Perceived integrity as a variable is more highly correlated with Consideration than Initiating Structure. Also the research concluded that as the strongest predictor, Perceived Integrity as a variable is more highly correlated to Perceived Effectiveness. This result is consistent with the notion that integrity is concerned with the needs and rights of other people.

17.6 Integrity and Performance

The ontological law of integrity states that "To the degree that integrity is diminished, the opportunity for performance (the opportunity set) is diminished" (Erhard et al. 2010). There is a relationship between integrity and performance, where integrity is a necessary condition for performance. Integrity not only exists as a virtue but rather than as a necessary condition for performance. Performance is defined as "the manner in which something or somebody functions, operates, or behaves; the effectiveness of the way somebody does his or her job" (Encarta Dictionary 2004). To maintain management performance centred in the human and ethical values is always an issue that requires being subject to pressures and tensions for the same nature of the management profession. Perceptions of the manager's integrity determine how much to trust the manager which, in turn, influences attitudes and performance.

Competency models that include integrity as a dimension are used by organizations to identify managerial performance capabilities (Boyatzis 1982) use subordinate ratings focusing on behaviours to evaluate the integrity of managers. Perceptions of manager's behavioural integrity created collective trust and were related to customer satisfaction and profitability which translated into higher performance (McLean Parks 1997). Behavioural ratings of observed ethical behaviour by co-workers measures integrity defined as a leadership competency suggests that only a small proportion of managers may have integrity issues without distinguishing high- from low-performing managers (Kaiser and Hogan 2010).

When nobody has an incentive to invest in firm-specific knowledge, the managerial integrity drops and consequently the performance of the firm, such as the case of external hires who step up the regression of integrity in firms (Rost et al. 2008). Regression of integrity in firms may result in the prevalence of outside hires. When followers believe their leader cannot be trusted because the leader is perceived not to have integrity, they divert energy diminishing work performance

(Mayer and Gavin 1999). Assuming that the integrity of the previous CEO has no effects on performance, Erhard et al. (2007) found that the managerial integrity of a former CEO pays off improving the performance of a firm at the time when the leadership change is stable.

Kaiser and Hogan (2010) conducted an empirical study of ratings on a competency-based integrity scale with psychometric properties to test the expectation that few managers are rated as lacking integrity, to prove that ratings of integrity fail to identify individuals at the low level and not predict managerial performance. The integrity competency analysis use subordinate ratings of integrity to predict overall performance. Subordinate ratings of a professional managerial integrity competency are consistent with performance ratings in organizations. Results of a research conducted by Kaiser and Hogan (2010) show that ratings on the integrity competency are unrelated to managerial performance. The proposed method by Kaiser and Hogan (2010) based on subordinate expectations about the likelihood that professional managers would misbehave and have unethically behaviours suggests that a larger proportion of managers may have professional integrity issues without distinctions performance.

Kaiser and Hogan (2010) found in their empirical research that manager's competency integrity is highly correlated with building talent showing concern for subordinates, although does not distinguish the level of management performance concluding that integrity competency does not predict performance. This finding is consistent with the definition of integrity as sensitivity for the needs and rights of other people. The empirical research conducted by Kaiser and Hogan (2010) found that the levels of manager's integrity is not correlated with the level of performance. This finding contradicts the research showing that personal integrity is a prerequisite for effective leadership.

17.7 Integrity and Leadership Effectiveness

Regarding integrity, most leaders follow a more Machiavellian view who wrote that a prince should appear a man of integrity (Machiavelli 1981: 101). Integrity as other values has an impact on effectiveness. The argument that leaders need integrity to function effectively is supported by Covey (1992: 61 and 108), who contends that followers become guarded of leaders with low level of integrity.

There are few empirical studies conducted to explore the role that integrity plays in leadership effectiveness. There is a lack of empirical research to analyze the relationship between integrity, leadership behaviours and effectiveness. The study of the impact that integrity has for effectiveness has not been clarified because integrity is to a greater or lesser extent being perceived as more effective when having honesty and fairness. Few empirical studies examine the relationship between integrity and leader effectiveness but not the impact integrity has on leader effectiveness. What may be good for the sense of integrity may not improve effectiveness. Direct reports have association between integrity and leadership effectiveness and are concerned about indicators of integrity of managers because of the need for consistent behaviour (Staw et al. 1980).

The assumption that integrity has a positive effect on leader and organizational effectiveness is questionable when research on leadership emphasizes behavioural approaches rather than integrity and actions that lack integrity can lead to success (Jackall 1988). Morgan (1989) developed a leadership assessment scales on integrity to analyze the relationship to leader effectiveness and found that integrity as a variable is related to trust. Trust reflects the integrity or capability of another party, thus trust in a leader's integrity may inspire followers because of the leader's adherence to certain values (McAllister 1995). Research on integrity and leadership effectiveness suggests a positive relationship. Badaracco and Ellsworth (1990) and Covey (1992) argue integrity has an impact for leadership effectiveness. Followers believing in the integrity of their leaders are more comfortable engaging in risky behaviours (Mayer et al. 1995). Hooijberg et al. (1997) call for the role of integrity as a value in leadership research.

Craig and Gustafson (1998) developed the Perceived Leader Integrity Scale (PLIS) to measure employee's perceptions of their leader's integrity and job satisfaction and found positive correlation. Craig and Gustafson (1998) provide a large pool of items. The global indicators of integrity (Craig and Gustafson 1998: 134) account for 81 % of the variance in perceptions of integrity. Becker (1998: 160) argues high personal integrity make excellent candidates for leadership positions. Simons (1999) used the concept of behavioural integrity and leader effectiveness and found that there is a significant positive correlation between perceived integrity and leader effectiveness. Morrison (2001: 65) states that integrity is necessary for managers to engender the goodwill and trust required for an effective leadership. Parry and Proctor-Thomson (2002) revised the PLIS to analyze the relationship.

Integrity is a cognitive form operating via different processes on outcomes such as the organizational citizenship behaviour (OCB). Thus, Dirks and Skarlicki (2004) argue that integrity may be a predictor of OCB and the leader may be seen as being with high integrity. This idea, according to the authors implies that integrity predicts employee OCB although the main effects for benevolence and integrity on OCB were not significant at low and moderate levels, however the authors found that when benevolence is high the relationship between integrity and OCB is positive. Mayer and Davis' (1999) trustworthiness scales assess trust in managers in terms of integrity and benevolence. Behavioral integrity and competence impact trust, although Salam (2000) argues that integrity and competence are not sufficient to increase trust for other parties.

Hooijberg and Lane (2005) examine the impact integrity has on people's perceptions of effectiveness and found that integrity has a small relevance for leadership effectiveness. To test the relationship between leadership behaviours, integrity, and managerial effectiveness, Hooijberg and Lane (2005) included in his research values associated with integrity and values in conflict with integrity. Hooijberg and Lane (2005) reported that is partially confirmed for all evaluators that integrity has a positive association with effectiveness for managers and their peers.

However, between integrity and direct reports or bosses' perceptions of effectiveness, they did not find a significant association between integrity and effectiveness. The results show a statistically significant association for the managers themselves and their peers, but there is not statistically significant association between Integrity and effectiveness for the direct reports and bosses. Their results also confirm that bosses associate goal-oriented behaviours had the strongest association, but not integrity with leadership effectiveness. These values have a stronger association with effectiveness than integrity, honesty, and fairness do. Integrity affects perceptions of managerial effectiveness when managers strongly associate being goal-oriented, monitoring and facilitation. Perceived competence and integrity are character-based factors make individuals willing to take the risk toward a common goal. Goal-oriented behaviours of managers are associated with effectiveness, but not integrity. Integrity as a key ingredient for effectiveness may be hard to maintain.

Competency ratings of integrity are not capable to identify managers who may lack integrity because there is an assumption that managers are at risk for misbehaving. Competency rating methods assume integrity in terms of desirable observed ethical behaviours in such a way that to identify managerial integrity underestimates the number of managers with integrity issues. Definitively, when an organization is lead by managerial integrity, interior life develops with integrity and generates an exemplar effect for all involved in the activities.

Kaiser and Hogan (2010) suggest that organizations conducting character and integrity audits consider other alternative approaches for detecting integrity such as simulations, assessment centres, enhanced background checks, specially designed interviews and rely on more than just competency ratings of integrity. There is the possibility to replace competency ratings with ratings based on the dubious reputation methods, the PLIS scale is in the public domain, by focusing on subordinates' expectations or create hybrid scales. The PLIS scale, a measure of the dubious reputation method identifies managers' integrity at the unethical end of the continuum. The dubious reputation analysis use subordinate ratings of integrity to predict ratings of job satisfaction and perceived effectiveness. Kaiser and Hogan (2010) propose the dubious reputation method to evaluate the integrity of managers based on expectations that managers behave unethically. The dubious reputation method is intended to replace the competency ratings to identify and evaluate the integrity of managers. Results of using PLIS are consistent with prior findings that leader integrity is determinant of leadership perceptions.

Integrity and ethics concern one's relationships with other people. The absence of ethics and integrity precluded leadership. Hooijberg and Lane (2005) examine the impact of some values including integrity on leadership behaviours and effectiveness finding that the value of integrity has a significant impact on effectiveness. The findings of Hooijberg and Lane (2005) do not support the notion that integrity is essential for leadership. They did not find a statistically significant association between integrity and effectiveness.

Personal integrity also plays a central role in transformational as well as charismatic leadership highlighted by research. Thus, Personal integrity is a prerequisite for leadership (Cohen 2009). Followers' perceptions of a leader's integrity are related to transformational leadership (Parry and Proctor-Thomson 2002). However, competency ratings do not measure low level of personal and managerial integrity because leadership research focuses on positive qualities (Padilla et al. 2007).

17.8 Materials and Methods/Experimental Details/ Methodology

The hypothesis of this research considers that there are some economic, social and cultural factors which appear to pressure management education to far outweigh to maintain professional integrity. This hypothesis is proved empirically confirmed by the finding that significant importance is placed on the professional's reputation for integrity, economic efficiency strength, organizational social capital, and a compliance ethical culture. This chapter outlines an approach in which professional integrity in management education is understood in the context of honesty, as having an ethical background, building trust and maintaining credibility. The chapter concludes by presenting a model of management education for professional integrity that can used to prescribe a more sensitive and dynamic human-ethical environment.

The research method employed is the ethnographic, documental and life's histories, complemented with field work supported by in-depth interviews and analyzed using a comparative method. Participants described several dimensions of professional integrity in management education. Discussion focuses on integrity as the basic principle of professionalism in management education to guide complex ethical reasoning, as well as the need for creating and sustaining professional integrity environments through ethical modelling and relational behaviours promoted by integrity as the essential element. This methodology puts in evidence that there is an urgent need to develop a model to approach professional integrity in economic and managerial careers.

In our own research conducted with information units involving teachers and students to determine the existence of program content oriented toward teaching ethics and professional integrity in the administration major at the university level as well as the existence of behaviour codes as a frame of reference (Paladino, Debeljuh and Del Bosco 2005). Results indicated that all the teachers coincide in affirming the need to incorporate a transversal program axis that would permeate the curriculum, oriented toward teaching ethics and professional integrity in the administration schools. Therefore, the study recommended setting up cooperation networks to implement common axes for teaching ethics at the national universities.

The outcomes of the research on the application in management education demonstrate that the drama of economic efficiency is centred on a dysfunctional professional integrity. This chapter provides a sound professional philosophy that empowers professionals to act with integrity, increases the probability for long-term success and professional fulfilment. The chapter offers practitioners, managers, leaders, etc., skills and moral frameworks of professional integrity that can be shared across and within professions, and used to compare and evaluate their professional practice. The results provide also the basis to develop a code of conduct and regulation policies to sustain management education for professional integrity which, can positively impact on business culture through influencing the behavior of key actors.

17.9 Results and Discussion

In general, there is a consensus that now a days it is required professionals with the capacity to live and share in harmony with others, sociability, self-control, professional integrity and adaptability in cultural diversity. To develop this type of professional, it is necessary to institute, teach and share with an example the values of the organization to the personnel on the basis of congruence between the word and the action of executives. The teaching of ethical professional based on the integrity must consider teaching at the university as an educative responsibility to satisfy the professional development programs. The ultimate end of any educative process is that human being achieve its plenitude to be capable to build everyday a more fair and equalitarian society where justice, tolerance and participation and of course, respect to others must prevail over any other interest. Being that, the economic progress will be possible on the behalf of human being integrity.

Personal sustainable development and success requires getting, restoring and maintaining professional integrity. To have, restore and maintain professional integrity behaviour for individuals, groups and organizations where it doesn't exist or it has been diminished requires a development program of professional integrity. As it has been signalled by Batteman and Snell (2001) ethics programs must be based on integrity and to go beyond to avoid illegality, to worry for the law, but also to inculcate on the people a personal responsibility for ethical behaviour. Ethical problems based on personal integrity, besides the legal aspects consider necessary to inculcate in the student personal responsibility for his/her ethical behaviour. Behaviours are manifestations and expressions of a value scale. As Humboldt had said: If we want to have professionals with ethics, we have to teach to be and how to be.

Professional development must inculcate the habits of professional integrity, in such a way to create confidence that those habits of professional integrity will be practiced by these same individuals when they become licensed professionals. However, determination to work in an ethical way and to be an integrity person is an individual process. The teaching of professional ethics and integrity is a factor contributed to an elemental human development in the global realm (Kliksberg 2002 and Etkin 1993). Professional ethics determine the essential bases of behaviours, to make decisions on the grounds of moral values and professional acts and keep on the relationship with vocation. The business ethics has an incidence in professional integrity. In this way, institutions of higher education must attend the specific needs of professional formation and development that society merits to the aim to guarantee the positioning of professionals in labor markets.

Learning models must integrate a holistic vision of professional managerial integrity formation and development, the institutions of higher education must foster formation and development of professional integrity of organizational administration according to the existent needs, achieving the requests by why they were created. The characteristics of professional integrity as part of the graduate profile of universities must be screened by the mechanisms of personnel selection of organizations and vice versa, according to the environment needs. It is required the existence of a major coordination between business organizations and the university to have an incidence in the formation and development of the managerial cadres in educative institutions as a product of this synchronization.

It has been under the study the need to achieve some changes centred on the formation and development of professional integrity in the professional practice (Rodríguez Ordoñez 2004). The components of the professional's moral integrity and their influence in the development of activities such as the academic formation and how it complements with learned values in the family nucleus which will generate in the professional an indisputable added value. Professional integrity of the manager's action in the development of competencies and capabilities are related to corporate social responsibility (CSR) that has a fundamental part in corporative governance.

An analysis of professional integrity and values across cultures and their interrelationships to increase or reduce human welfare is a new field of research. In this sense, Managers constantly associated integrity with honesty, merit and fairness but differ with other values. In some training situations penalties for tolerating lapses of integrity may be ameliorated, the same which may be fully enforced in the professional context. However, professional integrity must be so crucial in training situations where the stakes are not too high and some failures may be tolerated.

Some proposals can be implemented in the management teaching programs development addressed to the application of integrity and ethical values at the same level of knowledge, searching for coherent professional behaviours in order to avoid the forced interpretation of normative. Otherwise, when the occasion comes, it allows to treason without scrupulous the spirit of the norm, looking for meeting only the personal interests that nothing have to do with the pretended public interest that is equivalent to collective welfare of a community of persons and institutions served by the professional manager. The point to make here is that trust in his/her objectivity and integrity is vital to sustain the adequate functioning of the organizational activity.

Management's curriculum must be oriented towards the future and to must be enriched to include student's development in a systematic and ordered way of attitudes, attributes and personal qualities, such as professional integrity and independence, among others. All of these must be aligned with the concept of integral development, moreover because they are consubstantial to the successful practice of the profession (AICPA 1980: 16).

17.10 Implications for Management Education

Professions exist to serve society's needs through professionals using morally decent means to provide values and services. Professionals in administration and management must be able to effectively cultivate an image of personal integrity. When integrity-based trust in management professionals is high, organizations that espouse ethical and moral values are more willing to trust more important and crucial responsibilities and activities. The professional ethical principles give substance to different forms of professional behaviour included in the actions, such as how to focus justice to human beings, responsibility in performance of professional activities, discretion in information management and honesty in each one of his/her actions.

An individual maintains its professional integrity as long as it remains uncorrupted. Professionals that distort their essential service functions to society toward unreasonable profits, power, or greed, they may lose the trust and respect of their communities. The character-based perspective focusing on concerns about the managerial integrity, suggests that the referent trusted predicts the response or concern toward a specific individual integrity. The negligent professional manager in his/her actions despite that having necessary information to execute his/her functions, expose his/her professional integrity. In the case of conflicting duties, professional integrity tells us that the highest duty is to avoid harming others. Simons (1999) "… proposes that the divergence between words and deeds has profound costs as it renders managers untrustworthy and undermines their credibility and their ability to use their words to influence the actions of their subordinates". The manager must have and show absolute mental independence and criteria regarding to any interest, which can be considered incompatible with integrity and objectivity principles that can be affected without an application of autonomous and neutral criteria.

Management's professional must act with integrity which is achieved taking into account that must be immerse in each one of his/her functions, tasks and components of personal activities. The most important and significant aspects of management's professional services towards clients, customers and general public, cannot be defined as knowledge and experiences but in less precise terms, such as professional integrity, sense, wise, perception, imagination, circumspection, service to others, professional stability, personal benefits, professional honesty, respect to personal dignity, vocation, and so forth. Beyond the technological financial and of any other type aspects, the management's professional must have as a central axis his action and behaviour toward other human beings.

A reconstruction of professional ethics and integrity is necessary to recover credibility and respect of management's profession. According to the competencies of knowing to be and knowing to share, the attitudes, values, qualities, habits and dispositions imprinted in the citizens and professionals' character, make managers builders of a better society. Being capable of make sense on managerial knowledge and practices it is expected from personal integrity.

Society provides the necessary resources and opportunities for carrying out the professional integrity functions, the authority to act on its behalf and the autonomy required to provide social trust. Failures of social trust are related to breaches of professional integrity. Violations of the trust based on the relationship and on the authority to act on behalf of the entire society, are serious breaches of professional integrity. To refuse a professional assignment in such a way that breaks faith with all other members of the profession and the social interest, it may be considered a first-order violation of professional integrity. It is the equivalent of a manager to manage or abandoning managerial assignments that can be devastating to and organization and society. Manager's professional reputation and integrity in his/her relationships to other persons and stakeholder groups are important. The commitment to social welfare and preservation of environment is getting anchored in all managerial and economic fields' professions.

In conclusion to value integrity as a relevant aspect to individuals, is possible to work effectively for personal goodness and for the common good.

Recommendations for assessing professional managerial integrity in practice must urge the professional managers to consider the prevalence and impact of managerial misconduct. All the professions and management is not the exception, are ruled under social principles of honesty, integrity and collective responsibility that must be developed at the workplace. Integrity and responsibility must be part of the manager's professional life. This means that a good professional must know his/her legal, labour and entrepreneurial limitations which are aligned with the ethical values that generate a higher level of transparency. The management's professional is committed to carry on his/her functions with transparency and integrity generating a better quality of life.

It is necessary to promote a managerial culture to rescue the values and the attention to human being as a key factor to have organizations that every day achieves higher levels of development and productivity.

It is necessary to strengthen and consolidate plans and programs on management study with the ethical and human formation either in the teaching of specific courses strengthen them with the action of academic and administrative authorities.

Future research on professional and managerial integrity could conduct a more anthropological study and collect not only quantitative assessments but also qualitative assessments.

References

Adler, N. J., & Bird, F. B. (1988). International dimensions of executive integrity: Who is responsible for the world? In S. Srivastva & Associates (Eds.), *Executive integrity: The search for high human values in organizational life*. San Francisco, CA: Jossey-Bass.

AICPA (American Institute of Certified Public Accountants AICPA). (1980). Accounting for your Future. New York, 1980, p. 16.

Allport, G. W. (1937). *Personality: A psychological interpretation*. New York: Henry Holt & Company.

Argyris, C. (1991). *Teaching Smart People How to Learn*. Harvard Business Review: May–June, pp. 99–109.

Badaracco, J. L., & Ellsworth, R. R. (1990). Quest for integrity. *Executive Excellence, 7*, 3–4.

Batteman, T. S., & Snell, S. A. (2001). *Administración una ventaja competitiva*. México: Editorial Mc Graw Hill, Cuarta edición.

Becker, T. (1998). Integrity in organizations: Beyond honesty and conscientiousness. *Academy of Management Review, 23*, 154–161.

Boyatzis, R. E. (1982). *The competent manager: A model for effective performance*. New York: Wiley.

Brown, M. E., & Trevino, L. K. (2006). Ethical leadership: A review and future directions. *Leadership Quarterly, 17*, 595–616.

Cohen, W. A. (2009). *Drucker on leadership*. San Francisco: Jossey-Bass.

Cox, D., La Caze, M., & Levine, M. (2005). Integrity. The stanford encyclopedia of philosophy (Fall 2005 Edition).In E. N. Zalta (Ed.) Accessed April 9, 2006. http://plato.stanford.edu/archives/fall2005/entries/integrity/.

Covey, S. R. (1992). *Principle-centered leadership*. New York: Simon & Schuster.

Craig, S. B., & Gustafson, S. B. (1998). Perceived leader integrity scale. *Leadership Quarterly, 9*, 127–145.

Dirks, K. T., & Skarlicki, D. (2004). Trust in leaders: Existing research and emerging issues. In R. Kramer., & K. Cook (Eds.), *Trust and distrust in organizations: Dilemmas and approaches*. New York: Russell Sage.

Encarta Dictionary. (2004). *Encarta Dictionary* (Encarta, 2004, Microsoft® Encarta® Reference Library 2004: Microsoft Corporation.

Erhard, W., Jensen, M. C., & Zaffron, S. (2011). *Integridad: Un Modelo Positivo Que Incorpora Fenomenos Normativos de Moral, Etica y Legalidad—Abreviado (Integrity: A Positive Model that Incorporates the Normative Phenomena of Morality, Ethics, and Legality—Abridged)* (March 18, 2011). Harvard Business School NOM Unit Working Paper No. 10-061; Barbados Group Working Paper No. 10-01; Simon School Working Paper No. 10-07. Available at SSRN. http://ssrn.com/abstract=1756285.

Erhard, W., Jensen, M. C., & Zaffron, S. (2010) *Integrity: A Positive Model that Incorporates the Normative Phenomena of Morality, Ethics, and Legality—Abridged (English Language Version)* (March 7, 2010). Harvard Business School NOM Unit Working Paper No. 10-061; Barbados Group Working Paper No. 10-01; Simon School Working Paper No. 10-07. Available at SSRN. http://ssrn.com/abstract=1542759.

Erhard, W., Jensen, M. C., & Zaffron, S. (2009). *Integrity: A Positive Model that Incorporates the Normative Phenomena of Morality, Ethics and Legality* (March 23, 2009). Harvard Business School NOM Working Paper No. 06-11; Barbados Group Working Paper No. 06-03; Simon School Working Paper No. FR 08-05. Available at SSRN. http://ssrn.com/abstract=920625.

Erhard, W., Jensen, M. C., & Zaffron, S. (2008). *Integrity: A Positive Model that Incorporates the Normative Phenomena of Morality, Ethics and Legality* (March 23, 2008). Harvard Business School NOM Working Paper No. 06-11; Barbados Group Working Paper No. 06-03; Simon School Working Paper No. FR 08-05. Available at SSRN. http://ssrn.com/abstract=920625.

Erhard, W., Jensen, M., & Zaffron, S. (2007). A new model of integrity: without integrity nothing works. Negotiation, Organizations and Markets Research Papers, Harvard.

Etkin, J. (1993). *La doble moral de las organizaciones*. España: Mc Graw Hill.

Fritzche, D. J., & Becker, H. (1984). Linking management behavior to ethical philosophy: An empirical investigation. *Academy of Management Journal, 27*, 166–175.

Hernández, R., Silvestri, K., & Álvarez, A. (2007). Enseñanza de la ética en la formación gerencial. Revista de Ciencias Sociales, Vol. 13, no 3 Marcaibo dic.

Hooijberg, R., & Lane, N. (2005). Leader effectiveness and integrity: Wishful thinking? IMD 2005-1 IMD. International Institute for Management Development.

Hooijberg, R., Hunt, J. G., & Dodge, G. E. (1997). Leadership complexity and development of the leaderplex model. *Journal of Management, 23*, 375–408.

Jackall, R. (1988). *Moral mazes*. New York, NY: Oxford University Press, Inc.

Jensen, M. C. (2009). *Integrity: Without it nothing works (Jan 14, 2009)*. Rotman Magazine: The Magazine of the Rotman School of Management, pp. 16–20, Fall 2009; Harvard Business School NOM Unit Working Paper No. 10-042; Barbados Group Working Paper No. 09-04; Simon School Working Paper No. FR 10-01. Available at SSRN. http://ssrn.com/abstract=1511274.

Jensen, M. C., Granger, K. L., & Erhard, W. (2010). *A new model of integrity: the missing factor of production* (PDF file of Keynote and PowerPoint Slides) (March 26, 2010). Harvard Business School NOM Unit Working Paper 10-087; Barbados Group Working Paper No. 10-03. Available at SSRN. http://ssrn.com/abstract=1559827.

Kaptein, M. (2003). The diamond of managerial integrity. *European Management Journal, 21*, 98–108.

Kaiser, R. B. and Hogan, R. (2010). How to (and how not to) assess the integrity of managers. *Consulting Psychology Journal: Practice and Research American Psychological Association 2010, 62*(4), 216–234.

Kerr, S. (1988). Integrity in effective leadership. In S. Srivastva, et al. (Eds.), *Executive integrity: The search for high human values in organizational life*. San Francisco, CA: Jossey-Bass.

Kliksberg, B. (2002). *Ética y Desarrollo, La Relación Marginada* (con los premios Nóbel de Economía Amartya Sen, Joseph Stiglitz y otros). (El Ateneo 2002). ISBN 950-02-6366-1.

Kolthoff, E., Huberts, L., & Heuvel, H. (2003). *The Ethics of New Public Management: Is Integrity at Stake*? EGPA Study Group "Ethics and Integrity of Governance" Oeiras, Portugal, September 2003. July 2003.

Leslie, J. B., & Fleenor, J. W. (1998). *Feedback to managers: A review and comparison of multi-rater instruments for management development*. Greensboro, NC: Center for Creative Leadership.

Levinson, H. (1988). To thine own self be true: Coping with the dilemmas of integrity. In S. Srivastva, et al. (Eds.), *Executive integrity: The search for high human values in organizational life*. San Francisco, CA: Jossey-Bass.

Llano, C. (1997). *Empleo, Educación y Formación Permanente*. Lo mejor de Executive Excellence. Panorama Editorial, México.

Machiavelli, N. (1981). *The Prince. Translated by George Bull*. New York: Penguin Books.

Mayer, R. C., & Davis, J. H. (1999). The effect of the performance appraisal system on trust for management: A field quasi-experiment. *Journal of Applied Psychology, 84*, 123–136.

Mayer, R. C., Davis, J. H., & Schoorman, F. D. (1995). An integrative model of organizational trust. *Academy of Management Review, 20*, 709–734.

Mayer, R., & Gavin, M. (1999). *Trust for management and performance: Who minds the shop while the employees watch the boss?*. Paper presented at the Annual Meeting of the Academy of Management, Chicago, IL.

McDowell, D. (2010). *Core Values and Professional Integrity*. Retrieved from http://www.mncap.org/protocol/CoreValues_ProfIntegrity.pdf.

McLean, P. (1997). The fourth arm of justice: The art and science of revenge. In R. Lewicki., B. Sheppard.,& R. Bies (Eds), *Research on negotiation in organizations*. Greenwich: JAI Press, CT, pp. 113–144.

McAllister, D. J. (1995). Affect- and cognition-based trust as foundations for interpersonal cooperation in organizations. *Academy of Management Journal, 38*, 24–59.

Morgan, R. B. (1989). Reliability and validity of a factor analytically derived measure of leadership behavior and characteristics. *Educational Psychological Measurement, 49*, 911–919.

Morrison, A. (2001). Integrity and global leadership. *Journal of Business Ethics, 31*, 65–76.

Oxford dictionaries. (2011). Retrieved from http://oxforddictionaries.com.

Padilla, A., Hogan, R., & Kaiser, R. B. (2007). The toxic triangle: Destructive leaders, vulnerable followers, and conducive environments. *Leadership Quarterly, 18*, 176–194.

Paladino, M., Debeljuh, P., & Del Bosco, P. (2005). Integridad: respuesta superadora a los dilemas éticos del hombre de empresa. *Journal of Economic Finance and Administrative Science. Cuad. Difus. 10*(18-19), 9–37.

Parry, K., & Proctor-Thomson, S. B. (2002). Perceived integrity of transformational leaders in organizational settings. *Journal of Business Ethics, 35*, 75–96.

Pojman, L. P. (1995). *Ethical theory: Classical and contemporary readings* (2nd ed.). Belmont, CA: Wadsworth.

Rodríguez Ordoñez, J. A. (2004). Hacia la integralidad de la enseñanza y la práctica profesional en geotecnia. *Ing University Bogotá (Colombia), 8*(2), 159–171, julio-diciembre de 2004 159.

Rost, K., Salomo, S., & Osterloh, M. (2008). CEO appointments and the loss of firm-specific knowledge—putting integrity back into hiring decisions. *Corporate Ownership and Control, 5*(3), 86–98.

Salam, S. (2000). Foster trust through competence, honesty, and integrity. In E. Locke (Ed.), *Handbook of principles of organizational behavior* (pp. 274–288). Malden, MA: Blackwell.

Shakespeare, W. (1914). *The Oxford Shakespeare: The complete works of William Shakespeare.* Hamlet, Act II. London: Oxford University Press.

Simons, T. L. (2002). Behavioral integrity: The perceived alignment between manager's words and deeds as a research focus. *Organization Science, 13*(1), 18–35.

Simons, T. L. (1999). Behavioral integrity as a critical ingredient for transformational leadership. *Journal of Organizational Change Management, 12*(2), 89–104, p. 90.

Srivastva, S. and Associates (1988). *Executive integrity: The search for high human values in organizational life.* San Francisco, CA: Jossey-Bass.

Staw, B. M., & Ross, J. (1980). Commitment in an experimenting society: A study of the attribution of leadership from administrative scenarios. *Journal of Applied Psychology, 65*, 249–260.

Thompson, A. D., Grahek, M., Phillips, R. E., & Fay, C. L. (2008). The search for worthy leadership. *Consulting Psychology Journal: Practice and Research, 60*, 366–382.

Webster's. (1994). *Webster's New World Dictionary on PowerCD version 2.1, based on Webster's New World Dictionary*®, Third College Edition 1994.

Chapter 18
Do Institutional Investors Prefer to Invest in Socially Responsible Companies? An Empirical Analysis in Turkey

Ali Osman Gurbuz, Mehpare Karahan Gokmen and Aslı Aybars

Abstract Corporate social responsibility (CSR) has become an indispensible item on companies' agendas and even though the business discipline has been with us for a few decades, it started to attract much more attention recently. Companies are emphasizing the importance of addressing issues relating to the social, economic and environmental aspects of their operations which affect their stakeholders in addition to their core business activities. Actions undertaken by socially responsible companies may be considered as determinants in the decision making process of investors. This is especially the case with institutional investors, who have long term investment horizon and are more willing to invest in companies that are serious about CSR activities. Numerous analyses have been conducted in the literature regarding the relationship between institutional shareholding and corporate social performance mainly in developed countries. However, this study focuses on an emerging country—Turkey, and probes whether institutional investors have a tendency to invest in socially responsible companies utilizing logistic regression analysis. The empirical part of the study employs available dataset combining data relating to percentage of shares that are held by institutional investors with the financials and selected CSR measures for companies listed in Istanbul Stock Exchange.

A. O. Gurbuz (✉)
Istanbul Commerce University, Istanbul, Turkey
e-mail: aliosmangurbuz@yahoo.com

M. K. Gokmen
Ondokuz Mayıs University, Samsun, Turkey

A. Aybars
Marmara University, Istanbul, Turkey

A. Yüksel Mermod and S. O. Idowu (eds.), *Corporate Social Responsibility in the Global Business World*, DOI: 10.1007/978-3-642-37620-7_18,
© Springer-Verlag Berlin Heidelberg 2014

18.1 Introduction

The indispensible role played by corporate social responsibility (CSR) in the attainment of sustainable performance has driven the attention of academicians and practitioners on the hot debate regarding the amount of sources that has to be diverted to socially responsible activities. Due to the significance of the topic for the success of enterprises in avoiding the recent corporate scandals, theoretical evolution of CSR has gained momentum during the last few decades. The seminal work of Bowen (1953), which is regarded as the first attempt to investigate the link between society and corporations, defines CSR as 'the obligations of businessmen to pursue those policies, to make those decisions, or to follow those lines of action which are desirable in terms of the objectives and values of our society'. Later, Friedman (1970) made a major contribution to the development of CSR theory by emphasizing the responsibilities of management in exercising social responsibility. A recent definition of CSR can be regarded as that of the Commission of European Communities (2002), which describes CSR as 'a concept whereby companies integrate social and environmental concerns in their business operations and in their interaction with their stakeholders on a voluntary basis'.

The fundamental article of Carroll (1979) extends the concept of CSR into corporate social performance (CSP) and generates a more comprehensive notion that encompasses economic, legal, ethical and discretionary dimensions of business performance. This three dimensional model that includes the aspects of corporate social responsibility, social issues surrounding the organization and social responsiveness is further developed by the studies of Wartick and Cochran (1985), and Wood (1991), whereby the latter defines CSP as 'a business organization's configuration of principles of social responsibility, processes of social responsiveness, policies, programs, and observable outcomes as they relate to the firm's societal relationships'.

The substantial increase in the amount of shares that are held by institutional investors denotes the emergence of a new group of stakeholders recently. Due to the size of their investment, their mobility in terms of changing the composition of their portfolios is regarded to be less than those of individual investors. Thus, they are considered to be less capable of divesting their holdings. According to Graves and Waddock (1994a), institutional shareholders will have to impact the decisions of the firm when they are not satisfied by the investments that are undertaken as it is relatively difficult for them to disinvest. Pound (1992) also holds the same view in that the long-term orientation of these types of investors has led them to try to influence the decisions of top management. As a result, the impact of social criteria upon institutional shareholders' investment decisions has been widely analyzed in literature (Coffey and Fryxell 1991; Graves and Waddock 1994b; Waddock and Graves 1995; Mahoney and Roberts 2007). On the contrary, depending on the myopic institutions theory, institutional owners have a tendency to be short-term oriented since the performance of fund managers are evaluated regularly resulting in the need of frequent portfolio adjustments (Porter 1992). Based on Hansen and

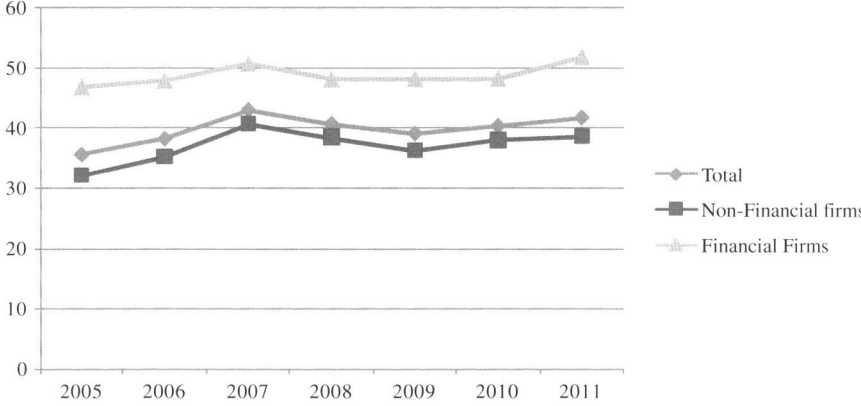

Fig. 18.1 Percentage of institutional ownership in publicly held companies

Hill (1991), the shortsightedness of institutional shareholders arises because of their performance appraisals' being based on annual or quarterly basis. Therefore, a growing array of literature has emerged regarding the controversial link between institutional shareholding and social investment of companies.

This study aims to contribute to this research area with empirical evidence in a developing country, Turkey. Besides greater emphasis on CSR investments in Turkey, increase in the percentage of shares held by institutional investors constitutes the motivation for this study. The latter fact is exhibited in Fig. 18.1[1] through the years 2005–2011. While percentage of shares held by institutional investors was 35.6 %, it raised to 41.7 by the end of 2011. Moreover this increase is slightly higher for non-financial firms in comparison to financial firms.

18.2 Measuring CSR

Measurement of CSR has turned out to be one of the most debatable issues in the array of literature that focuses on companies' social investments. As stated in the work of Shane and Spicer (1983), the difficulty of materializing the degree of firms' social responsibility arises from the voluntary nature of these investments and absence of mandatory reporting requirements. Based on the study of Ernst and Ernst (1978), which is further developed by Ng (1985), a checklist was generated to determine the major themes that can be considered as domains of responsible investments. These themes can be listed as environment, energy, products/consumers, community, and employee health and safety, employee other, general. The

---

[1] Figure 18.1 is formed utilizing the ownership data for firms which are listed on ISE consecutively for 2005–2011 periods. Financial firms are banks, insurance companies and investment trusts.

existence of a wide range of areas associated with these investments adds to the challenging nature of quantification.

Various methodologies have been applied in literature to enhance the measurement of CSR disclosures. Some of the earlier studies apply forced-choice survey methodology to quantify the degree of CSR in their samples (Aupperle 1984; Aupperle et al. 1985). Other studies utilize the scores driven from reputational indices such as Fortune database, which provides a comprehensive annual survey of most admired companies (Griffin and Mahon 1997; Wokutch and Spencer 1987; McGuire et al. 1988; Heinze et al. 1999). Graves and Waddock (1994b) define the drawbacks of surveys as low return rates and lack of consistency among the respondents, whereas; they consider overemphasis of corporate financial performance other than social performance as a problem of Fortune ratings. Another CSR ranking methodology can be named as social audits, which are assessments of companies' social performance by third parties focusing on issues like community services and environmental programs that are by being undertaken (Orlitzky et al. 2003).

One major method of disclosure-scoring is the use of content analysis of annual reports and some other corporate documents. This method as first utilized by Bowman and Haire (1975) and later used by many other academicians (Hoq et al. 2010; Aras et al. 2010; Hasseldin et al. 2005; Abbott and Monsen 1979; Toms 2002). Krippendorff (2004, p. 18) states that 'content analysis is a research technique for making replicable and valid inferences from texts (or other meaningful matter) to the contexts of their use'. However, this methodology is also considered to have certain drawbacks. Graves and Waddock (1994b) defines one of the limitations of content analysis as being too much dependent on the comprehensiveness of the documents subject to evaluation. Furthermore, the potential disparity between the actual actions of the companies and what is reported as being done in annual reports may be misleading. The subjective selection of the variables to be analyzed may also add to the problems associated with this method (Cochran and Wood 1984). Furthermore, significance of the analysis will be distorted by the difference of opinion among the coders (Janis et al. 1943).

Problems faced in terms of quantifying CSR has led to the development of certain indices that require the use of compatible processes across companies to enable consistency and comparison. One of the mostly referred databases that provide information concerning companies' social performance was developed by Kinder, Lydenberg, Domini (KLD) covering more than 650 listed companies traded on US stock exchanges. The independency of the rating agency in generation of KLD database results in its frequent usage in academic studies as well (Graves and Waddock 1994b; Waddock and Graves 1997; Tsoutsoura 2004; Griffin and Mahon 1997). Some other studies in literature utilize another database named as Canadian Social Investment Database (CSID) generated by Michael Jantzi Research Associates, Inc. in 1992 (Mahoney and Roberts 2007; Makni et al. 2009; Gargouri et al. 2010). Unfortunately no such index exists in Turkey that enhances the use of a consistent and objective measure of CSR for listed companies across time.

Due to the complications associated with the above stated methodologies and the nonexistence of a database proving reliable social responsibility measures in Turkey, this study utilizes the corporate governance rating scores attributed to companies listed on Istanbul Stock Exchange (ISE) Corporate Governance Index. These scores are issued by corporate governance rating institutions, which are licensed by Turkish Capital Markets Board. The overall corporate governance rating score includes four subsections which are named as shareholders, public disclosure and transparency, stakeholders and board of directors (Saha, Corporate Governance and Credit rating Services Inc.). The score attributed to the stakeholder subsection is used as a proxy for CSR in the empirical part of this study in-line with the work of Arsoy et al. (2012) since it encompasses seven parameters, namely; corporate policies related to stakeholders, stakeholder participation in corporate management, protection of corporate assets, human resource policies, customer and supplier relations, ethic rules and social responsibility. These dimensions are parallel to the areas covered by KLD scores which adhere to environmental performance, social contribution, corporate governance, and controversial business involvement (Chen and Delmas 2010). The overlapping nature of contents of stakeholder subsection of corporate governance rating in Turkey with the dimensions KLD strengthens to the accuracy of our CSR proxy.

18.3 Literature Review

Initial studies on the relationship between corporate social performance and institutional ownership are mainly conducted in developed countries. This is a natural outcome of emergence of CSR concept in those countries as many other major accounting and finance concepts. As CSR gained importance in other parts of the world, relevant academic research started to be conducted in developing countries as well. In this section, prominent studies on the specified relationship between socially responsible investments and institutional ownership will be examined firstly in developed countries and then in developing ones.

First empirical study that investigates the linkage between corporate social performance and institutional ownership is performed by Graves and Waddock (1994a). Prior studies were concentrating on impact of CSP on financial performance despite available CSR data. However, research evidence on that subject was inconclusive with contradictory results. One of the aims of this initial study is to explore whether institutional ownership may act as an intervening factor. It is hypothized that as far as investors are objectively informed about social responsibility investments, they prefer companies with CSR investments in order to decrease their risks. CSP proxy of the companies is measured with Domini Social Index, which is initially published in 1990 and tracks eight social attributes for a large sample of companies in U.S. In order to capture the behavior of institutional investors, the percentage of shares that are held by this type of investors before and after the availability of Domini Social Index is calculated for the years 1989 and

1991. Regression results indicate an insignificant positive relation between institutional ownership and CSP (Graves and Waddock 1994a).

Cox et al. (2004) investigate the relationship between institutional ownership and CSR investments with an emphasis on investment horizon in that they focus on long- term and short-term investors in U.K. Five types of institutional investors are analyzed in their study: pension funds, life insurance funds, charities, unit trusts and investment trust. While first three institutions are categorized as being long- term, remaining institutions are classified as being short-term oriented. Due to the accrual of CSR investments in the long run, it is expected that CSP should have a positive relation with long-term institutional investors and a negative relation with short term institutional investors. According to the results obtained for largest 600 companies in FTSE, controlling for firm size, risk, profitability, large block holders and industry differences, it is shown that there is a positive relation between CSP and long-tem institutional ownership. However, no significant relationship is found with short-term investors. Another contribution of this study to this area of research is the inclusion of separate measures for community, employee and environment besides an overall CSP measure (Cox et al. 2004).

Another comprehensive study is performed by Mahoney and Roberts (2007) for a large number of Canadian firms using panel data analysis. CSP of companies are evaluated according to a rating system developed by Michael Jantzi Research Associates. This rating system gauges individual components of CSP besides a general CSP rating for companies. These individual dimensions are listed as community issues, diversity in workplace, employee relations, environmental performance, international concerns, product and business practices and other. Test results on 1,189 observations for the period between the years 1996–1999 indicate that CSP investments attract institutional investors. Further analysis for individual components of CSP shows that investors give more emphasis to international and product dimensions of CSR investments than the others (Mahoney and Roberts 2007).

Fauzi et al. (2007) examine the subject in a developing country, Indonesia, using cross section analysis for 2005. An approach developed by Jantzi Research Inc., which is comparable to KLD, is used to measure CSR depending on annual reports. In contrast to the findings of other studies in U.S., Canada or European countries, no significant relation is revealed according to regression results, which are controlled for firm size, firm performance and industry. It is concluded that CSP does not make a change in the decision making process of institutional investors. This conclusion should be interpreted taking into account the limited time span of the analysis conducted. Different results could be obtained, if test period were extended. (Fauzi et al. 2007).

Hoq et al. (2010) analyze the relationship for Malaysia motivated by the lack of empirical evidence for socially responsible investments in this developing country. Thus, they focus on the link between CSR and institutional ownership to fill the gap for academic research. In this study, institutional ownership is measured by number of shares held by institutional investors and the percentage of firms' outstanding shares held by institutional investors while CSP is measured by scores, which are determined with content analysis of annual reports. Content analysis covers four key areas which are employee relations, environment, community involvement and product. Hypothesis testing, which is made on 200 largest companies selected from main board of Bursa Malaysia for the years 2000–2005, indicates a positive relation between institutional ownership and CSP (Hoq et al. 2010).

Another recent study in developing countries is performed by Kangarluie and Bayazidi (2011) in Tehran Stock Exchange. The aim of the study is to investigate the relationship between CSR and corporate governance mechanism. Institutional ownership is analyzed in the study as a sub-hypothesis within the external corporate mechanism. Due the absence of an objective scoring system for companies listed in Tehran Stock Exchange, a questionnaire is used to gauge the level of CSR for the period of 2003–2009. Results of the regression models indicate a positive relation between CSR and institutional ownership, which is measured with the percentage of institutionally owned stock of the firm (Kangarluie and Bayazidi 2011).

Oh et al. (2011) investigate the association of CSR rating with different types of ownership variables including institutional ownership on 118 Korean companies. KEJI index, which calculates CSR rating for Korean companies, is used in this study. As this index is available by 2006, only data relating to year 2005 could be included in the sample. Test results exhibit a positive relation between the institutional ownership and CSR rating. When the same relation is examined for foreign investors, CSR is found to be negatively associated with shares of top managers. Additionally, the relation is slightly stronger for long term investors compared to short term oriented investors in terms of institutional investors (Oh et al. 2011).

18.4 Hypothesis Development

Based on the literature review provided above, it can be clearly stated that there is tendency towards a positive relationship between institutional ownership and CSR. Nevertheless, an opposite association may also be expected. Theoretical background for the hypothesis development with both views will be provided in the following section.

It is important to understand the reasons that make companies engage in social responsibility investments to explain why institutional investors would select socially responsible companies. There are basically four hypotheses that may be useful in clarifying this issue. The first hypothesis depends on the agency theory and states that managers (agents) make social responsibility investments in order to restore a good 'personal' reputation (over- investment hypothesis). Depending on the second hypothesis, which is called as 'strategic choice', managers engage in that kind of activities in order to gain social and environmental support that would reduce the risk of executive turnovers. According to the third hypothesis, which is named as product signaling, social responsibility investments are used to differentiate company products. Lastly, CSR activities may be utilized in order to eliminate any conflict of interest among various parties in relation with the company such as managers and any type of stakeholders (conflict resolution hypothesis) (Harjoto and Jo 2011). Harjoto and Jo (2011) prove that these investments occur as a result of the last hypothesis, named as conflict resolution hypothesis, in contrast to over investment or strategic choice hypotheses indicating a positive impact on institutional investors. Furthermore, only weak support has been found for the product signaling hypothesis.

Institutional investors are attributed to be 'superior investors' who act rationally while making their investment decisions. Thus, favorable investments that would accrue in the long term are not disregarded by them (Mahoney and Roberts 2007). Increasing dominance of institutional investors in the market provides them with economies of scale in the evaluation of alternatives and therefore they are able to acquire a better quality of knowledge (Black 1992). This notion is one of the underlying factors for institutional investors to be long term oriented. Additionally, exit problems that occur due to high level of ownership in a company (Pound 1988) or inconvenience to find new attractive investments (David et al. 1998) reinforce the need for longer term investments. In accordance with the superior investor view and long term focus, CSR investments, which usually accrue in the longer terms, are not avoided but rather preferred by institutional investors (Mahoney and Roberts 2007).

As an opposing view, Cox et al. (2004) suggest that institutional investors could be either short-term or long-term investors due the role of investment horizon. Long-term investors are willing to wait for the return of CSR investments that accrue in long period of time. Additionally company reputation that increase through CSR investments increase the confidence of investors about the company. On the contrary, short term investors seek liquidity and they may not prefer companies with CSR investments that deteriorate the profits and depress market prices in near terms. In this study, it is assumed that all institutional investors have long term horizon. Therefore, the hypothesis is constructed as follows:

Hypothesis: Companies that have higher CSR scores are majorly preferred by institutional investors.

18.5 Research

In this section, hypothesis testing for the research question of our study will be presented using logistic regression model for companies listed in Istanbul Stock Exchange (ISE).

18.5.1 Data

Due to the lack of an objective scoring system for companies listed in ISE, 'stake-holder' category of corporate governance scores are used as the measurement benchmark in this study. This limitation urged us to only include the companies which are listed in Corporate Governance Index (CGI) in ISE. CGI has been calculated since 30.08.2007 and the number of firms that are being included in the index is continuously increasing. Initially 7 companies were included in the index for the year 2007. However, this number has reached 38 as of 2011. In order to have the maximum amount of companies in our sample, 2011 is selected as the year for the test period. Therefore, number of companies in the sample is determined to be 38.

18.5.2   Variables

The recent surge in the amount of shares that are held by institutional investors and accompanying the concentration of ownership in fewer institutions has made institutionalization of savings an important issue in the capital markets. Institutional investors encompass mutual funds, pension funds, insurance companies and certain private firms. As Mahoney and Roberts (2007) describe, some of their significant features can be summarized as their being rational and risk adverse investors with long term orientation. This study defines institutional ownership in line with Nofsinger and Sias (1999), Mahoney and Roberts (2007) and Hoq et al. (2010), whereby fractional institutional ownership is calculated as the ratio of the number of shares held by institutional investors to the number of shares outstanding. Thus, the percentage of firms' shares held by institutional owners is modeled as the dependent variable of the analysis and denoted by INST. Under logistic regression analysis, which is employed in our study in the empirical section, the dependent variable needs to be defined as a categorical variable. Thus, if percentage of shares held by institutional investors is above 50 %, it is attributed to be majorly held by institutional investors and labeled as 1. Otherwise, the variable is labeled as 0.

CSR is defined as the independent variable in this study and is measured with the component of corporate governance scores for companies listed in CGI. Corporate governance scores are composed of four sub-scores, which are calculated for shareholders, public disclosures and transparency, stakeholders and board of directors' categories. Following Arsoy et al. (2012), company scores calculated for stakeholders' category is used as the independent variable.

The economic decisions of institutional investors may be affected by some other intervening factors besides CSR investments of companies. Thus, in order to eliminate the impact of those factors, certain control variables are included in the model. Firm size and firm risk are selected as proxies of control in line with the work of Cox et al. (2004).

Firm size may influence the tendency of institutional owners to invest in firms' stock in either a positive or negative way. Institutional investors would prefer to invest in small firms with the aim of keeping their levels of ownership high (Graves and Waddock 1994b). Inversely, small companies may be more feasible for relatively small investors (Cox et al. 2004). Log of sales' amount for each company is taken as the proxy for firm size.

Firm risk may also be a decision criterion for institutional investors. Leverage is incorporated into the model to control for the level of firm risk. Risk averse institutional investors may avoid firms with high level of leverage with the reasoning that they can encounter a problem of insolvency. On the other hand, institutional investors, who seek higher levels of profit, may seek those kinds of companies (Cox et al. 2004).

18.6 Methodology

Limited number of firms and years included in the sample constraints the selection of an appropriate methodology that can be employed in our study. Accordingly, logistic regression model that overcomes the limitations of Ordinary Least Square (OLS) relating to sampling issues is chosen as the method of analysis. Selection of data from a multivariate normal distribution with equal variances and covariances for all variables is not required under logit regression model. In contrast to many other regression models, the response variable (Y) is not defined quantitatively, but qualitatively as a categorical variable in logit. Therefore, logistic regression models attempt to predict a probable relation between a categorical variable and one or more predictor variables using the occurrence probability of the regressand (Peng and So 2002).

The dependent variable of the analysis which is chosen to be institutional ownership is defined as categorical in accordance with the requirements of logistic regression. The model aims to explain the level of institutional ownership with the degree companies' corporate social responsibility. Additionally, as clarified above, firm size and firm risk are included in the model as control variables. Within the light of these facts, our model is formed as below:

$$predicted\ logit\ INST_p = \alpha + \beta_1 CSR + \beta_2 lnSales + \beta_3 Lev \quad (\text{Model 1})$$

where;

$INST_p$ is equal to 1 if percentage of shares owned by institutional investors is higher than 50 %; otherwise 0
CSR   CSR scores for companies in the sample
lnSales   Natural logarithm of sales amount for companies in the sample
Lev   Leverage for companies in the sample (Total Liabilities/Total Equity)

18.6.1 Test Results

Table 18.1 shows the results of descriptive statistics for the variables used in the model. While full sample includes 38 companies, 23 companies are included in the institutionally owned category and remaining 15 companies are grouped into

Table 18.1 descriptive statistics for companies in the sample

	No. of obs.	Mean	St. Dev.	Min.	Max.
CSR					
Full Sample	38	9.01	0.76	6.82	9.79
Inst. Own.[*]	23	9.28	0.52	8.10	9.79
Non- Inst. Own.	15	8.59	0.90	6.82	9.76
Total Sales (TL million)					
Full Sample	38	3.258	6.941	0	41.385
Inst. Own.	23	4.836	8.570	10	41.385
Non- Inst. Own.	15	836	1.241	0	3.891
Leverage					
Full Sample	38	0.56	0.27	0.01	0.91
Inst. Own.	23	0.63	0.24	0.01	0.91
Non- Inst. Own.	15	0.47	0.28	0.01	0.81

[*] If institutional ownership is higher than 50 %, then the firm is categorized as majorly institutionally owned. Otherwise it is grouped into the other category

Table 18.2 Test results for the logistic regression model

$predicted\ logit\ INST_p = \alpha + \beta_1 CSR + \beta_2 lnSales + \beta_3 Lev$

Variable	Parameter estimate	Standard error
Constant	−17.889	6.6186
	(−2.7029)	
CSR	1.1797	0.6336
	(1.8617)[***]	
LnSales	0.3646	0.2583
	(1.4117)	
Leverage	0.7899	1.6849
	(0.4688)	
McFadden R^2	0.3112	

+ Values in parentheses indicate z-values. [*], [**], [***] represent p—values $\leq 0.01, \leq 0.05$ and ≤ 0.01 respectively

the other category. Mean of the CSR scores is 9.01 for the full sample. For companies, which are majorly owned by institutional investors, it is calculated to be higher (9.28) and for the other group it is calculated to be lower than the mean of full sample (8.59). Same results are also found for the control variables, namely, total sales and leverage. This may indicate that institutional investors prefer larger firms and firms that take higher risk.

Regression model (Model 1) is tested using binary logistic regression method and test results are reported in Table 18.2. According to test results, a significant positive relationship between institutional ownership and CSR scores (z-value is 1.8617 and $p \leq 0.1$) is determined. However, no significant relationship is observed for control variables denoted as sales and leverage.

R^2 is used to measure the goodness of fit for logistic regression models as it is also the case with Ordinary Least Squares (OLS) models. Among various R^2s,

McFadden R^2 is determined to be superior (Menard 2000). McFadden R^2 is 0.3112 indicating explanatory power of the model. Although coefficients for control variables are found to be insignificant, they are included in the model based on the reasoning that test results for models excluding one control variable or both of them induce a decrease in McFadden R^2. As these models do not affect the interpretations, they are not reported in the study.

18.7 Conclusion

CSR (Corporate Social Responsibility) activities, which have accelerated in recent years, are attracting the attention of both academicians and practitioners. Growing literature on CSR covers many areas and majorly concentrates on financial performance. The purpose of this study is to evaluate the issue from point of view for institutional investors. It is investigated whether institutional investors consider CSR activities while making economic decisions. Empirical evidence on publicly held companies in Istanbul Stock Exchange indicates a positive relationship between CSR scores and percentage of shares held by institutional investors. This result is consistent with the findings of Cox et al. (2004), Mahoney and Roberts (2007), Hoq et al. (2010), Kangarluie and Bayazidi (2011) and Oh et al. (2011). It can also be concluded that companies that are interested in constructing long term relations with institutional investors would find it valuable to enhance the level of CSR investments.

References

Abbott, W. F., & Monsen, R. J. (1979). On the measurement of corporate social responsibility: Self-reported disclosures as a method of measuring corporate social involvement. *The Academy of Management Journal, 22*(3), 501–515.

Aras, G., Aybars, A., & Kutlu, O. (2010). Managing corporate performance: Investigating the relationship between corporate social responsibility and financial performance in emerging markets. *International Journal of Productivity and Performance Management, 59*(3), 229–254.

Arsoy, A. P., Arabacı, Ö., & Çiftçioğlu, A. (2012). Corporate social responsibility and financial performance relationship: The case of Turkey. *The Journal of Accounting and Finance, 53*, 159–176.

Aupperle, K. E. (1984). An empirical measure of corporate social orientation, Lee Preston's corporation and society research: Studies in theory and measurement. Greenwich: JAI Press, 1990, 237–264. Reprinted article from 1984.

Aupperle, K. E., Carroll, A. B., & Hatfield, J. D. (1985). An empirical examination of the relationship between corporate social responsibility and profitability. *Academy of Management Journal, 28*(2), 446–463.

Black, B. S. (1992). Agents watching agents: The promise of institutional investor voice. *UCLA Law Review, 39*(4), 811–893.

Bowen, H. R. (1953). *Social responsibilities of the businessman*. New York, NY: Harper & Brothers Publishers.

Bowman, E. H., & Haire, M. (1975). A strategic posture toward corporate social responsibility. *California Management Review, 18*, 49–58.

Carroll, A. B. (1979). A three-dimensional conceptual model of corporate performance. *Academy of Management Review, 4*(4), 497–505.

Chen, C. M., & Delmas, M. (2010). Measuring corporate social performance: an efficiency perspective. *Production and Operations Management, 20*(6), 789–804.

Cochran, P. L., & Wood, R. A. (1984). Corporate social responsibility and financial performance. *The Academy of Management Journal, 27*(1), 42–56.

Coffey, B. S., & Fryxell, G. E. (1991). Institutional ownership of stock and dimensions of corporate social performance: An empirical examination. *Journal of Business Ethics, 10*, 437–444.

Commission of the European Communities. (2002). Corporate social responsibility: A business contribution to sustainable development, Brussels.

Cox, P., Brammer, S., & Millington, A. (2004). An empirical examination of institutional investor preferences for corporate social performance. *Journal of Business Ethics, 52*(1), 27–43.

David, P., Kochhar, R., & Levitas, E. (1998). The effect of institutional investors on the level and mix of CEO compensation. *Academy of Management Journal, 41*(2), 200–208.

Ernst & Ernst. (1978). Social responsibility disclosure, 1978 survey. Cleveland, OH: Ernst & Ernst.

Fauzi, H., Mahoney, L., & Rahman, A. A. (2007). Institutional ownership and corporate social performance: Empirical evidence from Indonesian companies. *Issues in Social and Environmental Accounting, 1*(2), 334–347.

Friedman, M. (1970). The responsibility of business is to increase its profits. *The New York Times, 33*, 122–126.

Gargouri, R. M., Shabou, R., & Francoeur, C. (2010). The relationship between corporate social performance and earnings management. *Canadian Journal of Administrative Sciences, 27*(4), 320–334.

Graves, S. B., & Waddock, S. A. (1994a). Responses of institutional investors to corporate social performance measures. *International Journal of Value-Based Management, 7*(2), 165–180.

Graves, S. B., & Waddock, S. A. (1994b). Institutional owners and corporate social performance. *Academy of Management Journal, 37*(4), 1034–1046.

Griffin, J. J., & Mahon, J. F. (1997). The corporate social performance and corporate financial performance debate. *Business and Society, 36*(1), 5–31.

Harjoto, M. A., & Jo, H. (2011). Corporate Governance and CSR Nexus. *Journal of Business Ethics, 100*, 45–67.

Hoq, M. Z., Saleh, M., Zubayer, M., & Mahmud, K. T. (2010). The effect of CSR disclosure on institutional ownership. *Pakistan Journal of Commerce and Social Sciences, 4*(1), 22–39.

Hansen, G. S., & Hill, G. W. L. (1991). Are institutional investors myopic? A time series study of four technology driven industries. *Strategic Management Journal, 12*, 1–16.

Hasseldine, J., Salama, A. I., & Toms, J. S. (2005). Quantity versus quality: The impact of environmental disclosures on the reputations of UK Plcs. *The British Accounting Review, 37*, 231–248.

Heinze, D., Sibary, S., & Sikula, A. (1999). Relations among corporate social responsibility, financial soundness, and investment value in 22 manufacturing industry groups. *Ethics and Behavior, 9*(4), 331–347.

Janis, I. L., Fadner, R. H., & Janowitz, M. (1943). The reliability of a content analysis technique. *The Public Opinion Quarterly, 7*(2), 293–296.

Krippendorff, K. (2004). *Content analysis: An introduction to its methodology*. London: Sage Publications.

Kangarluie, S. J., & Bayazidi, A. (2011). Corporate governance mechanism and corporate social responsibility (CSR): Evidence from Iran. *Australian Journal of Basic and Applies Sciences, 5*(9), 1591–1598.

Mahoney, L., & Roberts, R. W. (2007). Corporate social performance, financial performance and institutional ownership in Canadian firms. *Accounting Forum, 31*, 233–253.

Makni, R., Francoeur, C., & Bellavance, F. (2009). Causality between corporate social performance and financial performance: Evidence from Canadian firms. *Journal of Business Ethics, 89*, 409–422.

McGuire, J. B., Sundgren, A., & Schneeweis, T. (1988). Corporate social responsibility and firm financial performance. *The Academy of Management Journal, 31*(4), 854–872.

Menard, S. (2000). Coefficients of determination for multiple logistic regression analysis. *The American Statistician, 54*, 17–24.

Ng, L. W. (1985). Social responsibility disclosures of selected New Zealand companies for 1981, 1982 and 1983, occasional paper, (vol. 54). Palmerston North: Massey University.

Nofsinger, J. R., & Sias, R. W. (1999). Herding and feedback Trading by institutional and individual investors. *The Journal of Finance, 54*(6), 2263–2295.

Oh, W. Y., Chang, Y. K., & Martynov, A. (2011). The effect of ownership structure on corporate social responsibility: Empirical evidence from Korea. *Journal of Business Ethics, 104*, 283–297.

Orlitzky, M., Schmidt, F. L., & Rynes, S. L. (2003). Corporate social and financial performance: A meta-analysis. *Organization Studies, 24*(3), 403–441.

Peng, C. Y. J., & So, T. S. H. (2002). Logistic regression analysis and reporting. *Understanding Statistics, 1*(1), 31–70.

Porter, M. E. (1992). Capital choices: Changing the Way America invests in industry. *Journal of Applied Corporate Finance, 5*, 4–16.

Pound, J. (1988). Proxy contests and the efficiency of shareholder oversight. *Journal of Financial Economics, 20*, 237–265.

Pound, J. (1992). Beyond takeovers: politics comes to corporate control. *Harvard Business Review, 70*(2), 83–93.

Shane, P. B., & Spicer, B. H. (1983). Market response to environmental information produced outside the firm. *Accounting Review, 58*(3), 521–536.

Toms, J. S. (2002). Firm resources quality signals and the determinants of corporate environmental reputation: Some UK evidence. *British Accounting Review, 34*, 257–282.

Tsoutsoura, M. (2004). Corporate social responsibility and financial performance (Vol. 7). Center for Responsible Business Working Paper Series.

Waddock, S. A., & Graves, S. B. (1995). Attraction or repulsion: How institutional owners react to corporate social performance. *Management Research News, 18*(12), 20–24.

Waddock, S. A., & Graves, Samuel B. (1997). The corporate social performance-financial performance link. *Strategic Management Journal, 18*(4), 303–319.

Wartick, S. L., & Cochran, P. L. (1985). The evolution of the corporate social performance model. *Academy of Management Review, 10*(4), 758–769.

Wokutch, R. E., & Spencer, B. A. (1987). Corporate saints and sinners: The effect of Philanthropic and illegal activity on organizational performance. *California Management Review, 29*(2), 62–77.

Wood, D. J. (1991). Corporate social performance revisited. *Academy of Management Review, 16*(4), 691–718.

Chapter 19
Investing Peacefully: A Global Overview of Socially Responsible Investing

Asli Yuksel Mermod and Samuel O. Idowu

Abstract The term 'Socially responsible investing (SRI)' has become increasingly popular since the 1980s. It's becoming one of the trendiest investment approaches in the world especially after the financial crises of recent times. Socially responsible investing is not only interesting for the investors but also for companies and governments of different countries. SRI allows people to invest their funds based on their own personal ethical and moral values. These investments are mostly used to make positive contributions to society in economic, social and environmental terms. Financial intermediaries are finding it harder and socially unacceptable to justify investing in companies which care less about the environment. There are not many socially irresponsible companies left in any event. Financial intermediaries, particularly banks should prolong their goals like making long-lasting profits and maximizing their stock values, but they should also consider protecting their reputation as well as their credibility by supporting socially responsible companies since good reputation means a lot in modern banking. This chapter seeks to demonstrate the importance of ethics and social responsibility in financial markets and to discuss the notion of 'socially responsible investing'. It traces the history of SRIs from its origins, discusses the benefits of Socially Responsible Investing (SRI) and finally discusses the contributions of SRI Indexes and states Turkey's position in SRI.

A. Y. Mermod (✉)
Marmara University, Istanbul, Turkey
e-mail: asli@asliyuksel.com

S. O. Idowu
London Metropolitan University, London, UK

A. Yüksel Mermod and S. O. Idowu (eds.), *Corporate Social Responsibility in the Global Business World*, DOI: 10.1007/978-3-642-37620-7_19,
© Springer-Verlag Berlin Heidelberg 2014

19.1 Introduction

Investors make immeasurable contributions to corporate expansion and growth everywhere in the world. The valuable decisions they make in this regard are not only important for their own investments and wealth creation, but also for the good of societies around the world, for helping the natural environment and for the overall peace and happiness of everyone living in this planet. On another hand their choices of their investment portfolios could have some negative impacts on societies; for example if those companies they have invested in were to divert funds to the so called 'sin investments' activities e. g. making weapons for war, alcohol or cigarettes or helping regimes involved in human rights abuses etc. These examples are no exaggerations; they are true reflections of what still go on in our world, even in the 21st century. The stocks we invest in can be either for good causes or some socially unacceptable activities; some of which might be in the so called 'sinful stocks' with potential high returns through 'dirty business' such as terrorism, gambling, large consumption of alcohol and cigarettes. Profits are good but conversely how would we feel when we go to bed if we knew that some part of our money was used in financing weapons used in fighting wars which killed innocent children or made them orphans or disabled them for the rest of their lives? Socially responsible individual would certainly feel uncomfortable about this sort of events. Would you still feel peaceful inside you owning that sinful stock when you gaze at your own children playing happily in front room or in your garden and enjoying their time? We wouldn't really want to make money off other people's demise, would we? Socially Responsible Investment basically stems from this simple idea where. Risky investments which risk our consciousness our inner health makes responsible investors avoid investing on sinful stocks. These evil stocks may bring real good profits but would you really prefer to become rich through this way? If yes perhaps you would buy a beach house near the sea with the profits of that sinful stock, but every time you drive your Ferrari down to the hill, wouldn't you feel like driving over the graves of all the people who died to make you rich? Social responsible investing is a blessing not to have that feeling. (Cabaniss 2012).

All investors have to make an assessment, of which stocks they don't feel comfortable with, and why. We would always face some conflicts during the evaluation between good or bad, for some products or some companies which some of the investors would say unethical whereas some others might think they are useful. SRI does not yet make a good distinction between them. There are some grey areas, which might cause diverse results for different investors. One stock as a good example for those conflicts can be McDonalds; many people proclaim they don't like is that of McDonald's, most often because they believe that McDonald's sells unhealthy, obesity-causing food. But in another way McDonald's can be considered as the only provider of hot, cheap accessible food. McDonald's sells their food so cheap that even the poorest can find enough change for a burger. For the poorest among us, the homeless, the alcoholics, weight gain is the least of their worries. A calorie is simply a unit of energy to protect homeless people stay alive outdoors in a cold environment. Some people may blame McDonald's menus for being irresponsible because of their "high-calorie foods", but for the extremely poor, those high-calorie foods can be survival foods (Cabaniss 2012). This difference of varied perceptions makes a problem area for selecting the 'good companies' in SRI decisions. Investors are still humans, so they would prefer to invest in 'good' companies and be in peaceful thoughts when they lie down. That's how the concept of social responsible investing has begun.

This chapter is structured as follows; it first differentiates the concepts of CSR and SRI and provides some definitions for SRI. It next proceeds to outline briefly the history of SRIs. The next section presents some major SRI indices and examines socially responsible investing strategies. The penultimate section provides an example of how SRI operates in an emerging market; namely Turkey and finally we conclude the chapter.

19.2 Defining SRI

Social responsibility in financial markets is becoming more and more crucial nowadays as the majority of investors prefer investing their monies in sustainable, socially responsible companies acting on the basis of morally acceptable ethical practices. It is becoming harder for companies that pollute the environment and are criticized by the media and stakeholders for being socially irresponsible to find new potential investors in the ever more competitive capital markets.

The term CSR is closely linked with SRI. The Social Investment Forum states that SRI involves evaluating companies on CSR issues, analyzing corporate social and environmental risks, and engaging corporations to improve their CSR policies and practices. SRI is often confused with "corporate social responsibility" (CSR). The two concepts have repeatedly been taken as identical concepts particularly in popular media sources. However, it is important to make a distinction between the concepts of "socially responsible investing" and "corporate social responsibility investment". The former one is a whole new business model, which relies on a customer base demanding that their investment should be allocated in a socially responsible manner. The latter can be considered as a "giving back" mechanism which has some marketing connotations for the firm, through which corporations aim to improve their public image and reputation. The second version can be easily used by financial institutions and banks to augment their reputation.

It should be noted that SRI investors deepen their standard financial criteria with corporate social responsibility criteria including the environment, working practices, treatment of employees, corporate ethics and governance, charitable and community contributions as well as screening to avoid products which might be considered socially damaging to health and life such as tobacco and weapon.

There is no general agreement on the role of these criteria in investment management; but Lowry, a promoter of social responsibility, identified some goals of SRI. First, it involves strategies to democratize the economy in some different ways: encouragement of the hiring, retention, and promotion of women and minorities. Second, SRI humanizes the working environment in a clean, safe and rewarding way. Third goal involves rethinking the ways profit has been traditionally used and distributed. Finally all these goals are related to a fourth goal: convincing the business world that a corporate conscience can pay (Hamilton et al. 1993).

The Forum for Sustainable and Responsible Investment (**US SIF**) – Formerly known as the Social Investment Forum (SIF 2005) describes sustainable and socially responsible investing. as "an investment process that integrates the environmental, ethical, social, and governance consequences of corporate policies and practices, both positive and negative, within the context of precise financial analysis to generate long-term competitive financial returns and positive societal impact".

Many different opinions are advanced by various authors about SRI: e.g. when investors invest their money in socially responsible investing funds, they contribute to building healthy communities, promote economic equity and create a cleaner environment while also delivering competitive rates of return (Petty 2003). Investors consider their ethical, religious, social and other normative preferences to make their investment decisions (Humphrey and Lee 2011). Individual investors and investment institutions should be free to make their investment decisions and governments should not interfere with them (Pan and Mardfin 2001).

Socially responsible investment indices, provides performance criteria of listed companies that are supposed to fulfill some particular socially responsible requirements which are determined by the issuers of the indices (Hamilton et al. 1993). These indices are of assistance to investors and beneficial to those companies listed in the indicator. Unlike the traditional type of investments, SRI applies a set of investment screening criteria to choose or reject some specific firms for a 'socially responsible portfolio' based on ecological, social, corporate governance or ethical criteria. Businesses involved in industries in activities such as arms, alcohol, tobacco, gambling, animal testing and nuclear power are mostly unwelcomed sectors for SRI investors whereas companies that are engaged in sustainable and environmentally friendly areas such as environmental management, alternative energy, green technology, green construction, sustainable living, equal treatment of minorities and fair trade are mostly welcomed stocks in the portfolio of SRI investors (Leahy 2008).

The idea of sustainable investments strikes the financial markets nowadays and investors increasingly consider non-financial aspects in their assessment of companies. Private and institutional investors become more aware of social and environmental factors which plays an important role in their financial considerations (Koellner et al. 2005).

SRI has experienced an explosive growth around the world reflecting the increasing awareness of investors to social, environmental, ethical and corporate governance issues (Yilmaz 2011). SRI investors encourage corporations to improve their practices on environmental, social, and governance issues. Investing approaches like SRI can also be referred to as mission investing, responsible investing, double or triple bottom line investing, ethical investing, sustainable investing, or green investing.

SRI identifies that corporate responsibility and societal concerns are official parts of investment decisions. SRI considers both the investor's financial needs and an investment's impact on society. SRI investors encourage corporations to improve their practices on environmental, social, and governance issues.

> *During the last few years Socially Responsible Investment strategies started to have been quiet popular in the media, regulators, fund managers, institutional investors and other stakeholders* (Vyvyan et al. 2007).

As a result of its investing strategies, SRI also works to enhance the bottom lines of the companies in question and, by so doing, brings more long-term wealth to shareholders. Responsible investing takes a longer term perspective, recognizing that environmental and social benefits and costs are rarely expressed on a quarterly cycle (Dalheim 2006). Regarding financial markets, the most important player, namely banks acting in similar fashion to investors on the capital markets have to define also their ethics and guidelines in detail. Banks need to make lasting profits and on the other hand they have to protect their reputation as well as their credibility by supporting socially responsible companies.

The Research of Eurosif (2010) demonstrates that SRI has exhibited a rapid and continuous growth over the last two decades and as of 2010, it encompasses an estimated $10,9 trillion (€7,594 trillion) out of $79.3 trillion in the global investment market today. As noted in Table 19.1

Eurosif utilises Core SRI and Broad SRI criteria to make a distinction between positive and negative screening in the SRI market. Core SRI activities (estimated at €1.2 trillion) consist of norms- and values- based exclusions and different types of positive screens while Broad SRI (estimated at €3.8 trillion) encompasses simple exclusion, engagement and integration approaches of negative screens.

It is important to note that there are no standards for defining what a SRI product is. It may be regarded like that financial experts dispose of a range of both

Table 19.1 Global SRI Data (2010)

			Total SRI (bn)	Total SRI (€ bn)
United States (2010)	Total SRI	US$3,069	US$3,069	2,141
Canada	Core SRI	Cnd $54.2	Cnd$609.2	405
	Broad SRI	Cnd$555.0		
Australia/NZ (2010)	Core SRI	Au$18.2	Au$93	58
	Broad SRI	Au$74.8		
Japan (2009)		¥579	¥579	4
Europe (2009)	Core SRI	£1,150	€4,986	4,986
	Broad SRI	€3,836		
TOTAL WORLD	€7,594			

Source Eurosif 2010 Trends Report: http://www.eurosif.org/research/eurosif-sri-study/2010
Download date: 30.11.2012

formal arrangements and informal conventions and customs in order to exercise SRI and thereby judge the CSR of potential companies. To exercise such an activity, several tactics have been developed which can be used separately or simultaneously (Boxenbaum and Gond 2006). SRI investors make an expanded investment analysis besides common financial analysis by including CSR criteria such as the environment, working practices, treatment of employees, corporate ethics and governance, charitable and community contributions and on the other hand screening to avoid products which are socially damaging; namely tobacco and weapon (Yuksel Mermod 2009).

Socially responsible investors consist of individuals and also institutions, such as corporations, universities, hospitals, foundations, insurance companies, public and private pension funds, nonprofit organizations, and religious institutions. Institutional investors represent the largest and fastest growing segment of the SRI world.

19.3 SRI: Its Evolution

Although for many, SRI appears to be a modern phenomenon but its history dates back to several hundred years. Socially responsible investing started to show its power in USA in 1970s and in Europe around 1990s. But the roots of this subject are very much related to the European religions. During its early stages of development, religious beliefs and values (such as Jewish Law, Catholic edicts, and Quaker and Methodist determinations and activism) were already important factors in terms of investing (Vyvyan et al. 2007). "Extremist" Christians used SRI to make payments in large amounts and even offer their wealth to Rome in order to be forgiven their sins and religious shortcomings by God. History suggests that the Islamic, Jewish, and Christian religions have tended to support economic actions that match directly with their beliefs. In biblical times, the Jewish laws laid down directives on how to invest according to ethical values. In the 1920s, the Methodist Church in the UK stayed away from investing in firms that were involved in production of alcohol, tobacco, weapons and gambling. John Wesley (1703–1791), was a famous name during his time for being one of the founders of Methodism. Wesley underlined his main principles in his work "The Use of Money" about social investing. Wesley emphasized that the use of money should be the second most important subject of New Testament teachings (Schulet 2006). Religious investors following his advice decided to abstain from investing in companies engaged in alcohol, gambling and tobacco. In his study it was clear encouraging doing no harm to ones neighbor through business practices and avoiding investing in destructive industries, harmful chemical productions and not to damage the health of workers were issues of importance. In the U.S., the Quakers Group practiced socially responsible investing as early as the 16th century, based on their beliefs in human equality and non-violence. Quakers in the US colonies refused to profit from weapons and slave trade when they settled in North America Idowu (2009).

At the beginning of the 20th century, the model of ethical and ecological investments was enhanced in USA and prohibited many sensible US investors to invest in 'sin stocks'; the stocks that implicated the production of alcohol, tobacco, weapons, pornography and gambling and therefore the first eco- ethic investment fund was founded in Boston in 1928 (Schmid 2001). In 1928, Pioneer Group created a "sin" screen that was later used to screen out certain investments when practicing socially responsible investing (SRI). Hence, the first official SRI Fund, the Pioneer Fund was born. The evolution of ethical investments in Europe was later. It started many years after USA as a consequence of the ecological crises like the danger of having less forests and oxygen. The first ecological green funds in Europe were about technologies that protect the environment. These firms have become successful just after the 1990s.

During the Vietnam War in the 1960s, the civil rights actions, and environmental issues caused individuals to reconsider their investment practices in a socially conscious manner, enhancing the growth of SRI. In 1960s social concerns like civil rights, the environment, and militarism were augmented. During Vietnam War years, the first model mutual fund, the Pax World Fund, avoided investments in weapon contractors.

In the 1980s, the anti-apartheid movement against the regime in South Africa had prevented socially responsible investors from touching the shares of companies which traded or operated in South Africa. SRI investors in US and Europe exerted pressure on companies that were doing business in South Africa to divert operations to other countries. SRI grew rapidly throughout the 1970s and 1980s as investors utilized both screening and shareholder advocacy to express concerns about apartheid in South Africa. SRI was finally recognized as an official movement with the main financial resources coming from churches, universities and colleges. Calvert was one of the first mutual fund companies to take a stand on apartheid in 1983 (http://ussif.org/pdf/research/Trends/1997%20Trends%20 Report.PDF). Meanwhile, SRI became global, spreading to other countries such as the United Kingdom, Australia, Japan, Austria, France, Germany and Switzerland (www.goodmoney.com).

In 1984, The Social Investment Forum (SIF) conducted the first industry-wide survey to identify assets involved in social investing, finding that it totalled $40 billion. Issues like environmental protection, human rights and labor relations have become common in SRI investment screening. Also in recent years some corporate scandals have turned corporate governance and responsibility into another focal point of SRI investors.

Since the early 1990s, SRI industry has experienced growth all over the world. In the late 1980s, interest in SRI began to expand throughout the world as it spread from North America to both the East and the West; to Australia, Japan, Austria, France, Germany, Switzerland, and many more countries (http://www. goodmoney.com/srihist.htm).

Today there are many environmental and social concerns for socially responsible investors to bring together. Incidents like Chernobyl accident 1986, the Exxon Valdez oil spill 1989or the Bhopal Union Carbide plant disaster in 1984, warnings about toxic wastes, global warming, and other environmental threats, continue to reinforce the seriousness of environmental concerns for responsible investors. Pressing social issues such as diversity in the workplace, employee issues, human rights in overseas factories, and socially destructive products such as tobacco, now provide fertile ground for investors to base their choices on (http://www.socialfunds.com/page.cgi/article1.html).

The new millennium brought into the spotlight a new dimension of SRI. The Enron and WorldCom accounting scandals of 2001, the Sarbanes–Oxley Act of 2002 and the "subprime mortgage" crisis of 2008 heightened the public sensitivity regarding corporate governance aspect of SRI. Researches show that corporations with good social records, regardless what the social issues were, rewarded investors better than unscreened investment portfolios. In other words, investors and businesspeople could do good socially while also doing well financially. The portfolios of churches, universities and colleges, and state and city pension funds were among the largest financial assets involved with SRI.

19.4 Major SRI Indices

SRI indices are designed to be benchmarked to non-SRI indexes, such as the S&P 500 or MSCI World Index. These indices have proved to be important tools for assessing the performance of SRI. In June 2011, there were 116 SRI indexes in the world. Dow Jones Sustainability Index, Domini 400 Index, S&P 500 Index, FTSE4Good Index, KLD Sustainability Index, FTSE KLD Global Sustainability Index and MSCI SRI Index are the most popular SRI indices in the world.

In the last several years, the pool of assets engaged in SRI strategies has grown more rapidly than the overall investment universe due to a number of factors, including net inflows into existing SRI products, the development of new SRI products and the adoption of SRI strategies by fund managers and institutions not previously involved in the field. For example, in the United States, from the start of 2007 to the beginning of 2010, a three-year period when broad market indices such as the S&P 500 declined and the broader universe of professionally managed assets increased less than 1 percent, assets involved in sustainable and socially responsible investing increased more than 13 percent (Social Investment Forum Foundation 2010). That's a dramatic growth for SRI funds (Chart 19.1).

The longest-running SRI index, the Domini 400 (now the name has changed to KLD 400) has commenced in May 1990. It kept on performing competitively with average annualized total returns of 9.51 percent through December 2009 compared with 8.66 percent for the S&P 500. KLD's Domini 400 index (or shortly DS400) is chosen to represent the negative screening strategy for U.S. market (Chart 19.2).

DOING GOOD AND DOING WELL

For the past decade, the leading VBI index has generally outperformed the major broad-market measures.

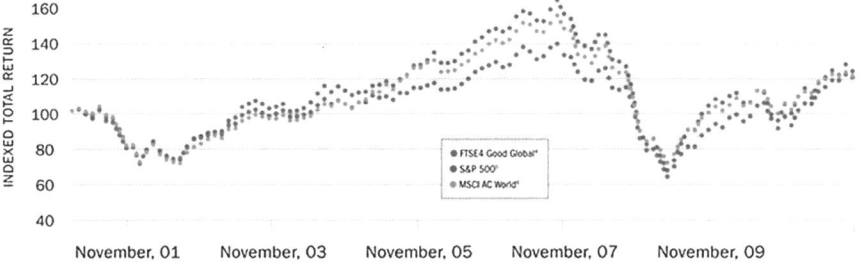

Data from November 30, 2001, to May 31, 2011. Price return is denominated in local currency as defined by the index provider. S&P 500 is denominated in USD.

PAST PERFORMANCE IS NO GUARANTEE OF FUTURE RESULTS. The information provided is for illustrative purposes and is not meant to represent the performance of any particular investment. It is not possible to invest directly in an index. Please note that IMPORTANT DISCLOSURES are listed at the end of the online article.

Chart. 19.1 Comparison of FTSE4 Good- S&P 500-MSCI AC World between 2001–2009 http://www.pbig.ml.com/pwa/pages/values-based-investing-comes-of-age.aspx   Accessed   on 11.12.2012

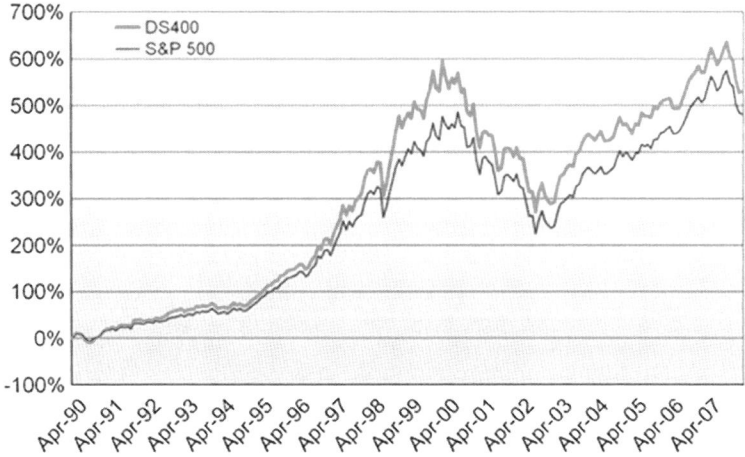

Chart. 19.2 DS400 Cumulative PERFORMANCE as of March 31, 2008 *Source* http://www.sproutly.com/2008/05/08/value-of-social-responsibility-in-the-us-530-billion/ Downloaded on: Feb. 7, 2010

KLD 400 Index (DS 400) is independently selected by the well known research firm KLD Research & Analytics, and aims to include primarily large cap stocks in the S&P 500; Approximately 250 companies for DS400 are selected from the S&P 500. 100 companies not in the S&P 500, but providing sector diversification and exceeding pre determined market cap limitations and the rest of the 50 companies are special companies that have shown excellence in their social and environmental dealings.

It is obvious above that The Domini 400 Social Index has been consistently outpacing the growth of the S&P 500 since 1990.

Analyzing the last 4 years, the comparison chart of the performance of KLD400 Social Index Fund and the S & P 500 during the period from January 2nd, 2008 to March 30th, 2012 shows that KLD 400 Social Index Fund has outperformed the S&P500 (Chart 19.3).

Calvert Social Index is a broad-based, thoroughly constructed benchmark for measuring the performance of US-based sustainable and responsible companies (Chart 19.4).

Calvert starts by taking the 1,000 largest companies in the US, based on total market capitalization, included in the Dow Jones Total Market Index (the Dow Jones TMI). Calvert's Social Research Department then analyzes each company. A social audit is conducted in the following areas: Products, Environment, Workplace, and Integrity. The stocks that meet Calvert's social criteria make up the Calvert Social Index. As of 6/30/2011, there are 656 companies in the Index.

Dow Jones Sustainability World Index (DJSI World), a collaboration between Dow Jones& Company, Inc. (United States) and SAM (Sustainable Asset Management) Group (Switzerland), is a global stock price index that captures the top 10 % of companies from the largest 2,500 companies worldwide by evaluating their sustainability based on economic, environmental and social criteria. Currently, 342 companies from all over the world are listed as members of DJSI World (as of September 2011) (Chart. 19.5).

Chart. 19.3 S&P versus KLD400 Index Fund (DS400) http://www.springwaterasset management.com/blog/ downloaded: 11.12.2012

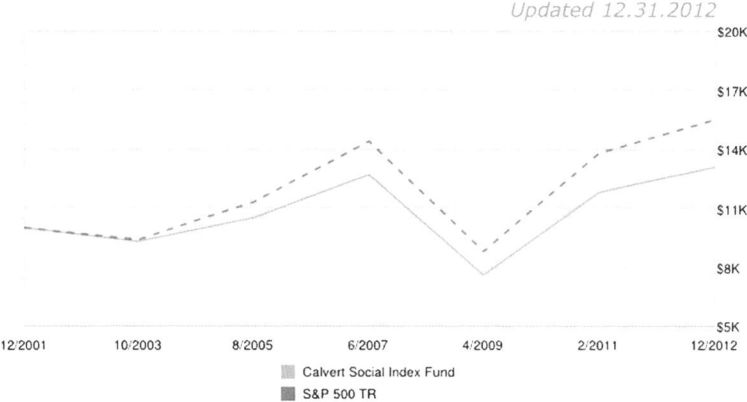

Chart. 19.4 Calvert Social Index versus S&P500 Hypothetical Growth of $10,000 *source* http://money.usnews.com/funds/mutual-funds/large-growth/calvert-social-index-fund/csxax downloaded: 11.01.2013

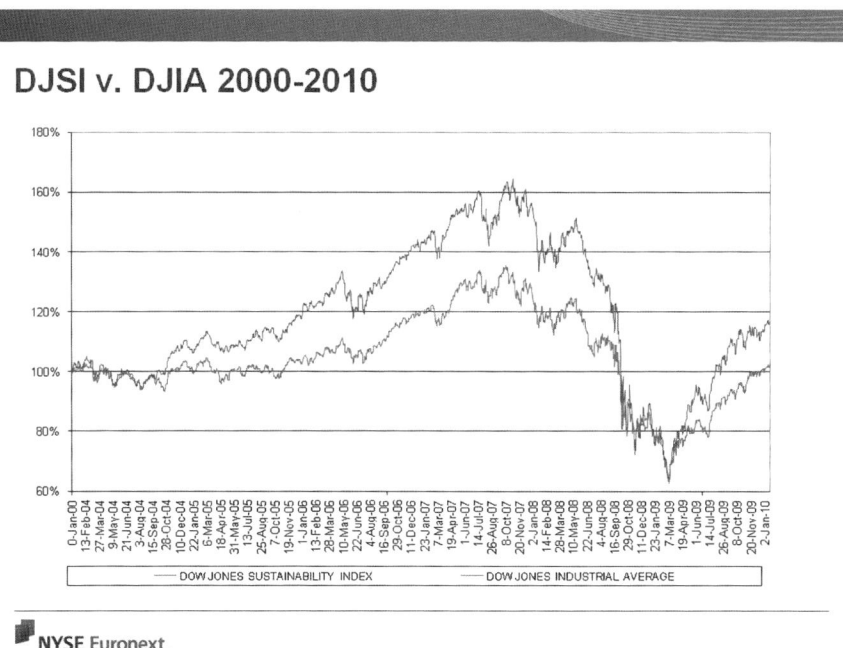

Chart. 19.5 Dow Jones Sustainability Index (DJSI) vs Dow Jones Industrial Index (DJIA) http://exchanges.nyx.com/fr/tdziedzic/it-pays-be-bullish-csr Downloaded: 6.2.2013

Chart. 19.6 The FTSE4Good Global Index http://www.ftse.com/Indices/FTSE4Good_Index_
Series/Performance_Analysis.jsp Downloaded: 8.2.2013

When the performance of the Dow Jones Sustainability Index (DJSI) is compared with the Dow Jones Industrial Index (DJIA), the DJSI outperformed the
DJIA over the last 10 years. In addition, the average trading of The World's Most
Ethical Companies outperformed the S&P 500 from 2007 to date. It seems that the
companies and executives who uphold strong social values, governance practices,
and transparency are more and forward-thinking. (Dziedzic 2011).

The FTSE4Good Global Index is a stock price index that was developed and
established by the FTSE (Financial Times Stock Exchange), a company owned
jointly by The Financial Times and the London Stock Exchange. It evaluates
companies based on their environmental sustainability measures, relationships
with their stakeholders, human rights protection, assurance of supply chain labor
standards, and prevention of bribery (Chart. 19.6).

The Morningstar Socially Responsible Investment Index (MS-SRI) is the
first socially responsible investment index in Japan. Morningstar Japan K.K. selects
150 companies from among approximately 3,600 listed companies in Japan by
assessing their social responsibility, and converts their stock prices into the index
(Chart. 19.7).

19.5 Research Regarding SRI Performance

Numerous studies have been conducted since 1970s to measure whether SRI was a
financially sound strategy, capable of providing its investors returns competitive
with traditional investments. Many studies concluded that there was not a statistically significant differential between SRI and traditional fund management
except a clear conscience for the investor. However there were also some studies

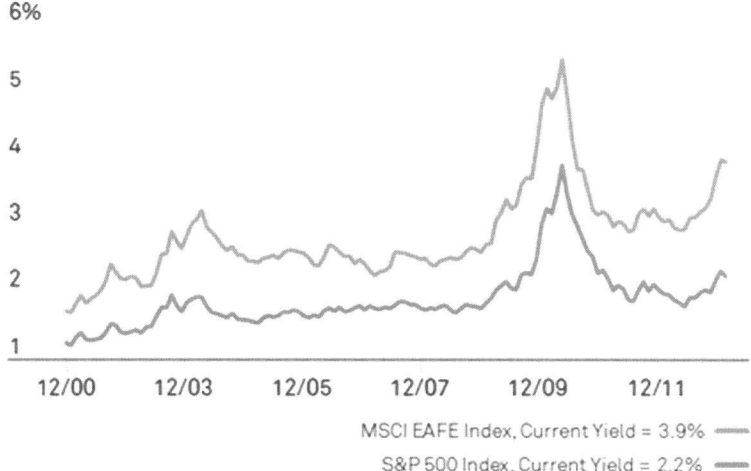

Chart. 19.7 The Morningstar Socially Responsible Investment Index (MSCI) https://www2.blackrock.com/us/financial-professionals/market-insight/market-commentary/point-of-view-with-richard-turnill-and-stuart-reeve Downloaded: 8.2.2013 *source* MSCI and Ned Davis, 12/31/11

that concluded in favour of SRI and some that concluded that SRI funds under-performed traditional funds.

Milton Moskowitz' study in 1972 has been widely accepted as a leading research in this area, and his conclusions were as follows:

> From a performance standpoint it might make more sense to concentrate on avoiding the "socially irresponsible" companies than to try to profit from a portfolio of the most responsible companies. Social irresponsibility may be only the tip of the corporate iceberg with many other problems lying under the surface (Moskowitz 1972).

Hamilton, Jo and Statman's study was published in 1993 compared the returns of the 17 SRI funds established before 1985 with a benchmark of 170 traditional funds. Over the study period of Jan. 1981 to Dec. 1990, the SRI funds under-performed the benchmark by a mere 0.76 % annually, which was not found to be statistically significant. Looking at the individual SRI funds, 15 funds performed statistically at par with the benchmark, one fund (Transamerica Capital Appreciation Fund) outperformed the benchmark, whereas, another fund (SFT Environmental Awareness Fund) underperformed the benchmark. They concluded "the investors can expect to lose nothing by investing in a socially responsible mutual fund (Hamilton et al. 1993).

DiBartolomeo and Kurtz (1999) compared the performance of Standart and Poor 500(S&P) Index and Domini Social Index (DSI) in the period between May 1990 and January 1999. Their aim was comparing their results with the previous researches made. They used Fundamental Risk Model and Arbitrage Pricing

Theory for their analysis. According to their analysis DSI outperformed the S&P 500 during that period. Because DSI portfolio was more sensitive to market movements, had more exposure to better performing industries and had a growth bias during a period when investing was in favor DiBartolomeo and Kurtz (1999).

Statman published another study in 2000, where he compared the Domini Social Index (DSI) with S&P 500 Index. The review of the Domini Social Index covered the May 1990–September 1998 time period and concluded that, using a modified form of the Sharpe ratio, that the DSI's risk-adjusted returns for this period were higher than those of the S&P 500 (Statman 2000).

In another study Statman (2005) compared the content and returns of S&P500 with 4 SRI Indexes (Domini 400 Social Index (DS 400 Index), the Calvert Social Index, the Citizens Index, and the U.S. portion of the Dow Jones Sustainability Index) in the period between the late 1990s and early 2000s. He could finally state that S&P500 Index performed worse than the 4 SRI Indexes (Statman 2005).

Mallin et al. (1995) analysed the monthly returns of 29 ethical trusts and 29 non-ethical trusts in the U.K. in 1993. They found that on the mean excess returns, ethical trusts appeared to underperform both non-ethical trusts and the market in general, however, on a risk adjusted basis ethical trusts outperformed non-ethical trusts. They also concluded that both ethical and non-ethical trusts underperformed the market in general (Mallin et al. 1995).

Jones et al. (2008) investigated the returns performance of 89 ethical funds in Australia over the period 1986–2005. Using a multi-factor CAPM model, they concluded that ethical funds significantly underperformed the market in Australia, particularly in the last 5 years of the sample period (2000–2005). Risk adjusted returns (using Jensen's alpha) indicated an average annual underperformance of 1.52 % in the 2000–2005 period for the sample and .88 % over the whole study period(Jones et al. 2008).

In an international study, Schröder (2004) investigated the performance of 16 German and Swiss funds and 30 U.S. funds that concentrate on socially responsible investing; he also investigated the returns of 10 SRI indices. He concluded that most of the German, Swiss and U.S. SRI Investment funds did not significantly underperform their benchmarks. He also identified a difference between the funds such that U.S. funds were more invested in blue chip stocks whereas the German and Swiss funds tended to invest in smaller companies. The results of the performance analysis for the SRI indices exhibited that only the Calvin index clearly underperformed the benchmarks, but also the Europe-wide FTSE4Good-index had a significantly negative Jensen's alpha in one of the two model versions used. But most of the SRI indices exhibited a positive, although insignificant, Jensen's alpha. Overall, he concluded that the performance of SRI assets was not worse than those of conventional assets except for two of the ten SRI indices (Schröder 2004).

Based on the research he has conducted for his recent book, Cary Krosinsky demonstrated that "sustainable investment funds" (which is an emerging subgroup of socially responsible funds) significantly outperformed mainstream indices between December 2002 and December 2007, returning +18.7 %, on average, versus the MSCI World, S&P 500 and FTSE 100's returns of +17.0 %, +13.2 % and +13.0 %, respectively. Particularly, the Winslow Green Growth Fund significantly outperformed even Warren Buffett. Between 2002 and 2007, Buffett's holding company Berkshire Hathaway increased by 100 %, while the Winslow Green Growth Fund saw over 200 % growth (Krosinsky and Robins 2009).

In their study D'Antonio et al. (1997), compared the returns of bonds in Domini 400 and Lehman Brothers Corporate Bond Index. They found no significantly differences in average portfolio performance (D'Antonio et al. 1997).

Bollen (2007) compared SRI funds with traditional funds in terms of their asset stability. His study confirmed that SRI assets to be more stable than traditional funds. He found that social responsible investors hold their funds longer due to their moral motivation as SRI funds have both financial sense and moral sense to investors (Bollen 2007).

But contrary to Bollen's findings, Renneboog et al. (2006) note that SRI assets to be less stable than traditional funds., Renneboog et al. evaluated international SRI funds to UK equity funds (Renneboog et al. 2006).

Derwal and Koedijk (2009) compared the performance of SRI bonds and traditional bonds by using multi-index performance evaluation models. They expressed that there was no significantly differences between SRI funds and traditional funds (Derwall and Koedijk 2009).

Diltz (1995), compared with 14 socially screened stock portfolios and 14 unscreened stock portfolios by using CAAR analyses in the year between 1989 and 1991. He concluded that abnormal returns could only be observed in three of the portfolios (Diltz 1995).

Reander et al. (2005) used 60 investment funds from four countries to measure performance of SRI funds and traditional funds. They applied four criteria for this study, namely: age, size, country and investment universe. Their study used Jensen's alpha, Sharpe ratio and Treynor ratio to analyze their performances. They come across with the idea that SRI and traditional funds exhibit a very similar performance (Reander et al. 2005).

Some of the authors insist that SRI funds end up with lower returns when compared to traditional funds. Teper argues that social investors must assume a charge of estimated 1 % per annum for equity accounts. He compares unrestricted accounts with SRI screened accounts in other words 'sin free accounts' and finds that the SRI accounts incurred a risk-adjusted cost of 1.1 % in the period of December 1984 to September 1990. (Teper 1992).

Rudd (1981), notes down that traditional portfolios outperform the SRI portfolios. One of the reason for that is SRI portfolio returns do not cover the additional residual risks (Rudd 1981).

Geczy et al. (2003) examined the costs of SRI's and their discovery included a range of losses to risk-adjusted return. (Geczy et al. (2003).

There are some studies exploring the relationship between screening and SRI performances. One of the examples is the study from Renneboog et al. (2007a, b) which examined the impact of the screening activity on risk-adjusted returns and risk loading. They established that number of social screens decreased significantly the performance of the SRI funds but the number of sin, ethical or environmental screens do not affect significantly to financial performance of SRI. They also added in their study that funds with higher number of SRI screens had higher returns even after controlling for well-known risk factors (Renneboog et al. (2007a, b).

Barnett and Salomon (2003) noticed that environmental and labor relations screens (positive screening) reduced SRI fund performance but on the other side screening out companies (negative screening) improved SRI fund performance (Barnett and Salomon 2003).

Some researchers looked for the impact of screening intensity on the risk and return of SRI funds. Their result was screening intensity caused lower systematic risk. SRI can be costly in this aspect (Renneboog et al. 2007a, b) and (Lee et al. 2010).

The costs of SRI investing depend on the skill of the managers, the portfolio size and investment universe. SRI asset management institutions spend time on transforming several variables in their data, which was given by rating vendors into the investment decisions. (Adler and Kritzman 2008).

Some authors made their researches about SRI in Europe. Garz et al. (2002) compared with the Dow Jones Sustainability Index (DJSI) for Europe and DJ STOXX 600 Index for the period between January 1999 and October 2002. They concluded that DJSI had better performance than DJ STOXX (Garz et al. 2002).

Bauer et al. (2002) used SRI funds in Germany, UK and US. They compared these funds with traditional funds. They used 4-factor model of Carhart. End of the study they found that UK funds had better performance than US, German and traditional funds. Also SRI funds have different investment styles than traditional funds (Bauer et al. 2002).

Schwartz (2003) asked the question if the SRI funds are really ethical or not in his study. He reasoned that some SRI's sometimes behave unethically (Schwartz 2003).

Petty (2003) scrutinized the critics regarding to SRI in his study. Even though SRI has a very old history it is still untested. Negative screening makes people content because of moral sense, but if they are really effective in encouraging the social changes and environmental improvement is a big question mark. Investors, who have no idea about social responsible companies, can be cheated easily. Companies that are supposed to be social responsible can give them wrong information about their returns and social responsible activities. To avoid deception, investors need to have knowledge about funds past investment practices and reputation in SRI community, before they invest their money. Screens are not strict enough because of the life cycle effects of products; for instance electronic devices (Petty 2003).

19.6 Socially Responsible Investing Strategies

Socially responsible investing started in the 17th century. The Quakers refused to participate in slave-trade, war-related activities in 17th century and Methodists declined to profit from sinful companies which were consisting of businesses like alcohol, tobacco, weapons and gambling in 1920s (Renneboog et al. 2007a, b). Also Muslim investors rejected to invest their money on pork production, pornography, gambling companies and interest-based financial institutions due to restrictions in their religious book; namely: Koran. These examples are the first examples about negative screening. In 1960 there had been many noteworthy events in relation to the environment, civil rights, and militarism in the world. For example Anti-war activists in U.S. during the Vietnam War urged people not to invest in Dow Chemical, because it was the largest producer napalm at that time. Antiwar activists convinced investors that investing in Dow Chemical would mean a contribution to the war. In the 1980s the modern concept of SRI emerged. Social responsible investors invest their money in the light of climate changes, environmental issues and pollution. In the year between 1980 and 1990 SRI was finally recognized as an official movement. Social investment funds like Calvert and Working Assets and Social Investment Forum were founded. This was the beginning of the positive screening. SRI had become a global practice in the 21st century. According to 2011 Socially Responsible Investing Report (TIAA-CREF 2011) SRI continues to expand faster than conventional assets under management.

During the financial crisis of 2007–2010, the overall universe of managed assets has remained roughly flat, while SRI assets have grown to more than $3 trillion in the United States alone at the beginning of 2010. According to Social Investment Forum 2010 Report on Trends in SRI Investing, SRI assets increased 182 % from $202 billion to $569 billion in the year between 2007 and 2010.

There are three main types of strategies in SRI:

First one is called "shareholder advocacy". It refers to the usage of shareholders' rights to make companies act more socially responsible. It means directly confronting management on social or environmental issues, as well as earnings, by applying pressure or support (Kawamura 2002). Shareholder advocacy consists in the practice of monitoring corporate behavior and seeking changes through dialogue with companies or through the use of share ownership rights, such as filing shareholder resolutions. The more confrontational approach of engagement is called shareholder activism (Bettignies and Lepineux 2009). Companies must pay attention to their reputation in order to keep profit margins high in the long term, because they are forced by socially responsible investors to reduce pollution, provide safer work places, follow human rights standards and become more accountable to the society. SRI assets are expected to grow around the world in the future. Governments and investors are more aware of the issues like global warming, the Kyoto Protocol, emissions trading, corporate governance, community investing, and microfinance. As in Europe and US, entrepreneurs in Turkey and in other emerging countries should be aware of those issues and keep in mind when making investment decisions (Yuksel Mermod 2009).

According to Social Investment Forum, shareholder advocacy increased from $739 billion to $1497 billion between the years 2007 and 2010.

Second type is called as "community investing". Finance textbooks tell us that companies should maximize the value of their shareholders'equity. In other words, companies 'only responsibility is a financial one. In recent years, CSR has become a focal point of policy makers (and the public), who demand that corporations assume responsibility towards society, the environment, or the stakeholders in general. SRI investors thus aim at promoting socially and environmentally sound corporate behavior. Community investing directs capital to people and institutions underserved by traditional providers of financial services. These include low-income individuals, small businesses, and vital community services such as affordable housing, child care, and health care (Statman 2007).

It offers to make funds available to help "poorest of the poor" in areas such as affordable housing, small business, and community development (Pan and Mardfin 2001). According to Social Investment Forum, assets in community investing institutions rose more than 60 % from $25 billion in 2007 to $41.7 billion at the beginning of 2010 in U.S. Also for many investors this type of investment represents a further step beyond positive and negative screening.

Third type is called portfolio screening which can be divided into two categories.

Negative and positive screens related to community relations come next in popularity, followed by screens related to the environment, labor relations, products and services, and equal employment. Shareholder advocacy involves actions by shareholders to encourage CSR, such as filing shareholder resolutions and voting on them.

Screening means the use of criteria to select companies to be part of the investment universe. There are two broad categories of screens. Negative screening excludes or reduces the portfolio weights of companies with weak environmental, social, or governance records, and positive screening includes or increases the portfolio weights of companies with strong records. Negative or exclusionary screening is usually related to controversial business areas such as human rights, corruption, weapons, and controversial projects. Companies involved in those activities are excluded from the investment universe. Negative screening is the oldest investment approach in the history, which has come to the investment scene around the 17th century. They avoid companies producing goods that may cause health hazards or exploit employees either in developed or developing countries. Negative Screening involves the exclusion of sin stocks like alcohol, tobacco, weapons and gambling. For example many investors rejected to invest on South-land Corporation because its 7-Eleven stores sold Playboy and Penthouse magazines in 1980s. It can also involve avoiding poor corporate social responsibility performers. Domini Social Equity Fund removed Wal-Mart from its portfolio in 2001, because of its labor management policies (http://articles.latimes.com/2001/may/18/business/fi-64987). But this kind of screening has negative sides. For example Humphrey and Lee (2011) in their article confirmed that it gives limited investment opportunity to investors because of exclusion of many profitable stocks and having access to unconstrained investment opportunity is impossible and also it reduces funds' abilities to form diversified investment portfolios. Many companies are excluded in SRI indices because they do not comply with the social, environmental sustainable development.

Last portfolio screening type is positive screening. Portfolio managers select companies with sound social and environmental records and with good corporate governance (positive screening). Positive screening, which is also called the best in class approach, refers to the selection of companies on the basis of positive criteria, such as good governance, environmental management, climate protection, stakeholder dialogue, community awareness and outreach. In this type investors prefer to invest their money in the funds which contribute to the development of society such as, companies are environmental aware, responsible corporate citizens, seek to reduce pollution, have progressive hiring policies and possess a good human rights record and exercise good labor relations (Benson et al. 2006). For instance investors invest their money to Toyota cars, but not to Mitsubishi in Japan. Because Toyota cars have well established corporate governance structure, respected for environmental friendly products, contributed to society. But Mitsubishi failed to recall vehicles, filed false safety reports with regulators and clutch defect contributed to accidents and fatalities (Schuman 2006) (Table 19.2).

In general, SRI investors expect companies to focus on social welfare in addition to value maximization. According to the finance theory, it is impossible to beat the market and this rule applies to SRI funds too. Therefore as long as SRI funds are sufficiently diversified, they have no reason to perform poorly. Excluding some stocks from the portfolio of is not detrimental, except possibly if these stocks are negatively correlated with the stock market index. It can be concluded that, it is entirely possible to align financial investments and moral convictions. SRI funds should not perform significantly better or worse than other funds (Capelle-Blancard and Monjon 2011).The securities of socially responsible companies are not an exception for the portfolio theory and ethical investors can add those securities to their portfolio without an extraordinary loss estimate.

As the name suggests, the starting point for "socially responsible" investment activity should be answering the subjective threshold question: what is social good and how is it defined?

Sinful stocks can be defined as stocks from the companies which are involved in activities that can be considered as unethical or immoral. Here is a contradiction in this definition; one situation that could sound unethical to one investor might not be so bad for another investor. For instance aggressive marketing and advertising campaigns can be considered waste of money and wrong information for an investor but for another that would not cause any problem. There is always a gray area about ethics.

The perspectives of the wide variety of SRI practitioners differ from one another (religious, environmentalist, human rights activist etc.), and therefore, it is hard to generalize about the ambitions and methods of socially responsible

Table 19.2 Social responsible investing trends

	Definition	Positive/Negative Screen
Aerospace/Defence/ Weapons	Avoid investing in companies involved in the production/marketing of weapons	Negative
Animal Testing/ Animal- related	Firms practicing product testing on animals, as well as those that manufacturing hunting equipment, are avoided (negative). Investments in companies that support welfare of animals are encouraged by positive screening funds	Positive and/or Negative Screen
Tobacco/Alcohol- related	Investments in tobacco and alcoholic beverage businesses are avoided	Negative
Gambling-related	Investments in casinos and gambling equipment suppliers are avoided	Negative
Pornography/Child Labour	Investments in the porn industry are avoided. Firms that employ child labour anywhere in the supply chain are also avoided	Negative
Environment	Seek and support firms with proactive involvement in ecologically friendly business activities	Positive and/or Negative Screen
Human Rights	Seek and support firms with a good human rights track record while avoiding those with poor records	Positive and/or Negative Screen
Employee Benefits/ Labour	Funds invest in those firms that meet high standards of positive labour policies while those firms with a track record of exploitation are avoided	Positive and/or Negative Screen
Customer/Product Advocacy	Seek firms acting in the best interest of the consumers and using ethical advertising in their product marketing. Avoid firms making spurious claims and products.	Positive and/or Negative Screen
Nuclear Power	Seek firms using nuclear power to reduce our dependence upon oil/coal powered energy. Ignore firms involved in the production and operation of nuclear reactors used for producing weapons of mass destruction	Positive and/or Negative Screen
Alternative Energy/ Biotechnology	Seek and support firms with a proactive approach to harnessing environmentally friendly and renewable sources of energy	Positive
Corporate Governance	Invest in firms that maintain high standards of responsibility and transparency in CSR issues. Avoid firms with a record of scandals and fraudulent activities	Positive and/or Negative Screen

(continued)

Table 19.2 (continued)

	Definition	Positive/Negative Screen
Company Investments/ Foreign Operations	Seek companies committed to research and development, both home and abroad with considerable positive social benefits. Ignore companies investing in technology or infrastructure that harms the environment Firms with operations in countries with unfair organizations are also avoided	Positive and/or Negative Screen
Community/Social Issues	Invest in firms that are involved in community building projects by sponsoring employee volunteering projects and other such programs	

Source   http://eurekahedge.blogspot.ch/2010/07/2010-key-trends-in-socially-responsible.html downloaded on 9.2.2013

investors. However, it is still possible to categorize SRI strategies under three widely practiced methods of investing and a fourth emerging strategy that has been derived from "positive screening".

19.7 SRI in Turkey

Despite considerable growth in the CSR investments by major Turkish corporations, on the SRI front, it would be fair to state that Turkey has remained behind the curve in SRI. SRI is a comparatively new investment approach in Turkey and for many emerging countries there is still a need to make huge improvements for socially responsible investing. For example since May 2008 "IsBank Type B Tema Environmental Responsible Fund" has been offered by Turkiye Is Bankası and on 10 August 2010 the Istanbul Stock Exchange Sustainability Index (ISESI 2010) Project was launched by the Istanbul Stock Exchange and the Turkey Business Council for Sustainable Development. The Project's aim is to review listed companies on the ISE based on their management of sustainability issues and to create an index that will demonstrate the leadership of listed Turkish companies.

19.7.1 İş Bankası TEMA Environmental Fund

This is the first socially responsible fund in Turkey, issued by Isbank. Registered to SPK on the 27th of May 2008 and offered to public on the 30th May 2008 with a total value of 20,000,000TL. The Fund Strategy: In the selection of capital market instruments that will be invested on fund management, instruments with easy conversion into cash and low risk are preferred. T.C. İş Bankası has co-sponsored the fund with TEMA foundation, and the fund has been named "İş Bankası B Type TEMA Environment Fund". The managers utilize traditional "negative screening" investment strategy and avoids investing in the stocks of corporations which (1) has recently been penalized for environmental damage charges, (2) produces weapons and tobacco products, (3) operates gold mines. The fund also requires corporations (except financial institutions) to obtain TSEN ISO 14001 Environmental Management System Certificate in order to qualify for investment. In addition, the fund makes monthly contributions to TEMA Foundation as license and consulting fee. This fund avoids investing in companies that increase pollution, produce tobacco and weapons, engaged in search gold. It managed the investments by the principles of environmental responsibility. According to its charter, a certain amount has to be paid for TEMA as the licensing and consulting fees each month. Investors have to be TEMA volunteer if they want to be a part of this fund. On June 2008 it invest in 6 companies including, Turkiye Sınai Kalkınma Bankası (TSKB), Zorlu Enerji, Tofas Oto Fabrika, Aygaz, Eczacı Ilac and Arcelik as beginning portfolio(Alp 2008). On the December 2011, value of the portfolio is 9.506.917, 48 billion TL and it has 1.349 investors. When we compared with its return for the period between January 2011 and December 2011, it has lower return than beginning of the year. It is −11, 42 % (http://www.isteyatirim.com.tr/). According to this return we can say that Tema Cevre Fonu is not successful financially.

According to the data set obtained from Turkiye İş Bankası upon request, between the IPO and 20 December 2011, the fund has generated a return of 30.38 % compared with the Istanbul Stock Exchange100 (ISE100) index return of %34,87 and ISE equally weighted fixed income index return of 52,69 %. The index data was obtained from Matrix (a financial data provider). According to the November 2011 monthly report, the fund's assets are comprised of 2,5 Million TL worth of stocks and 7,3 Million TL worth of Turkish government debt instruments, which indicates a stock weight of 25,55 % and fixed income weight of 74,45 %. In order to analyze the performance of the fund, a combined benchmark is created by calculating the weighted average of ISE 100 index returns and ISE equally weighted fixed income index returns based on the asset weights of the funds.

$$Combined\ Benchmark = 25.55\ \% \times 34,87\ \% + 74.45\ \% \times 52.69\ \% = 39.42\ \%$$

The combined benchmark exhibited an underperformance of 9.04 % over a period of 42 months. In addition, the total asset figure of 9.8 Million TL points to a considerable negative growth in the size of the fund.

19.7.2 The Istanbul Stock Exchange Sustainability Index

All entities and institutions that are related to the capital markets including both companies and regulatory authorities are involved in CSR and sustainability issues. Stock exchanges around the world assume more dynamic roles in social responsibility studies and many of them expand gradually more projects related to social life and environment. Those studies are carried out through a task force set up within the World Federation of Exchanges (WFE) with a view to categorizing the role of the exchanges in creating a sustainable community. Istanbul Stock Exchange (ISE) has become a member of UN Global Compact and UN Principles of Responsible Investment (UNPRI). The strategies of WFE-member exchanges relating to sustainability are classified in three general categories:

1. To create awareness in listed companies on environment, social responsibility, and corporate governance issues;
2. To create sustainability indices, to develop information services and products for investors,
3. To set up specialized markets for specific sustainable investment niches.

Within this context; ISE started a sustainability index project in cooperation with the Business World and Sustainable Development Association. ISE plans to develop an ISE Sustainability Index which will be comprised of ISE-listed companies that incorporate sustainability criteria into their investment processes and activities will be launched upon the completion of the project. It will be beneficial if all the activities aimed at increasing environmental and social sensitivity and improving corporate governance are carried out under a single program, and where applicable, the suggestions resulting from such activities are integrated into the decision-making processes and applications of ISE.

On 10 August 2010 in Istanbul, the Istanbul Stock Exchange (ISE) and Turkey Business Council for Sustainable Development (TBCSD) launched the Istanbul Stock Exchange Sustainability Index (ISESI) Project. The Project's aim is to review listed companies on the ISE based on their management of sustainability issues and to create an index that will demonstrate the leadership of listed Turkish companies (ISE 2010).

The Istanbul Stock Exchange Sustainability Index (ISESI) Project is a multi-stakeholder project which aims to build best practices and set a Turkish sustainability benchmark for ISE-listed companies. ISESI is also expected to be a platform for the institutional investors to demonstrate their commitment to companies managing environmental, social and governance (ESG) issues with high performance. ISE also developed a Corporate Governance Index (XKURY) which is comprised of companies applying Corporate Governance Principles. The index aims to measure the price and return performances of companies traded in ISE Markets with a corporate governance rating of minimum 7 over 10. The corporate governance rating is determined by the rating institutions incorporated by CMB in its list of rating agencies as a result of their assessment of the company's compliance with the corporate governance principles as a whole(ISE,2011). Istanbul Stock Exchange Sustainability Index (ISESI) Project which was prepared by Istanbul Stock Exchange (ISE) and Turkey Business Council for Sustainable Development (TBCSD). This index seek to provide competitive advantage for leading Turkish companies by raising the profile of sustainability leaders, similar to companies listed on global sustainability indexes, as well as indexes recently launched in emerging markets like Brazil, China, Egypt, Korea, India and South Africa. This Project will develop an index of companies listed on the ISE to act as a benchmark encouraging and enabling major companies in Turkey to compete successfully today in a world where.

Corporate environmental, social and corporate governance (ESG) performance is necessary for long term success (ISESI-Project Briefing, 2010–2011). Like Johannesburg Stock Exchange's socially responsible investment index (SRIX), ISESI will help increase the awareness about environmental and sustainability issues.

The selection of companies is very important part of this project. There are some leading Turkish companies, investors and international social responsibility expert advice about to create selection criteria. According to ISESI draft sustainability criteria (http://www.ise.org/Indexes/StockIndexesHome/Sustainability_Index.aspx?sfopl=true), selection of companies were connected with their environmental performance, resource management, business in society, usage of water, effecting the climate change, management issues, social characteristics like health and safety, contribution of society, activities about human rights and labor rights and reporting and transparency policies.

A survey has been conducted by Pricewaterhouse Coopers (PWC 2011) among Turkish companies to examine their opinions towards sustainability in companies, the existing sustainability practices of companies and the aims to explore the future expectations and trends. 45 questions were asked and 215 companies from 11 different industries joined the survey (PWC 2011). According to this survey, (95 %) of companies answered that sustainability is related with their business activities, (93 %) of companies considered that sustainable investments have positive impact on the financial performance of the companies, (93 %) of companies followed the sustainability activities in private sector and (80 %) in public sector. For the majority of the companies' economic and social dimensions of sustainability has more importance than environmental dimensions. According to the answers of questioned companies; reputation, legal regulation and competition are perceived by the companies as the most significant driving forces of sustainability practices. (62 %) of the companies have sustainability strategies. The above mentioned percentage can be considered quiet low due to the costs and required knowledge to apply the right strategies. The majority of the mentioned companies have policies about transparency, labor education, occupational safety and health. For (75 %) of companies energy using is an important issue. Water pollution and waste products are other essential concerns for these companies. But Greenhouse Gas and other harmful gas emissions are less important subjects for them. (86 %) of 191 companies do not publish any sustainability report. (12 %) publish sustainability report every year in order to be able to use the advantage of competitive and brand awareness. (83 %) of 190 companies indicated that they want to have a place in ISESI index. Companies in communication industries seemed more ambitious to take a part in ISESI than the other companies. (6 %) of companies had never heard about ISESI.

ISESI will assess how businesses are addressing urgent sustainability issues important for Turkey such as climate change, the depletion of natural resources and ecosystems, diminishing water supplies, health and safety, community relations, employee relations and their consequences on the Turkish economic development. All listed companies in the ISE will be eligible to apply for inclusion in the index, however the main prerequisite will be meeting the Environmental, Social and Corporate Governance (ESG) criteria set forth by ISESI. The sustainability ratings will be administered by a third party vendor of company sustainability performance, which will be supported with conceptual input from Sustainable Asset Management (SAM), research provider of the Dow Jones Sustainability Indices (DJSI) since 1999.

There are also two other SRI funds which have a small portion in portfolio management in Turkish Financial Markets:

19.7.3 Type B 100 % Capital Guaranteed Clean Energy Fund

This fund was issued by Yapıkredi Bank and offered to public at 01.04.2011. Minimum investment required is 2000TL. This is the 19th sub-fund of guaranteed funds issued by the bank. Fund Strategy is to create initial investment by investing in government bonds and to create profit from "S&P Global Clean Energy Daily Risk Control 12 % Excess Return Index (EUR)" Portfolio structure is static and portfolio management is quiet passive. There will be no changes about management, structure or type of the fund since we there will be no investment acceptance after the offering period. To provide guaranteed capital 95 % of the investment will be done to TC Government Bonds and 5 % will be invested in "S&P Global Clean Energy Daily Risk Control 12 % Excess Return Index(EUR)" (http://www.yapikredi.com.tr/trTR/yatirim/yatirim_fonlari/ykb_fonlari/rehber/v_yatirim_fonu.aspx).

19.7.4 Type 10 % Return Guaranteed Clean Energy Fund

This was the first return guaranteed responsible investment fund issued by Turkiye Sanayi Kalkinma Bankasi (TSKB). It was offered to the public on the 12th and 16th January 2009 and ended on 19th January 2010. Minimum investment was

1,000TL. Fund Strategy: Amount providing capital and 10 % return at the end of maturity is invested in Turkish treasury bills and bonds or Reverse Repo (IMKB market or OTC market, about 92 % of the portfolio). The remaining amount of the portfolio is invested in a single index option contract to participate positive return which includes basket of indices (about 8 % of the portfolio) consisting of an equal ratio between International Renewable Energy Index, International Energy Efficiency Index and International Waste Management Index (ratio of each of Index is 33 %). http://www.tskb.com.tr/images/yatirim_hizmetleri/TEF_Brosur_son.pdf.

19.7.5 Islamic Banking in Turkey

Turkey has one of the world's biggest Muslim population, but religion has until recently played little part in its banking system. It is obvious to see that socially responsible investing would be a much more important topic for Turkey in the future. The Turkish people prove that ethics are more important to them than interests when we looked at their system of banking. We noted that share prices in the participating banks (Islamic banking) have generally increased rapidly. There are four participating banks in Turkey at the moment, some are publicly traded Albaraka Turk and Bank Asya, and others are unlisted Kuveyt Turk and Turkiye Finans. These four "participating banks" held just 4.318 % of the sector's assets as of March 2011. Since their drive for socially responsible investing takes its roots from religious laws, participating banks are great examples. If we look at statistical data, we will see that participating banks are growing every year in a stable way. (See Table 19.1) Thus, we can say that investors take religious matters into consideration when they invest in emerging countries like Turkey for example. Moreover, when we look at participating banks –or Islamic banks- in

Table 19.3 Asset growth of Turkish participating banks. (Thousand TRY)TKKB

Years	PB.s	Growth (%)	Banking Sector	Share (%)
2000	2.266.000		106.549.000	2.13
2001	2.365.000	4.37	218.873.000	1.08
2002	3.962.000	67.53	216.637.000	1.83
2003	5.112.934	29.05	254.863.000	2.01
2004	7.298.601	42.75	313.751.000	2.33
2005	9.945.431	36.26	406.915.000	2.44
2006	13.729.720	38.05	498.587.000	2.75
2007	19.435.082	41.55	580.607.000	3.35
2008	25.769.427	32.59	731.640.000	3.52
2009	33.628.038	30.50	833.968.000	4.03
2010	43.423.000	29.13	1.007.031.000	4.31

Source The participation banks association of Turkey–TKKB

global terms, we can see some systematic improvement in the system especially in the gulf countries. They have specialized banking tools and their market share is nearly one third of the system. In 2009 the shariah-compliant assets reached about 400 billion US dollars throughout the world and the potential market is 4 trillion US dollars. This confirms to us that there is a great potential for participating banks in Turkey. Lastly, we must add that participating banks have an advantage over other banks: since they do not consider interest rates (*riba*) when they make lending decisions, they are not affected by central banks' interest rate changes. Growth ratios of Turkish participating banks are good examples of this as depicted in Table 19.3.

19.8 Conclusion

Socially Responsible Investing, as part of the broader "sustainable living and social responsibility" theme has its roots way back into history, however the concept has gone through considerable evolution and has become one of the major trends of the new millennium. Socially responsible funds are still exhibiting significantly higher growth rates than conventional mutual funds. The strategies and principles of SRI are being adopted by alternative investment areas such as venture capital, real estate development, microfinance and other debt financing vehicles and so on.

Socially responsible investing affects investors, companies and countries. It allows people to invest their monies based on their own personal values. Investors place their social, environmental and governance concerns in the balance. According to different studies, SRI funds are also comparative and can perform just as traditional funds. But some authors argue that SRI funds have lower returns than traditional funds. Studies about SRI indexes show that the most successful index in SRI indices is the Domini 400. If we want to leave a better future for our children and grandchildren, we can invest our monies in socially responsible companies.

Turkey, with its claim of becoming a regional financial centre, has no other alternative but to catch the wave and advocate SRI practices. The ISE's attempt to launch a sustainability index is an important component of elevating the Turkish capital market to the forefront of the global investment marketplace; however this attempt needs to be supported by not only the government, but also the private sectors and Turkish companies.

Compliance with ESG criteria has the potential to provide Turkish companies access into an exclusive $11 Trillion global investment market, which is not available to "non-member" firms. Turkey, being an emerging economy, depends highly on such long-term capital in order to accelerate its economic development.

SRI is a new investment approach in Turkey. In May 2008 Turkiye Is Bankası offered a SRI mutual fund called "B Tipi Değişkenli Tema Cevre Fonu". It managed the investment by the principle of environmental responsibility. But according to its financial data, we can say that it is still not successful.

Another step to improve SRI in Turkey, is the Istanbul Stock Exchange Sustainability.

Index (ISESI) Project. It was launched by the Istanbul Stock Exchange (ISE) and the Turkey Business Council for Sustainable Development (TBCSD). The selection of companies is the most important issue about ISESI. PWC carried out a survey among 215 Turkish companies about their views on the sustainability issues, the existing sustainability practices of companies and aims to explore the future expectations and trends. According to survey, Turkish companies have followed sustainability activities and it shows that they are not indifferent to sustainability issues compare with their counterparts elsewhere. They stated that sustainability investment has positive impact on the companies' both financial and ethical performance and these provide them some competitive advantages.

They currently take into consideration social and economic aspects of sustainability but in the future they will probably extend this to include their environmental aspect of sustainability. Reputation, legal regulation and competition are considered as some important driving force for the companies. It shows that in the future with the implementation of the necessary arrangements, companies will be more interested in sustainability issues. According to survey, we could see that majority of companies care about the ISESI. In addition, companies' decision about entering the ISESI, competitive advantage, competition and costs are the most important factors. In the light of this survey, we can say that Turkish companies are ready to perform in line with the requirements of the ISESI.

It is expected that there is a potential for considerable growth by the Turkish SRI Markets in future. One of the reasons for this assumption is the growth rate of the participating banks (Islamic banks). People are more likely to invest in socially responsible companies than in those companies which only profit oriented. Investors are affected strongly by religious views and therefore are more sensible in terms of social, governmental or environmental issues which indicate that the growth in socially responsible investment market will continue to expand and grow in Turkey in the very near future.

References

Adler, T., & Kritzman, M. (2008). The cost of socially responsible investing. *Journal of Portfolio Management, 35*(1), 52–56.

Barnett, M. L., & Salomon, R. M. (2003). Throwing a curve at socially responsible investing research. *Organization & Environment, 16*(3), 381–389.

Bauer, R., Koedijk, K., & Otten, R. (2002). International evidence on ethical mutual fund performance and investment style. LIFE Working Paper, University of Maastricht, No. 02.59.

Benson, K. L., Brailsford, T. J., & Humphrey, J. E. (2006). Do socially responsible fund managers really invest differently? *Journal of Business Ethics, 65*, 337, SpringerLink.

Bettignies, H. C., & Lepineux, F. (2009). Finance for a better world: The shift toward sustainability (pp. 124–125), Palgrave Macmillan.

Bollen, N. P. B. (2007). Mutual Fund Attributes and Investor Behavior. *Journal of Financial and Quantitative Analysis, 42*(3), 683–708.

Boxenbaum, E., & Gond, J.-P. (2006). Micro-strategies of contextualization: Cross-national transfer of socially responsible investment. DRUID Summer Conference 2006, pp. 3–4.

Cabaniss, M. (2012). Socially responsible investing and McDonald's http://beta.fool.com/boriskabinov/2012/08/21/socially-responsible-investing-and-mcdonalds/9783/ accessed: 18.1.2013.

Capelle-Blancard, G., & Monjon, S. (2011). The Performance of Socially Responsible Funds: does the screening process matter? Working Papers 2011–2012, CEPII research center.

D'Antonio, L., Johnsen, T., & Hutton, R. B. (1997). Expanding socially screened portfolios: An attribution analysis of bond performance. *Journal of Investing, 6*(4), 79–86.

Dalheim, Stu, (2006). Socially responsible investing, an introduction. Presentation at Calvert Foundation, p.2, http://www.rivernetwork.org/rally/2006-files/Rally06_10G2.pdf accessed 13.11.2012.

Lee, D. D., Humphrey, J. E., Benson, K. L., & Ahn, J. Y. K. (2010). Socially responsible investment fund performance: The impact of screening intensity. *Accounting and Finance, 50,* 351–370.

Derwall, J., & Koedijk, K. (2009). Socially responsible fixed-income funds. *Journal of Business Finance & Accounting, 36*(1–2), 210–229.

DiBartolomeo, D., & Kurtz, L. (1999). Managing risk exposures of socially screened portfolios. *Northfield Information Services,* September 1999, pp. 1–17.

Diltz, J. D. (1995). The private cost of socially responsible investing. *Applied Financial Economics, 5,* 69–77.

Dziedzic, T. (2011). http://exchanges.nyx.com/fr/tdziedzic/it-pays-be-bullish-csr Dow Jones It pays to be bullish.

Eurosif (2010). European SRI Study 2010 Revised Edition", http://www.eurosif.org/research/eurosif-sri-study/2010 p. 59.

Garz, H., Volk, C., & Gilles, M. (2002). More gain than pain—SRI: sustainability pays off. *WestLB Panmure.*

Geczy, C. C., Stambaugh, R. F., & Levin, D. (2003). *Investing in socially responsible mutual fund.* Philadelphia: The Wharton School, University of Pennsylvania.

Hamilton, S., Jo, H., & Statman, M. (1993). Doing well while doing good? The investment performance of socially responsible mutual funds. *Financial Analysts Journal, 49*(6), 62–66.

Humphrey, J. E., & Lee, D. D. (2011). Australian socially responsible funds: Performance, risk and screening intensity. *Journal of Business Ethics, 102,* 519. SpringerLink.

Idowu, S. O. (2009). Practicing corporate social responsibility in the UK. In S. O. Idowu, & W. Leal Filho (Eds.) Global Practices of Corporate Social Responsibility. Berlin: Springer.

Istanbul Stock Exchange Sustainability Index (ISESI) Project 2010–2011 Briefing, Istanbul, August 2010.

Kawamura, M. (2002). How socially responsible investment (SRI) could redefine corporate excellence in the 21st century. *NLI Research Institute, 160,* 16.

Koellner, T., Weber, O., Fenchel, M., & Scholz, R. (2005). Principles for sustainability rating of investment funds. *Business Strategy and the Environment, 14,* 54–70.

Krosinsky, C., & Robins, N. (2009). Sustainable investing: The art of long term performance. press release by the publisher, March 26, 2009, http://www.csrwire.com/ press_releases/13587-Over-US-5-Trillion-of-Sustainable-Investing-Funds-Available-to-Relaunch-the-Global-Economy.

Leahy, J. (2008). Socially responsible investing: The quest for financial return and social good. *Accountancy Ireland, 40*(6), 47–49.

Mallin, C. A., Saadouni, B., & Briston, R. J. (1995). The Financial Performance of Ethical Investment Funds. *Journal of Business Finance and Accounting, 22*(4), 495.

Moskowitz, M. (1972). Choosing socially responsible stocks. *Business and Society Review, 1*(1), 71–75.

Pan, P. G., & Mardfin, J. K. (2001). *Socially Responsible Investing*, Report No:6, Hawaii Legislative Reference Bureau. pp. 2. http://www.sristudies.org/Pan+and+Mardfin+(2001).

Petty, A. W. B. (2003). *Screening investments of stakeholders: Socially responsible investing in the united states*. University of Virginia, Darden Business Publishing, USA, pp. 10.

PWC (2011). *Turk Is Dunyası'nda surdurulebilirlik uygulamaları değerlendirme raporu*, September 2011. p. 41.

Reander, N. K., Ray, R. H. G., Ower, D. M. P., & Sinclair, C. D. (2005). Evaluating the performance of ethical and non-ethical funds: A matched pair analysis. *Journal of Business Finance & Accounting, 32*(7–8), 1465–1493.

Renneboog, L., ter Horst, J., & Zhang, C. (2006). Is Ethical Money Financially Smart? *TILEC Discussion Paper*, February 2006, pp. 1–49.

Renneboog, L., ter Horst, J., & Zhang, C. (2007). Socially responsible investments: Methodology, risk exposure and performance, *ECGI Working Paper Series in Finance*, No. 175, pp. 2.

Renneboog, L., ter Horst, J., & Zhang, C. (2007). The price of ethics: Evidence from socially responsible mutual funds. *European corporate governance institution Finance Working Paper*, No. 168, p. 10.

Rudd, A. (1981). Social responsibility and portfolio performance. *California Management Review, 23*(4), 55–61.

Schmid, H. D. (2001) *Grünes Geld*.St.Gallen: Texte zur Tagung in Boldern 2000, pp. 9.

Schröder, M. (2004). The performance of socially responsible investments: Investment funds and indices. *Financial Markets and Portfolio Management, 18*(2), 131.

Schulet, S., Schuet, J. (2006). Socially responsible investing in the United States, March, 2006, www.sriinvesting.com.

Schwartz, M. S. (2003). The ethics of ethical investing. *Journal of Business Ethics, 43*, 195–213.

Schuman, J., (2006). Doing good while doing well—Why SRI is booming. http://apafs.org/event/2006pdf/jonathan_schuman.pdf.

Simone, M. (2010). *Social Responsible Investing Retail Investors' Preferences*. (Master Thesis, Maastricht University Master International Business Finance), pp. 5.

Social Investment Forum (2005). Report on socially responsible investing trends in the United States. http://www.socialinvest.org. Accessed: 23.05.2009.

Social Investment Forum Foundation (2010) Report on socially responsible investing trends in the United States, pp. 8.

Statman, M. (2000). Socially Responsible Mutual Funds. *Financial Analysts Journal, 56*(3), May-June, pp 30–39.

Statman, M. (2005). Socially responsible indexes: Composition, performance and tracking errors. May 2005, Santa Clara University Leavey School of Business, pp. 1–29. 8 http://www.msci.com/products/esg/.

Statman, M. (2007). Socially responsible investments. *Journal of Investment Consulting, 8*(2), pp 22–24.

Jones, S., van der Laan, S., Frost, G., & Loftus, J. (2008). The investment performance of socially responsible investments in australia. *Journal of Business Ethics, 80*, 181.

Alp, S. (2008). *Is Bankası'nın cevre fonu 6 sirkete yatırım yaptı*, 2008. http://v3.arkitera.com/news.php?action=displayNewsItem&ID=30796.

Teper, J. (1992). *Evaluating the cost of socially responsible investing*. New York: The Social Investment Almanac.

TIAA-CREF (2011). *Socially Responsible Investing Report*, USA, pp. 4.

Vyvyan, V., Ng, C., & Brimble, M. (2007). Socially responsible investing: The green attitudes and grey choices of australian investors. *Corporate Governance, 15*(2), 370–381.

Waxenberger, B. (2005). Prinzipiengeleitetes Investment—Orientierungen und kritische Bemerkungen. In: Waxenberger. B., Grin Verlag.

Yilmaz, I. (2011). *Corporate social responsibility disclosures as an indicator of social performance and its relation with financial performance*. PhD Thesis, Marmara University, Istanbul, pp. 46.

Yuksel Mermod, A. (2009) Revolution in financial markets: Using social responsible investing (SRI) funds as a new instrument in a competitive financial environments. 1st International Conference on Governance, Fraud, Ethics& Social Responsibility, pp. 538–539.

Internet Resources

A Brief History of Socially Responsible Investing, pp. 1 www.goodmoney.com/srihist.htm accessed: 23.11.2009 http://www.goodmoney.com/srihist.htm.

Blackrock Financial Professionals Website: https://www2.blackrock.com/us/financial-professionals/market-insight/market-commentary/point-of-view-with-richard-turnill-and-stuart-reeve.

Eurokahedge News Website: http://eurekahedge.blogspot.ch/2010/07/2010-key-trends-in-socially-responsible.html.

FTSE Indices: http://www.ftse.com/Indices/FTSE4Good_Index_Series/Performance_Analysis.jsp.

Hector R. Rodriguez Course Presentation http://fr.slideshare.net/hecrod/7-bse-socially-responsible-investing#btnNext Hector R. Rodriguez course presentation, Downloaded on: Feb.7, 2010.

Is Bankasi Website: http://www.isteyatirim.com.tr/Fon/FonKartiDetay.aspx?FonKodu=TMC 12.

Istanbul Stock Exchange Website: http://www.ise.org/Indexes/StockIndexesHome/Sustainability_Index.aspx?sfopl=true.

Istanbul Stock Exchange, (2010), "Istanbul Stock Exchange Sustainability Index (ISESI) Project 2010-2011 Briefing", p.1, http://www.isesi.org/ISESI__ENG/About_ISESI_files/ISESI_Project_Brief_Aug.pdf www.ise.org, access date: 25.05.2011.

Merrill Lynch Private Banking; Values Investing comes of age: http://www.pbig.ml.com/pwa/pages/values-based-investing-comes-of-age.aspx Downloaded on 11.12.2012.

NYSE Euronext Exchanges: http://exchanges.nyx.com/fr/tdziedzic/it-pays-be-bullish-csr.

Social Index Fund Dumps Wal-Mart Shares (2001). http://articles.latimes.com/2001/may/18/business/fi-64987.

Social Funds: http://www.socialfunds.com/page.cgi/article1.html.

Social Responsible Investing Trends (2010): http://eurekahedge.blogspot.ch/2010/07/2010-key-trends-in-socially-responsible.html.

Springwater Asset management website: http://www.springwaterassetmanagement.com/blog/downloaded: 11.12.2012.

Sproutly A Blog for Young and Growing Entrepreneurs: http://www.sproutly.com/2008/05/08/value-of-social-responsibility-in-the-us-530-billion/.

The Forum for Sustainable and Responsible Investment, http://ussif.org/about/, accessed 16.11.2012. http://www.sproutly.com/2008/05/08/value-of-social-responsibility-in-the-us-530-billion/.

The Forum for Sustainable and Responsible Investment: http://ussif.org/pdf/research/Trends/1997%20Trends%20Report.PDF.

TSKB Website: http://www.tskb.com.tr/images/yatirim_hizmetleri/TEF_Brosur_son.pdf.

Yapi Kredi Bank Website: http://www.yapikredi.com.tr/trTR/yatirim/yatirim_fonlari/ykb_fonlari/rehber/v_yatirim_fonu.aspx.

US News World Report: http://money.usnews.com/funds/mutual-funds/large-growth/calvert-social-index-fund/csxax.

Index

A. Yüksel Mermod and S. O. Idowu (eds.), *Corporate Social Responsibility
in the Global Business World*, DOI: 10.1007/978-3-642-37620-7,
© Springer-Verlag Berlin Heidelberg 2014

Printed by Printforce, the Netherlands